Native on the Net

Is the global village a real possibility in cyberspace? *Native on the Net* explores the influence of the internet on the lives and routines of indigenous and diasporic peoples. With case studies ranging from the Arctic to the Australian outback, Kyra Landzelius leads a team of expert anthropologists and ethnographers who go on-site and online to explore how a diverse range of indigenous and transnational diasporic communities actually use the internet. From the Taino Indians of the Carribbean to the U'wa of the Amazon rainforest, from the Turcomans and Assyrians of Iraq to the Tongas and Zapatistas, *Native on the Net* is a lively and intriguing exploration of how new technologies have enabled these previously isolated peoples to reach new levels of communication and community: creating new communities online, confronting global corporations, or even challenging their own native traditions.

As well as offering a rich exploration of local use of the internet, important recurrent themes such as the relationship between identity and place, community, traditional cultures, and the nature of the 'indigenous' are explored in varying contexts, providing a unique contribution to our knowledge of the impact of new global communication technologies on those who have traditionally been geographically, politically and economically marginalised.

Kyra Landzelius is an anthropologist (PhD, University of Pennsylvania) and currently a researcher at the University of Gothenburg. She has been an Assistant Professor at Centre College, a Visiting Scholar at the Department of Anthropology, Cambridge University, and a Lise Meitner Fellow at the Institute for Advanced Studies in Science, Technology and Society in Graz. Her work has appeared in *Social Science and Medicine*, the *Journal of Material Culture*, and *Indigenous Affairs*.

Native on the Net

Indigenous and Diasporic Peoples in the Virtual Age

Edited by Kyra Landzelius

Routledge
Taylor & Francis Group

LONDON AND NEW YORK

First published 2006
by Routledge
2 Park Square, Milton Park, Abingdon, Oxon OX14 4RN

Simultaneously published in the USA and Canada
by Routledge
270 Madison Ave, New York, NY 10016

Routledge is an imprint of the Taylor & Francis Group, an informa business

© 2006 Kyra Landzelius

Typeset in Goudy and Gill Sans by Taylor & Francis Books
Printed and bound in Great Britain by TJ International Ltd, Padstow, Cornwall

British Library Cataloguing in Publication Data
A catalogue record for this book is available from the British Library

Library of Congress Cataloging-in-Publication Data
A catalog record for this book has been requested

ISBN10: 0–415–26599–1   ISBN13: 978–0–415–26599–7 (hbk)
ISBN10: 0–415–26600–9   ISBN13: 978–0–415–26600–0 (pbk)
ISBN13: 978–0–203–48714–7 (ebk)

Contents

Contributors   *vii*

Acknowledgements   *x*

1 Introduction: Native on the net   1
  KYRA LANDZELIUS

2 Remote indigenous communities in Australia: Questions
  of access, information, and self-determination   43
  ALOPI S. LATUKEFU

3 Canadian aboriginal peoples tackle e-health: Seeking
  ownership versus integration   61
  VALERIE GIDEON

4 A screen of snow and recognition reigned supreme?
  Journeys into the homeland of a Greenlandic webpage   80
  NEIL BLAIR CHRISTENSEN

5 On line, off line and in line: The Zapatista rebellion
  and the uses of technology by Indian women   97
  MARISA BELAUSTEGUIGOITIA

6 The meta-native and the militant activist: Virtually
  saving the rainforest   112
  KYRA LANDZELIUS

7 Amerindian@Caribbean: Internet indigeneity
  in the electronic generation of Carib and Taino identities   132
  MAXIMILIAN C. FORTE

8 Debating language and identity online: Tongans on
   the net   152
   HELEN LEE

9 Deterritorialized people in hyberspace: Creating and
   debating Harari identity over the internet   169
   CAMILLA GIBB

10 Negotiating nationhood on the net: The case of the
   Turcomans and Assyrians of Iraq   186
   HALA FATTAH

11 Discussion lists and public policy on iGhana: Chimps
   and feral activists   202
   JOHN PHILIP SCHAEFER

12 The transformation of discourse online: Toward a
   holistic diagnosis of the nature of social inequality
   in Burundi   220
   ROSE M. KADENDE-KAISER

13 Ch(c0de): Virtual occupations, encrypted identities, and
   the Al-Aqsa intifada   238
   WILLIAM C. TAGGART

14 Internet *counter* counter-insurgency: *TamilNet.com*
   and ethnic conflict in Sri Lanka   255
   MARK WHITAKER

15 Cyberethnography: Reading South Asian
   digital diasporas   272
   RADHIKA GAJJALA

16 Postscript: *Vox populi* from the margins?   292
   KYRA LANDZELIUS

   Index   305

Contributors

Marisa Belausteguigoitia is a Director of the Program in University Studies, National University of Mexico. She received her doctorate in Cultural Studies from the University of California, Berkeley, in 2000. She has published numerous articles on the Zapatista rebellion and on indigenous women, including in *women@internet* (edited by Wendy Harcourt) and the *Politics of Place*, edited by Wendy Harcourt and Arturo Escobar.

Neil Blair Christensen is an editor at Nature Publishing Group. He holds an MA in Eskimology from the University of Copenhagen, and has conducted research at the Arkleton Centre for Rural Development Research, University of Aberdeen. He has previously been employed at the University of Copenhagen, Munksgaard International Publishers, and Blackwell Publishing. His research and publications focus on cyber anthropology from an Arctic perspective, and include the book *Inuit in Cyberspace: Embedding Offline Identities Online*.

Hala Fattah, an Iraqi-born academic, completed her PhD in Modern Middle East History at UCLA (1986) and taught at Georgetown University (1990–93). In 2004, she assumed responsibilities as the first Resident Director of the American Academic Research Institute in Iraq, serving in Amman, Jordan, where it is temporarily located. She is the author of *The Politics of Regional Trade in Iraq, Arabia and the Gulf, 1746–1900* (1997) and *A Brief History of Iraq* (2005).

Maximilian C. Forte is an Assistant Professor in Anthropology at Concordia University, Montreal. He is the author of *Ruins of Absence, Presence of Caribs: (Post) Colonial Representations of Aboriginality in Trinidad and Tobago* (2005). He is also the Founding Editor of the Caribbean Amerindian Centrelink (www.centrelink.org) and *KACIKE: The Journal of Caribbean Amerindian History and Anthropology*.

Radhika Gajjala is Associate Professor in Interpersonal Communication/ Communication Studies at Bowling Green State University, Ohio. She received her PhD in 1998 from the University of Pittsburgh. Her articles have appeared in *Feminist Media Studies, International and Intercultural Annual, Contemporary South Asia* and *Works and Days,* and in the books *Technospaces: Inside the New Media* (2001) and *Domain Errors! Cyberfeminist Practices* (2003). She is author of *Cyberselves: Feminist Ethnographies of South Asian Women.*

Camilla Gibb has a DPhil in social anthropology from Oxford University and held a postdoctoral position at the University of Toronto from 1998 to 2000. She has since left the world of academia to write full-time. She is the author of three novels, which have been published in 18 countries: *Mouthing the Words* (1999), *The Petty Details of So-and-so's Life* (2002), and *Sweetness in the Belly* (2005). Her latest novel is set in Ethiopia and amongst Ethiopian refugees in London.

Valerie Gideon is a member of the Mik'maq Nation of Gesgapegiag, Quebec, Canada. She is currently Director of Health and Social Development at the Assembly of First Nations in Ottawa. She previously held the position of Director of the First Nations Centre at the National Aboriginal Health Organization. She graduated from McGill University in 2000 with a PhD in Communications, and is a founding member of the Canadian Society of Telehealth.

Rose M. Kadende-Kaiser, a native of Burundi, is currently working with Geneva Global, a company that advises philanthropic investment for community development projects in developing countries. She also teaches at the University of Pennsylvania's Women's Studies Program and African Studies Center. She has been a visiting scholar at the Solomon Asch Center for Study of Ethnopolitical Conflict (University of Pennsylvania), and an Assistant Professor of Cultural Anthropology and Director of the Women's Studies Program at Mississippi State University.

Kyra Landzelius is an anthropologist (PhD, University of Pennsylvania) and currently a researcher at the University of Gothenburg. She has been an Assistant Professor at Centre College, a Visiting Scholar at the Department of Anthropology, Cambridge University, and a Lise Meitner Fellow at the Institute for Advanced Studies in Science, Technology and Society in Graz. Her work has appeared in *Social Science and Medicine,* the *Journal of Material Culture,* and *Indigenous Affairs.*

Alopi S. Latukefu is currently working for the Australian Agency for International Development (AusAID). He is a former Chief Executive Officer of Goolarri Media in Broome and has held various senior management roles within the Outback Digital Network. Latukefu has conducted research in e-commerce and other aspects of the information economy for many groups, including the University of New South Wales, the Commonwealth

Government of Australia, as well as looking at knowledge assessment within Pacific Island Countries for the World Bank.

Helen Lee is a Senior Lecturer in anthropology at La Trobe University. Her research has been primarily with Tongans, both in the islands and in the diaspora. She has published two monographs on these issues: *Tongans Overseas* (2003) and *Becoming Tongan* (1996, under the name of Helen Morton). Her work combines traditional ethnography with cyberspace research, an approach that continues in her current study of second-generation Tongan transnationalism.

John Philip. Schaefer is a cultural anthropologist with interests in cultural studies, ethnomusicology and transnationalism. Born and raised in Ghana, he went to the United States in 1991 and is currently completing a doctorate in anthropology at the University of Texas, Austin. His doctoral research interests have taken him to Morocco to study a musical and religious community in the North African black diaspora.

William C. Taggart, a PhD student at the Massachusetts Institute of Technology, is an anthropologist who works on issues related to technology, culture, and identity. He is interested in marginal and transnational political movements, and especially in the use they make of new information technologies. He recently launched a long-term ethnographic project focusing on advanced robotics research in the United States and Japan.

Mark Whitaker is an Associate Professor of Anthropology at the University of South Carolina, Aiken. His work in Batticaloa, Sri Lanka, focuses on politics, nationalism, religion, and the Tamil diaspora. He is the author of the 1999 monograph, *Amiable Incoherence: Manipulating Histories and Modernities in a Batticaloa Hindu Temple* (Vanderbilt University Press), as well as a number of book chapters and articles. His book, *Learning Politics from Sivaram*, is forthcoming from Pluto Press.

Acknowledgements

In an era of instantaneous and cross-planetary relays it is somewhat astonishing, perhaps even humbling, that some communicative projects can still clock-in on existential and not digital time. Such is the case with this volume. It was first seeded nearly a decade ago as a border idea alongside other research, yet it persisted, to grow into an international workshop held in Gothenburg on 8–11 June 2001. Due to an avalanche of unfortunate circumstances, it then lay dormant for more seasons than one cares to count. Its re-growth owes thanks to a dedicated ensemble of players, without whom it could never have borne fruit.

The aforementioned workshop benefited immensely from the stewardship of Mikael Johansson, Kim Wistedt and Nicholas Waller of the Gothenburg chapter of the International Work Group for Indigenous Affairs (a Copenhagen-based nonprofit organization). This voluntary group of enthusiasts was a vital force in bringing the workshop to life. Their logistical support was a godsend, and their ideas a welcome inspiration. As an outgrowth of their creative initiative, the workshop received coverage in Sweden on morning radio (8 June 2001) and on *Rapport*, a TV evening news program (9 June 2001). A special thanks goes to Kim for fulfilling the role of interviewee on the radio program, and for rising to the occasion with such professional finesse and eloquence.

In the context of the workshop, I appreciate this opportunity to thank Sven Gabrielsson, of the School of Business, Economics and Law (Gothenburg University), for accommodating the workshop on the School's premises, and his warm geniality in making resources available to us. I further appreciate the goodwill of Wil Burghoorn and Sven Cederroth (both at the Center for Asian Studies, University of Gothenburg) and the supportive words of Marita Eastmond from the Department of Social Anthropology there. The workshop's inaugural seminar – open to the university community and the general public – was held on the premises of the Department of Social Anthropology, which proved a helpful arrangement. Per Jonas Parffa superbly launched the workshop with a fascinating lecture-presentation about SameNet, the information-communications network linking Saami peoples; and I am grateful to Henrik Micael Kuhmunen for recommending Per Jonas. I am indebted, clearly, to the dozen workshop participants, many of whom traveled from afar to attend. The writings of most of them are represented in the chapters here.

Financial support for the workshop was provided by the Swedish Research Council (*Vetenskapsrådet*), The Axel Wenner-Gren Foundation for International Exchange of Scholars (*Wenner-Gren Stiftelserna*, based in Stockholm) and The Wenner-Gren Foundation for Anthropological Research, Incorporated, based in New York (note: the latter two foundations are not affiliated). I wish to thank Laurie Obbink of the latter for her administrative assistance. My own research on this topic and my editorial work came about through a research grant from the Swedish Research Council (*Forskningsrådsnämden*, 1998–2002). I am honored by the substantive support this work has received.

The editorial commitment on the part of our publisher, Routledge, provided a veritable cornucopia of support and encouragement through the trials that weathered and threatened to erode this project. Foremost among them I wish to express my heartfelt thanks to Senior Editor Lesley Riddle for her warm humanity alongside her exquisite professionalism. Lesley's graciousness and unwavering faith in this project were essential to its rejuvenation. I appreciate also the engagements of many committed Routledge staff (past and present), including Amy Laurens, Claire Johnsson, Neil O'Regan, Gemma Dunn, Melisa Whorley, Lucie Ewin, Julene Knox and others – all of whom were in attendance at some point during the book's germination. All but one of the chapters were written expressly for this volume; an earlier version of Camilla Gibb's chapter was published in *Anthropologica* (the Journal of the Canadian Anthropology Society), and we extend our appreciation to *Anthropologica* for permission to include it here.

My deepest debt of gratitude – individually and collectively – extends, of course, to the many contributors whose chapters are presented here. I am beholden to these fellow gardeners for graciously bearing what was in some cases a heavy-handed editorial plowing on my part. I am touched, as well, by their spirited and steadfast commitment to this harvest over time. We are each of us indebted to numerous persons – interviewees, informants, colleagues, administrators, financers, etc. – who have helped to make possible our respective work and writings herein. We take this opportunity to collectively acknowledge this wide-ranging cast of major and minor players who have essentially chaperoned this volume, yet who are too numerous to list here. Bound summarily, I alone am accountable for the volume's coherence (or lack thereof) and its tardy debut.

Chapter 1

Introduction

Native on the Net

Kyra Landzelius

Homing in on cyberspace

Connectivity on the margins

A view of the electronic frontier from the user's terminal makes clear that the information superhighway is well on the way to paving everyday work and play habits for mainstream citizens virtually everywhere. Interoperability, connectivity, universality, fluidity, transparency – such are the buzzwords of our digital age. But what do they mean to, and for, peoples outside the mainstream? What do they deliver for indigenous peoples on the fringes of power; for subaltern minority populations in diaspora? Can the info-superhighway be a fast track to greater empowerment for the historically disenfranchised? Or do they risk becoming "roadkill": casualties of hyper-media and the drive to electronically map everything?

Information-communications technologies (ICTs) – and their productions via internet, email, chat sites, homepages, and the like – have become standard agents of global intercourse, bequeathing the information age and hyperlinking contemporary lives to the pace and (non)places of cyber-networking. ICTs are not only vital to the performance of dominant institutions and logics, they play an increasingly ubiquitous role in the choreography of everyday modes of being and doing and thinking across the planet. By reconfiguring space/time equations, cyberspace[1] is re-configuring a broad range of human transactions, in the arenas of commerce, education, governance, healthcare, and not least sociality. There is a vast and ever-growing literature on how these interactive technologies mediate practices and influence personhood for groups in the mainstream.[2] Far less is known about the uses and experiences of ICTs by groups decentered from dominant institutions and idioms. This is especially true for indigenous peoples, who have long been delegitimized by ruling cultural norms and isolated (economically, politically, geographically) from centers of influence. It is also true for many in diaspora, peoples who are often juggling attachments (and alienations) to and from homelands, host countries and fellow travelers in diaspora. Questions abound concerning relatively straightforward matters of ICT access, deployment, agendas, use and content of engagements. What is the reach of cross-planetary communications media into the meaning-making routines of indigenous and/or diasporic peoples? How are indigenous voices, in turn, electronically reaching new audiences and creating new horizons for speakers as well as listeners? How do marginalized peoples perceive and position themselves in relation to global computer networkings, and how do these sociotechnical apparatuses figure in local lifeworlds? In what ways are interactive media environments changing the subjectivities and practices, both online and offline, of peoples historically de-centered from "the action"?

Questions also abound concerning more complex matters, including technological challenges to co-relations of place, history, language, and identity; the implications and imagery of digital politics for equations of power and subversion; the meeting of different worldviews in relatively autonomous, relatively anonymous virtual places. How are digital "mediascapes" (Appadurai 1990) transforming cultural dispositions, and in turn being transformed by them? How do virtual networks – migrating independently of space/time – provide new anchors that bring about a virtual "rooting" of diasporic communities (dispersed across space/time), whilst also "routing" new cosmopolitanism forms? Just what does it mean to be indigenous in the information age?

This volume ventures towards such questions by grounding cyberspace in 14 local adventures that map some of the basic *who, what, when, where, why* and *how* of ICT activity on the part of indigenous and/or diasporic peoples. To chart the initial movements/moments of indigenous cyberactivism, and gauge the momentum of virtual diasporas, the collection brings together ethnographically-oriented researchers (mainly anthropologists) engaged in both on-site and online fieldwork. In ethnographically mapping cyberspace into marginalized, sometimes remote communities (not, however, to be conceived as internally homogeneous or bounded collectives) we take steps towards asking how these technologies are being "indigenized": that is, how are they being creatively integrated and indexed into practices and beliefs rooted in a local cultural logic? This perspective marks a move to situate the workings of a global cyberspace into ethnographic snapshots that hint at the "internal diversity of globalization", and interrogate "assumptions about the 'local' as a source of cultural continuity, and 'the global' as a source of change" (Hannerz 1996: 9). It also marks a move to situate this project within a new generation of internet research that employs "ethnographic particularity" in order better to analyze the "very different universes of social and technical possibility that have developed around the Internet" at particular historical conjunctures (Miller and Slater 2001: 1; see also Hakken 1999, Hine 2000, Jones 1995, 1997).[3]

The different worlds of internet activity mapped here span from the Arctic to the Australian outback, from Africa to the Americas. Our essays are variously concerned with questions of access and application, ideologies and intentions, values and visions with respect to ICT media, and the articulation of alterity across spatial, temporal, and cultural divides, yet within global fields of power and discourse. Each of these cases will be elaborated more fully over the course of this introduction; and some general reflections put forth in the Postscript.

While our presentations here highlight the virtual, it is worth keeping in mind that offline fieldwork informs interpretation: all of the contributors have undertaken conventional on-site fieldwork, a few have been working in the field for decades, several are "native anthropologists". The suturing of virtual with conventional methods endeavors to deconstruct the binaries of online/offline, and to better probe the dialectical ways in which digital media technologies-in-action are being socialized and (trans)localized through signifying practices and exchanges. In their research into the dynamics of internet use in Trinidad, Miller and Slater write: "we are not simply asking about the 'use' or 'effects' of a new medium: rather, we are looking at how members of a specific culture attempt to make themselves a(t) home in a transforming communicative environment, how they can find themselves in this environment and at the same time try to mould it in their own image" (2001: 1).

To make oneself "a(t) home" in cyberspace is to problematize the nature of home. To do so in the name of culture and/or ethnicity, as many indigenous and diasporic ICT users expressly do, is to complicate further the relationship between identity and place. Home and identity – always already in play through local–global articulations – become newly inflected by virtual flows of images and ideas; newly refracted, in the mediated politics of representation and (dis)information; and newly reflective, even meta-reflective, as subjectivities are traversed by mediascapes and other cosmopolitan influences. Via information-communications technologies, home and identity also become newly equipped to respond to such challenges and opportunities. Our writings empirically explore these trends with respect to indigenous and/or diasporic peoples, peoples for whom the question of home – or lack thereof – constitutes a key (perhaps the key) determinant of identity, as place and as symbol. This is not to imply that for any social group "home" is a simple construct. To the contrary, it is to permit that, despite its seeming inertia, home is a rather fragile "production of locality": "increasingly a struggle" that constantly needs to be shored up through "hard and regular work" (Appadurai 1995: 206, 213). Moreover, the task of producing locality – which Appadurai defines as "a structure of feeling, a property of social life and an ideology of situated community" – is "now more than ever shot through with contradictions" (1995: 213, 221). Such contradictions arise in part as a result of technological and resource disjunctures and global flows; but it is equally true that these very processes – precisely because of their simultaneous globality but also their plasticity (or what we might call their capacity for indigenization) – represent a "significant new element" in the production of locality (1995: 220). The ethnographies presented here, in their respective ways, are attempts at "worlding cyberspace" (Fischer 1999a) by exploring how these global information-communications resources entangle (with) the micro and macro-dynamics of locality's challenges and of challenges to locality. Our work queries the positioning and performance of identities mediated electronically; and as authored by (and in some cases for) subaltern persons taking the role of webpage designer, online author, message poster, virtual interlocutor and myriad other practices in the capacity of new techno-scientific actors.

The facet of titles

Before embarking on a discussion of the ethnographic moments presented here, some words about the book's title are in order. *Native on the Net* is intended prismatically, as an attempt to refract five facets of online engagements on behalf of peoples conventionally distanced from the mainstream. First, it marks a relatively straightforward reflection that indigenous peoples are increasingly appropriating ICTs to their own ends and purposes. Second, the title poses an examination of the prolific use of the net as a forum for making claims in the name of ethnicity – with inventiveness and momentum towards intensification of a more-or-less essentialized identity staked in a kind of "indigeneity" (whether or not the peoples in question are in fact "indigenous" in the strictest sense of the term). Third, it explores the use of the net as a forum, not only for making claims in the name of ethnicity, but for *naming* ethnicity – to claim "nativeness" as it were. Fourth, "native on the net" questions the role of new media in shifting the semantics of the term "native", and the ways in which "indigeneity" may be re-thought, re-worked, re-positioned, re-vitalized and (in some cases, alas) re-colonized online. Fifth, the phrase is intended to invoke and conceptually jostle with a once-classic professional taboo in anthropology, in the form of a fuzzy proscription against "going native" whilst doing fieldwork with the anthropological "Other". Each of these five facets provides a framework for orienting us to the chapters and themes in this volume.

Indigenous cyberactivism

Locating indigenous presence online

The question of locating "authentic" indigenous cyber-presence raises the conundrum of verifying identity – an always potentially tricky matter made perennial in the age of digerati, as any web cruiser who has come across a virtual rabbit or other digital conspecific can well attest![4] Typing "indigenous", "aboriginal", "native peoples" and like descriptors into a major search engine yields hundreds of thousands of "hits", a weighty percentage of which undoubtedly have little real connection with *bona fide* indigenous authors or authorizations. Nevertheless, whether factual or fictional, legitimate or not, taken collectively these hits orchestrate the online *re-presentation* of indigenous peoples. They give us a profile, if you will, of the *virtual face of indigeneity*. In its most immediate form, this face marks an expression of the online projects, aims and agendas undertaken by indigenous peoples themselves; this includes: websites authored and/or commissioned by indigenous governing bodies (i.e. the official leadership); webpages sponsored by native-owned businesses; personal homepages posted by indigenous persons; and chatrooms or discussion lists linking participants from and across different indigenous groups. Less direct expressions of virtual indigeneity are manifest in the online presence of, for example: pan-indigenous organizations; international bodies such as the UN and its *Task Force on Indigenous Peoples*; non-governmental organizations and pedagogical institutions such as libraries, museums and universities. How the larger face of virtual indigeneity reflects, refracts, embellishes or distorts indigenous self-representations (in the form of individual, collective, or pan-collective endeavors) is a matter for further study. We touch upon such questions here in chapters that examine specific instances of indigenous online engagements. I refer to these directly self-authored, or at least *authorized*, engagements as indigenous *cyberactivism*; and chart some of its coordinates below.

Indigenous peoples across the globe are becoming ever more cyberactive: using and assimilating ICTs to and for their own ends and purposes (as conversations with indigenous leaders and activists, a growing literature on the topic, and my own concerted tracking of the phenomenon since the late 1990s, attest).[5] Given that "indigenous" – more so than most identity descriptors – is hardly an uncontested or unambiguous one, it bears note that we adopt the term largely in its conventional sense;[6] albeit it is precisely changing dynamics in the articulations of indigenous identities (on- and offline) that we ponder in our discussions and chapters.[7] While still emergent, indigenous cyber-presence has rapidly accelerated and amplified over the past decade: currently hundreds of official and unofficial websites are operated by and/or on behalf of indigenous peoples worldwide, and thousands more indigenous peoples are using chat, email and other applications for myriad purposes ranging from recreation to business to information-gathering to networking. Not surprisingly, most indigenous cyberactivists to-date reside in Western(ized) countries, yet indigenous usage is geographically spreading and diversifying alongside and in keeping with global trends. In underscoring its rapid momentum, at least one author has conjectured that a drive to "enhance [indigenous] life chances through rebalancing of power" may account for an "eager embrace of the new ICTs that, on the face of it, seem more likely to be part of the problem than part of the solution" (Havemann 2000: 19). We might argue that problems and solutions are ultimately matters of local and trans-local determination, differentially contributing to the production of locality (and/or its sabotage). In sketching indigenous ICT engagements in distinct locales, several chapters in this volume pinpoint a range of problems and solutions put in motion.

Despite the heterogeneous range of indigenous cyberactivism, its varied expressions might be seen to gravitate towards one of two predominant orientations: those geared towards an internal public comprised of fellow group members, and those geared towards an external public (which may target non-indigenous peoples and/or indigenous peoples from other groups). We might describe the former initiative as predominantly *inreach*, and the latter as predominantly *outreach*. For heuristic purposes we can conceptualize specific engagements along an *inreach–outreach* continuum, bearing in mind however that most embed multiple layers of intentionality, with tiers of primary and secondary agendas, purposeful and coincidental ones. By and large, most genres of engagement are driven by a primary orientation. Four such are highlighted for discussion here: community services (the circulation of information and resources to local residents); image management (oriented towards public relations and presentations of self, in terms of past or present, collective or personal identities); sovereignty campaigns or movements (including solidarity networks); and indigenous cosmopolitan networks. In the coming sections, I inventory in more detail these four *inreach–outreach* orientations, but first it is important to tackle questions of materiality. Before any group can go online, they must first be connected; that is, they must navigate the pragmatics and problematics of crossing the digital divide.

Wiring the Outback

To cross the digital divide one must have access to the necessary materials (e.g., servers, keyboards, terminals, electricity), identify and install the appropriate programming, and command the technical know-how – a trio that has been dubbed the hardware, software and wetware of ICT management. Indigenous groups differ in terms of their capacity or proclivity to storm these triple gates; yet many an indigenous community, particularly in so-called "First World" countries,[8] has made procuring this trio a top priority. Proactive indigenous initiatives to establish ICT literacy and resources locally serve as keen reminders that paths to the information superhighway do not follow a simple urban–rural continuum, nor indeed follow upon any linear technological progression or prerequisite. The rise in wireless and satellite technologies, which circumvent the need for certain pre-existing infrastructures (such as telephone cables); and the rise in public–private partnerships that target ICT development in remote regions (the characteristic homelands of present-day indigenous peoples) are making it increasingly possible for some indigenous communities to "skip ranks" in attaining connectivity. Indeed, for some, entering the digital age may mean bypassing industrial modernity altogether and catapulting (in certain material or "artifactual" respects) into hyper- or post-modernity.

A case in point is provided by Alopi Latukefu in Chapter 2. Latukefu discusses the trials and tribulations of a multi-actor, multi-tiered plan to bring connectivity to the hinterlands of northern Australia. A collaborative government–corporate effort, the Outback Digital Network is working not only to integrate remote regions into a global grid of web-based communications, but ultimately to put the ownership and control of these media into the hands of Aboriginal peoples. The indigenous leadership who champion the Network view its greatest potential in terms of the politico-economic autonomy that Australian Aborigines seek and which the information age promises (in theory at least) to provide. Seeing strength in numbers, they strive to link and hyperlink different indigenous groups in order to bolster a national indigenous

substantial results. By far the biggest success story of any indigenous cyber-campaign to date belongs to the Zapatista netwar, however: a virtual uprising which mirrored and broadcast the "real-time, real-life" uprisings of the indi-genista and mestizo peasants of Chiapas in their armed confrontations with the Mexican government. Under the charismatic leadership of subcomandante Marcos, this "first informational guerrilla movement" (Castells 1997) became a tour de force of cyberactivism, and the premier example of the web's potential to precipitate empowerment.

The high-profile Zapatista campaign was initially launched to protest against neoliberal "free" trade schemes and other "modernization" policies poised to exclude and thus further disadvantage the flailing Chiapas peasant economies. Along the way it coalesced into an embryonic "indigenous" movement, joined by leftists and grassroots activists, liberation theologians and members of the Catholic Church, plus various non-governmental organizations – all pushing for greater political representation and social welfare for the indigenous peoples of Mexico. Essential to the campaign's success was its tactical use of computer-mediated communications to diffuse "a fiesta of the word" (Nash 1997) and images to Mexican society and to the world at large, resulting in a transnational network of support that made it literally impossible for the Mexican govern-ment to ignore the movement's demands or to enact large-scale repression under the eyes and ears of a watching world (Rich and Reyes 1996; Routledge 1998). ICTs enabled the movement to propel what otherwise would have been "a local, weak insurgent group to the forefront of world politics"; yet they also provided a key arena in which a "most innovative theatrics of revolution" could play out (Castells 1997: 79, 80). In a paradoxical twist (predicated upon the kind of magic worked in/by cyberspace), the Zapatista movement rising from the dense jungles of Chiapas successfully deployed planetary information-communications technologies to wage a fundamental insurgency against the new geopolitical order (Parra 1995).

Marisa Belausteguigotia's chapter in this volume provides an important angle on the Zapatista movement, by bringing into sharper focus the strategic role of feminist-based non-governmental organizations and their capillary solidarity links to activists situated elsewhere (i.e. at workplaces, universities, agencies, etc.). The strategic networking of these eclectic, electronically mobilized "brigades" (Glusker 1998) proved invaluable in helping to voice the gender-specific demands of Zapatista women eclipsed by the movement as such and its broader politico-economic goals. It might even be argued that, by opening up a heterogeneous space within the movement, the Zapatista women's agenda posed a direct challenge to the very constitution of the larger campaign. This might especially hold true with respect to calls for liberation from a patriarchy (and its corollary institutional and domestic violences) that in praxis was intrinsic to "tradition" as contemporarily enacted (and historically mutated). Such calls invariably foreground a more composite and less rosy picture of "indigenous cultures" than an idyllic or monolithic stereotype might allow. The question of

tangible empowerment or distributed justice has been made even more problematic by the Zapatista women's pronouncement of a "right to rest", by which
is meant the right to a measure of emancipation from domestic drudgery,
unskilled wage laboring, and daily chores to maintain the family unit that
disproportionately fall on indigenous women. Here, at the millennial shift, we
witness an intriguing twist in the global feminist initiative: a twentieth-century,
originally elite movement distinguished by its indefatigable campaigns for the
"right to work" has come to find itself challenged, by indigenous "sisters" at the
dawn of the twenty-first century, to embrace a new and vastly different agenda –
that of campaigns for the "right to rest". While few Zapatista women were
themselves cyber-active, their cyber-savvy leadership clinched a tactical success
to find their cause a(t) home in cyberspace.

To be successful, indigenous movements (like social movements everywhere)
must cultivate and engage an audience. In the age of conventional media, this
challenge translated into capturing the media spotlight and convincing (or
circumventing) its gatekeepers as to the "newsworthiness" of the resistors'
performance, if not necessarily their cause. Digital interactive media theoretically democratize these channels by universalizing access to a (hypothesized)
public sphere where anyone/everyone is potential author and/or participant.
Yet, in an era of information overload and endless "good causes" where the
"medium is the message" (McLuhan 1965), enhanced visibility may do little to
lessen the sensationalism often required to ignite the kind of moral outrage that
best mobilizes sustained support. The phenomenal publicity accorded to the
Zapatista uprising was directly hinged on the strength of the solidarity networks
that ensued from recruitment of non-native allies. That hotchpotch cross-planetary alliances can prove vital to indigenous movements is likewise illustrated
by the sovereignty campaign of the U'wa peoples of the Colombian Amazon,
discussed here by Kyra Landzelius in Chapter 6. In striving to prevent a multinational oil company from petroleum "development" on their ancestral lands,
the U'wa joined forces with grassroots environmental organizations whose
public-relations teams helped orchestrate a two-pronged attack. They combined
ordinary take-it-to-the-streets boycotts with an extraordinary cyber-campaign.
This included displaying the U'wa against a colorful backdrop of rainforest
photos and transcripts of native cosmology, a framing that went far in garnering
sympathy for the plight of the natives and the fate of the rainforest.

Such framing of "Other-ness" provides another angle on being "native on
the net", where ICTs are being used to make claims in the name of ethnicity. In
distinction to "virtual stomping grounds" where Lakota shamans seize the
opportunity to correct perennial misrepresentations about "who we are", the
U'wa's virtual re-presentations – via the mediating role of non-U'wa
strategists – could fit cozily within generic expectations about "who natives
are". Contrary to actively refuting stereotypes, the U'wa campaign reproduced a
few. This is not to imply that the collective U'wa "online persona" is in any way
"inauthentic"; it is rather to point out that the success of sovereignty missions

in certain cases is likely hinged on performative strategies that exhibit the native Other along caricatured lines, highlighting harmony and downplaying diversity (this may further risk circumscribing indigenous agency and/or its public expressions). Despite having greater leeway as "autoethnographers", there may be extent pressures and/or incentives for indigenous peoples to "world cyberspace" (or at least their bit of it) according to tropes of indigeneity – in effect to "go native" – even (or perhaps especially) *vis-à-vis* sympathetic constituencies such as grassroots activists or non-governmental organizations (Beckett 1996: 10; see also Conklin 1997 and Mato 1996). This brings us to a deeper consideration of the essentially inter-subjective nature of indigenous identities.

Situating indigeneity

Viewing indigeneity through an historical lens situates it as an "articulation" that has taken shape in the zone of contact with the dominant order (cf. Clifford 2001).[11] Given the thesis that all articulations of identity are (at least) a two-way street, it follows that indigeneity and its properties have been made intelligible with respect to the logic of the conqueror and *vice versa*, in an historical and dialectical process of co-intelligibility. Put in terms of the question of locality, it can be said that both indigenous and colonial locales (and trans-locales) were indebted to a relational consciousness of the ethnic projects of each other (their "ethnoscapes") – against which [their own] local practices and projects [were] imagined to take place (Appadurai 1995: 209). As many scholars have noted, this "dialogic coproduction of 'indigenous' rhetoric" has been "rarely a 'coproduction' between equals", however (Rogers 1996: 79; see Forte 2001: 365). Whereas naming – and thereby controlling – the native Other constituted an essentially Western power prerogative from the start, the concept of indigeneity has clearly transformed over time, bringing us today's plurality of meanings and "full range of indigenous ways to be modern" (Clifford 2001: 470). Under certain circumstances and in some contexts, indigeneity may prove a platform for cultural-political empowerment: the qualifying basis on which to seek retribution for past wrongs, to gain recognition as a minority group, to assert autonomy as sovereign peoples with jurisdiction over lands, language and lifeways. Indeed, some groups may see "an historical opening" (see Brown 1997) and a ray of politico-economic hope in attempting to make their indigenous ethnicity "work" for them; in effect "turning the tables" to make a past liability into a potential asset.

Perhaps seizing an historical moment, a growing number of indigenous persons, individually and collectively, are seeking political and human rights based precisely on difference. These initiatives are creating new zones of contact where indigeneity is being debated and defended, performed and represented, implicitly re-conceptualized. With their capacity to erase distance and permit "realtime" dialogue, ICTs are obviously well poised to facilitate cross-indigenous networking and chaperone this meta-reflexive momentum in the semantics of indigeneity. Computer-mediated communications thus become the historically-latest interactive technologies in an ongoing dialectic that produces and situates indigeneity within globality. Moreover, as implicit and explicit tools of solidarity-building, digital contact zones may become pivotal spaces for determining the "*quest* of indigeneity within globality" (Landzelius 2003). What effects these quests will have on the "*question* of indigeneity within globality" – that is, on what it means to be indigenous and what forms a global indigeneous movement might take – remain to be seen. However, it seems a safe bet that ICTs will play an increasingly significant role in the articulation of emergent forms of indigenous cosmopolitanism.

The Ngati Awa of present-day New Zealand are one of many indigenous groups "tapping into" the "virtual we" of indigenous solidarity movements in their campaign to (re)claim an indigeneity historically denied them (see also Barcham 2000). Some branches of the Ngati Awa were so thoroughly acculturated that they "lost" their native religion and language: two qualifications for claiming indigenous status in the eyes of the present New Zealand government. This example serves to illustrate the specter of debate about who is indigenous and who not, and again pinpoints the situatedness of identity in-the-making. What Jackson notes about the identity-constructions of native Amazonians holds true for all indigenous groups: their "vision of themselves as Indian is generated out of their fundamental embeddedness in the larger society" (Jackson 1989: 138; Conklin 1997). The desire to re-embed oneself as "Indian" with respect to one's immediate society and the world at large is precisely the topic of Chapter 7 in this volume, by Maximilian Forte, who documents two movements to "re-engineer indigeneity" in the Caribbean. Given the official view that the native peoples of the Caribbean were driven to extinction, these re-engineering campaigns are challenged with the task, not simply to breathe life into tenuous indigenous identities, but verily to invoke the reality of a Carib indigeneity. Their impassioned online rally, "We are not extinct!", proclaims an alternative version of the legacy of displacements. If, under the dominant interpretation, "the supposed continuity of the transplanted [colonizer] was thus a function of the discontinuity of the indigenous [native]" (Forte 2001: 364), then for those Caribbean groups laying claim to indigeneity, the task lies in proving "continuity". It appears that the world wide web confers a relatively accessible global arena in which to do just this: to stage continuity and perform authenticity via displays of native *pow-wows* and the like. Indeed, it might be said that recognition has been forthcoming in the "symbolic capital" (Bourdieu 1990) of hyperlink "endorsements" connecting Caribbean websites with those of other, more established, indigenous groups and pan-indigenous organizations worldwide. The Caribbean case gives us a vivid example of "the dynamics of positioning" (Miller and Slater 2001: 10, 18–20 and *passim*), whereby revivalists for an aboriginal Carib heritage are writing and wiring themselves into an indigenous cosmopolitanism and its spectacles.

These enterprises of and for Carib revitalization evince a performative quest to legitimize a desired identity-construction not exactly avowed or allowed by dominant society. To "make claims in the name of ethnicity" is here supplanted by a prior ontological claim to "name ethnicity". Such a state of affairs illustrates a third facet of our title, wherein "native on the net" represents a jostling for authenticity, for the right to author oneself, to govern one's alterity or difference. Thus far in this introduction we have considered several instances (namely, the Caribs, U'wa, Zapatistas, Inuit, First Nations of Canada, and Australian Aborigines) where the internet has provided a space for worlding indigenous self-representations. In the process, some indigenous groups are emerging as politicized forces to be reckoned with – in regional, national, and transnational contexts. Whereas indigenous cyberactivisms play out globally and circuitously to accrue clout and redress wrongs, at the end of the day the aims are firmly sedimented in the "enduring spatial nexus" (Clifford 2001: 482) of any given group: its production of locality and shapings of (home) place.

Campaigns (virtual and otherwise) that give greater visibility and voice to native peoples, coupled with greater attention accorded their circumstances (by supporters and detractors alike) are bound to influence notions of "what it means to be indigenous", and ways of being so. Indigenous homepages that seek to defend native religion from alleged poachers, websites that become vehicles for broadcasting internal tribal debates, distance learning projects to revive native languages – all represent radically new venues for practicing and configuring indigeneity. They are at once exercises in cultural positioning and survival, but also templates for change, transformative steps in the production of culture. The amplification of indigenous cosmopolitanism via electronic solidarity networks arguably further contributes to, and may possibly accelerate, shifts in the meanings inscribed upon "indigeneity" over time. Such processes of resemanticization hint that indigenous identities are being problematized, appropriated, transformed; open to re-interpretation, re-rehabilitation, re-invention. As native identity-constructions become newly articulated via new media, the everyday practices and the lives of indigenous peoples are also coming to be shaped (directly and indirectly) by computer-mediated communications.

In the book's remaining chapters we turn to ways in which computer-mediated communications are shaping the lives of diasporic peoples, by similarly influencing "what it means to be diasporic" and by changing ways of being so. Diasporist identities, like indigenous ones (and it bears reiterating that the two are not mutually exclusive) are equally tricky to characterize: caught betwixt and between norms of nation-states, on the one hand, and indigenous claims on the other (cf. Clifford 1997, 2001). Somewhere in the self-consciousness of any given diasporist identity lie concepts of aboriginality – albeit one staked not in proximity and immediacy, but predicated on distance (geographic, historic, symbolic) – from an originary place/point. Discourses of diaspora hence are arguably informed by a kind of "nativeness", although with connotations uprooted from anchorage (or imagined anchorage) in a (naturalized, embodied, grounded) contiguity and performance, to mark instead disjunctures and deferrals, to mark substitutions that embody longings. Under this definition, neither exodus nor memory nor corporeal knowing nor even once-upon-a-time physical residency need be prerequisites of diaspora. In some cases, as we shall see, it is less the geophysical reality of homeland than its symbolic potency or imaginary that is essential to diasporist subjectivity and consciousness. In understanding oneself as diasporic, attachment to an idea – an idea often embedding fictionalized notions of ethnic purity, priority, and placement – may take precedence.

In the following section we explore the online brokering and broadcasting of diaspora and diasporist conceptualizations. Our data mainly derive from cyberethnographic excursions into electronic discussion forums – arguably the lifeline of virtual diasporas.

Virtual diasporas

Locating diaspora

In considering experiences and identities predicated on diaspora, it is of significance that the term has acquired new connotations and a new currency in recent decades. As Clifford (1997: 255) explains, the "language of diaspora is increasingly invoked by displaced peoples who feel (maintain, revive, invent) a connection with a prior home". It is the substance of such felt connection that is of particular interest here. Often infused with nostalgic remembrance of things past and bearing a certain degree of alienation and resistance in the present, diaspora is inherently wedded to an "ideal return" as a potent antidote to displacement. Being "displaced" seems epidemic, even symptomatic, in today's world; and the current cachet of the term "diaspora" may simply reflect, in part, the geopolitical scene (Brah 1996; Cohen 1997). Nevertheless, the proliferation of border crossings in our times (e.g., global tides of economic migrants, political refugees, expatriates, professional classes and others) does not in and of itself explain why the notion now seems so fitting. If conceived simply as mass population flows, diaspora is certainly nothing new; in modern times alone it harks back to the so-called "Age of Discovery": that earlier era of globalization when human traffic on a planetary scale (e.g., settlers, soldiers, slaves, merchants, natives) fueled and forged the capitalist order. Present trends in globalization are assuredly more volatile and intense, driving itinerancy to record highs. However, the argument might be put forth that the contemporary logic of diaspora reflects current historical conditions of displacement, in which people can be uprooted, yet keep in touch, have homes in a "host" country, yet simultaneously consider themselves "homeless". Unlike the immigrants of yesteryear, the displaced of today can "stay connected" in ways that were inconceivable to their forebears. "Infrastructural technologies" (Calhoun 1992: 208, in Hannerz 1996: 95) afford the means for regular physical, symbolic and/or fantasized "return" for many, via transport, communications and entertainment media. Undoubtedly, ICTs give an unprecedented technological edge to quests to "maintain, revive, invent" connections – connections to an actual homeland and to people still there and/or connections to a dream of homeland and displaced others who share this dream. It might further be suggested that cyberspace not only assists in the emplotment and mediation of diaspora, it actively keeps the ideology of diaspora alive. For example, in their study of the potential of cyberspace to "reorder relations between diaspora Iranians", Graham and Khosravi (2002: 10–11) point out that participation in online forums has enabled Iranians abroad "to appreciate the size and range of the diaspora communities" and has enhanced "awareness of oneself as part of a far-flung diaspora". The role of cyberspace in reordering relations – and, importantly, in reordering the worldviews and experiences that undergird relations – arguably boosts the value of "being diasporic" as a sustainable identity-construction.

In and between multiple worlds

The first virtual diaspora considered here presents a case of indigenous peoples in diaspora; it thereby serves to bridge categories whilst problematizing them. Helen Lee's chapter in this volume invites us into online conversations on *Planet Tonga* and the *Kava Bowl*: two chat sites frequented by both native Tongan youth living on the Pacific island of Tonga and their peers in diaspora. Alongside the typical banter of youth culture (i.e. gossip about romance, popular music, jobs and school) there is a clear thematic concern with what it means to "be Tongan" and how best to go about being so in today's world. Such concerns are given voice in lively debates: one such studied by Lee is centered on the question of online language. Participants in favor of reserving *Planet Tonga* as a virtual arena for "keeping the Tongan language alive" implicitly assign mother tongue to the role of a keeper of identity. Those who advocate using English in order to disseminate Tongan culture to as large a cyber-audience as possible tend to hold the view that being Tongan transcends language. The language-identity debate has had repercussions, moreover, in bifurcating second-generation immigrants along the lines of language proficiency, with the more skilled speakers emerging as elite self-appointed defenders of Tongan, and the less skilled gravitating towards a greater pan-Polynesian identity. As it turns out, cyberspace is also inspiring youth to broach taboo topics (e.g., about sexuality, delinquency, the corruption of Tongan royalty) that propriety has decreed off-limits in face-to-face discussion. Armed with the latest communications technologies, Tongan youth are thus pushing the boundaries of tradition, and changing the culture's conventions from within its ranks, yet on a world wide web scale.

Tongan discussion forums give us a glimpse into how indigenous/diasporic youth are meta-reflexively grappling, in a surprisingly impassioned and probing manner, with the hardships and opportunities of living in, or between, two worlds: of having a "traditional" culture of origin and dominant one(s) of acculturation. Online negotiation of the challenges faced by these youth – as "islanders in the world" (see Lee, this volume) – might be said to represent "the generation of virtual diaspora" in both senses of the term: meaning the discursive engendering of diasporist subjectivities articulated in electronic space; and the first generation of Tongans to forge a virtual community. Similar themes of balancing disparate worlds, and reflecting upon such balancing-acts, have been identified from other contexts. In their study of Bedouin youth online in Israel, Gad and Grabea (2005) propose that users perceive their chat sites as "mirrors" (i.e. places for "self-examination and the testing of possible identities"); and also as "a bypass" (a "secure place in which one can push the envelope of traditional restrictions and see what happens").

In Chapter 9 here, Camilla Gibb further examines the role of the internet in the lives of diasporic youth. Gibb demonstrates how Harari youth whose parents emigrated from Ethiopia to "the West" use ICTs not simply to express a diasporic identity, but verily to author one into existence. Most of these second-generation Harari youth have never lived in their Ethiopian "homeland" (i.e. the birthplace of their parents), have never visited there, and have no plans to go "back". Nevertheless, they discursively attach themselves to this geographical point-on-the-map in their online chats; and from their words it becomes clear that their relationships to this sign are emotionally and politically charged. For them, being diasporic rests on a largely-invented, ambiguously-inherited attachment that not only supercedes or eclipses corporeal knowing – it substitutes for it. There is yet another twist to this digital diaspora: given that Harari people are a small group hailing from a tiny hilltop city in Ethiopia, in the scale of things there are few fellow Harari with whom to exchange stories. In situating themselves virtually, Harari frequently emphasize their Islamic roots, and accordingly gravitate towards the relatively populous and dynamic Muslim online networks. While pan-Islam provides a readily-available font for diasporic identity-constructions, these may well come with strings attached. To the extent that online networks become substitutes for "real-world" counterparts, the risk is that a spiral effect of alienation and discrimination might ensue for translocal historical subjects in diaspora or "second-generation" diaspora. Under this scenario, making oneself a(t) home online may subvert opportunities and/or inclinations to compose a life offline.

The production of locality for Harari youth in diaspora aptly illustrates "the reflexive project of the self" (Giddens 1991) at several conjunctures. Young Harari become subjects by actively navigating and reconciling several imagined communities: an immediate urban, typically Western "second-home", an abstracted Ethiopian homeland, and online communities forged with fellow Harari along with more populous pan-Muslim virtual "homesteading". Their project further exemplifies how the internet is being recruited to broker relations in the name of ethnicity, even to reconfigure and situate that ethnicity. It invokes as well the third facet of our title, where "native on the net" refers to quests for validation as well as exercises in personal and collective self invention. This echoes some of the issues raised by the examples of indigenous cyber-activism given above. In diaspora, however, these issues – recitations on heritage, campaigns to safeguard tradition and/or territory, performances of cultural legitimacy – take on different inflections when the presumed isomorphism between place and identity is ruptured. Whereas in the case of indigenous cyberactivism, cyberspace often presents a staging ground for the defense of authenticity or a meeting ground for networking, for those in diaspora it may well pose an alternative "territory" where a transnational virtual neighborhood might be constructed *tout de suite* (see Graham and Khosravi 2002: 13). This is not to imply that spatiality is superfluous with respect to virtuality. To the contrary, as these ethnographies attest, geospace is often omnipresent – discursively, graphically, ideologically, affectively – in virtual world-building.

The recurring "presence" of geospace in cyberspace is, for example, to be found in many homepages posted by Kurds, a stateless and historically marginalized peoples whose body politic is widely dispersed. Approached with regard to the production of virtual community – as "structures of feeling" (Williams 1977) and properties of social life – it is of interest that the homepages of Kurds in diaspora (as well as the websites of official Kurdish organizations) exhibit a remarkably patterned theme, at least as perceived by the casual, outside observer (based on my random excursion through roughly one hundred Kurdish homepages available in English or part/optional English). The intertextuality of Kurdish homepages is readily apparent in their formulaic and cross-referential contents: nearly each one posts a map of Kurdistan, a history of the Kurdish peoples, a delineation of their struggles for self-determination, links to official Kurdish organizations and media sites, and the ubiquitous personal narrative recounting the homepage author's own exodus to a Western land. One popular link leads to *www.aka.kurdistan's* "Unknown Image Archive", which posts (mainly historic) photographs of anonymous Kurds, and implores site visitors to come forward with any information they might have in order to put a name to a face, and thereby, one image at a time, to "unlock the life within each photograph" in a joint effort to reclaim lost histories, lost trans-generational connections, lost worlds.

Such re-presentations can be read as sites of recovery: at once reclamations of a fragmented and silenced collective, whilst equally pledges of continued solidarity. The recitation of alternate histories (history being always-already a political project, more of invention than reconstruction) arguably assumes heightened significance for a people whose collective past has been a casualty of multiple erasures and censorship. Hereby, mapping the world in the absence of a *bona fide* nation-state may well assume subversive undertones as an act of forbidden nationalism. To circulate electronic maps and fly digital flags is (metonymically) to rehearse nationalist aspirations in cyberspace, where the map of Kurdistan becomes a sign with a referent, if clearly not to sovereignty, then to geopolitical machinations and dis-orderings. Via a "dynamics of objectification", cyberactive Kurds are authoring "their internet" as a relatively safe haven to emplot the nation-state dream. This usage skirts the fine line between what Miller and Slater refer to as the "expansive realization" that the internet offers to "deliver on pledges" that people have made to themselves in taking up "their rightful place" on the one hand, and the "expansive potential" of the internet as "a mode of imagining the future", on the other (2001: 10–14, and *passim*). We might add another dynamic of objectification in play on *www.aka.kurdistan*: a *re-inscription of the past* via narratives of lamentation.

A similar instance of how politically-marginalized groups might annex the internet as an instrument to "deliver on pledges" and as a horizon to re-imagine the future, is presented here in Chapter 10, by Hala Fattah, who researches the online discussions of Turcomans and Assyrians in diaspora. Although these are two distinct Iraqi minorities, there are clear parallels in the uses and agendas that frame their respective cyber-engagements. Both groups have found virtuality to be a fertile place to fashion an idealized, quasi-mythic past – forgetting certain chapters of their history and over-inflating others in quests to recapture their respective "golden ages" (e.g., the Assyrian civilization (see also Gabrial 1998), and the days of the Turcoman empire). Such "ever-morphing" spectacles of the use and abuse of history undoubtedly serve multifarious contemporary purposes. In part, their moves stem from a desire to exercise the new freedoms of expression available in diaspora. As Fattah notes, "there is nothing as exhilarating as letting off steam in cyberspace", especially for those who have "grown up believing that freedom of expression is for others". In part, their moves are declarations of intent: they are "putting Iraq, and the world, on notice of their programs and intentions, and so beginning a vital and necessary dialogue to reopen the question of their long-awaited 'return' to the homeland". As with the case of Kurdish homepages, geospace casts its shadow over the virtual communities of interest and imagination that are articulated in and through Assyrian and Turcoman chat sites. In aspiring to shape the future body politic, both groups in diaspora are reordering ties with the Iraq of today and jockeying to position themselves into the ongoing dialogue (and eventual project) to remake the Iraq of tomorrow. Herein we witness another instance of how the world wide web becomes a "field of dreams" for nation-building, at least virtually. We also witness again its attraction for asserting distinction and claims in the name of an original ethnicity grounded in monuments of yesteryear and victorious moments past.

Cyber-wounds and cyber-healing

Thus far, our estimations of the ways the internet reorders the diasporic condition have largely considered how peoples (Harari, Kurds, Turcomans, Assyrians) write themselves into larger histories (like that of pan-Islam) and/or glorified ones (like past golden ages) as part of contemporary political projects and articulations of identity. Herein, it seems that making oneself a(t) home in cyberspace furnishes a platform for conjecturing an alternative home in geospace (whether it be sovereign, democratic, pluralist, separatist, etc.). Each virtual landscape of words and dreams, in its own way, poses a critique and reha-bilitation of home place; we now turn to an example of cyberspace deployed as a weapon to *defend* home territory by those who have left it behind.

In Chapter 11 of this book, John Philip Schaefer presents a picture of iGhana, a virtual "e-nation" that exists as an electronic space/nonspace of imagination and interest, traversed via texts and images, terminals and satel-lites by a "netizen" public comprised of Ghanaians in diaspora. Schaefer follows one particularly defining moment in the birth of iGhana: a virtual brawl escalating in the digital badlands of discussion forums. The discord was triggered by the proposal, on the part of an American animal-rights organiza-tion, to relocate captive chimpanzees from US zoos and research laboratories to a nature reserve/ecotourism park in Ghana. In rejecting this idea, iGhanaians rallied to defend their homeland from becoming what they feared would be a dumping ground for "throw-away" chimps, possibly infected with disease or worse. The battle was fought on two fronts. The first front staged a contest for influence on the domestic political scene – by charging that the ecotourism park marked a case of playing regional favoritism. The second front mobilized a trans-nationally dispersed resistance in postcolonial spirit against centuries of foreign incursions – wounds re-opened by this latest "good intentions" act, read as veiled superpower hegemony. On this front, iGhanaians summoned forth (to revisit upon the West) the colonial language long used to delegitimize the black African "Other". They tellingly invoked accusations of contamination and subjection, bestiality and primitivity, in a summary rejection of the animal-rights petition. It might be said that the highly-charged, almost histrionic chimp scheme "took on a virtual life of its own", becoming a scapegoat onto which were hurled raw anger over colonial atrocities, grievances about contemporary political corruption, and diasporic feelings of estrangement. It simultaneously became a test case for the exercise of power-at-a-distance for an absent body politic. Hereby, the internet empowered iGhanaians (a group whose very dispersion is a direct conse-quence of politico-economic differentials) to virtually annihilate distance and wield "real-time" influence on affairs "back home". Given that the influence of ex-pats in diaspora was in significant respects more compelling than that of fellow compatriots who had never left, it must be conceded that iGhana wielded or at least galvanized geopolitical clout in its own right. In this manner it established itself as a political entity to be reckoned with – not despite, but essentially because of, its virtuality.[12] In addition to proffering alternative, un-sanitized versions of colonialism through native eyes, iGhanaians are using the web to scour the political horizon and keep (alleged) neocolonialism in check.

Whereas iGhana presents a case of digital technologies pushed into service to wage a war of words against a perceived foreign threat, the next case we consider gives us a promising glimpse into the mobilization of cyberspace to combat an even more insidious and dangerous foe – that of enmity from within. In her chapter (Chapter 12), Rose Kadende-Kaiser studies two online discussion forums where Hutu and Tutsi in Burundi and in diaspora meet to debate and decimate the roots of the bloody civil war which took more than a million lives in the mid-1990s. The first bulletin board of its kind, Burundinet was active in the immediate post-war period, while the wounds of inter-ethnic violence were still fresh and the topic of ethnicity dominated discussions. At best, exchanges on *Burundinet* represented good-faith endeavors to learn from the mistakes of the past; but at worst they devolved into tit-for-tat accusations and blanket attempts at blaming the other. Nevertheless, as Kadende-Kaiser points out, the very fact that Tutsi and Hutu – whose interrelations had so recently been consumed by murderous rage – were even engaging in dialogue (a delicate one at that) marked a positive step towards bridging ideological differences. The second discussion list, the *Burundi Youth Council*, was launched seven years after the war with the explicit goal to move beyond the ethnic divide. Its rules of conduct specifically forbid discussion around the sensitive topic of ethnicity, whilst permitting ventures into traditionally-tabooed subjects, such as conversations about homosexuality, teenage pregnancy, abortion, and women in governance. By side-stepping the potentially explosive issue of ethnicity, yet liberalizing debate on serious and sensitive concerns that cross-cut ethnicity, the online youth forum may prove more successful at engendering the kind of tolerance needed not only for immediate conflict resolution but for realizing and forging a vibrant public sphere. While quintessentially Burundi, this experimental discursive forum nevertheless moves in a direction that imports (for better or worse) Western ideas, a trend that may well challenge the grounds of tradition.

The dialogic success of Hutu–Tutsi online exchanges gives a promising example of the unique communicative advantage of virtuality: to be recruited as a relatively "safe" refuge in which to begin the tentative process of community healing – a (virtual) reconciliation with the potential for real rapprochement. Whereas Hutu–Tutsi cyber-locutions certainly give cause for optimism about the prospects of digital democracy or at least digital diplomacy, Chapter 13 on cyber-terrorism serves as a sobering reminder of the annexation of cyberspace to more divisive ends. In the chapter William Taggart explores "virtual occupations": in the form of the cyberwars of pro-Palestinian hackers who deface Israeli websites and pro-Israeli hackers who deface Palestinian ones. For the virtual terrorist, the "safety" of cyberspace assumes new meanings, wherein anonymity becomes a resource in the execution of electronic hate crimes and the graffiti of humiliation. Hence, before appointing abstraction a safer medium or designating communicative exchange an inevitable good, it would be wise to recall the decisive role played by radio broadcasts in inciting the interethnic violence in Burundi, and thereby come face-to-face with the caustic and spiraling "real-world" effects of verbal aggression, propoganda and disinformation. Surely graphics of Arafat in a monkey suit or the Israeli flag in flames come with a real-life punch. Complicating the matter further, the scope of electronic sabotage spreads far beyond that of the immediate zone of physical conflict, involving not just hackers but participants/viewers worldwide.[13]

The virtual terrorist's anonymity raises interesting methodological issues for the virtual ethnographer. From Taggart's fieldwork we learn that anti-Israeli hackers are likely to be computer-savvy Arab teenagers: boys and young men resident in Pakistan or other Arab countries, or perhaps in diaspora. For them, hacking is an opportunity to manifest solidarity: indeed, to participate (virtually) in defense of the Muslim brotherhood. It is improbable that covert computer activities are taking place in refugee camps or the Occupied Territories in Palestine. There, access to ICTs is limited and potentially under surveillance, and when given half a chance, as Taggart reminds us, Palestinian youth are more inclined to embrace cyberspace as an escape from the violence of everyday life, an alternative world of gaming, chatting, cruising music channels and porn sites. After all, for them resistance is literally only a stone's throw away; albeit, hacking – throwing digital "stones" – may come with less risk of bodily harm. In the case of anti-Palestinian hackers, a large number appear to be Russian-Jewish male youth recently immigrated to Israel. Having reached their "homeland" (according to Jewish prophecy and its codification in Israel's right of "return" law) these new arrivals must none the less find and assert their "native" identity as belongers within the ethnically-plural Israeli state. For some, perhaps, these challenges are being met through ultra-nationalistic activities like defacing Arab websites, whereby newcomers can "world" their loyalty via cyberspace, whilst also overcoming alienation and demonstrating technical prowess.[14]

The experiential (and rhetorical) infinities of cyberspace suggest it to be a boundless *terra nullius* where room enough for everyone is virtually guaranteed (granted the hardware, software, wetware are "in place" and free from sabotage or censorship, of course). In contradistinction, hacking demonstrably implies that some cyber-plots are more equal, or at least more desired, than others. To deface another's website is to violently wrest that locality, however temporarily, from its aboriginal colonizers. The dot.com planet – despite (or perhaps because of?) the multiplicity of sites and their ephemeral nature – is clearly regarded a convenient (symbolic) battlefield into which to import territorial and other contests.

Counter-reflexes and meta-reflexivities

The cyberethnographies considered above – iGhanaians fighting perceived neocolonialism; Hutus and Tutsis talking reconciliation; pro-Palestinians and pro-Israelis waging electronic warfare – attest to the ready annexation of cyberspace as a place to export geopolitical conflict, for the purposes either of exacerbating or alleviating it, fomenting it or resisting it. In keeping with this focus on the role of virtuality in the transplantation and transmutation of offline geopolitical relations, the next chapter examines the strategic enlistment of cyberspace in the all-important terrain of public opinion management.

In Chapter 14, Mark Whitaker details the methodical creation of the online news forum, *Tamilnet*, a journalistic site designed to add an indigenous public sphere to the government-dominated one that has "officially" framed representations of Sri Lanka's conflict. *Contra Burundinet*, *Tamilnet.com* is not an endeavor to dialogically heal the wounds of war; rather, it is an agenda to recast images of war and its aftermath through the little-heard voices of the independence movement. Likewise, as distinct from iGhana, which (as we have seen) was authored by diasporic Ghanaians on the outskirts of homeland and as a means to influence events back home, *Tamilnet* is authored from within, by "on the ground" witnesses, perpetrators, resistors, narrators, etc. Moreover, it was launched expressly for the purpose of mobilizing those in diaspora, and through them, reaching a global public. Theirs was a message aimed to counterbalance the Western media's alarming indifference to, and even negative type-casting of, the independence movement – an aim made all the more urgent by keen recognition of the need to gain distance from the loosely-applied "terrorist" labels being bandied about as rhetorical weapons to (legitimately or otherwise) dismiss resistance movements of every stripe in post-9/11 geopolitics.

Towards the goal of founding an alternative public sphere, *Tamilnet* site organizers adopted the neutrality standards and operating models of Western media. In little over a year, they achieved a news forum whose reporting is 99 percent accurate and is widely recognized as such, with a track record for credibility that has facilitated its uptake and distribution by international wire services. The site, nevertheless, is biased – as indeed and inevitably is *all* journalism, a crucial point that Whitaker aptly reminds us applies in equal force to Western media. What holds true for conventional newscasts seems to hold true for virtual ones as well: that is, that journalism is biased *tout court* and at the outset, biased in prioritizing (or conversely erasing) some issues over others; biased in following, writing and posting certain stories in lieu of alternatives, and so on. Few were more savvy about media's bias under the aspiration (or pretext) of neutrality than *Tamilnet's* leading editor; in fact, his proposal to model the forum according to professional standards evinced both a sincere appreciation of the market for factual reporting, and an experienced understanding of media clout and its power – not simply to inform publics, but to strategically inform public opinion. With respect to the site's design and implementation, *Tamilnet's* founders exhibited remarkable foresight and a meta-reflexive insight into the workings of representational power, publics, performance, and global positioning. Their "counter counter-insurgency" – one that "talks back to power using the tools of power" – grasped the significance of re-formatting one's cause in line with protocols that define the very terms of credibility, and then effectively enlisted electronic media to broadcast this newly-forged (claim to) legitimacy.[15]

Questions about reflexivity and its multiple layerings also loom large in our next and last cyberethnography, which journeys into the online discussions of South Asian women in diaspora, exchanging communiqués via the list-server known as *SAWnet*. In Chapter 15, Radhika Gajjala, a native ethnographer and herself a list member/participant, introduces us to the "*SAWnet* refusal" – when list members are to prohibit scholarly study of their forums, on the grounds that virtual chat is akin to being "in a friend's living room" where one is apt to forget (indeed, one wants to forget) that there are "microphones to many other living rooms [and one's] message is being transmitted all over the world". In opting to preserve their sense of safety online, *SAWnetters* in effect voted their refusal to become ethnographic subjects.

The *SAWnet* refusal did more than subvert Gajjala's "attempted cyberethnography"; it also helped to highlight challenges specific to fieldwork online and the newly-problematized relations between cyber-anthropologist and ethnographic virtual Other (challenges we shall consider in more detail). It is interesting in this context that Gajjala's work itself focuses on the question of the representativeness of a digital diaspora and the often-static and stale images of "homeland" engendered by its participants/members. In having access to cyberspace – understood as a discursive/material realm of cultural production – *SAWnet* women (like many an elite group in diaspora) have tended to be in a privileged position to re-present their homeland largely on their own terms. This has empowered these relatively affluent women to deconstruct the monolithic notion of a "Third-world woman": a notion constructed by dominant stereotypes, with the dual complicity of Indian nationalist rhetoric alongside Western feminism. On the one hand, ICTs have implicitly granted diasporic *SAWnetters* the power to speak on behalf of their less privileged sisters "back home"; yet on the other hand, discourses of diaspora run the risk of marginalizing and silencing the "subaltern" subject who has not moved West. As Gajjala points out, however, the balance of power is shifting by virtue of shifts in technology access: as ever-greater numbers of resident South Asian women get online, they are in a virtual position to extend rejoinders to diasporist discourses and counter impressions of homeland and home peoples seemingly "frozen in time". Here, internet affords a vehicle whereby the subaltern can resist "mummification" as a seductive stereotype of nostalgia, whether neocolonial or diasporic in tenor.

As the *SAWnet* refusal makes clear, interactive media technologies can blur, even subvert, the conventional power asymmetries between research subject and researcher, enabling "virtual informants" to "talk back" to the ethnographer as well, perhaps inciting them to openly reflect upon acts of representation. The prospect of cyberethnography of/on *SAWnet* invoked collective and reflexive dialogues regarding rights to privacy in chat's quasi-public "small world" space-time. Virtual feedback from cyber-locutors "back home" is poised to deepen and reproduce such reflexive musings upon the politics and ethics of speaking for others. It seems clear that, despite (or perhaps because of) their seamless appearance/experience, computer-mediated communications have the capacity to invoke a great deal of meditation, precisely on questions of locality, identity, positionality, visibility. In this context, cyber-ethnography is sure to push further anthropology's own meta-reflexive turn.[16] This possibility brings us to a consideration of the dynamics of an ethnography in/of virtuality, where ethnography is arguably made more indeterminate, or at least more conscious of its indeterminacy. The next and final section reflects upon some problematics and prospects of making anthropology a(t) home in cyberspace.

Virtual tricksters and virtual taboos

The globality and virtuality of cyberspace challenge for new methodological and analytical tools that are better equipped: to grasp relations of temporality, spatiality, agency and materiality; to engage with identities that are mobile, volatile, composite, (potentially) anonymous, experimental, deceptive or archived; to apprehend communities that are fluid; to negotiate an ethics of representation in the absence of face-to-face accountability. In short, cyberspace acutely problematizes the "production of locality" central to the ethnographic project's "governing telos", a telos in unwitting complicity with the social projects (i.e. the "cultures") it studies (Appadurai 1995: 207). Acts of signification brokered by digital, cross-planetary media assuredly comprise one of humankind's most ambitious and reflexively-charged exercises in meaning-making; and one that confronts anthropology, even an anthropology wizened by its reflexive turn, with incomparable interpretive challenges.

Virtuality's multiple indeterminacies raise a thicket of unsettling questions: Just where (or what) is the virtual field site? Where and when is the virtual ethnographer? Which media forms will most aptly re-present virtual ethnography? How and with whom should professional fieldwork ethics be applied? Just how should the virtual informant be interpreted – as textualized subject or interactive text? And so on. By mediating the material and the symbolic in radically new ways (Bell 2001: 2) virtuality dis- and re-assembles (or, to plunder an anthropological concept, we might say plays "trickster" with) the relative ground of conventional social and dialogical forms. Trickster technologies slip through our certainties, twisting taken-for-granted ontological categories and interactive modalities. For example, they simultaneously evoke rooted qualities of place/venue (e.g., website, homepage, multi-user dungeon, digital archive, etc.) and fluid qualities of process/vehicles (e.g., information superhighway, electronic mail, networking, cruising the web). Poster (1998) considers the internet to work like a tool but also like a society; similarly, Hine (2000) approaches it as both a "cultural artifact" and equally as a "culture" in its own right. Jones (1995: 16) pluralizes the conceptual framework by apprehending computer-mediated communication to be "at once technology, medium, and engine of social relations". Fischer (1999a) provides us with a rich list of cyberspace's transformative capacities, in a manner somewhat reminiscent of the enumerated definitions of "culture" that Kroeber and Kluckhohn (1952) famously and usefully problematized for anthropologists over half a century ago. Fischer's list is a kind of pedagogical enticement to encourage "anthropologies of late modernity" to heed calls for "worlding cyberspace" through contextualized, situated studies realized upon the hunch that computer-mediated communication provides "a design studio for social theory" (Fischer 1999b: 469).

It is by dint of capturing the ways cyberspace collapses and convolutes certain disciplinary conventions that we intend a fifth facet of our title. *Native on the Net* puns upon a once-canonical professional taboo: as anthropologists of yesteryear set off into "the field" (or so the story goes), they were admonished not to "go native"; that is, to avoid over-identifying with the locals' perspective. This fuzzy proscription against an even fuzzier occupational hazard cautioned ethnographers to remain "neutral" (i.e. to be rational as opposed to emotional observers of inner cultural workings), or otherwise risk losing an ostensibly objective scientific distance *vis-à-vis* the anthropological subject/object – traditionally, the indigenous Other. Space precludes us from here interrogating this taboo-turned-parable, one moreover with an aura of hubris about it.[17] A mere glance none the less suggests that it iterates dichotomous distinctions between home and field, here and there, center and periphery, etc. – distinctions which are to remain in place upon return with the "now" act of writing-up of field notes from "then" accounts of participatory witnessing-turned-scientific truth. Viewed from the reference point of communicative praxes taking place instantaneously and planet-wide, such dichotomies seem artifacts of thought lingering from a nigh-obsolete analog age. These fictional constructs and the binary logic undergirding them are fundamentally challenged – distorted, blurred, unraveled – by virtuality's prolific capacity to reshuffle relations – between anthropologist and informant, locality and identity, subjects and texts, centers and peripheries. Hence, on the one hand we can take note of how cyberspace challenges anew anthropological ways of knowing and any residual anchorings in static researcher/informant configurations. On the other hand, we might say that, far from dissipating, binary thinking has undergone a qualitative shift: has been upgraded, as it were, in/for an internet-age. By this I refer to the dichotomous logic that echoes in the dualistic (and dueling) tropes mobilized to capture the ICT experience. This bevy of new signifiers coined to connote pre-cyber days and non-cyber moments has spawned: "real life" as a counterpart to "virtual life", offline versus online, screened versus face-to-face, etc. Indeed, it might be asserted that a *mana*-like power – ineffable, unique, evasive, unlocalizeable – figures in these metaphorical evocations of the nature of ICTs.

In thus jostling with the taboo against "going native" (a taboo still thinly in circulation and one which is not without its measure of value and professional acumen), we here enlist it by dint of shorthand, as a condensed sign that encapsulates and caricatures essentialized notions of all kinds, both those implied in the simplistic dividing lines of classic anthropology, and those spawned to unproductively sever virtual technologies from situated being and doing. We intend our *double entendre* to poke fun at, whilst seeking to seriously problematize, these essentializing trends.

In the first instance, our pun is by way of suggesting that cyberspace "itself" fundamentally "takes to task" lingering anthropological divisions and presumptions implied in the "going native" taboo. Posed thus, we might query whether anthropology indeed can even "go native" when the field and/or informants are (on occasion) virtual? The supposition becomes, if not completely nonsensical (given cyberspace's potential to erode certain distinctions), then at least maladaptive to the characteristics of the medium; and the issue is moot. Clearly, with cyberspace as field site, there is no "there" or "then" in the typical sense: the field is here/there, everywhere/nowhere, perpetually open to immediate (re)visitation, and moreover poised to (re)visit us, the fieldworker. Indeed, as the fieldwork experience increasingly attests, electronic communications chase anthropologists (even those not concerned with things virtual) "back home" – not simply keeping us connected and connectable to the (real life) field at a distance (via emailing, chatting, homepaging, etc.) – but moreover and intriguingly, presenting us with new "satellite" fields for contemplation, virtual arenas of sociality and/or conflict, of symbolic actions and reactions which informants animate and which inevitably influence events in "the" field and may even ironically call into question that field and the anthropologist's place there (cf. Whitaker 2004). We are accordingly closer to the field than ever – it's just at our fingertips; and yet further from it than ever, to the extent that we may never (need to?) leave home to converse with "the locals". Indeed, several of the ethnographers whose writings are included in this volume first embarked upon online research only after, and because, the peoples they knew and/or studied were already "there". With "natives" (implying here simply any research "informant", "subject", or better, interlocutor) themselves going online in increasing numbers, then any discipline intent upon studying "the human condition" can ill afford to ignore or exorcise these meaning-making acts and enactments. In the face of researcher–informant "meetings" in virtual (non)places, dichotomies and their premises collapse in ways that mandate critical deconstruction: what happens to power, to place, to representation, to resistance, to authority, to authenticity? These assuredly do not resolve, but they do reconstitute.

In the second instance, thus, our "going native" pun is intended by way of proposing that anthropology "itself" can fruitfully be tapped to task our split conceptualization of the world wide web as an alien, unfathomable terrain. Here, echoing others (Escobar 1994; Hakken 1999; Miller and Slater 2001; Wilson and Peterson 2002), we suggest that a discipline committed to fieldwork is especially well equipped to enrich our grasp of virtual media as a prosthetic animation of signifying propensities that, far from being divorced from everyday being-in-the-world, exhibit an intriguingly dynamic, multivalent role in (cross)cultural productions, in near and far relations, in personal and collective identity-constructions, in navigating the ordinary and performing the extraordinary. Tools forged in the "abandonment of a commitment to realism" arguably give ethnographers a firmer "ontological footing" (Wilson and Peterson 2002: 451) as we venture into cyber or virtual territories apprehended to be "fields of relations" (Hine 2000: 56; see also Hastrup and Olwig 1997). While for certain ethnographic projects (depending on intentions, aims, etc.) the analytical design may "stay within" the virtual field(s) in order to explore "communities in cyberspace", it is a truism that, in all cases, the offline inflects the online and *vice versa*.[18] Some things moreover remain the same: whereas the digital/virtual field-worker moves through time rather than space, the delicate bartering intrinsic to any kind of travel (physical, virtual, metaphorical) nonetheless holds. Anthropologists on the web must still find access, establish rapport, learn the rules for being competent participants, receive permission to undertake research, etc. (or fail to accomplish some or all of these endeavors, as the *SAWnet* "refusal to be studied" aptly shows). In short, fieldworkers must still negotiate place. It follows that multi-sited ethnographies that (re)position virtuality as yet another locality help shed light on the diversity and specificity of online social (and *asocial*) forms as interactive (non)spaces, which perform and transform the local (within the global and *vice versa*). Anthropology's strongest contribution is likely to be found, furthermore, in a potential to situate fieldwork at the culturally-constructed (and hence shifting) interface between offline and online: a divide that itself represents a "crisis of boundaries" (Shields 1996: 7) involving two "consensual loci" each accorded a reality that calls for interpretation (Stone 1991); and, we would further argue, that calls for conceptual integration. While there is clearly something "different" about cyberspace, something exceptional and extraordinary, it is incumbent upon us to unravel just how this difference is woven/filtered into lives and becomes aspectual of identities.

When the theater of fieldwork includes indigeneity and globality, diaspora and virtual return, anthropologists face a renewed challenge to capture the dynamics of "native" (i.e. "local") identities: how do they traffic, transform, artic-ulate, adapt, strengthen, subvert, triumph and/or tumble online? Approached thus, we might pose the query of whether cyberspace can "go native". By this, we imply the question of whether virtual technologies can be indigenized, meaning not only assimilated into local perspectives and for local agendas, but actively inscribed and shaped by them: indelibly stamped with the objectives (grand or otherwise) and logic of a (non-dominant) culture-sharing collective. In contrast to the aforegoing question of whether anthropology can go native in cyberspace (a question we basically dismissed as moot), the "answer" to this second query is, at present, wide open. The varied chapters here – all informed by on- and offline fieldwork (whilst prioritizing or highlighting one or the other angle) – represent a modest step towards this issue, one we revisit in the Postscript. First, however, we turn our attention to the 14 ethnographic portraits that explore the ways in which indigenous and diasporic publics are attempting to make themselves a(t) home in cyberspace, going global and going local with friends and virtual strangers, with electronic homesteaders from near and far, with interlocutors who are, as Hakken aptly notes (1999: 68), equally "the Other" online. After all, we are all native in cyberspace.[19]

Notes

1   Throughout this introduction I use cyberspace, internet, new media and the worldwide web in a rather sloppy and overlapping matter to cover both infrastructure and the uses

to which it is put (Wilson and Peterson 2002: 452); this loose and generic refer-encing places emphasis on effects as "a cluster of different technologies . . . all of which have in common the ability to stimulate environments within which humans can interact" (Featherstone and Burrows 1995: 3).

2   The literature on the social implications of ICTs is vast; albeit much early scholar-ship was sensational and speculative: polarized by tendencies to conceptually domesticate "the new" according to either utopian or dystopic type-casting. A second generation of empirical studies is proving more adept at navigating the terri-tory and guiding our interpretations through it, so that we can better map, for example, how global media technologies are coming to be "commonsense" (Jones 1997), at least in and across certain contexts. This collection further seeks to de-mythologize cyberspace, focusing on ICT usages by marginalized peoples. The introduction, however, makes no attempt to span the literature, referring the reader instead to some of the reviews and collections available (Jones 1995, 1997; Shields 1996; Porter 1997; Smith and Kollack 1998; Hakken 1999; Herman and Swiss 2000; Bell and Kennedy 2000; Ess 2001; Wilson and Leighton 2002; McChaughey and Ayers 2003).

3   In the spirit of colloquialism, my introduction and the chapters in this book in general talk about "the internet". Nonetheless, I am in conceptual agreement with Miller and Slater's (2001: 15) refutation of "the idea of a pregiven entity called 'the Internet,'" which they note is better understood as a place-embedded assembly of technical possibilities and disparate media that are forged into what we might call customized internets. Accordingly, they explore how Trinidadians construct "their internet" (ibid: 14, italics in the original); in a similar manner Bell (2001) explores "cybercultures," and Dodge and Kitchin (2001) map "cyberspaces". In working towards a situated, heterogenous view of new media, I hope the chapters here shed light on how different indigenous and/or diasporic groups are not only orienting themselves to these technical possibilities, but are assembling respective internets, cyberplaces, cybercultures, etc. from among these tools. This is akin to what we might query as *indigenizing the internet*.

4   In her work into online experimentation with alternative identities, Turkle (1997) encounters a range of such creative identity performances amongst her research subjects.

5   Several studies consider the emergent use of ICT's by indigenous peoples (Arnold and Plymire 2000; Bray-Crawford 1999; Cleaver 1998; Fair 2000; Kuhmunen 2001; Lee 1996; Mizrach 1999; Parra 1995; Routledge 1998; Trahant 1996; Wood 1995; Vitali 2001). See also the theme issues on this topic by: *Cultural Survival Quarterly* (1998) and Volume 21 of the *Electronic Library*, edited by Roy and Raitt (2003); see also the 2003 special issue of *Indigenous Affairs* published by IWGIA (International Work Group for Indigenous Affairs).

6   The website of the International Work Group for Indigenous Affairs (a non-profit, non-governmental organization in support of indigenous rights) gives a definition of indigenous that might be taken as conventional. Indigenous refers to the frequently "disadvantaged descendants of those peoples that inhabited a territory prior to formation of a state" (www.iwgia.org). Distinguished from "dominant sectors of society", they are "determined to preserve, develop and transmit to future genera-tions their ancestral territories, and their ethnic identity, as the basis of their continued existence as peoples, in accordance with their own cultural patterns, social institutions and legal systems" (IWGIA 2001; see also 2000). Under this defi-nition, "indigenous peoples make up 5% of the world's population, occupy over 20% of the earth's landmass and pursue self-determination and sovereignty in all 73 coun-tries in which they dwell" (MacIntosh, n.d.). There are currently an estimated 350 million peoples, representing 5,000 distinct groups worldwide, who claim and are

recognized to be indigenous by the United Nations and by non-governmental organizations, such as IWGIA and Cultural Survival.

7 Given the nature of the medium, the virtual face of indigeneity also subsumes
second-person representations of indigenous peoples by non-natives – for purposes of
profit (e.g., trade in native arts and goods), prestige, self-promotion (as in some New
Age expropriations), or what-have-you; in extreme unauthorized cases, what appears
to be indigenous presence online is more correctly deemed indigenous *pretense*.
Whilst distinguishing real from counterfeit indigenous cyber-presence is admittedly
difficult, the data currently under assembly and my own surveying on- and offline
give reason to believe that a growing percentage of indigenous virtual actors and
sites are "authentic". Moreover, indigenous groups are proving increasingly adept at
meeting the challenge of finding ways – if not to police imposter sites outright (an
admittedly difficult task) – then to at least expose counterfeits and better arm themselves against them.

8 "First World" references a hegemonic and much-weathered term originally used to
aggrandize (largely Western) "developed" countries (countries some now propose be
aptly dubbed "over-developed"). The ranking of worlds articulated, of course, the
modernist project and its progress myth, wherein it was implied that "Third World"
"developing" countries would and should progress into and toward First World ones
(once "Second World" "communist" countries were toppled and hence categorically
arrested in this schema with its unmistakably capitalist predilections). Much of this
mythologizing and indeed the failure of the modernist project have been critically
analyzed by numerous scholars and activists (see, especially, the work of economist
Amartya Sen 2000). For our purposes here, it bears note that this schema assigned
indigenous peoples to a "Fourth World" standing – a term some indigenous communities subsequently have appropriated as affirmation of their rightful sovereignty. To
the extent that the "First" and "Third" terms (whose specters still circulate amongst
us) are deployed here, they are intended critically and with irony; albeit it remains to
be seen what positive or negative values will adhere to the "Fourth" term. The move
to re-define and claim anew a trans- or supranational category of "Fourth World
peoples" is itself an interesting political twist on the modernist pyramid – a nominal
survival carrying new significations for the 21st century.

9 The statement by National Chief M. Coon Come, Assembly of Canadian First
Nations is available online at http://www.broadband.gc.ca/binder/ncacl061102_e.pdf.

10 The document can be found at http://www.aics.org/war.html.

11 To here assert the inventedness of indigeneity is by no means to deny the "reality" of
indigenous peoples, nor the genuineness of their claims. Virtually all indigenous
groups worldwide have been (at one time or another), and most continue to be,
victims of forced de-traditionalization in the wake of colonialism, religious conver-
sions, globalization, state-sponsored civilizing projects (e.g., education, assimilation,
welfare dependency, etc.), market economies, and so forth. (Maybury-Lewis 1997).
Pushed into remote corners of the world, their dispossession has been profound and
their calls for self-determination righteous (see Friedman 1999). To assert the
inventedness of indigeneity is, however, to concede that indigeneity (like all identities) emerges relationally and transactionally, undergoing transformation and
re-signification in relation to shifting contexts, values, agendas, worldviews.

12 iGhana is an e-nation with a real-world counterpart, with which it has a complex set
of inter-relations and a measure of influence. Taking virtual nations to their logical
extreme, however, puts us on the border of such entities as the Republic of Lomar, a
facsimile of a nation-state absent the referent (yet rumored to be located somewhere
between Canada and the USA). By simply logging onto the Republic's website and
paying a small fee, as did Schaefer, one can apply for a Lomar passport and a driver's
license – credentials that confer no substantive rights or powers, and appear (to

borrow the pun of the neo-Lomarian Schaefer) "perfectly meaningless" (except perhaps as symbolic capital). These simulacra might be read as anti-documents that lampoon the nation-state and its bureaucratic logic, perhaps even taking to task its self-seriousness and *raison d'être*. Whatever the intent or interrogation, it ultimately confirms the grave dominion of the nation-state: for, while the Republic of Lomar may have seemed the ultimate in cyber-play and ploy, it was not necessarily an innocent game. The site drew numerous, misguided asylum seekers, would-be émigrés hoping in vein that Lomarian "citizenship" could be a stepping-stone into North America – as if, through the magic of things cyber, this online home might morph into, or at least leverage, a real-life double. Whatever the initial motives for imagining Lomar into existence (its creators insist it was not a hoax), over the course of its first year as an e-nation, the Republic came to adopt the refugee cause – a rather interesting chapter in its own history. In a case of life imitating art, what may have started as caricature has since evolved into a "do-good" organization that circulates information for refugees.

13 See also Sean Lawson's work on Palestinian and Israeli hackers (http://www.geocities.com/db8r.geo/). Offline conflict "spilling over" into online social spaces has been well documented, in discussions of flaming, email jamming, etc.; less has been said about conflicts first triggered virtually that are then exported into real life situations and relations. Siamak Rezaei (2001) gives us one such example: involving disinformation circulated online that, presumed true, began to negatively effect relations between different Kurdish political factions.

14 In further pondering the identity of those engaged in virtual colonization, we can not eliminate the possibility that official military and intelligence teams might well be hackers too: trained digital combatants in the sabotage of enemy computers, or alternatively masquerading as enemy hacker/terrorists in a covert strategy to recruit international sympathies and secure public compliance. In similar vein, being "the most computer literate, connected country in the Middle East" may make Israel better armed to crack-down on virtual terrorists, but ironically also makes it a more prominent target for cyber-attacks (see Lawson n.d.).

15 For a similar case whereby virtual counter-journalism on the part of ethnic minorities has forced oppressive regimes into a "dialogue of sorts" with resistors, see Fink's (1998) work on the various forms of online activism by Burmese in exile.

16 With the reflexive turn, anthropology itself became an object of critique, confronted by challengers on all fronts: ranging from deconstruction of the field site, to calls for transparency regarding the ethnographic project, to counter voices from peoples "under study", to ethical and representational dilemmas in the act of "writing culture". A plethora of new approaches blossomed from this disciplinary "rethinking" and "re-capturing", including: experimentation with auto-anthropology, interpretive ethnography and, informant co-authorship; queries about "constructing the field" (Amit 2000) or about "siting culture" (Olwig and Hastrup 1997); proposals for "multi-sited" fieldwork (Marcus 1995), fieldwork of "non-places" (Auge 1995) or of hybrid places, "anthropology at home" (Jackson 1987) or conversely a call for "native anthropologists"; theorizations about the "predicament of culture" (Clifford 1988), the "global ecumene" (Hannerz 1996), and "writing against culture" (Abu-Lughod 1991); and anthropological inquiry into new terrains, such as science and technology, media, social movements, and conflict zones, to name a few. The reflexive turn has been mapped at length, with many influential works to date (these include: Stocking 1985; Clifford and Marcus 1986; Marcus and Fischer 1986; Geertz 1990; Atkinson 1990; Fox 1991; Behar and Gordon 1996; Gupta and Ferguson 1997; van Maanen 1995).

17 It remains a fascinating exercise to probe the concepts of culture and knowledge implied in the "going native" taboo (culture as contagion, blindspot, portable

attire...?). Fieldwork relations between the anthropologist and the "natives" are, for obvious and not-so-obvious reasons, extraordinarily complex and intricate, spanning the full spectrum of human possibilities and inevitably grappling with issues of power, privacy, protection, property and prying. While we can not here entertain a spicy debate about "going native" or why it was deemed a matter of such poor professional habit, the aspirations (and inferiorities) of anthropology to be a "science of man" undoubtedly lay at the heart of this long-held (if not necessarily upheld) taboo. An ideal anthropology was presumably one unsullied by the capriciousness of volatile sentiment, yet the very existence of the taboo, like all such, bespeaks the prospect of its transgression – of acculturation towards (even) the radical "Other". Anthropological history is indeed peppered with rumors of such transgressions; but equally of anecdotes attesting to the taboo's redundancy. I might here relay a colleague's candor on the matter: a tall blond Scandinavian who jokingly recounted his fieldwork experiences in a Southeast Asian village "for me going native was never a problem because the 'natives' kept reminding me that I shouldn't be there!"

18　There is moreover some evidence that conventional status differentials (e.g., gender, race, class) "transfer over" in cyberspace (albeit in multifarious ways), calling into question its emancipatory potential (see Burkhalter 1999). In addition, language mixing, slang use, idioms, and other heteroglossic tendencies that everywhere drive the communicative project across divides, seem particularly prolific and reflexively-tinged in online forums. These practices simultaneously liberalize and police signifying exchanges across ingroup/outgroup cultural boundaries, as communicative agents code-switch between opening their comments to a larger public and/or catering them to select (intended) recipients (as we see here in the online ventures of Inuit, Tongans, Burundians, iGhanaians, and Native Americans who move back and forth between English and their respective native tongues). This implies meta-consciousness about audience(s) and about localities.

19　Albeit, this is not to imply that some may not, in true Orwellian fashion, be more "native" than others.

References

Abu-Lughod, Lila (1991) "Writing Against Culture", in Fox, R. G. (ed.), *Recapturing Anthropology: Working in the Present*. Santa Fe: School of American Research Press, pp. 137–64.

Amit, Vered (2000) "Introduction: Constructing the Field", in Amit, V. (ed.), *Constructing the Field: Ethnographic Fieldwork in the Contemporary World*. London: Routledge, pp. 1–18.

Appadurai, Arjun (1990) "Disjuncture and Difference in the Global Cultural Economy", *Public Culture* 2: 1–24.

—(1995) "The Production of Locality", in Fardon, R. (ed.), *Counterworks: Managing the Diversity of Knowledge*. London: Routledge, pp. 204–25.

Arnold, Ellen L. and Plymire, Darcy C. (2000). "The Cherokee Indians and the Internet", in Gauntlett, D. (ed.), *Web.Studies: Re-Wiring Media Studies for the Digital Age*. London: Arnold Press, pp. 186–93.

Atkinson, Paul (1990) *The Ethnographic Imagination: Textual Constructions of Reality*. London: Routledge.

Auge, Mark (1995) *Non-places: Introduction to an Anthropology of Supermodernity*. London: Verso.

Barcham, Manuhuia (2000) "(De)Constructing the Politics of Indigeneity", in Ivison, D., Patton, P. and Sanders, W. (eds), *Political Theory and the Rights of Indigenous Peoples*. Cambridge: Cambridge University Press, pp. 137–51.

Becker, Marc and Delgado-P., Guillermo (1998) "Latin America: The Internet and Indigenous Texts", *Cultural Survival Quarterly* 21(4). Available online: www.cultural-survival.org/publications

Beckett, Jeremy (1996) "Contested Images: Perspectives on the Indigenous Terrain in the Late 20th Century", *Identities: Global Studies in Culture and Power* 3(1–2): 1–13.

Behar, Ruth and Gordon, Deborah A. (eds) (1996) *Women Writing Culture*. Berkeley: University of California Press.

Bell, David (2001) *An Introduction to Cyberculture*. London: Routledge.

Bell, David and Kennedy, Barbara M. (2000) *The Cybercultures Reader*. London: Routledge.

Bourdieu, Pierre (1990) *The Logic of Practice*. Stanford: Stanford University Press.

Brah, Avtar (1996) *Cartographies of Diaspora: Contesting Identities*. London: Routledge.

Bray-Crawford, K. P. (1999) "The Ho'okele Netwarriors in the Liquid Continent", in Harcourt, W. (ed.), *women@internet: Creating New Cultures in Cyberspace*. London: Zed Books, pp. 162–72.

Bromberg, Heather (1996) "Are MUDs Communities? Identity, Belonging and Consciousness in Virtual Worlds", in Shields, R. (ed.), *Cultures of Internet*. London: Sage, pp. 143–52.

Brown, Wendy (1997) "The Time of the Political", *Theory & Event* 1(1).

Burkhalter, Byron (1999) "Reading Race Online: Discovering Racial Identity in Usenet Discussions", in Smith, M. A. and Kollock, P. (eds), *Communities in Cyberspace*. London: Routledge, pp. 60–75.

Calhoun, Craig (1992) "The Infrastructure of Modernity: Indirect Social Relationships, Information Technology, and Social Integration", in Haferkamp, H. and Smelser, N. J. (eds), *Social Change and Modernity*. Berkeley: University of California Press, pp. 205-36.

Castells, Manuel (1997) *The Information Age: Economy, Society and Culture*. Volume 2, *The Power of Identity*. Malden, MA: Blackwell.

Cheung, Charles (2000) "A Home on the Web: Presentations of Self on Personal Home-pages", in Gauntlett, D. (ed.), *Web.Studies*. London: Arnold, pp. 43–51.

Cleaver, H. M. (1998) "The Zapatista Effect: The Internet and the Rise of an Alternative Political Fabric", *Journal of International Affairs* 51(2): 621–40.

Clifford, James (1988) *The Predicament of Culture: Twentieth Century Ethnography, Literature and Art*. Cambridge, MA: Harvard University Press.

——(1997) *Routes: Travel and Translation in the Late Twentieth Century*. Cambridge, MA: Harvard University Press.

——(2001) "Indigenous Articulations", *The Contemporary Pacific* 13(2): 468–90.

Clifford, James and Marcus, George E. (eds) (1986) *Writing Culture: The Poetics and Politics of Ethnography*. Berkeley: University of California Press.

Cohen, Robin (1997) *Global Diasporas: An Introduction*. London: UCL Press.

Conklin, Beth A. (1997) "Body Paint, Feathers, and VCRs: Aesthetics and Authenticity in Amazonian Activism", *American Ethnologist* 24(4): 711–37.

Cultural Survival Quarterly (1998) Special Theme Issue: *The Internet and Indigenous Groups*, (21)4.

Dodge, Martin and Kitchin, Rob (eds) (2001) *Mapping Cyberspace*. London: Routledge.

Donaghy, Keola (1998) "Olelo Hawai'I: A Rich Oral History, A Bright Digital Future", *Cultural Survival Quarterly* 21(4). Available online: www.culturalsurvival.org/publications

Escobar, Arturo (1994) "Welcome to Cyberia: Notes on the Anthropology of Cyberculture", *Current Anthropology* 35: 211–32.

Ess, Charles (ed.) (2001) *Culture, Technology, Communication: Towards an Intercultural Global Village*. Albany: SUNY Press.

Fair, R. S. (2000) "Becoming the White Man's Indian: An Examination of Native American Tribal Web Sites", *Plains Anthropologist* (45)172: 203–13.

Featherstone, Mike and Burrows, Roger (1995) "Cultures of Technological Embodiment: An Introduction", in Featherstone, M. and Burrows, R. (eds), *Cyberspace, Cyberbodies, Cyberpunk*. London: Sage, pp. 1–19.

Fink, Christina (1998) "Burma: Constructive Engagement in Cyberspace?", *Cultural Survival Quarterly* 21(4). Available online: www.culturalsurvival.org/publications

Fischer, Michael M. J. (1999a) "Worlding Cyberspace: Toward a Critical Ethnography in Time, Space, and Theory", in Marcus, G. (ed.), *Critical Anthropology Now: Unexpected Contexts, Shifting Constituencies, Changing Agendas*. Santa Fe: School of American Research Press, pp. 245–304.

——(1999b) "Emergent Forms of Life: Anthropologies of Late of Postmodernities", *Annual Review of Anthropology* 28: 455–78.

Forsgren, Aanta (1998) "Use of Internet Communication among the Sami People", *Cultural Survival Quarterly* 21(4). Available online: www.culturalsurvival.org/publications

Forte, Maximilian (2001) *Re-engineering Indigeneity: Cultural Brokerage, the Political Economy of Tradition and the Santa Rosa Carib Community of Arima, Trinidad and Tobago*. PhD dissertation, Adelaide University.

Fox, Richard G. (1991) *Recapturing Anthropology: Working in the Present*. Santa Fe: School of American Research Press.

Friedman, Jonathan (1999) "Indigenous Struggles and the Discreet Charm of the Bourgeoisie", *The Australian Journal of Anthropology* 10(1): 1–14.

Gabrial, Albert (1998) "Assyrians: 3,000 Years of Hisory, yet the Internet is our Only Home", *Cultural Survival Quarterly* 21(4). Available online: www.culturalsurvival.org/publications

Gad, Alexander and Grabea, A'dnan (2005) *Chats behind the Chig: Bedouin Youth Online Chat as a Mirror, Rescue, Bypass and Bridge*. Unpublished manuscript.

Geertz, Clifford (1990) *Works and Lives: The Anthropologist as Author*. Stanford: Stanford University Press.

Giddens, Anthony (1991) *Modernity and Self-Identity: Self and Society in the Late Modern Age*. Stanford: Stanford University Press.

Glusker, Susannah (1998) "Women Networking for Peace and Survival in Chiapas: Militants, Celebrities, Academics, Survivors, and the Stiletto Heel Brigade", *Sex Roles* 39(7–8): 539–57.

Gordon, Andrew C., Gordon, Margaret and Dorr, Jessica (2003) "Native American Technology Access: The Gates Foundation in Four Corners", *Electronic Library* 21(3): 428–34.

Graham, Mark and Khosravi, Shahram (2002) "Reordering Public and Private in Iranian Cyberspace: Identity, Politics and Mobilization", *Identities: Global Studies in Culture and Power* 9(2): 219–46.

Gupta, Akhil and Ferguson, James (eds) (1997) *Anthropological Locations: Boundaries and Grounds of a Field Science*. Berkeley: University of California Press.

Hakken, David 1999 *Cyborgs@cyberspace? An Ethnographer Looks to the Future*. London: Routledge.

Hannerz, Ulf (1996) *Transnational Connections: Culture, People, Places*. London: Routledge.

Hansen, Klaus Georg (2000) *The Gap between Potentials and Realities: Analysing the Use of Computer and Internet in Greenland*. Paper presented at the 12th Inuit Studies Conference, 23–26 August, University of Aberdeen.

Hastrup, Kerstin and Olwig, Karen F. (1997) "Introduction", in Olwig, K. F. and Hastrup, K. (eds), *Siting Culture: The Shifting Anthropological Object*. London: Routledge, pp. 1–14.

Havemann, Paul (2000) "Enmeshed in the Web? Indigenous Peoples' Rights in the Network Society", in Cohen, R. and Rai, S. M. (eds), *Global Social Movements*. London: The Athlone Press, pp. 18–32.

Herman, Andrew and Swiss, Thomas (eds) (2000) *The World Wide Web and Contemporary Cultural Theory: Magic, Metaphor, Power*. London: Routledge.

Hine, Christine (2000) *Virtual Ethnography*. London: Sage.

Hornborg, Anne-Christine (2000) *Kluskap – As Local Culture Hero and Global Green Warrior: Types of Narratives among the Mi'kmaq Indians of Eastern Canada*. Paper presented at the 20th American Indian Workshop, 26–28 April, Lund University.

Huhndorf, Shari M. (2001) *Going Native: Indians in the American Cultural Imagination*. Ithaca: Cornell University Press.

IWGIA (2000) *The Indigenous World 1999–2000*. Copenhagen: International Work Group for Indigenous Affairs.

——(2001) *Indigenous Issues: Indigenous Peoples – Who are They?* Copenhagen: International Work Group for Indigenous Affairs

——(2003) "Indigenous Peoples and Information Technology", Special Theme Issue: *Indigenous Affairs*. Copenhagen: International Work Group for Indigenous Affairs.

Jackson, Anthony (ed.) (1987) *Anthropology at Home: ASA Monographs*. London: Routledge & Kegan Paul.

Jackson, Jean (1989) "Is there a Way to Talk about Making Culture without Making Enemies?" *Dialectical Anthropology* 14: 127–43.

Jones, Steven G. (1995) "Understanding Community in the Information Age", in Jones, S. G. (ed.), *CyberSociety: Computer-Mediated Communication and Community*. Thousand Oaks: Sage Publications, pp 10–35.

——(1997) "The Internet and Its Social Landscape", in Jones, S. G. (ed.), *Virtual Culture: Identity and Communication in Cybersociety*. London: Sage Publications, pp. 7–35.

Kolko, Beth E., Nakamura, Lisa and Rodman, Gilbert B. (eds) (2000) *Race in Cyberspace*. New York: Routledge.

Kroeber, A. L. and Kluckhohn, C. (1952) *Culture: A Critical Review of Concepts and Definitions (Vol. 47)* Cambridge. MA: Peabody Museum.

Kuhmunen, Henrik Micael (2001) *SameNet*. Available online: www.sapmi.net/ajtte

Landzelius, Kyra (2003) "Paths of Indigenous Cyber-Activism", in Indigenous Peoples and Information Technology, Special Theme Issue: *Indigenous Affairs*. Copenhagen: International Work Group for Indigenous Affairs, pp. 6–13.

Lawson, Sean (n.d.) *The Cyber-Intifada Resource Guide: A Resource for Tracking the Intifada in Cyberspace.* Available online: www.geocities.com/db8r.geo

Lee, Gary Yia (1996) "Cultural Identity in Postmodern Society: Reflections on What is a Hmong?", *Hmong Studies Journal* 1(5): pp. 1-4.

MacIntosh, Ian (n.d.) *Cultural Survival.* Available online: www.cs.org

Marcus, George E. (1995) "Ethnography in/of the World System: The Emergence of Multi-Sited Ethnography", *Annual Review of Anthropology* 24: 95–117.

Marcus, George E. and Fischer, Michael M. J. (1986) *Anthropology as Cultural Critique: An Experimental Moment in the Human Sciences.* Chicago: University of Chicago Press.

Mato, Daniel (1996) "On the Theory, Epistemology, and Politics of the Social Construction of 'Cultural Identities' in the Age of Globalisation: Introductory Remarks to Ongoing Debates", *Identities: Global Studies in Culture and Power* 3 (1–2): 61–72.

Maybury-Lewis, David (1997) *Indigenous Peoples, Ethnic Groups, and the State.* Boston: Allyn and Bacon.

McChaughey, Barabara and Ayers, Michael D. (eds) (2003) *Cyberactivism: Online Activism in Theory and Practice.* London: Routledge.

McLuhan, Marshall (1965) *Understanding Media.* New York: McGraw Hill.

Miller, Daniel and Slater, Don (2001) *The Internet: An Ethnographic Approach.* Oxford: Berg.

Mizrach, Steven (1999) *Natives on the Electronic Frontier: Technology and Culture on the Cheyenne River Sioux Reservation.* PhD dissertation, University of Florida.

Nash, June (1997) "The Fiesta of the Word: The Zapatista Uprising and Radical Democracy in Mexico", *American Anthropologist* 2: 261–74.

Olwig, Karen Fog and Hastrup, Kirsten (eds) (1997) *Siting Culture: The Shifting Anthropological Object.* London: Routledge.

Parffa, Per Jonas (2001) *SameNet: Sápmi Online. The Saami Intranet and Meeting Point.* Paper presented at the International Workshop on Indigenous and Diasporic Internet Use, 8–11 June, University of Gothenburg.

Parra, Max (1995) "The Politics of Representation: The Literature of the Revolution and the Zapatista Uprising in Chiapas", *Journal of Latin American Cultural Studies* 4(1): 65–71.

Polly, Jean Armour (1998) "Standing Stones in Cyberspace: The Oneida Indian Nation's Territory on the Web", *Cultural Survival Quarterly* 21(4). Available online: www.culturalsurvival.org/publications

Porter, David (ed.) (1997) *Internet Culture.* London: Routledge.

Poster, Mark (1998) "Cyberdemocracy: The Internet and the Public Sphere", in Holmes, D. (ed.), *Virtual Politics: Identity and Community in Cyberspace.* Thousand Oaks, CA: Sage, pp. 212–28.

Powers, Marla N. (1999) "Cyberspirituality: Lakota On Line", *Acta Americana* 7(2): 47–59.

Pratt, Mary-Louise (1992) *Imperial Eye: Travel Writing and Transculturation.* London: Routledge.

Rezaei, Siamak (2001) *Evolution of Media on the Internet: Kurdish Case.* Paper presented at the International Workshop on Indigenous and Diasporic Internet Use, 8–11 June, University of Gothenburg.

Rich, Paul and Reyes, Guillermo de los (1996) "The Internet Insurrection: Chiapas and the Laptop". Paper prepared for the American Sociological Association.

Rogers, Mark (1996) "Beyond Authenticity: Conservation, Tourism, and the Politics of Representation in the Ecuadorian Amazon", *Identities: Global Studies in Culture and Power* 3(1–2): 73–125.

Routledge, Paul (1998) "Going Globile: Spatiality, Embodiment, and Media-tion in the Zapatista Insurgency", in Tuathail, G. Ó. and Dalby, S. (eds), *Rethinking Geopolitics*. London: Routledge, pp. 240–60.

Roy, L. and Raitt, D. (eds) (2003) "The Impact of IT on Indigenous Peoples", *Electronic Library* 21(5): 411–13.

Sen, Amartya (2000) *Development as Freedom*. New York: Anchor.

Shields, Rob (ed.) (1996) *Cultures of Internet: Virtual Spaces, Real Histories, Living Bodies*. London: Sage.

Smith, Marc A. and Kollock, Peter (eds) (1998) *Communities in Cyberspace*. London: Routledge.

Stocking, George W. (ed.) (1985) *Observers Observed: Essays of Ethnographic Fieldwork*. Madison: University of Wisconsin Press.

Stone, Allucquere Rosanne (1991) "Will the Real Body Please Stand Up? Boundary Stories about Virtual Cultures", in Benedikt, M. (ed.), *Cyberspace: First Steps*. Cambridge, MA: MIT Press, pp. 81–113.

Trahant, Mark N. (1996) "The Power of Stories: Native Words and Images on the Internet", *Native Americas* 13(1): 15–21.

Turkle, Sherry (1997) *Life on the Screen: Identity in the Age of the Internet*. New York: Simon and Schuster.

Uimonen, Paula (2001) *Transnational.Dynamics@Development.Net: Internet, Modernization and Globalization*. Stockholm: Stockholm Studies in Social Anthropology.

Uimonen, Paula (2001) *Network Culture and Pioneer NGO's: internet Frontiers in Laos, Malaysia and Geneva*. Paper presented at the International Workshop of Indigenous and Diasporc Internet use, 8-11 June, University of Gothenburg.

van Maanen, John (1995) "An End to Innocence: The Ethnography of Ethnography", in van Maanen, J. (ed.), *Representation in Ethnography*. Thousand Oaks, CA: Sage, pp. 1–35.

Vitali, Frances (2000) *Navajo Cybersovereignty: Digital Diné Weaving the World Wide Web into an Oral Culture*. PhD dissertation, Emporia State University.

Whitaker, Mark (2004) "Tamilnet.com: Some Reflections on Popular Anthropology, Nationalism, and the Internet", *Anthropological Quarterly* 77(3): 469–98.

Williams, Raymond (1977) *Marxism and Literature*. Oxford: Oxford University Press.

Wilson, Samuel M. and Peterson, Leighton C. (2002) "The Anthropology of Online Communities", *Annual Review of Anthropology* 31: 449–67.

Chapter 2

Remote Indigenous Communities in Australia

Questions of access, information, and self-determination

Alopi S. Latukefu

Introduction

The internet has become an established form of communication for millions of people throughout the world. Its humble beginnings, as a Cold War means of information-exchange based on a distributed as opposed to centralized network, seem a universe away from the complex tool that is quickly becoming the most important information and knowledge distribution device since the printing press. Yet the seeming ubiquity of the internet appears a façade of First World illusions when it is remembered that more than 80 percent of the world's populations have yet to hear a basic telephone dial tone.[1] Australia is little different in this regard to most other countries where there exists still a clear urban–rural technological divide, a divide that privileges metropolitan regions and leaves rural communities with limited access to communications infrastructures and the human resources to use these effectively. The Outback Digital Network (ODN) is a project funded by the federal government of Australia that is attempting to bridge such divisions by providing connectivity and access to some of the most remote indigenous communities in the world.

As information management in government, business and community-based organizations increasingly moves to digital platforms, questions of technology access become of renewed critical importance to all citizens, including indigenous peoples. Already back in 1989, Nugget Coombs, a long-term advocate of the rights of indigenous Australians, wrote about the need for an effective "Aboriginal mechanism" to coordinate local collective action and parlay it into national influence on behalf of indigenous peoples within the remote regions of Northern Australia, in particular in the Kimberley region.

> Political effectiveness on the part of Aboriginal people requires well-coordinated collective action. With the exception of the KLC [Kimberley Land Council] ... Aboriginal organizations ... have been predominantly local, small, with restricted objectives and informal in structure and style ... Their ability to influence government policy, particularly in relation to the amount and allocation of financial resources, is limited. This is partly due to the difficulty of coordinating a number of organizations to design and

give effect to common strategies and to speak with one voice to apply political pressure at State and Commonwealth levels. They are unlikely to
increase their political effectiveness until there is an Aboriginal mechanism
within which their locally-oriented planning and political advocacy can be
coordinated.

(Coombs *et al.* 1989: 121).

Since 1996, a number of key leaders in the indigenous community, including
the directors of the ODN,[2] have been lobbying the commonwealth government
of Australia to provide effective communications links to and within remote,
regional and rural Aboriginal communities in Australia. They see the internet –
or more specifically, a digitally-based broadband network for the carriage of
multimedia information and communications – as the answer to the
"Aboriginal mechanism" highlighted by Coombs. As the regional manager of
the (ODN) in the Kimberley and Pilbara regions of western Australia, I have
had the privilege of working with a number of indigenous organizations and
individuals leading the information and communications agenda within northwestern Australia. I have also witnessed much of the frustration that the
Aboriginal leadership in Australia experience on a day-by-day basis in their
dealings with government at all levels and in their endeavor to bring change on
behalf of the communities they represent. Given the dynamics of traditional
culture, even the issue of who actually has the right to speak on behalf of a
community is itself problematic.[3]

In this chapter, I discuss the major challenges confronting organizations,
communities and individuals involved in projects like the ODN in their attempt
to develop robust, accessible and equitable information-telecommunications
environments for indigenous communities. Specifically, I focus on questions of
access, information, knowledge and control. A brief overview of current sociopolitical trends within Australia highlights the complex array of issues facing
remote indigenous communities at the dawn of the twenty-first century. These
challenges include environmental, economic, and social issues that are inherent
to remote regions of Australia, as well as the political struggles of Aboriginal
peoples. Given the dark lessons from colonial history, it remains to be seen
whether information and communications technologies can become agents of
positive change for indigenous peoples, or whether they will simply entail a
further cooption of indigenous communities to Western hegemony through
knowledge control and the processes of "globalization".

Historical forces and knowledge control

In considering the internet and its potential, it is important to query its place
within an historical trajectory as well as a contemporary context where information and knowledge control are tools of power. For the past five hundred years
since the so-called Age of Discovery, Western nations wielded global influence

and largely dictated the course of interaction between indigenous and non-indigenous communities worldwide. The development of modernity over this time was fueled by the strategic uses of knowledge in military-political domination, technological innovations, and population management systems. Modernity also coincided with the rise of democratic movements, which theoretically recognized the rights of "man" to universal franchise alongside a number of other entitlements accorded to citizens (a category that was far from inclusive, however). The irony of the emergence of colonialism and modernity was that they were tightly integrated into the imperial juggernaut which was to destroy, subjugate and disenfranchise many non-Western cultures around the world, including indigenous societies.

During the early period of mercantilism and colonial expansion, pressure was mounting on small fragmented kingdoms and republics within Europe to consolidate into larger nation-states (defined geographically as well as linguistically and culturally) for purposes of both trade and war. Such consolidation was facilitated by the greater circulation of the printed word (made possible by the invention of the printing press), the growth of literacy and numeracy within the general population, and the increasingly effective use of information and communications as tools for framing how members of a society perceived themselves as part of a collective (Anderson 1983). Along with these trends came the ability to manage large populations from a relatively small number of centers. This system was to prove effective within nation-states, and also for managing the colonial administrations that were part of the wider imperial base of Europe during this era. Information and communications management not only equipped the state to handle the logistics of exploration, war, commerce, migrations, deportments and other initiatives, they also provided the means to inscribe the general populace with "grand narratives" celebrating the progress of these initiatives and decreeing the inferiority of the indigenous primitive. European ideology categorically legitimated a sharp division between the perceived state of enlightened superiority of white peoples to that of the bestial – or, at best, "noble" – savage.

In Australia (as in other countries where indigenous populations were subjugated under colonial rule) capitalism emerged as the dominant commercial model and mode of development. Capitalism as a system requires the concentration of capital (be it land, labor, or other means of production, including knowledge-production) in the hands of an elite minority, who are then able to leverage off the capital to further increase their wealth and power. When it is recognized that capital is in fact itself a function of knowledge and information, in line with Castells's (1996: 14) division of modes of production versus modes of development, we simultaneously acknowledge that property, infrastructure and labor are all determined by the function of information. Since the time of British colonization two hundred years ago, and the subsequent federation of Australia as a nation-state, the experience of indigenous communities with respect to colonialism, capitalism and other practices of modernity has run the full spectrum. Thus, while information and communications paved the path for the political enlightenment of European subject-citizens, they also sealed the fate of Aboriginal peoples subject to displacement, enslavement, exploitation, persecution and in some cases genocide. With the emergence of the modern nation-state, information and knowledge-control were further intensified in the areas of public health, education, transport, defense and other administrative systems. However, racism towards Aboriginal peoples not only continued to be practiced in and through these new systems, it became further institutionalized in campaigns to "civilize" native peoples into the "White Australian" nation, established with the Act of Federation in 1901 (and the subsequent ratification of the "White Australia Policy" which gave white Australians overarching rights both internally and externally above all other Australians). Assimilation actively sought to destroy Aboriginal cultures, languages, lifeways and traditions – in short, to decimate their entire knowledge base. One particularly brutal campaign involved the forced removal of Aboriginal children from their families for purposes of being schooled in white ways and culture (resulting in the formation of the "Stolen Generation").

For centuries, Aboriginal cultures were thus regarded as impediments to progress. It was not until the 1960s that Aboriginal peoples were even granted citizenship and gained the right to vote (in 1961) and to be counted in the National Census (in 1967). Slowness to formulate political solutions, and the continuing struggles to forge an equitable social contract, affected relationships at all levels between Aboriginal governing leaders and the commonwealth (federal), state and local governments. The legislative framework that eventually developed with particular regard to Aboriginal affairs gave a concentration of power to the commonwealth. Governance structures originally designed at the state level to manage indigenous affairs were largely removed from the governance equation by the federal government through what was a paternalistic, yet at the same time benevolent, agenda to protect the interests of indigenous communities in the face of rampant disregard from colonial times of their social and economic rights under consecutive local and state bodies. As a result, whereas non-indigenous Australian communities have two layers of government between themselves and the commonwealth (whose bureaucracy is designed mainly for dealing with national and not local issues), Aboriginal communities deal directly with the commonwealth on many issues of concern to their daily lives, from health and education to basic infrastructure and services. Because of the small and fragmented nature of Aboriginal organizations in the past, the ability to leverage a lobbying presence at either local, state or national levels has been hampered by the fact that Aboriginal people are not a single homogenous grouping, but rather a number of diverse communities with different cultures, languages, experiences and outlooks.[4] Moreover, cultural, infrastructural and geographic barriers have limited their ability to effectively communicate over large distances. Nonetheless, over the past thirty years substantial political gains have been made. Certain myths legitimating the

British annexation of Australia have been effectively challenged in the nation's High Court. This has included the rejection of the notion that at the time of contact Australia was a "Terra Nullius" or empty land – a concept used by the British to justify invading and confiscating the lands of Aboriginal peoples in Australia without entering into treaties (as they had done with the indigenous communities of Aotearoa in New Zealand; see Broome 1994). The later decades of the twentieth century also witnessed a rise in Aboriginal protest movements. These have gained popular support, including from non-indigenous citizens, and have redressed some of the more extreme forms of legal and economic discrimination. Reforms have included re-enfranchisement over various means of production, be they labor (as in the case of the Pindan Mob's struggle for equal wages in Western Australia in the 1950s, and the Arbitration Commission wage case of 1965 leading to the strike by the Gurindji people),[5] land (with the land rights movement of the 1970s and 80s and establishment of land councils), cultural self-determination and rights to political enfranchisement, and the ongoing fight for welfare and social justice.

In sum, a dark historical legacy underpins many of the current political and social problems and technological backwardness facing remote Aboriginal communities in Australia today, a legacy that they have only recently begun to challenge successfully. Given this situation and given lessons from history, it might not be a surprise to learn that within Aboriginal communities there still exists an uneasy tension about different systems of knowledge and information and who controls them. Despite this, a number of indigenous communities and their leaders have proposed the establishment of an information and communications base within their region. This reflects the many ways in which modernity has had an enormous impact on the debate and ideologies within indigenous politics in Australia. Aspirations for ICT development are tied into ongoing struggles for self-determination: for example, in each of the landmark political events noted above, the media and the public's access to information played important roles in achieving outcomes. Aboriginal communities still have relatively limited means to air their grievances and make their needs known to a wider audience nationally or even internationally. The dynamics that have characterized how remote communities are working to achieve a voice in the wider public policy debates are being repeated in the online environment. In some cases external non-indigenous organizations have been providing online presence and information management to indigenous groups. However, this has implications for the ways in which Aboriginal organizations, communities and individuals operate, as they are drawn into a sort of benign dependency relationship in terms of their own information and knowledge management.

Incentives to develop ICTs are linked to a campaign for recognition of the rights of Aboriginal peoples to the same level of access and quality of services (including telecommunications) enjoyed by non-indigenous Australians, yet in a way that reflects and respects Aboriginal cultural and social dynamics.

Understanding and mediating these issues are prerequisite to successfully introducing global information-communications technologies into indigenous
societies and economies. First, however, fundamental environmental and socioeconomic hurdles must be surmounted.

Access and conditions in Aboriginal communities

Indigenous communities, particularly in northern Australia, are so hampered by
a dearth of material, social and human resources for the delivery of basic
services that it is difficult to envision, let alone implement, advanced ICTs.
Environmental factors have long posed obstacles to infrastructural development. Relative to other societies entering the information age, remote
Australian indigenous communities are faced with the arduous task of building
the required technological and economic bases upon which in turn to build and
sustain a network. There have always been difficulties in finding appropriate
technical solutions for regions such as the Pilbara and Kimberley. The environments that many of these communities exist within are some of the harshest in
the world. The existing digital radio concentrator systems infrastructure, which
has delivered telephony into remote communities in the north for the past
thirty years, was itself specially designed by Telecom Australia and the Swedish-
based Ericsson as an innovative solution for remote regions. These areas of
Australia suffer from extreme temperatures, repeated flooding, and even insect
problems (with voracious termites and ants causing problems with terrestrial
cabling). To bring telephone lines or fibre-optic cabling into every community
within the northwest (which in the Pilbara and Kimberley regions covers
almost one million square kilometres), where communities are small isolated
groups with very little disposable income, is difficult to justify in terms of public
spending and nearly impossible to justify in commercial terms. Only in 2002 did
Telstra (Australia's formerly publicly-owned national telecommunications
provider) secure sufficient funding to upgrade the existing network through a
federal government program (Department of Communications Information
Technology and the Arts 2001).

Socioeconomic problems commonly found in remote Aboriginal communities further exacerbate the issue. Over the past few decades, entrenched poverty,
unemployment, welfare dependency, public health deficiencies, violence,
alcohol and other substance abuse, and in some cases political and economic
corruption, have all taken their toll on communities. Educational deficiencies
are widespread, resulting in poor literacy and numeracy skills that negatively
affect indigenous employment opportunities not only in remote regions but
Australia-wide (Commonwealth of Australia 1999). While there do exist industries that could provide greater job opportunities to indigenous people within
remote regions, problems of unemployment and under-employment spiral due to
lack of a skilled indigenous workforce and/or racially-motivated discrimination.
This is a sensitive issue, as it is often tied to basic cultural clashes between

indigenous and non-indigenous worlds. Until industrially-based organizations become more flexible in handling the social and cultural responsibilities faced by many indigenous people in their daily lives (for example, when deaths occur or kinship obligations demand their participation), change will be slow. Social problems pose a constant concern to current providers, and a possible deterrent to prospective providers of sustainable services into these communities. The low penetration of even basic telephone services is both a sign and a symptom of such dysfunction and anomie. Due to service limitations and costs, it has largely been beyond the reach of most individuals in remote communities to have home telephone access. Where there are phones (for example, in schools, shops or community offices), access tends to be filtered through a non-indigenous teacher, shopkeeper or community administrator. This has resulted in very low levels of community usage and regular vandalism. Recent rationalization of the economy by the government has resulted in further cutbacks in public services. This, coupled with the pull-out of other historical sources of assistance such as the Catholic Church, has led to further pressures on existing facilities.

Indigenous residents in remote communities thus generally do not possess many of the required resources and skills to permit successful levels of engagement with computers, the internet and other ICTs. Solutions to the networking and communications needs (and aspirations) within these communities must not only find cost-effective ways to deliver sophisticated services, like broadband internet, but must also educate community members. This includes educating them in the uses and even in the value of these services, and demonstrating the capacity of what are, after all, radically new tools. It further includes adapting these tools to align with the traditional practices and values held by the community itself. Such goals have defined the work undertaken by the ODN and its member organizations.

The Outback Digital Network is a consortium of five community-based Aboriginal organizations across the north of Australia. It was formed to address the telecommunications needs of remote communities, needs ranging from standard telephone services to broadband access. The five centers work on similar developments of the network in their respective region, yet each also contributes particular aspects to the development of the network as a whole. In Queensland, the contribution of the Balkanu Cape York Development Corporation has been in the linking of the network to issues of economic and social development. In the Tanami communities, the Tanami Project was the first videoconferencing network established in the early 1990s; it thus brings almost ten years of experience of broadband usage and applications to the ODN. The Tenant Creek Regional Infrastructure Project, part of the planning and development of infrastructure needs within the Barkley region of the Northern Territory, has important links to both territorial and commonwealth government planning. Within their respective regions, both the Top End Aboriginal Bush Broadcasting Association and the Broome Aboriginal Media Association have been involved in the development of broadcast media. The latter has 100 percent community ownership of a commercial media arm, which already develops traditional Aboriginal media forms through radio and television. It is currently moving into multimedia and online applications through its membership in the Outback Digital Network.

As an organization fully owned by indigenous people, the ODN has established a framework for access that ties into traditional cultural notions. For example, the idea of servicing individual households is, at present, less of a priority than the delivery of broader community access and affordability. The assumption within the ODN is that a community as a whole will buy into the network. Access therefore will not be restricted by protocols, practicalities and/ or problems that commonly arise in cases where access is provided externally, whether by commercial, occupational, administrative, or educational bodies. This autonomy is seen as the key to both the sustainability and the value of the ODN project. It is also in alignment with the objective to empower communities through information, skills and knowledge, as well as through cross-community partnerships (between both public and private sectors). This requires training community members and employing them to maintain the network in their local communities. Over time, this will provide communities with their own effective communications, management and governance tool.

Hence, the aspiration of the ODN is to work to create many types of partnership that will allow indigenous people to be employed within their own respective communities, and also will allow them to fully participate in the larger Australian society. These goals fit within the overall vision of Aboriginal leaders concerning the potential benefits of information-communications technologies for native peoples. The main incentives driving ICT development in remote regions are considered next.

Incentives and trends in ICT development

Incentives for ICT development in the remote northwestern communities span economic, social, cultural and political agendas. For both indigenous and non-indigenous communities in the region, visions of economic opportunity and social mobility are key motivators, and include the creation of new jobs and a better-educated workforce and regional development schemes, particularly in the tourist sector. On the Aboriginal side, incentives for development further include political empowerment and greater overall indigenous autonomy. The current Aboriginal leadership in northwestern Australia views the internet and other types of distributed information-based systems as a possible solution to the ongoing dilemmas that face remote Aboriginal communities in harmonizing traditional systems of knowledge (which tend to be fluid in character) with the powerful applications of Western knowledge systems (which, relatively speaking, are more rigid in character). At a 2001 meeting of the Global Islands Network in Germany, the following statement was made concerning some of the issues that small islands have encountered in their direct dealings with larger nation-state governments and/or international agencies: "Bureaucracy hates anything small and complex." Aboriginal communities, particularly those in isolated and remote areas of Australia, have precisely such qualities. Governance structures within traditional societies in areas like the Kimberley have been described as small "tribal" units with intricate and crosscutting obligations. As Elkins notes:

> A tribe usually consists of several localized groups which are the real political and economic units, and it is they which tend to make one tribe dovetail as it were into its neighbours. This is mainly the effect of the kinship system, for all persons with whom any person comes into contact must be brought into the kinship system and therefore given a place in a common life of economics and general behaviour.
>
> (Elkins 1954: 29)

Traditional systems are thus complexly based in numerous multi-dialogues of relationships, protocols and laws. They are generally powerful within the community-based system of governance, but become more diluted and less powerful as one moves into regional groupings and cross-community ties. The difficulties of Aboriginal governing bodies to achieve effective representation and voice at the national level are tied to contradictions between complex traditional politics of governance and classifications of knowledge, and those of larger, linear and hierarchically-based politics, as modelled in Western representation, management and development systems. While the former is very effective in dealing with issues at the community level, the latter is far more effective in dealing with the imposed requirements of the federative system in Australia. This state of affairs complicates relationships between Aboriginal communities and governments at all levels – be they commonwealth, state or local. Governments in Australia have tried to fashion a response to indigenous issues largely by creating structures which best suited the federated units that emerged out of the colonial system. Needless to say, these characteristically have not reflected indigenous forms of governance or their power structures, nor have they recognized the diversity of cultures, languages and societies that make up what is monolithically regarded as "Aboriginal Australia". Members of Aboriginal communities, particularly those living in remote regions under both traditional and Western systems of law and culture, face the difficult task of harmonizing these two systems.[6]

The leadership's almost universally-accepted proposal is to provide information-communications technologies in order to fuel opportunities for indigenous communities to work with each other and with various organizations to coordinate their actions and governance. Inherent in this process are themes of autonomy, self-determination, rights and responsibility, and the overarching idea that by working together communities can overcome the difficulties that they face in isolation. Kevin Fong, a director on the board of the Outback

Digital Network and the Managing Director of Goolarri Media Enterprises, put it this way:

> Only by acting as a network can we leverage off the economic and social opportunities of the information economy. As the old people always used to say: "ten sticks are harder to break than one".
>
> (Fong, personal communication)

What needs to be put in place is a system that develops from the ways that traditional Aboriginal communities within and across the north and south of Australia have dealt with their own heterogeneity. They have developed "communities", linked together by knowledge of tradition, songs, genealogies and mythology (Elkins 1954: 44). The term "community" is still used today within the Kimberley region to refer to the populations living outside of cities or regional townships who have close ties and knowledge of their lands and tradition. When Aboriginal people refer to traditional sociocultural, linguistic or economic ties (particularly in regard to their family relationships and ties to land) the terms "community" or "country" are used. Interestingly, the notion of "community" as a loose confederacy of groups tied to information and knowledge linkages, neatly describes the networked-based structures that indigenous and non-indigenous governing bodies seek to emulate within an ICT-based economy. While these systems of knowledge and relationships often have not mapped well onto the modern and post-modern political landscape, it remains to be seen if ICTs might prove an exception.

With respect to other (and largely non-indigenous) motivations for bringing ICTs to these remote regions, tourism comes to the fore as a main incentive. Because of its relative isolation and harsh environs, north Australia from Kimberley through to Cape York has been spared the huge demographic changes that regions elsewhere in Australia with more temperate climates and accommodating landscapes have experienced since colonization. For instance, it was only in the 1880s (100 years after the colonization of New South Wales) that pastoralism as a livelihood finally came to the Kimberley region. These regions cover diverse lands and environments, including the Great Sandy Desert, which links into the Tanami and other great desert regions of Australia, the plains country of the Fitzroy Plateau and the tropical regions of the Top End of Northern Territory and Cape York. Contemporary occupations and development schemes have generally been limited to primary industries such as fishing, pearling, mining and pastoralism. Because primary industries located their main transportation routes in hubs like Perth, Adelaide, Sydney and Brisbane, there was very little incentive to "informationalize"[7] remote regions. Only in the past twenty years (with investment in better road systems) have these regions been opened up to tourism – an increasingly important industry in the north of Australia, which has some of the most spectacular terrain in the world, including Kakadu National Park and Uluru in the Northern Territory, and the Bungle-Bungle ranges and gorges in the Kimberley and Pilbara regions. As an industry, tourism has singularly provided incentives to investment and informationalization within the regions and for the residents who inhabit them. Because of the increasingly positive valuation of the "indigenous experience", tourism operators and private and public development agencies are seeing value in traditional cultures, which otherwise for two centuries have been either actively destroyed or maliciously ignored by dominant society. However, for Aboriginal peoples, questions about the direct benefit to indigenous societies and cultures, coupled with fears of being commodified by tourism, largely dampen the incentive to back tourism schemes.

The politics of ICT development

The issue of remote indigenous communications is a political minefield at all levels of government, local, state and federal. For local governments within many of the shires of the Kimberley and Pilbara regions, as is true elsewhere in Australia at the local level, indigenous needs and affairs have traditionally not been considered high-priority matters. This changed considerably over the closing decade of the twentieth century, as Aboriginal peoples used their demographic numbers and electoral power to bring about changes in local government structures and to enhance their representation within these agencies. For example, in 2000 the shire of Broome signed service agreements with surrounding indigenous communities to cover environmental issues, community planning and building codes. While this marks an important first step towards politically reintegrating regions and bringing indigenous and non-indigenous residents together under an umbrella of regional concerns, there is still a long way to go before local governments and remote indigenous communities have equitable and mutually beneficial relationships. State-level politics have followed similar trends. Until recently in western Australia, indigenous affairs at the level of state governance have generally been pigeon-holed into a Department of Aboriginal Affairs (now called the Department of Indigenous Affairs) and sub-departmental bodies like the Office of Aboriginal Economic Development, Aboriginal Health, and Aboriginal Education. Under the previous conservative government of the western region, the structures that were established within state sectors had greater resemblance to colonial administration offices than to a viable and equitable government liaison in the region. This situation was to improve, however, with the election of a Labor government in Western Australia in 2001, which brought about better terms of engagement between state-level and indigenous agencies. Some such trends have subsequently remained. In October 2001, the state government of western Australia and the state council of the Aboriginal and Torres Strait Islander Commission signed a *Statement of Commitment to a Just Relationship* binding the government of western Australia and indigenous western Australians. While in some ways a rhetorical document, the *Statement of Commitment* does provide a foundation onto which partnerships and other ways of forging closer ties can be achieved. These changes directly feed agendas to develop ICTs in the northwestern regions.

Public planning and funding of ICT development has customarily fallen within the domain of the federal commonwealth government, like most other telecommunications in Australia. In considering the recent political history of telecommunications development, it is worth reviewing some of the actions, and the lingering effects, of Australia's conservative coalition governments at the turn of the century. This government was hardly pro-indigenous; in fact, whenever it seemed politically salient, the Prime Minister cynically exploited indigenous issues, such as famously refusing to issue an official apology to the Stolen Generation.[8] Nevertheless, its frequent use of divide-and-rule tactics in order to appease constituencies and balance varied political interests did affect ICT planning. For example, the conservative government deliberately muddied the distinction as to who is ultimately responsible for telecommunications in a legislative and political sense, while at the same time they distributed funds in a manner that undercut state jurisdiction. Interestingly, one way in which they managed this was by introducing programs like Networking the Nation, a body established after the government's privatization of 51 percent of its national telecommunications carrier, Telstra – a move that sparked considerable debate among the electorate. To add to the complexity, the Outback Digital Network is itself funded in part through Networking the Nation.

Such debates about ICT development are made complicated by the fact that rural non-indigenous Australians in certain remote regions themselves suffer disparities in terms of public services. This has caused considerable conflict within the current federal government whose coalition represents interests that have historically felt antipathy if not antagonism towards indigenous communities who inhabit these same regions. Moreover, recent high court decisions setting common law precedents have allowed Aboriginal peoples throughout Australia the right to be considered prior and traditional owners of lands with which their families have had continuing connections (Netheim 1999). Given the information-based nature of establishing such claims, it becomes apparent that these processes are linked into communications infrastructure issues, particularly in regions like the north, where legal challenges are underway with regard to traditional lands. Such issues further problematize local relations between indigenous and non-indigenous communities. The political issues surrounding the establishment of a network which targets the needs of remote indigenous communities thus must be sensitively established. Conceptual gains need to be made to link all levels of government with Aboriginal communities as well as to bridge diverse Aboriginal communities. Moreover, it is worth repeating that there is a need to learn from, and reformulate, the traditional strengths of indigenous political systems and to enhance their relevance within the new information economy.

This brings us to the issue of the collective involvement of Aboriginal peoples in their own community welfare. This relates to their role in the planning and uses of ICTs in their communities, and the question of direct engagement – which stands as one of the goals of the ODN. A controversial book by Noel Pearson, entitled *Our Right to Take Responsibility* (2000), reflects the current debate about rights and responsibilities. Pearson calls for revision of the existing structures of Aboriginal governance that have left communities in the northern Cape York region demoralized by a combination of welfare dependency and a general sense of hopelessness in their abilities to determine their own economic, social and cultural existence, which would thus include technological development schemes. Through what he terms a partnership approach, Pearson suggests that it is only through proper engagement with the political-economic and social realities of Australia as a whole in the present historical moment that Aboriginal communities can truly actualize their rights to be given the same opportunities as fellow Australian citizens. At the same time, he argues that indigenous communities must recognize that with rights come responsibilities. Through this balancing of rights and responsibilities, he believes that Cape York communities can achieve greater self-determination and the ability to act autonomously, and thereby rid themselves of the conditions of dependency and anomie in which they currently exist.

Interestingly, as indigenous communities are encouraged to assume the "right to responsibility", government and agencies at the local level are simultaneously being charged with the need to take more responsibility for indigenous communities in their region. This, too, is echoed in Pearson's book, which calls for implementation of tiers of governance for Aboriginal communities as a step to reverse their thirty-year reliance on the federal government for basic services. Important first steps have indeed been taken towards politically reintegrating regions and bringing indigenous and non-indigenous residents together under an umbrella of regional concerns. In his vision, Pearson further advocates rationalization of existing government structures that have duplicated, yet in the end not delivered on, basic services. This ties into an overarching ideology that holds that the public sectors should be streamlined and private-sector engagements introduced in working to foster more equitable knowledge-based networking relations with Aboriginal organizations and communities. The program fits with the Australian government's own deregulation and privatization of telecommunications, a trend found throughout the Western world.[9] As previously noted, however, given the currently low financial incentive for infrastructural investment in indigenous communities, government support will continue to be essential for ICT development in remote regions. It is of relevance in this regard that, when the Commonwealth government partially privatized its telecoms industry in 1996, the capital expenditure budget for extending the network to planned remote areas of the north was capped, and in some cases suspended indefinitely, due to the shift from a planned to a retail-oriented process.

Pros and cons: self-determination or buy-in?

This chapter has attempted to give the reader an insight into some of the complexities that face remote Aboriginal communities in Australia in their quest and aspirations to improve their position within the wider Australian society, and the management of their own communities through the use of information and communications technologies. In conclusion I would like to critique some of the mystique surrounding the magic of internet and digital technologies, and question the implications in development terms for regions which have been so eager to "buy in" to their hype. This is not to question the power and efficacy of networking and digitally-based tools in the creation of managed societies. The Outback Digital Network is itself committed to increasing the networking of remote indigenous communities at a sustainable financial cost to them.

Given all of the competing agendas and substantial hurdles confronting the development of ICTs in remote indigenous communities, it may be premature to ask if there will be harmonization of indigenous and non-indigenous systems of information, knowledge, management and control. Yet, in beginning to ponder this question, I am reminded of the danger of implementing any seemingly benign tool of management without considering its ideological and technological roots. I would like to introduce here the concept of the panopticon, an optical tool developed for the surveillance of nineteenth-century prisoners (Foucault 1979). Situated as an observation closet in a courtyard surrounded by prison cells and holding a guard-observer inside, hidden from view, the panopticon could spy at any or all times unbeknown to the prisoners. Its creator, Jeremy Bentham, envisaged the panopticon as the optimal management tool for prison populations by virtue of the fact that it afforded the possibility and threat – if not necessarily the actuality – of continuous surveillance. Inevitably, as the theory goes, the prisoner would internalize this surveillance and police himself. I suggest that what we see today with network-based distribution systems of knowledge and information can either be interpreted as a great step forward in liberal democratic governance, or alternatively, as another kind of panopticon.

In drawing an analogy from the panopticon, we might note that governments around the world have been keen to reorganize themselves to accommodate the "networked" society phenomenon. Despite the retraction of the dot.com industry in 2001, global trends suggest the ongoing investment into online, digitally-based information-communications services as a cornerstone of development in all nations. A main interest on the part of governments has been in the way that these technologies promise to lower the cost of delivering public services by reducing or removing altogether the expense of providing a physical presence, in the form, for example, of a government office, education or medical institution.[10] There is an especially strong incentive to achieve this in the case of distant and remote communities. Concurrently, governments are always seeking more effective methods to collect feedback about remote communities than those which traditional servicing and surveying have been able to provide. The potential to link remote communities to outside services and applications (such as telemedicine, distance learning, or governmental processes) and simultaneously to collate data on each transaction, make information and communications technologies important and attractive tools of power. As noted, the Australian government at national and state levels currently remains the main source of capital funding to bring ICT networks and services to indigenous communities, and will continue to play a major role even in the event of private funding. Its influence could be regarded as having a double nature, however.

From a standpoint positive to the options for indigenous communities, it is of note that the introduction of mass-distributed media into the nation-state superstructure has brought important gains for mobilization of historically subdued identities. In discussing these trends within the history of modernity and current postcolonialism, Castells writes:

> Once a nation became established, under the territorial control of a given state, the sharing of history did induce social and cultural bonds, as well as economic and political interest, among its members. Yet, the uneven representation of social interests, cultures, and territories in the nation-state skewed national institutions towards the interests of originating elites and their geometry of alliances, thus opening up the way for institutional crises when subdued identities historically rooted or ideologically revived, were able to mobilize for a renegotiation of the historical national contract.
>
> (Castells 1997: 270)

Taking a straightforward view, the internet is a tool that indigenous communities can use to manage information, communications and distance with the power, speed and flexibility of computing, and a seemingly limitless reach (although, as we have seen in this chapter, access is a more complex issue than is immediately apparent). Through its ability to frame knowledge and information in ways not achievable by other forms of media and distribution channels, it promises a means of empowering communities, giving them access to information and knowledge which they can in turn weave into their own knowledge and skill base.

The negative interpretation from the point of view of indigenous communities takes into account that the technologies and implementation of any information and communications systems are already framed by a complex array of external political, economic and social relationships. Computer technology itself is framed within a strict logical binary system. It has been noted, with respect to the historic forces that have shaped the modern information age, that imperialism and colonialism were themselves binary systems, creating binary oppositions between imperialist Europe and anything outside of it (Said 1978). It might further be remembered that modern citizens were successively brought under the management of government through the control of knowledge and information. So seductive is the power of the ICT medium that it might only appear to move centralized control out of the hands of government and into the hands of the people, merely giving them the notion of self-determination and empowerment.

While ongoing struggles for self-determination play a complex role in the drive to bring the information age to indigenous communities, for indigenous communities in Australia and possibly around the world it can be argued that self-determination within one system may well be a further buy-in to another.

The issue that needs to be raised before any question of indigenous usage of the internet is addressed is thus: whose information infrastructure or "info-structure" determines what is valued in an economy (whether in the local community or the greater global economy into which they are linked)? This dilemma is one which Aboriginal communities in Australia already face on a daily basis and in many arenas. The issue is also tied into questions surrounding governance and management within Aboriginal communities, although it is not unique to Aboriginal communities alone. The information economy and informationalism are only possible when the true value, and thus productivity, of knowledge and information – outside of restricted circles of material production and power – are recognized. By taking such an approach, the issue of access to the information superhighway becomes not simply one of infrastructure, or even of usage, but importantly one of the economic, social and cultural sustainability of such a network within a given community. Specifically, it is only when indigenous communities within the Kimberley, Pilbara, and other regions served by the ODN, have an active stake in the relationships that accrue from ICTs that there can be hope for an equitable, sustainable and workable process for all. Associated with this is the overarching issue of who determines knowledge within these remote communities and for the wider indigenous populations throughout Australia.

Should indigenous communities therefore follow the ICT path in their struggles for self-determination? This is ultimately a question only answerable by them. However, the full impact of these technological breakthroughs may not be apparent in the day-to-day management and delivery of networks. The true social and cultural costs to communities may well be hidden within the very fabric of what constitutes their difference in Australia today.

Notes

1   The International Telecommunications Union reports that only sixteen people in every hundred of the world's population are serviced with main telephone lines.
2   The Outback Digital Network is a federation of five community organizations that include Broome Aboriginal Media Association, the Top End Aboriginal Bush Broadcasting Association, the Tenant Creek Regional Infrastructure Project, the original Tanami videoconferencing network (within the Tanami desert communities), and Balkanu, Cape York Development Corporation.
3   In undertaking these discussions I must emphasize that I am in no way speaking on behalf of or for communities in the Pilbara and Kimberley regions, nor the wider Australian Aboriginal community, in this regard. Rather, this chapter is simply a statement of some of my own thoughts on the matter.
4   Aboriginal communities in the Kimberley may define themselves either through language group (such as Bardi-Jawi, Nyul-Nyul or Gidja peoples), or with classifications in terms of environment (e.g., Saltwater, Freshwater, or Desert Mob) and/or modern political experience (e.g., people from the Kimberley and Pilbara regions

will refer to themselves as the Kimberley or Pilbara Mob – which are quite distinct from the Territory or Queensland Mob). Traditional sociocultural relationships clearly link these communities across these classifications and regions.

5   In 1966, the Gurindji people in the Northern Territory walked off the Wave Hill pastoral station on which they worked in protest at wages and working conditions. This followed a 1965 decision by the Arbitration Commission, which ruled that Aboriginal workers should not be discriminated against in terms of wage awards. The pastoral industry argued successfully for a "'slow worker" caveat to be introduced in the decision, which allowed pastoralists to pay below the award wage if workers were considered to be under-productive. This resulted in a three-year delay in the implementation of equal wages to Aboriginal peoples. It also led to the decision by the Gurindji people to start the process of land claims, culminating in the Northern Territory Land Rights Act of 1976 that allowed Aboriginal people with "traditional and ongoing relationships to land" to make claims on Reserve or Crown Lands (Broome 1994). The Arbitration Commission's ruling led to the eventual decline in the pastoral industry as a whole, as the labor that Aboriginal people had provided in the past (which had been the major employment in the Pilbara and Kimberley regions) was no longer available for the industry to exploit. While groups such as the Gurindji people of Wave Hill in the Northern Territory were very active in defending their rights to land and wages within their particular sphere of influence, it was only with the backing of political parties and the Union movement in Australia that they could highlight their ongoing struggle at a national level, although in the end not all succeeded in their objectives.

6   The drive to empower indigenous elites has powered an agenda of consolidation and standardization for individuals, particularly those of mixed descent who were part of the "assimilationist" policy of twentieth-century white Australia. There have been continuing discussions of the implications of being "taken away", including the prominent Stolen Generations Report which emerged out of the National Inquiry into the Separation of Aboriginal and Torres Strait Islander Children from their Families (Australia) (Wilson 1997). One significant finding for present-day indigenous communities is that many of the "Stolen Generation" individuals, who have had access to the tools of informationalization (literacy and numeracy), possess the capacity to bridge discussions intra-nationally and internationally, liaisons which many of their relatives living within traditional communities have neither the access nor the capacity to undertake (Latukefu 2000).

7   In being sensitive to colonial and postcolonial legacies, I use the terms informationalize and informationalism to characterize the specific "Western" practice of building a codified information system around a single object or transaction. This differs slightly from Castells' use of informationalism as a specific mode of development upon which technological processes are based, which in his definition is "oriented toward the accumulation of knowledge and towards higher levels of complexity in information processing" (Castells 1996: 13–18).

8   It is of interest to note that, in the opinion of many Aboriginal leaders in the Pilbara and Kimberley regions, the eight-year rule of the conservative government in western Australia was not all bad for communities in the region. The conservatives were rigid on certain indigenous issues (e.g., Native Title, a concept introduced into Australian law to grant indigenous peoples legal claims to Crown Land under the classification of Native Title as opposed to some other title, such as freehold or pastoral). None the less, under the conservatives, major advances in remote indigenous communities were made in the areas of housing, electricity and water. This is in contrast with the former Liberal Party in the Northern Territory, whose relatively uncontested thirty-year rule brought little infrastructure into indigenous communities. What makes the situation in the Northern Territory also of note is that communities have had rights over their land for nearly the same period of time.

9   This trend marks a significant reversal of mid-twentieth-century policies, when telecommunications were regulated, consolidated and "nationalized" into government-led groups (and were themselves a switch from the individually-owned networks that were common at the turn of the twentieth century). Following upon and in line with the growing privatization of public telecommunications, there has been an international liberalization of telecommunications markets (bringing, for example, agreements on tariff rates and profits for telecommunications companies and governments). In 1998, the World Trade Organization agreed upon an accord on basic telecommunications aimed at liberalizing and standardizing telecommunications pricing and structures. At the time of the agreement, it covered up to 90 percent of the global revenue base in telecommunications.

10   This is not just a phenomenon of governments but also of certain private-sector organizations. For example, over the last decade banking institutions have largely closed their branch offices within rural and regional communities of Australia. Interestingly enough, although few remote communities were provided with banking services in the first place, the emergence of online services is allowing this to happen.

References

Anderson, Benedict (1983) *Imagined Communities: Reflections on the Origins and Spread of Nationalism*. London: Verso.

Broome, Richard (1994) *Aboriginal Australians: Black Responses to White Dominance 1788–1994*. St Leonards: Allen and Unwin.

Castells, Manuel (1996) *The Information Age: Economy, Society and Culture. Volume, 1: The Rise of the Network Society*. Malden, MA: Blackwell.

——(1997) *The Information Age: Economy, Society and Culture. Volume, 2: The Power of Identity*. Malden, MA: Blackwell.

Commonwealth of Australia (1999) *National Indigenous English Literacy and Numeracy Strategy 2000–2004*. Canberra: Commonwealth of Australia.

Coombs, H. C. et al. (1989) *Land of Promises: Aborigines and Development in the East Kimberley*. Canberra: Australian National University and Aboriginal Studies Press, Australian Institute of Aboriginal Studies.

Department of Communications Information Technology and the Arts (2001) *Untimed Local Calls Tender: Telecommunications Services Provided in Extended Zones*. Canberra: Commonwealth Government of Australia.

Elkins, A. P. (1954) *The Australian Aborigines: How to Understand Them*. Sydney: Angus and Robertson.

Foucault, Michel (1979) *Discipline and Punish: The Birth of the Prison*. New York: Vintage.

Latukefu, Alopi (2000) *PAKNET Strategy Paper: Smart Applications for Networked Communities*. Unpublished paper. Broome: Broome Aboriginal Media Association.

Netheim, G. (1999) "The Search for Certainty and the Native Title Amendment Act 1998", *University of New South Wales Law Journal* 22: 564–84.

Pearson, Noel (2000) *Our Right to Take Responsibility*. Cairns: Noel Pearson and Associates Pty Ltd.

Said, Edward (1978) *Orientalism*. London: Routledge and Kegan Paul.

Wilson, Ronald Darling (1997) *Bringing them Home: A Guide to the Findings and Recommendations of the National Inquiry into the Separation of Aboriginal and Torres Strait Islander Children from their Families*. Sydney: Human Rights and Equal Opportunity Commission.

Chapter 3

Canadian Aboriginal Peoples Tackle E-Health

Seeking ownership versus integration

Valerie Gideon

Introduction

Canadians take great pride in their healthcare system, thanks to its public character and universality. Its strong link to national identity has prompted high levels of investment and commitment on the part of government for over half a century. However, despite the fact that the Canadian healthcare system is celebrated as one of the best in the world, significant health inequities persist amongst the country's Aboriginal peoples. The Canadian government recognizes that these disparities are rooted in the lack of opportunities for the health of Aboriginal peoples. For example, over one third of Aboriginal communities, which tend to be in more remote regions of the country, are located more than 90 kilometers from physician services. Health programs and services delivered to Aboriginal communities are modeled on Western medicine, lacking the flexibility required to suit Aboriginal cultural beliefs and traditional values. Aboriginal leadership sees e-health as a way of improving access to, and control over, health services. E-health is defined as "the use in the health sector of digital data-transmitted, stored and retrieved electronically – for clinical, educational and administrative purposes, both at the local site and at a distance" (Picot and Cradduck 2000: 33). The most common e-health applications are telehealth/telemedicine (the delivery of medical/health services at a distance) and electronic patient record-keeping. The view that e-health may improve the quality of, and access to, healthcare for Aboriginal Canadians has been adopted by the Canadian government specifically in the context of its First Nations and Inuit Health Renewal Initiative (Assembly of First Nations 2001a: 29). The move towards e-health is also being implemented on a Canada-wide basis for all Canadians (whether indigenous or not) as the best way of meeting the healthcare challenges of the twenty-first century (Commission on the Future of Healthcare in Canada 2002).

This chapter explores the potential of e-health to respond to the needs and interests of Aboriginal peoples in Canada. It begins by contextualizing e-health's development in Canadian and Aboriginal healthcare systems, and reviews Aboriginal information and communication technology (ICT) settings (see Gideon 2000). Both national and grassroots Aboriginal e-health projects are described, and common Canadian and unique Aboriginal e-health issues compared. Current e-health applications are examined with respect to their potential to empower Aboriginal peoples. In concluding, I suggest an alternative model for Aboriginal e-health development geared towards collective empowerment. This model is intended to be applicable to other Aboriginal ICT undertakings in other sectors, within and outside Canada.

History and the contemporary dynamics of Aboriginal peoples

The 1996 Canadian Census counted 799,005 Aboriginal people, representing 2.4 percent of the Canadian population (Statistics Canada 1996; Royal Commission on Aboriginal Peoples 1996). The term Aboriginal peoples of Canada refers to First Nations, Inuit and Métis peoples. Each of these three groups has its own unique history, culture, and political agenda with respect to larger Canadian society.

First Nations are today comprised of 633 bands, representing 52 Nations or cultural groups and speaking over 50 different languages. Among these Nations are Dene, Cree, Blood, Blackfoot, Micmac, Mohawk, and Algonquin peoples. First Nations include Indians who received legal status under the Indian Act of 1876. Legal status, on a practical level, connotes access to limited tax exemptions, special federal education, and social, health, and economic programs. For a time, it also prevented Indians from voting, consuming alcohol and from access to certain public areas. Until 1981, women who married non-status Indians lost their legal status and that of their children. As a result of colonization, First Nations became the target of assimilationist policies, as evidenced by the British North America Act of 1867, which rendered "Indians, and Lands reserved for the Indians" matters of government regulation. The Indians Acts of 1876, 1880, 1884 and onward created the reservation system and delegated regulatory powers at the national level to the Department of the Interior and at the local level to federal "Indian" agents. Regulatory powers included the abolishment of traditional ceremonies (e.g., the Potlatch ceremony of western Canada, and the sundance ceremony of the Prairies), a pass system for outsiders onto reservations, and a network of residential schools. Today, the Department of Indian Affairs and Northern Development (formerly the Department of the Interior) "holds" and administers 0.3 percent of Canada's total area for Indian occupation.

Early in the nineteenth century, Métis peoples began to emerge as a distinct group, born from marriages of Cree, Ojibwa and Salteaux women with French and Scottish fur traders in the mid-1600s. Scandinavian, Irish and English heritages were later incorporated into the population, during the time of the continuing exploration of western Canada (Métis National Council 2001: 1). The Métis developed a language called Michif and worked as intermediaries between Europeans and Indians (as guides, interpreters and provisioners to new forts and trading companies). British and Canadian policies towards them were generally dismissive, however (Royal Commission 1996: 10). They were treated as "squatters" and uprooted from their land to make room for "legitimate" settlers. In 1885, the Métis of the Red River Valley, led by their leader Louis Riel, launched an unsuccessful struggle for recognition of their land and their own government which culminated in a crushing military confrontation. To this day, Métis claims for recognition have not been attained, although in 1992 Louis Riel was recognized as a founder of the Canadian Confederation. Today, Métis communities are established in Ontario, the Northern Territories, the Prairies and the West Coast.

Inuit reside throughout the far northern regions of the world. Characterized by language, environment and cultural features, they are divided principally into two closely-related groups: the Yupik and the Inupiat. In Canada, there are Yupik in Northern Quebec (Nunavik) and in the St. Lawrence Islands region. There are approximately 45,000 Inupiat in Arctic Canada. Despite European contact, it has been claimed that the network of living sites and travel routes connecting Inuit with seasonal land and marine hunting areas have remained largely intact since the first Inuit inhabitants (Inuit Tapirisat of Canada 2001: 2). With the exception of Labrador and the off-shore Nunavik communities, all Inuit have signed land claims agreements. These agreements reflect the changing times of Aboriginal–non-Aboriginal political relations in Canada and the increasing trend towards recognition.

The political history between Aboriginal and non-Aboriginal peoples of North America initially reflected "nation-to-nation relations" involving cautious cooperation formalized in treaties and arrangements, such as the Royal Proclamation of 1763 (Royal Commission 1996: 6). The Proclamation sought to "protect" tribes of Indians from molestation or disturbance on their lands – those regions of the Dominion not having already been purchased or ceded to the British colonial government. This colonial policy was "schizophrenic", in that it appears to recognize the nationhood of Aboriginal peoples on equal footing, all the while expecting Indians to acknowledge the authority of the British monarchy as well as to cede lands as required or requested (Royal Commission 1996: 7). With increasing immigrant populations, the retraction of the fur trade, the establishment of peace in the North American continent between French, British and American factions, and growing imperialist/colonialist ideologies, the situation for Aboriginal peoples was increasingly transformed "from respectful coexistence to domination by non-Aboriginal laws and institutions" (Royal Commission 1996: 8). The spirit of the first partnership agreements was lost; and the interpretation of "protection" moved away from safeguarding to assimilating Aboriginal peoples by means of non-Aboriginal institutions, including mandatory education, enforced socialization and political control.

A new struggle for recognition of Aboriginal peoples and their rights was fueled in 1969 by a revolt ignited against the federal government's White Paper document that sought to abolish provisions under the Indian Act, namely the Indian reservation system. First Nations interpreted this move as one that sought to annihilate their last form of recognition as distinct peoples in order to create a brand of integration-flavored equality. A dozen years of intense political struggle by Aboriginal peoples, including appeals to the Queen and the British Parliament, victoriously culminated in the Constitution Act of 1982 and its recognition of "existing Aboriginal and treaty rights" (Royal Commission 1996: 14). The definition of Aboriginal rights has never been successfully negotiated since this enactment. However, fiduciary obligations of the federal government towards Aboriginal peoples have been recognized concerning many issues. Notably, in 1997, these included matters of health.

A picture of health and health servicing of Aboriginal peoples

Despite mounting recognition of indigenous rights, Aboriginal peoples still experience health conditions that fall short of the standard enjoyed by the overall Canadian population, a standard praised by the United Nations as one of the best in the world. In fact, inequities between Canadian Aboriginal and non-Aboriginal populations are most evident in regard to health status. For instance, the infant mortality rate remains higher among First Nations (10.9 per 1,000 compared to 6.3 per 1,000 Canadians in 1993 (Health Canada 1996: 27). Life expectancy at birth is approximately seven to eight years less for Status First Nations than for Canadians in general (Assembly of First Nations 1998b: 25). Rates of death due to injury are three to six times higher among some First Nations than they are for most Canadians (Health Canada 2001a: iv). While the suicide rate for Canada is 13 per 100,000, Aboriginal suicide rates reach as high as 82 per 100,000 in some Inuit communities (Inuit Tapirisat of Canada 2000: 14). In terms of disease rates, tuberculosis and diabetes are seventeen times and three times higher, respectively, among Aboriginal peoples (Royal Commission 1996: 2).

The above health statistics illustrate some of the particularly acute health problems confronting Aboriginal peoples. The statistics further reflect inequities in healthcare services, inequities that are both apparent to Aboriginal peoples, and lived in the course of everyday life. According to a regional health survey conducted by First Nations and Inuit, approximately 60 percent of respondents believed that health services available to them remained unequal to those provided to the general Canadian population (Wien and McIntyre 1999: 241). This perception of service inequity is supported by statistics on physician/nurse shortages in Aboriginal and in rural and remote Canadian communities. In 1993, areas that did not comprise urban centers contained 23 percent of the Canadian population, but had access to only 9 percent of physicians (including 3 percent of specialists) (Ng et al. 1997: 22). The Canadian government has found that, depending on the region, anywhere from 15 percent to 53 percent of nursing positions in First Nations communities in 1999 were either vacant or filled only on a temporary basis (Health Canada 1999: 2).

The provision of health services to Aboriginal peoples is, in fact, neither explicitly supported nor denied by the legislative body that links Aboriginal peoples to the Canadian government. Rather, the provision of health services originally emerged as a policy exercise. Early federal involvement in health services delivery to First Nations and Inuit involved the construction of hospitals and community visits by field nurses. In 1930, government expenditures towards these services totaled less than one-third of those provided to the larger Canadian population. From 1930 to 1950, community health facilities were constructed and public health programs conducted (Assembly of First Nations 1998b: 20–1). In the 1940s, the Ministry of Health assumed responsibility for health services delivery to First Nations and Inuit, and it remains under the Ministry's jurisdiction today. The 1979 Indian Health Policy granted non-provincially insured health benefits, such as prescription drug coverage, eye and dental care, to all First Nations persons regardless of whether they reside on Indian reserve lands.

Despite decades of government sponsorship, however, barriers to an effective, sustained Aboriginal health strategy remain. Foremost among those identified by the Assembly of First Nations (the First Nations national leadership body) are basic structural impediments, including: the lack of attention to planning and research capacity in Aboriginal communities; the lack of integration of services with those delivered to other Canadians; the lack of integration of services delivered in other sectors that impact determinants of health (such as housing) (see Health Canada 2001b, 2001c, 2001d, 2001e). The Assembly has also articulated culturally-based complaints, such as the diminishment of women's traditional roles in healthcare and the overall lack of cultural-based programming. Of particular importance to note are the indigenous leadership's criticisms concerning the dominant health system's emphasis on clinical treatments instead of prevention of disease, and "the legacy of the enforced dependency on the Canadian government" that continues to position Aboriginal peoples as passive players in their own health destiny (Assembly of First Nations 1998b: 7). While this problem of "enforced dependency" indisputably remains, greater responsibility none the less has been asserted by Aboriginal peoples over the past twenty years. Influenced by the World Health Organization's Alma-Ata Declaration on Primary Healthcare, the 1979 Indian Health Policy offered First Nations a process by which they could develop health plans to control and manage services. It recognized the direct relationship of self-government to the improved health of Aboriginal peoples, a relationship explicitly put forth by the Assembly:

> For Aboriginal people, an integral component restoring balance and well-being to communities, involves community empowerment as well as individual well-being. To this end, health and social services delivery must be

under Aboriginal control, and services delivered by trained Aboriginal people. The ultimate expression of an Aboriginal health system that embodies both individual and community empowerment is self-government.

(Assembly of First Nations 1998b: 20)

Nearly 300 First Nations and Inuit communities have opted to negotiate the transfer of health services to more direct Aboriginal control, and an estimated additional 60 communities are in the pre-transfer stage. Some critics of such transfers, from the perspective of being sympathetic to Aboriginal rights, have viewed the transfer policy as a "dump and run" approach to self-government. However, a good case has been made that the transfer of health services administration to First Nations and Inuit communities has enabled greater flexibility in adapting healthcare delivery to suit local needs and has increased community involvement in healthcare (Assembly of First Nations 1998b: 22).

It is with an eye towards furthering self-determination over matters of health that e-health poses an attraction to Aboriginal peoples and their leadership. E-health is viewed as a means to:

1   assist Aboriginal peoples in addressing inequities in overall health status, and in accessing scarce healthcare resources at the time these are needed;
2   increase support to healthcare providers in order to improve the recruitment and retention of physicians, nurses and other medical staff;
3   achieve a more cost-efficient allocation of medical transportation and avoid unnecessary and high-risk travel of patients and healthcare providers;
4   increase the capability of Aboriginal peoples to hold the federal government accountable by facilitating access to information on the health status of Aboriginal peoples and their utilization of healthcare services;
5   provide a new continuum of care and information despite the fragmentation of healthcare across regional health authorities and shifts from institutional to multidisciplinary, community-based care promoted by Canadian healthcare reform.[1]

Aboriginal e-health initiatives have evolved from two trends: the increasing use of information and communications technologies ICTs by Aboriginal peoples and for multiple purposes; and the adoption of e-health in Canada as a whole. In the following sections, I trace these two underlying trends of Aboriginal e-health in order to highlight its current prevalence and potential for increasing Aboriginal peoples' opportunities for improved health.

The use of ICTs by Aboriginal peoples

On a Canada-wide basis, the use of ICTs has been influenced by the cumulative dependence on technology in social and economic sectors, as well as by the

Canadian government's intervention to delimit the impact of ICTs on certain key areas of "public interest", such as health. For instance, the country's main regulatory agency for communications, the Canadian Radio-Television and Telecommunications Commission, has instigated some strategic measures to provide universal and equal access to ICTs while also protecting personal privacy. Most notably, it has required telephone companies to supply the same basic service to all Canadians, including local access to the internet. To date, it is estimated that 145 (approximately 20 percent of) Aboriginal communities could benefit from an additional infusion of 41 million Canadian dollars to provide this required service baseline (Indian and Northern Affairs Canada 2002). A number of other actions have been undertaken by the federal government to promote uses of ICTs conducive to the "public interest". Since 1995, the Community Access Program has subsidized "e-centres" in 5,000 remote and rural communities to provide public internet access, and also school-base access programs. A similar initiative has created several Smart Communities, each viewed as:

> a community ranging from a neighbourhood to a nation-wide community of common or shared interest, whose members, organizations and governing institutions are working in partnership to use information and communication technologies to transform their circumstances in significant ways.
>
> (Panel on Smart Communities 1998: 3)

These federal programs have significantly increased the use of ICTs in Aboriginal communities. By 2002, a total of 304 Community Access projects were created in 211 Aboriginal communities (approximately 50 percent); and 429 SchoolNet projects were implemented in 309 communities (representing approximately 85 percent of First Nations schools).

These programs, still in their early stages, are thus far proving worthwhile. An example of a successful Smart Community Aboriginal project is the *Kuh-ke-nah Network* or *K-Net* (www.knet.ca). *K-Net* links First Nations e-centres in Deer Lake, Fort Severn, Keewaywin, McDowell Lake, North Spirit Lake and Poplar Hill – all of Northern Ontario (with an additional five communities planned in the near future). *K-Net* provides videoconferencing and web-based communication tools to Aboriginal schools, health facilities, Aboriginal local government offices, and other community service organizations. The Smart Community model has also featured prominently in the context of the establishment in 1999 of Nunavut – Canada's new Eastern Arctic Inuit territory. In June 1994, the Leo Ussak Elementary School at Rankin Inlet opened Nunavut's first Community Access Centre named *Igalaaq*, i.e. "window" on the world. Funded by the Community Access Program and by corporate donations, the Centre was celebrated in international news and visited by politicians and academics. Part of the success of these initiatives could be due to the cultural appeal of the Smart Community model in terms of traditional Aboriginal beliefs. The model supports the holistic view that all elements of life are inter-connected, and that all elements collectively contribute to community and individual well-being.

In order to expand the linkages of Smart Communities, the Assembly of First Nations leadership has also been lobbying strongly to implement a National First Nations Network to provide broadband access to all First Nations commu-nities. If realized, the Network will be utilized as part of a broader Aboriginal plan for economic, social, cultural and healthcare change (Assembly of First Nations 2001b; National Broadband Task Force 2001). E-health is one such intended application of the proposed Network. Aboriginal e-health has thus originated from the adoption of the Smart Community model by Aboriginal peoples in their general implementation and use of ICTs in their communities.

Working towards Aboriginal e-health

Aboriginal e-health initiatives were first conceived by the First Nations leader-ship in two "background papers" submitted to the Canadian government's Advisory Council on Health Infostructure (Assembly of First Nations 1998a, 1998b). The Council adopted the recommendations, and included them in its Canada-wide plans for a Canadian Health Infostructure, defined as:

> [the] application of communications and information technology in the health sector to allow the people of Canada (the general public, patients and caregivers, as well as healthcare providers, health managers, health policymakers and health researchers) to communicate with each other and make informed decisions about their own health, the health of others, and Canada's health system.
>
> (Advisory Council 1999: G-1)

The vision lends support to the dominance of a citizen/community paradigm in the healthcare system, and to better access to health information for all. To thus integrate medical services and health data requires a common technological infrastructure in managing network and computing, as well as standards in privacy and security. Substantial investments have been made by the federal government in order to build this common infrastructure (e.g. 500 million Canadian dollars for electronic patient records and 800 million for primary care, by 2002 alone; and investments continue.)

As noted above, Aboriginal e-health has featured prominently within overall Canadian e-health development since the outset. Indeed, an Aboriginal Health Infostructure has been envisioned as an autonomous and distinct institution concerned with "how Aboriginal peoples structure their own health informa-tion" using ICTs (Glover 2001). Yet, it is also strategically interconnected with the Canadian infostructure in order to enhance and operationalize the participation of Aboriginal peoples as active, recognized, and equal partners in Canadian initiatives (Brewer 2001a; Advisory Council 1999: 7–12). A partnership between the National Aboriginal Health Organization (the Assembly of First Nations, Inuit Tapirisat of Canada, and Métis National Council) is leading the development of this vision. The Organization is working at improving and promoting traditional healing practices, in addition to building Aboriginal partnerships in the areas of medical research and in the recruitment and training of health professionals.

Since the late 1990s, a number of e-health projects have been launched to benefit Aboriginal communities. Included among these are: projects that link tertiary care hospitals to community health centers (e.g., the Baffin Health Network, the Keewaytinok Okimakanak Telehealth Project); projects that target specific maladies (e.g., the Mental Health Evaluation and Community Consultation Unit, the National Native Addictions Information Management System, and SLICK – screen for Limbs, I-Sight, Cardiovascular and Kidney Complications Using Mobile Diabetes Clinics); or projects that focus on infrastructure (e.g., the Federal/Provincial/First Nations Telehealth Project). Some projects are regional in scope (e.g., the *Ikajuruti Inungnik Ungasiktumi* Network, which is a satellite-based network aimed at establishing telehealth in the Inuit territory of Nunavut, or the Nova Scotia Telehealth Network to support rural healthcare). Some are national in scope, such as the First Nations and Inuit Health Information System (FNIHIS). The latter targets all 566 First Nations communities, in addition to an unknown number of Inuit communities. Launched in 1997, FNIHIS has a long-term vision to transition healthcare management to First Nations control, and to allow information exchange between provincial/territorial and more central health information systems.

Despite the high levels of activity and coordination, significant gaps still remain in Aboriginal e-health development and implementation. Indeed, while there are some common problems shared by both Canadian e-health and Aboriginal e-health agendas, there are also problems unique to the situation of Aboriginal peoples that must be recognized and addressed (Brewer 2001b). Problems common to both often involve questions of universal access to ICTs (such as economic barriers and computer literacy) and the lack of a continuum of information (based on problems of interoperability and data sharing). Problems unique to Aboriginal e-health challenges, not surprisingly, tend to arise from ethnic or cultural differences and/or are a legacy of historical marginalization. They include inequities in health status and in non-medical factors that contribute to the poorer health status of Aboriginal Canadians relative to other Canadians. They also include a dearth of adequate information and health research concerning Aboriginal populations, a dearth brought about by, for example, the lack of inclusion of Aboriginal peoples in national health surveys. They are, in general, insufficiently tailored to the unique practice settings of Aboriginal communities. In order to meet the needs of Aboriginal peoples, e-health initiatives also need to consider medical care in adherence with the holistic view of health (and its determinants) that is characteristically espoused by traditional culture.

Foremost among the challenges unique to establishing e-health in Aboriginal communities, I would like to focus on questions of data ownership, control, access and possession (commonly referred to as OCAP). Self-regulation in matters of data OCAP is of particular importance for Aboriginal peoples because self-regulation will allow them to implement mechanisms that reflect traditional cultural understandings and practices. For example, the Inuit do not have a word for privacy in their language, and thus it is not unusual for an Inuk to broadcast on the local radio station a personal story, possibly related to health, about a fellow community member. An example of self-regulation is the privacy framework created by the Carcross Tagish First Nation that relies on a Council of Elders to provide oversight and hear appeals. In order to manage knowledge in ways consistent with culture and with the protection of personal and community health information, the Assembly of First Nations has put forth a number of recommendations for a community-centered data ownership framework (1998b: 30–2). These recommendations seek to balance the ethics of informed consent relating to the collection, use and disclosure of health information (at the individual and community levels) with respect for community governance structures. They also seek to protect both community property and cultural-intellectual property rights, and to protect the right to determine how data is to be used to address community needs. Reflected in these recommendations is the recognition that e-health management "is more than just computer training ... it is building capacity in self-determination and governance in healthcare which builds upon an individual and community development process" (Aboriginal Nurses Association of Canada 2000: 26). In short, e-health is challenging traditional culture as well as promoting it.

Aboriginal e-health in action

From 1998 to 2001, I was involved in the day-to-day management of First Nations community telehealth projects. In this capacity I observed numerous examples of the ways in which telehealth can substantially improve healthcare delivery and quality of care, and thus positively promote gains in the health status of Aboriginal peoples. For example, the Fort Chipewyan community has been using videoconferencing technology installed in its nursing station to provide physiotherapy, occupational therapy and speech therapy services at a distance. Accordingly, an assistant therapist on-site works electronically with therapists in the nearest city hospital, and, via this supervision, is able to deliver services to community members at the nursing station. In this case, telehealth enables patients to receive regular therapy sessions which they otherwise would have received only by travelling via airplane to the nearest city hospital at a prohibitive cost. A newspaper article describes the unique, holistic dimension of this service:

[To] assist the emotional well-being of patients, the system will also provide "televisitation sessions" which will let patients visit with family and friends hundreds of kilometres away. Mary Simpson of the Nunee Health Authority says there's a proved therapeutic value: "We've already linked Elders hospitalized in Fort McMurray with Elders in Fort Chipewyan, and it was a wonderful success."

(Napier 2001)

With e-health, both finances and time can be used more efficiently, and health-care made more accessible, especially for the elderly and for children. The success of the Fort Chipewyan project has led this community to seek to become a referral center of expertise for other neighboring First Nations communities. A Saskatchewan First Nations community named Southend used telehealth principally to conduct doctors' clinics and educational sessions for staff and patients. The community telehealth coordinator explains the value of the project as follows:

[The] education sessions and the specialist consults have been very benefi-cial for our staff and for the community members. The community staff enjoy coming to the education sessions and we usually have a large audi-ence. I have also found that some clients prefer to be seen through telehealth rather than travelling out to Saskatoon, which usually requires a two-day arrangement for travel.

(McInroy 2001)

By way of another example of e-health in action, I am currently involved in the development of an electronic health record system for First Nations communities (one that is based on the First Nations and Inuit Health Information System described above). The past trend has been characterized by little information exchange between, on the one hand, community health providers in the local setting and, on the other hand, physicians, specialists and other healthcare providers working in city hospitals. Typically, for example, no medical history records accompany a patient who is evacuated from a remote indigenous community to a regional hospital in order to receive emergency care. When the patient is released, the field nurse in the home community, in turn, generally has little or no information about the services the patient received while at the hospital. Much delay and confusion can result, and in the worse case, inappro-priate care might ensue from the lack of vital information exchange. An electronic health record would allow all healthcare providers involved in the care of the patient to access relevant information at the point of care.

E-health projects such as these still face a number of difficulties, many of which are related to the volatility of rural and remote healthcare delivery. For example, projects are often hindered by the frequent turnover of field nurses. Improving the overall capacity and involvement of Aboriginal community members in local healthcare delivery would go far in overcoming such an obstacle. E-health projects are also dependent on external resources (such as access to ICTs) and bureaucracies, and are therefore subject to conditions beyond their influence or control. I have found that the capacity of e-health to move the healthcare system in the direction of indigenous ownership and empowerment is different depending on the context. Moreover, these differences, and hence the outcome of any given e-health project, are determined to a large extent by the role played by Aboriginal individuals and communities. The types of role that Aboriginal individuals and communities presently take, or are tacitly assigned, in relation to e-health, are described further in the next section.

Aboriginal e-health as a "thing" or as a new "environment"

New tools do not necessarily translate into new ideas, new capacities, or new powers. The same holds true for information and communication technologies. ICT tools are developed and implemented in accordance with existing structures and policies that direct the actions of leaders and users. It is my contention that the outcome of e-health varies based upon whether it is used as an instrument of extension to facilitate or re-engineer current processes and practices of existing institutions, or used as a means of innovation to create new processes and practices and thus change the underlying values, roles and actions of existing institutions. Poster (1998) has suggested that the effects of the internet are more like those of a social space (such as Germany) than those of a thing (such as a hammer). In like fashion, I argue that e-health is used both as a thing and as a new environment. As a thing, its effects include reform, re-engineering, efficiency, cost-effectiveness, timely access to care, etc. Yet, it is its potential as a new environment that may well bring about social change, including political participation, empowerment, and thus better health.

The capacity of the internet to act as a new environment is rooted in the way it affects patterns of information flow. Meyrowitz (1995) argues that social roles are partly determined by social situations, themselves related to a specific physical location. He further contends that the logic of behaviors exhibited by social actors in a particular situation is influenced by patterns of information flow. When applied to the arena of healthcare, it is clear that the social role of physicians as primary decision-makers is tied to their ownership and control of medical information in hospitals and major healthcare locations. Electronic media may well change this pre-established pattern by weakening the relationship between information flow, physical locations and social situations. In the context of e-health, it could be posited that telemedicine threatens the dominance of Western medical expertise, in general, and the public health insurance system, in particular (at least, as it is currently structured in Canada). E-health may do so in part because it enables wider public access to health information outside the hospital walls.

This analysis of electronic media helps us to speculate on some other ways in which e-health might empower Aboriginal peoples by engendering new institutional developments and new policies. Gains may arise in the field of information exchange to build Aboriginal capacity in health planning and research. Gains might also be made in Aboriginal assertions of their rights to data ownership, control, access and possession. This could lead to self-regulation in matters of privacy and improvements in Aboriginal access to equitable connectivity. The potential of Aboriginal e-health towards empowerment can be more clearly elucidated by examining the main roles in which Aboriginal individuals and communities are and can be positioned by e-health applications.

Table 3.1 Aboriginal peoples' roles in relation to e-health

Role of aboriginal peoples	E-health as a thing	E-health as a new environment
As recipients of telemedical services	Persistent dehumanization of healthcare and centralization of authority in specialized medical centers at the expense of community-based health systems.	Delivery of alternative health practices by Aboriginal centers of expertise (e.g., in mental health, health promotion and traditional medicine) to other Aboriginal communities.
As objects of research and general data collection	Evidence-based decision-making facilitated by government health information networks.	Client/community involvement in health information and research networks, advancing the use of alternative research networks and sensitive to socio-structural inequities related to access.
As information-seekers	Promotion of lifestyle approach consisting of educating patients to comply with a certain regimented set of behaviors prescribed by Western medical practitioners.	Shared decision-making and self-management of care by the client.
As interactors	Provision of a virtual environment to promote patient compliance to a prescribed regime/forms of self-care.	*New tool that will enhance critical thinking, competency and empowerment* (Boscoe 1999:7). Adoption of a new zone of socialization through mutual aid and self-help networking.

Table 3.1 briefly describes these roles on the basis of whether e-health is used as a thing or as a new environment.

I suggest that the optimal model and application of e-health, in terms of the question of Aboriginal health empowerment, will best come about in cases where it functions in its capacity as an environment more than in its capacity as a thing. In comparing these perspectives, we can consider the Fort Chipewyan project as an example of e-health applied to create a new environment for Aboriginal individuals and communities as "recipients of telemedical services". Here, e-health through videoconferencing is helping to break down geographical isolation, and is allowing Aboriginal communities to share their health knowledge and practices with each other, as well as with other Canadians.[2] Although initially focused on physiotherapy and similar services, the Fort Chipewyan project is currently exploring the use of videoconferencing as a medium to deliver traditional medicine to Aboriginal communities. The term "telespirituality" has been coined to describe the linking of spiritual leaders to communities (Napier 2001). In offering this service, the community would position itself as a First Nations center of expertise, effectively using e-health to create a radically new way, or environment, of servicing healthcare to Canadian indigenous peoples. This application stands in sharp contrast to the standard use of e-health, which is often used to intensify the already-established authority of specialized medicine in university-affiliated hospitals. The intensification of the existing system tends to increase the unequal status of the patient relative to the physician, and thus threatens to further dehumanize healthcare (Bronzino *et al.* 1990).

Another example of the benefits of e-health as environment versus tool can be found in the way in which it positions Aboriginal individuals and communities as "objects of research and general data collection". In tacitly working with the "tool" assumption, the National Forum on Health (a major player in Canadian healthcare reform of the 1990s) recommended that ICT networks be established to build a culture of evidence-based decision-making. Now widely implemented across the country, evidence-based decision-making promotes a research design that is quantitative, scientific and empirical. In contrast, the e-health agendas of Canadian Aboriginal peoples have been working to reverse Aboriginal peoples' traditional relationship with medical research. For example, they have undertaken a First Nations and Inuit Longitudinal Regional Health Survey designed to offer an alternative to the electronic medical record. The typical electronic medical record is a legal document that establishes the physician as the core decision-maker and that reproduces the body politic of the medical clinic in several ways (e.g., its temporal structure, division of labor, geography and hierarchical design). Comparatively, the First Nations and Inuit Health Information System aims to heighten Aboriginal authority in their health programs and services. This is being accomplished by introducing community involvement in research design and analysis. In this manner, the

Aboriginal model has similarities with certain grassroots health movements, such as the recently-organized international Consumer Network (of the Cochrane collaboration) that has emerged to re-balance health authority. In her proposal to form this Consumer Network, Hilda Bastian states: "values cannot be measured with a ruler, and the pain of peoples' struggles with ill-health should not be homogenised till it is no longer recognisable" (1994: 5).

In considering another example of the application of e-health as a new environment, we can discuss the role accorded to Aboriginal individuals and communities as "information-seekers". Consumer health informatics commonly facilitate an approach to healthcare that focuses on educating patients to comply with a certain regimented set of behaviors (Bang *et al.* 1998: 104). In the scenario of e-health, such an approach might be regarded as a case of using ICTs as tools to discipline changes in lifestyle and health practices. An alternative approach suggests that ICTs can empower consumers to actively practice self-care. In fact, some advocates of this position have gone so far as to posit that self-care will become the central, organizing paradigm of healthcare in the information age (Ferguson 1992). In distinction to the three facets of health-care – tertiary, secondary and primary – during the industrial age, Ferguson maps six facets, or resources, for the information age. These are: individual self-care, friends and family, self-help groups and networks, and health professionals like facilitators, partners, and authorities. Indeed, studies that have evaluated e-health in terms of its contribution to self-care have noted that it "envisages . . . more opportunities for managed self-care and home-based service provision" (Tavistock Institute 1996: 2.2.iii). Aboriginal projects like the National Native Addictions Information Management System are being developed in ways that promote self-care opportunities.

Finally, the role assigned to Aboriginal individuals and communities as "interactors" makes an impact in determining whether any given e-health project may function more like an environment or like a tool. Interactive technologies are also commonly used to discipline health-related lifestyle behaviors, rather than to increase self-help. A cautionary note reflecting awareness of this common practice was put forth at the conceptual stage of the Canadian Women's Network: "are we trying to increase patient compliance with medical directives or are we creating a tool that will enhance critical thinking, competency and empowerment?" (Boscoe 1999: 7). According to Boscoe, interaction is the key to using electronic communications in order to create a new zone of socialization rather than to maintain the status quo. To create a new environment, interaction must involve multiple stakeholders in an atmosphere of mutual respect. With respect to the Aboriginal situation, the small population base of First Nations and Inuit communities has generally tended to limit the ability to form self-help groups locally. The use of e-health by individuals networking across communities is promising to provide the added advantage of anonymity often difficult to obtain in small localities.

"Our voice, our decisions, our responsibility"

A review of the potential of e-health to create a new healthcare environment leads me to suggest an alternative model for Aboriginal e-health development. This model is assembled from other models that have variously focused on technology, health/medicine and citizen/community participation and governance. As envisioned by this model, Aboriginal telemedicine would revolve around self-managing institutions with power at the grassroots level. It would operate in accordance with new social contracts that reflect broadened norms and values. Such broadened values could take into account traditional values concerning the interdependence of all living organisms: time, touch, human contact, compassion, justice, fairness, equality, reciprocity, conviviality, connectedness vs. causality, etc. In seeking to prevent the imposition of dominant viewpoints, the alternative model of e-health would allow for dissent as well as the expression of diverse viewpoints (see Boscoe 1999). Furthermore, it would envision technology as a tool of conviviality. As Illich (1973) has noted in his discussion of convivial design, the meaning and impact of technology is context-specific and determined in concert with human and non-human actors who are themselves influenced by technological development. Conviviality thus allows for the interpretive flexibility of a given technological artifact. Indeed, I propose that the integration of e-health within an overall strategy that goes *beyond* health is fundamental to the successful contribution of e-health to improvements in Aboriginal health empowerment.

At the present time, the question remains as to whether and how the Aboriginal Health Infostructure can or will be implemented in accordance with an alternative e-health model. I have argued here that the success of e-health projects is related to the degree to which the potential of ICTs can be harnessed to create new environments. E-health offers an unprecedented opportunity to break down barriers in geographical isolation and in expert knowledge systems and, thereby, to empower Aboriginal peoples. It is just such new environments for envisioning healthcare, for data ownership, access, control and the like, that may be determinant for the expression of Aboriginal voices, decisions and responsibility with respect to their own health futures (Assembly of First Nations 2001a).

Notes

1   While outside the scope of this article, the ability of e-health applications to address these aims has been demonstrated to varying extents by researchers. For instance, telehealth's ability to improve the management of workloads and professional training of health practitioners in rural and remote settings has been extensively observed (Watanabe and Casebeer 1999; Gilmour *et al.* 1998; Jennett *et al.* 1995; Mitchell *et al.* 1996; Doze and Sampson 1997; Miyasaka *et al.* 1997). As well, economic analyses of the impact of telehealth reveal positive savings in practitioner travel times and medical transportation costs (Baer *et al.* 1997; Doolittle *et al.* 1998; Navein *et al.* 1996; Vincent *et al.* 1997; Afset *et al.*1996; Finley *et al.* 1997; Pavan-Kickoloff 1999).

2   Another instance in the making is the National Native American HIV/AIDS Integrated Services Network (www.nnaapc.org), a collaboration between several Native American organizations. The network establishes contractual relationships with local service providers to ensure access to services by Native Americans infected with HIV, including services emphasizing spirituality, traditional healing, and cultural awareness. Although not yet electronic, the network is an ideal project for e-health, and especially its potential to build and ensure wide access to Native healthcare models.

References

Aboriginal Nurses Association of Canada (ANAC) (2000) *Survey of Nurses in Isolated First Nations Communities: Recruitment and Retention Issues*. Ottawa: ANAC.

Advisory Council on Health Infostructure (1999) *Canada Health Infoway: Paths to Better Health*. Ottawa: Health Canada.

Afset, J. E., Lunde, P. and Rasmussen, K. (1996) "Accuracy of Routine Echocardiographic Measurements Made by an Inexperienced Examiner through Tele-instruction", *Journal of Telemedicine and Telecare* 2: 148–54.

Assembly of First Nations (AFN) (1998a) *An Aboriginal Health Info-Structure: Critical Issues and Initiatives*. Ottawa: AFN.

——(1998b) *An Aboriginal Health Info-structure: Social/Political/Operational Issues*. Ottawa: AFN.

——(2001a) *First Nations Health: Our Voice, Our Decisions, Our Responsibility*. Ottawa: AFN.

——(2001b) *Executive Summary to the Government of Canada for the Deployment of Broadband Services to First Nations*. Ottawa: AFN.

Baer, L., Elford, R. and Cukor, P. (1997) "Telepsychiatry at Forty: What Have We Learned?", *Harvard Review of Psychiatry* 5(1): 7–17.

Bang, Debbie L., Farrar, Sheryl, Sellors, John W. and Buchanan, Don H. (1998) "Consumer Health Information Services: Preliminary Findings about Who is Using Them", *Journal of Medical Systems* 22(2): 103–15.

Bastian, Hilda (1994) *The Power of Sharing Knowledge: Consumer Participation in the Cochrane Collaboration*. Canadian Cochrane Centre, McMaster University. Electronic document.

Berg, Marc and Bowker, Geoffrey (1997) "The Multiple Bodies of the Medical Record: Toward a Sociology of an Artifact", *The Sociological Quarterly*. 38(3): 513–37.

Boscoe, Madeline (1999) *Women and Health Information I-way*, in *Proceedings from Conference: Digital Knowledge II: Building Electronic Space for Community Health Information, 1997*. Toronto: Coalition for Public Information.

Brewer, Alexa (Health Canada) (2001a) *Working Towards an Aboriginal Health Infostructure*. Paper presented at the Canadian Society of Telehealth meeting, Toronto.

——(2001b) *The Aboriginal Health Infostructure: Towards a New Continuum of Information*. Paper presented at the National Inuit Health Information Conference, Inuvik.

Bronzino, Joseph D., Smith, Vincent H. and Wade, Maurice L. (1990) *Medical Technology and Society: An Interdisciplinary Perspective*. Cambridge, MA: MIT Press.

Commission on the Future of Healthcare in Canada (2002) *Shape the Future of Healthcare: Interim Report*. Ottawa: Commission on the Future of Healthcare in Canada.

Doolittle, G. C., Williams, A., Harmon, A., Allen, A., Boysen, C. D., Wittman, C., Mair, F. and Carlson, E. (1998) "A Cost Measurement Study for a Tele-Oncology Practice", *Journal of Telemedicine and Telecare* 4(2): 84–8.

Doze, S. and Sampson, J. (1997) *Telepsychiatry: Pilot Project Evaluation.* Winnipeg: Alberta Heritage Foundation for Medical Research.

Ferguson, Tom (1992) "Consumer Health Informatics", *Healthcare Forum Journal* 38(1): 28–32.

Finley, J. P., Sharratt, G. P., Nanton, M. A., Chen, R.P., Bryan, P., Wolstenholme, J. and MacDonald, C. (1997) "Pediatric Echocardiography by Telemedicine – Nine Years' Experience", *Journal of Telemedicine and Telecare* 3(4): 200–4.

Gideon, Valerie (2000) *Telehealth and Citizen Involvement.* PhD dissertation, McGill University.

Gilmour, E., Campbell, S. M., Loane, M. A., Esmail, A., Griffiths, C. E., Roland, M. O., Parry, E. J., Corbett, R. O., Eedy, D., Gore, H. E., Mathews, C., Steel, K., and Wootton, R. (1998) "Comparison of Teleconsultations and Face-to-face Consultations: Preliminary Results of a United Kingdom Multicentre Teledermatology Study", *British Journal of Dermatology* 139: 81–7.

Glover, Paul (Health Canada) (2001) *The Aboriginal Health Infostructure: Towards a New Continuum of Information.* Paper presented at Assembly of First Nations Health Conference, Ottawa.

Health Canada, First Nations and Inuit Health Branch (1996) *Trends in First Nations' Mortality 1979–1993.* Ottawa: Health Canada.

——(1999) *Action on Nursing: National Nurse Retention and Recruitment Strategy.* Ottawa: Health Canada.

——(2001a) *Unintentional and Intentional Injury Profile for Aboriginal People in Canada 1990–1999.* Ottawa: Health Canada.

——(2001b) *Community Services in the 21st Century: First Nations and Inuit Telehealth Services. National First Nations Telehealth Research Project HTF-NA402 1998–2001.* Ottawa: Health Canada.

——(2001c) *The Alberta First Nations' Project to Screen for Limbs, I-Sight, Cardiovascular and Kidney (SLICK) Complications using Mobile Diabetes Clinics.* Ottawa: Health Canada.

——(2001d) *ICTs in Health Infoway: Canada Health Infostructure Partnerships Program.* Ottawa: Health Canada. Available online: www.hc-sc.gc.ca/ohih-bsi/whatfund/chipp-ppics/proj/projti_e.html

——(2001e) *Yukon Territory.* Ottawa: Health Canada. Available online: www.hc-sc.gc.ca/ohih-bsi/chi_sc/fpt/yt2_e.html

Illich, Ivan (1973) *Tools for Conviviality.* New York: Harper & Row.

Indian and Northern Affairs Canada (2002) *Report on Aboriginal Connectivity.* Paper presented at the National Connecting Aboriginal Canadians Forum, Ottawa.

Inuit Tapirisat of Canada (ITC) (2000) *Evaluation of Models of Healthcare Delivery in Inuit Regions.* Ottawa: ITC.

——(2001) *Inuit of Canada: Our 5000 Years Heritage.* Ottawa: ITC. Available online: www.itk.ca/sitemap/i_heritage/i_heritage2/i_heritage2.html.

Jennett, P., Hall, W. G., Morin, J. E. and Watanabe, Mo (1995) "Evaluation of a Distance Consulting Service Based on Interactive Video and Integrated Computerized Technology", *Journal of Telemedicine and Telecare* 1(2) pp. 69-78.

Kuh-Ke-Nah Network of Smart First Nations (KNSFN) (2002) *Keewaytinok Okimakanak's K-Net to Deliver Expanded Satellite Services to Remote Communities.* Thunder Bay: KNSFN.

McInroy, Lorna (2001) "Telehealth System in Saskatchewan Makes 'Virtual' Doctor Visits Possible", *Canadian Healthcare Technology* 16.

Métis National Council (2001) *Who are the Métis?* Available online: www.metisnation.ca/MNC/home.html

Meyrowitz, Joshua (1995) *No Sense of Place: The Impact of Electronic Media on Social Behavior.* New York: Oxford University Press.

Mitchell, B. R., Mitchell, J. G. and Disney, A. P. S. (1996) "User Adoption Issues in Renal Telemedicine", *Journal of Telemedicine and Telecare* 2: 81–6.

Miyasaka, K., Suzuki, Y., Sakai, H. and Kondo, Y. (1997) "Interactive Technology in High-Technology Home Care: Videophones for Pediatric Ventilatory Care", *Pediatrics* 99(1): E1.

Napier, JoAnn (2001) "Telehealth Program Brings Care to Remote Areas", *Ottawa Citizen*, 29 May.

National Broadband Task Force (2001) *The New National Dream: Networking the Nation for Broadband Access.* Ottawa: Industry Canada.

Navein, J., Arose, D. and Pietermich, A. (1996) "A Business Model for Telemedicine", *Journal of Telemedicine and Telecare* 5(1): 76–7.

Ng, Edward, Wilkins, Russell, Pole, Jason, and Adams, Owen B. (1997) "How Far to the Nearest Physician?", *Health Reports* 8(4): 19–31.

Panel on Smart Communities (1998) *Smart Communities: A Report of the Panel on Smart Communities.* Ottawa: Industry Canada.

Pavan-Kickoloff, Angela (1999) *Participant Satisfaction and Comfort with Multidisciplinary Pediatric Telemedicine Consultations.* Paper presented at Inter@ctive Health, Fredericton.

Picot, Jocelyne and Cradduck, Trevor (2000) *The Telehealth Industry in Canada: Industry Profile and Capability Analysis.* Ottawa: Industry Canada.

Poster, Mark (1998) "Cyberdemocracy: The Internet and the Public Sphere", in D. Holmes (ed.), *Virtual Politics: Identity and Community in Cyberspace.* Thousand Oaks, CA: Sage, pp. 212–28.

Royal Commission on Aboriginal Peoples (1996) *Final Report, Four Volumes.* Ottawa: Canada Communications Group.

Statistics Canada (1996) *Canadian Census.*

Tavistock Institute (1996) *TELMED: The Impact of Telematics on the Healthcare Sector in Europe.* Brussels: European Health Telematics Observatory.

Vincent, J. A., Cavitt, D.L. and Karpawich, P.P. (1997) "Diagnostic and Cost-Effectiveness of Telemonitoring the Pediatric Pacemaker Patient", *Pediatric Cardiology* 18(2): 86–90.

Watanabe, Mo and Casebeer, Ann (1999) *Rural Health Research: The Quest for Equitable Health Status for all Canadians. Report of The Rural Health Research Summit, Prince George.* Ottawa: Health Canada.

Wien, Fred and McIntyre, Lynn (1999) "Health and Dental Services for Aboriginal People", in First Nations and Inuit Regional Health Survey National Steering Committee (eds), *First Nations and Inuit Regional Health Survey National Report.* Ottawa: First Nations and Inuit Regional Health Survey National Steering Committee, pp. 217–45.

Chapter 4

A Screen of Snow and Recognition Reigned Supreme?

Journeys into the homeland of a Greenlandic webpage

Neil Blair Christensen

Spaces of identity

I remember once paying a visit to local fisherman, kiosk-owner and politician Adam Grim in Aappilattoq, a small Greenlandic community where a combination of fishing and hunting is the most common way of making a living.[1] It was during winter, and the village of some 220 inhabitants, located on an island off the west coast of Greenland, was surrounded by frozen sea and covered in snow. Together with nine other villages and the small town of Upernavik, Aappilattoq comprises the Municipality of Upernavik and is home to some 3,000 people.[2] The size of the municipality is breathtaking. It stretches 450 kilometers from north to south along the northwestern coast of Greenland, covering a total area of 200,000 square kilometers, and, by comparison, is only slightly smaller than the entire United Kingdom. It was a mixed group of strangers, friends and family visiting Adam, who welcomed everyone at the front door of his "home". Inside, some of his guests were looking through photo albums full of picturesque images, most of which had been taken outdoors and were thus dominated by snow and ice – icebergs floating in dark blue fjords or frozen to a standstill in a sea of ice – along with views of the two communities Aappilattoq and Upernavik, as well as photographs of local events and family members. Adam drew our attention to the many pictures of the physical space of the community, which appeared isolated as it lay there surrounded by barren land- and seascapes. In simply expressing his reality, Adam somehow anticipated that we recognized and accepted these symbols of Greenlandicness. Maybe he did not really think about it: it was just his way of being, his everyday lived space. We did not really think about it either, because we expected something along those lines. After all, we were in Greenland. It seemed that the wider the social network amongst those present extended in geographical terms, the more our perceptions tuned into mapping the geo-spatial particularity of the small Greenlandic community in comparison to the places from whence we had come. We were experiencing space and boundaries that were foreign to each of our own everyday space(s). Being confronted with an assertion of local community, with Adam taking on the role of mediator, we reacted by placing ourselves on the geographical map. The feeling or illusion of an isolated Arctic indigenous community in comparison to the "rest of the world" was a boundary that recursively negotiated the social sense of place and identity, born in the dynamic exchange of how this Greenlandic family and its members perceived themselves and how outside others were being invited to perceive them. Some of us visitors, including myself, came from afar, yet only stayed for a couple of minutes. Despite the warm welcoming, my presence went unnoticed – and I was not offered that cup of coffee that is customary for any social call in Greenland.

So I left my computer and walked into the kitchen of my Copenhagen apartment, to fix myself a coffee and rest my eyes in the midst of some online fieldwork in Greenland. I was a semi-nomadic anthropologist, a habitué; traveling thousands of kilometers online to visit homepages such as Adam's. I was following up a seemingly banal point by French philosopher Henri Lefebvre, who questioned if space was a social relationship – to which he answered in the affirmative by launching into a complex sociology of space as a phenomenon interlinked with property relationships, nature and materiality, social labor and forces of production that impose a form on the land (Lefebvre 1991: 85 and *passim*). The variety of space(s) on the web and the situations that emerge in and around webpages present us with an approach to space and modernity that is interesting in the light of Lefebvre's sociological and philosophical ideas. This chapter will try to uncover some of the social relationships that are sometimes concealed, sometimes not, but are certainly embedded and thus re-appropriated in the spaces of many Greenlandic homepages with the help of their maps, pictures, links, text and guestbooks. My approach seeks to disconnect itself from the ideology of a cyberspace myth that envisions a sharp divide between what goes on offline and online.

Welcome to Aappilattoq

A banner at the top of Adam Grim's family homepage reads: "Welcome to Aappilattoq". The welcoming text is accompanied by a photograph of a snow-covered landscape, with some thirty buildings scattered across what appears to be a hilltop but actually turns out to be an island surrounded by ice and snow. The picture has been taken from outside the village, across a frozen body of water, covered in snow and thus revealing a frequently used trail winding off to the left towards the village. It is a sunny day with a clear blue sky. The thick blanket of snow makes the landscape look barren, and Aappilattoq seems quite isolated lying there all by itself on its rocky island. The background of the webpage is dark blue and dotted with something that appears to be light blue ice crystals. The dark background helps to accentuate the photo. The spatial effect is immediate: "we are here – where are you?" In this fashion, Adam's welcome page exemplifies how Inuit often design webpages that (re)produce an imagined Arctic remoteness – a remoteness that is a key aspect of asserting Inuit identities, cultures and histories of occupancy, and signifies the otherness of their social space in comparison to that of other peoples.[3]

A menu with thirteen items stretches across the page just below the photo of Aappilattoq, and the page reads: "Welcome to Family Adam Grim's homepage in Aappilattoq" in three languages, English, Danish and Greenlandic. Two maps appear. One depicts Greenland, with a highlighted area of the northwestern coast, and is accompanied by the legend "Upernavik area". When clicked, the enlarged version of the map divides Greenland into its different municipalities. The other map, with the legend "Aappilattoq area", shows a coastline with dots and place names, Aappilattoq being one of them. The remainder of the welcome page contains external links to the official Greenlandic Santa Claus website, a Greenlandic web portal by the name of *Igloo*, a Greenlandic search engine, a Danish tabloid newspaper, and some banner advertisements for outdoor equipment.

Appropriation of space – an open invitation

I click the first menu item, Aappilattoq, on Adam's welcome page. A new page appears with a large photo at the top. It pictures some children sitting on an outdoor staircase at the side of a house. The rooftops of houses appear below their feet on the sloping hillside, and a large iceberg floating around in the blue water of a small bay beyond is centered in the picture. Sixteen other photos depict the village from the east and the west: all snow-covered with buildings, dogs and people. They are dated 13/14 March 2001. The header of the page informs us that Aappilattoq was established in 1850 and is 150 years old. I go back to the previous page and click the menu item, Upernavik, and I am informed by a header that the small town had its 225th anniversary in 1997. The header is accompanied by an aerial shot of Upernavik, similar to that of Aappilattoq, located across an island that appears to be isolated. Again, the picture is taken during winter. Thirteen other pictures show the small town – or large village, if you will. Included are shots of the supply ship *Irena Arctica* from the Royal Arctic Line, arriving with fresh supplies for the communities and new cars for the newly-opened fixed-wing airstrip, making the expensive helicopter traffic obsolete and aiming to pull Greenland even more together as a country. The large satellite dish that connects Upernavik to the outside world is also present among the photos, sitting by itself on the top of the island. The very bottom of the page portrays a large picture of local politicians. Clicking the image will take me straight to the official tri-lingual page for Upernavik. There, the usual snow-covered outdoor pictures, dogsleds and buildings greet me. The page offers me photographs, a welcoming preface by the mayor, official data, and links to 13 homepages from the Upernavik district as well as to the Danish friendship town Odense. Adam Grim's homepage appears among the links and I return to his pages after this short detour. "You are always welcome to Aappilattoq", I am greeted, after clicking the menu item *Foto*, meaning "photo" in English. The welcome message is written in English and Greenlandic. The Grim family welcomes us with seven pictures – one for each family member –

with legends that give me their dates of birth. Two other pictures show their house and the daughter's dog, lying outside stretched out across the snow. The next item on the menu is *Interest* and informs the visitor in Danish and Greenlandic about Adam's interests, his work as a local politician and as the captain of a fishing boat. He has been a local politician in Siumut since 1997, as a Social Democrat, where he also holds a post on Siumut's board at the national level. The page contains links to the official Upernavik page maintained by the municipality and the Danish Social Democratic Party, as well as Siumut. Clicking on the link to Siumut I arrive at a page that features debate forums, a multitude of online articles on hot topics in Greenlandic society, and links to a variety of online resources in Greenland. After a while I return to Adam's "Interest" page and look at the single photo without a credit that pictures a group of politicians dressed in national costumes with the municipal insignia hanging on the wall behind them, in what appears to be the meeting room of the Upernavik town hall.

I decide to check out the remainder of Adam's pages before moving on. A weather page provides yet another set of outdoor winter photos of the community, as well as a link to ice charts and weather forecasts for Greenland. The next page from the menu is called "A. G. Kiosk", and is a short page advertising offers from Adam's kiosk. The specials at the time of my visit are snowmobile accessories such as covers, bearings and wheels. Other pages include one with eighteen photos and the scores from the Winter Games 2000 in Aappilattoq where the local communities met and competed at football (i.e. soccer). The 2001 News Page contains a photo of a tall iceberg in the bay outside Upernavik town, and a sequence of three photos of the first sun appearing in Aappilattoq from 2 to 4 February 2001, after the long period of winter darkness. A similar 2000 News Page exists with as many as 65 photos, showing everything from a grandchild's fifth birthday, the first plane to touch down at the new airport, a heard of musk ox, the first supply ship to arrive in May 2000 when ice conditions allowed after a long winter, to a visit to the village by a top government official – and much more. At the time of my visit, Adam's website is made up of 13 pages as well as a guestbook, and contains as many as 140 photos, a couple of maps and some 90 links to other websites.

The guestbook icon, blinking at the bottom of his homepage, invites people to visit and submit entries – in English, Danish and Greenlandic. On the day of my visit, the guestbook contains 102 entries, of which 91 are in Greenlandic; and it has been accessed 2,298 times. The web counter informs me that Adam's page has had a total of 5,126 visits since 3 March 2000. The date for my own visit is 7 October 2001, so that averages nine visits per day during its first year and a half. By matching the guestbook counter with the counter on the welcome page, we see that the guestbook is evidently a very active part of Adam's website. Almost half of all visits to the website are likely to be combined with a visit to his guestbook, but only a fraction of the visitors sign the book, and an entry only occurs for each 22nd visit to the guestbook on average. It seems clear that a majority of visitors go there only to read the entries made by others. Many of those who do actually sign also appear to be frequent visitors, judging from the number of their entries as well as their statements, such as comments on the long-term development of Adam's pages, or notes that make explicit their offline relationships with Adam, his family and his community. I would here like to give some brief examples, in order to indicate what kinds of comments visitors make, and thus what kinds of identities they articulate in relation to Adam's website. Some of the core users stand out, and a particularly-defined social space develops when reading their comments and visiting their own homepages.

One such core user is Imina Heilmann who lives in Upernavik town. When I first visited his homepage in 1999 he had recently moved there from Qaanaaq, located in the very north of Greenland, and he maintained pages with ample photographs and information from that area. When Adam launched his site in late 1999 it did not take long before Imina left an entry in Adam's guestbook, and vice versa. The two also linked to each other's homepages from their links sections, and it was apparent that they knew each other quite well. During the summer of 2000 Imina was on holiday in Aalborg, Denmark, and wrote to Adam about the hot weather by way of an entry into Adam's guestbook, rather than sending him a personal e-mail – even leaving his mobile telephone number so that Adam could reach him. Other visitors to Adam's guestbook include members of the Grim family, who use the guestbook for short greetings once in a while, including Adam himself. Some visitors leave not only their email addresses, but include links to their own webpages. Quite a few of the names appear familiar; they belong to some of the people from Upernavik whose homepages Adam links to himself. I follow some of the links in the guestbook entries, and before long I notice that many have entries by Adam in their own guestbooks, similar to the case of Imina's guestbook. Their entries combined with the interlinking of each other's homepages create a sense of community and belonging. However, there are also entries from complete strangers. Guestbook entry by Judith Ann in England: "I loved seeing the photographs of Greenland. This is a place I would love to visit one day. Thank you for allowing me the chance to see some of the scenery here and also your family. Best wishes from England."

While the pages interact with the world wide web, and thus with the global Gesellschaft of the present, they do not create a picture of a homogenous global Gemeinschaft as much as they give an impression of Greenlandic space(s) that inter-exist with many other spaces.[4] For Lefebvre, visualizations of space are representations, which, although abstracted, do not necessarily obey consistency or coherence. They do, however, have practical impact because they are architectonic constructions: agents of social and political practice that link our understanding of objects and people through a knowledge that is "always relative and in the process of change" (1991: 41). The spaces of Adam's and Imina's websites are more than semi-static representational spaces; they undergo change whenever they alter the contents, or whenever a visitor modifies the space by inserting a comment or a link in the guestbooks. Adam and Imina are webmasters, but they are not gatekeepers in total control of the traffic at their respective websites, nor to the links and search engines that direct visitors to their pages from other social spaces.

The links page is divided into five sections: a nameless set of general links, Greenlandic links, Danish links, links from the Faroe Islands and a section called Other. The general links direct the visitor to quite diverse locations, such as the homepage of a recent expedition, the Upernavik official pages, a Greenlandic online resource called *Atagu*, the national travel agency's guide, a Y2K page by Microsoft, a download site with free software for kids, as well as a page that provides satellite views of the USA. This categorization of links represents the superstructure for many of Adam's social spaces: the Danish Kingdom, consisting of Greenland, the Faroe Islands and Denmark; transnational companies and services . . . and eventually onto something for the kids. The Greenlandic link section includes four personal homepages, the Home Rule Government pages, the national travel agency, a number of nationally-owned corporations, some web portals for shopping and chat, and a career directory for upcoming students. The Greenlandic links on Adam's page are not overly excessive in number, but provide visitors with a broad opportunity to visit other websites from within and outside of Upernavik, key government and commercial pages, and even more extensive resources through web portals. In contrast to a vision of cyberspace in which powerful individuals no longer need the more-or-less useless shell we know as physical space because all its social meaning has been transplanted into cyberspace, Greenlandic internet users such as Adam and Imina approach cyberspace much more pragmatically and "lived".

The selection of links (re)produces a multitude of political, economic, social, personal, cultural and physical spaces. They appear situationally, depending on the content of a webpage, the links clicked on by the visitor, the entries in a guestbook, the internet connection speed. They are all somehow interconnected; some directly and others through third or fourth intermediate webpages. Nevertheless, it becomes an almost impossible task to map them, because they change directions all the time and multiply rapidly. Yet, when roaming the many pages, one will soon discover that the pages link recursively to each other, and by doing so give visitors a feeling of "exploring" Greenlandic space(s). Thus, as a simple example, I can click onto the Home Rule government page, find the Upernavik page and again find Adam's page from there, but depending on the situation I could click another route and, despite the similarities, such as the excessive use of photos, my experience could turn out differently. The social localities that emerge from this production of space with its explicit links, guestbook entries, photos, mixture of three languages and explicit as well as implicit meanings are beyond the descriptive reach of this chapter because of their sheer diversity. Yet, we clearly witness how cyberspace is being appropriated as another layer of communication and integration at a very local level. Here, Adam's presence on the web draws upon and affects many of the dynamics in his society. Nevertheless, the simple fact that Adam is interacting with a much more dispersed and differentiated group than he would normally meet away from the web also forces us to recognize that, at the same time, Adam's engagement on the web greatly exceeds the local.

Periphery in a networked world

Innaarsuit, a community of 135 people in the Municipality of Upernavik, whence many of the homepages in this chapter originate, became the center of attention in November 1997 when the world's northernmost internet café opened there. In this small community, where dogs are more than twice as numerous as people, two computers with extra hardware were set up in the school kitchen with the help of technicians and sponsorships from the national operator, TELE Greenland, and KNI, the national trading and supply company. At that time, the internet had been available in Greenland for about a year, since late 1996 when the country was introduced to a 100 percent digitized telecommunications network, being only the second country in the world to achieve this status. The interest of the villagers was significant in the beginning, but they, especially the adults, soon realized that the amount of Greenlandic content available on the web did not satisfy their needs or expectations. Soon, the novelty of the medium faded at the same speed that it had first appeared. The leader of the project moved from the village, and his successor, another outsider, basically took over the café for personal use. In 1998, he left as well, and the computers were packed away to make room for the May celebrations of school graduates – only half a year after they had first been installed. Later, in August 1998, a new principal arrived at the school and the computers were once more unpacked (Hansen 1999).

Today, however, the connection speed is modest, the sponsorship is gone, access is now paid for by the minute, and users experience frequent network failures because heavy traffic in the large towns further south, such as Sisimiut and the capital Nuuk, burdens the server capabilities. Users have no alternative service provider since the government-owned operator holds the monopoly on all telecommunication services in Greenland. Greenland may be among the countries in the world with the most modern communication infrastructures – for example, it operates one of the world's most modern, but also most expensive communication infrastructures in which 55,000 people use an estimated 12,000 cellular phones and up to 40 percent of the population have internet access. Yet it remains a peripheral country; and, despite internet access, periphery continues to matter. Located in a small village in the middle of nowhere, paying expensive rates by the minute for internet access with frequent network failures does as least as much to remind people of where they live as it does to make them forget. The feeling of periphery, be it physical, social, political or economic, helps to define and (re)produce the sense of belonging for the villagers in Upernavik, online as well as offline. Despite the increasing use of cyberspace, Greenlandic society remains on the periphery of the world, and Greenlandic villages, such as Aappilattoq and Innaarsuit, remain on the periphery of Greenlandic society.[5]

Pages such as Adam's seem to be simultaneously staging and resisting periphery by appropriating or colonizing bits and pieces of cyberspace. The more that Greenlanders communicate with outside others, the more they position themselves as members or non-members of an enlarged social space, a world where it becomes increasingly important for peoples to appropriate and dominate their own space. A simple way to achieve this end is to present space to outsiders that is uniquely related to one's own immediate space. At the same time, while outside information and communications are increasingly pouring into the country, members of the Greenlandic population are increasingly communicating internally with one another. Here, cyberspace plays a role in transforming existing personal, local, cultural and national spaces and discussions, similar to the role played by print media (particularly newspapers) in the Greenlandic nationalist discourses of the early twentieth century.

The birth of Greenlandicness

As a nationally recognized identity, Greenlandic identity is not much older than 80 or 90 years, when it was first discussed in a series of newspaper articles from 1911 to 1920 in the two newspapers *Atuagagliutit* and *Avangnâmiok* (see Berthelsen 1976). In those days, Greenlandic identity was considered quite static and singular in its nature, including only those who were hunters, spoke Greenlandic, and lived off the land. With the introduction of a large-scale occupational change towards commercial fishing, some Greenlanders started to question the relevance of the occupational status of "hunter" as the key symbol of Greenlandic identity and instead stressed the importance of mastering Greenlandic language. These early discussions on the definition of *Kalaaliussuseq* (Greenlandicness) took place over the course of a decade. Only residents in the respective hometowns of the two newspapers had a chance to read and comment on the issue, on a monthly basis. The remaining population in Greenland had to wait for their yearly supply of newspapers, and thus up to two years to read their own replies. Despite the slowness of this process, the level of increased communication, for its day, did have a tremendous effect on Greenlandic society. As people in different parts of the country started communicating through newspapers, colonial institutions and eventually radio, the collective consciousness of a national identity gained strength. However, growing communications did not erase local identities; rather, a differentiation in local identities ensued, with national identity becoming a supra-identity. Greenlanders increasingly found their country explicitly entangled in world processes as a nation in its own right, rather than as a region within Denmark.[6]

Spurred by geopolitical events, the negotiation of Greenlandic identity further expanded over the century from local to national to international levels. One might say that Greenlandicness, far from being erased or displaced, has been the product of increased communications. The multitude of different nationalities appearing in the guestbooks of Greenlandic webpages bears witness to this process.

The context is one of lived time and space wherein the relations we experience on the homepage are situational, whether temporary or lasting. Our experience and understanding of the social space depends on the links we follow, the photos we view, the bits of text we read, as well as the purpose and extent of our visits. Adam's homepage is one of approximately 130 personal homepages registered under the Greenlandic domain *iserit.gl* used by the national service provider to host homepages without domain names of their own, and some 170 pages for businesses, institutions, schools, administrations, etc., which exist in Greenland under the top-level domain. *gl*. In addition, there exists an unknown number of Greenlandic websites under top-level domains. *dk* and *.com*, as well as in web communities such as *geocities.com*. Having monitored Greenlandic webpages since 1998, my own conservative estimate totals approximately 350 websites made by Greenlanders, or businesses and institutions that serve Greenland (as of 2002). With a population of 55,000, this amounts to one website per 150 people. We could also choose to measure the presence of Greenland in cyberspace on a given day by searching for the word Greenland through a search engine and receive, say, 822,000 hits; the same process might deliver 272 for Aappilattoq. By any means of measurement, Greenlanders are virtually negotiating Greenlandicness, as well as appropriating space, in cyberspace.

Myth and reality: noble "net-savvyges" meet everyday users

The different Inuit peoples of the circumpolar Arctic have long been defined by their isolation, which comes from living in a sparsely populated and peripheral region of the globe. Nonetheless, this isolation has not left these societies in a social vacuum, for they have always taken an active part in the larger world. Sejersen exemplifies the continuum by which Inuit have always been part of global processes: he describes how a Western explorer by the name of Murdoch thought in 1826 that he had "discovered" Iñupiat in Northern Alaska, but was amazed to find these people smoking tobacco, which turned out to have been traded around the globe through elaborate networks running from South America to Europe and through Siberia and into North America (Sejersen 1996: 43–44). An analogy to these trade networks persists in the networks of cyberspace, where identities, alongside goods and political ideas, are traded and negotiated. Today, communications technologies are decidedly changing the relative isolation of Inuit peoples. Yet, despite their continuous and increasing interaction with the world alongside processes of change, Inuit are often stigmatized as either happy Eskimos or sad victims of (post- or hyper)modernity. This simplification seems linked to a supposed, but neverthe-less misunderstood, conflict between indigeneity on the one hand and wage economy and modern technology on the other, such as in the anti-sealing campaigns by Greenpeace and other "conservationist" approaches by outsiders to Inuit resource management and/or development. Indigenous peoples throughout the Arctic have experienced similar contradictions, often in the form of "do-good" initiatives and attitudes that implicitly deny them a coherent contemporary identity. In her discussion on how the Yupiit of Alaska differ from the stereotype of peaceful igloo-dwellers, Fienup-Riordan concludes that, "Contrary to the view that would see them as either traditional or modern, many Yupiit are . . . striving to be both" (Fienup-Riordan 1990: 231). Even though Inuit identities and cultures are often thought of in a somewhat "museo-logical" context by outsiders, their contents and dynamics are and have always been subject to continuous change. Lefebvre recognized that "No space disap-pears in the course of growth and development: the worldwide does not abolish the local" (1991: 86). In its simple way, Adam's homepage illustrates Lefebvre's argument.

In attempting to assess how Inuit peoples feel about the internet and how they envision its role in their lives, I conducted an online pilot survey with Inuit participants from Alaska, Arctic Canada and Greenland (see Christensen 1999). The majority of respondents held the opinion that, while the internet brought development to the Arctic, this was not automatically a trend towards homogeneity, democratization or togetherness for the Arctic region. Many Inuit web users made reference to the practicalities of increased communication, especially when living on the periphery of world society compared to those living in political-economic centers.

> Not the least, [online shopping is] also a nice thing, that all different types of merchandise can be examined and ordered through the internet, again in regard to where one lives here where the choice in goods is very limited.
> (Survey respondent, adult male from Ammassalik, Greenland)

> We live in an isolated town. The airplane tickets to go anywhere are very expensive. We are hope [sic] the Internet will bring long distance education for student research and long distance communication for both individuals and business/corporations/associations etc.
> (Survey respondent, adult female from Rankin Inlet, Nunavut, Canada)

People may look into a screen, but their "looking" is shaped by their lives outside the screen. Although many survey respondents were keenly aware of the pan-Arctic potential that the internet held for Inuit peoples, few had concrete examples of uses that might contribute to the ideal of an Arctic cooperating region.[7] Generally, respondents to my survey were much more likely to use the internet to write about personal, local or regional issues. One Greenlandic participant was of the opinion that, "As it is now, the use of the internet and information and communication between Arctic people is accidental." None the less, many did articulate the desire for global communications to enhance cross-cultural understanding. As one Greenlander expressed the matter: "It is my hope that information about Inuit and all aspects of our culture will bring more understanding and interest for the Inuit people, and our sustainable ways of life."

Melting snow: social space under change

Many dystopians and utopians throughout the 1980s and most of the 1990s created and sustained the myth that identity and culture would suffer from and/or evolve into a complex web of new cyber identities and cultures. However, at present, the cyberspace myth seems to have developed into exactly what it originally set out to escape: namely, a limited world. The utopian and dystopian cyberspaces generally had one thing in common: their narrow focus on cyberspace as an abstract organism somewhat devoid of human action: a "Giant Worm", in the words of Lanier (1990). Whereas much cyber research has focused on the dynamics of new online identities and/or cultures (see Curtis 1996; Lyon 1997; North 1994; Reid 1991; Rheingold 2000; Turkle 1995) this paper has focused on the online (re)production and assertion of offline identities – identities that do not depend upon cyberspace for their existence. In a convincing line of arguments, Robins addresses this widespread resistance to consider offline and online as part of a whole encompassing world and reminds us that "We can all too easily think of cyberspace and virtual reality in terms of an alternative space and reality" (1995: 153). The myth often fails to realize that cyberspace is driven by human agency that continuously defines and thus interpenetrates each and every corner of interaction. Here, I have tried to deal with a combined analysis of personal self on the web (Chandler 1998), cultural identities (Lillie 1998; Mitra 1997) and continuity between on- and offline spaces (Hamman 1996). The recursive relations between online and offline through webpages such as Adam Grim's are a testimony to the re-appropriation of cyberspace in different ways. Visualizing through its many hyperlinks, guestbook entries and photographs a process influenced by and influencing many things great and small, Adam's cyberspace is more than a sealed environment of electronic networks, but a lively, "dirty" and unpredictable social process.

What Lefebvre theorized, by pointing out that new communication networks do not eradicate older ones from their context, was in fact what Adam was doing on the web (1991: 86). Adam was forming a variety of social space(s) by asserting existing spatially-articulated phenomena, such as family, identity, occupation, physicality, economy, politics, nationality and internationality on the web. Some people would mistakenly claim that his homepage was purely representational, but (taking into account that space is a social relationship)

Adam was more than simply mirroring and representing his existing offline spaces. He and his visitors were working the properties of cyberspace into new forms and contexts that recursively asserted and were asserted by his own social space, as well as those of his visitors and their actions. Adam's homepage was situated somewhere between the dominating space of technocratic ideology that Lefebvre opposed, and the practical appropriation of space as a resistance to alienation in (post-)modern times that Lefebvre heralded. Adam was yet another personal homepage owner on the web, but he was also a Greenlander, an Aappilattormioq, a politician, a fisherman, a kiosk owner, a family man, a father. He (and we, vicariously and temporarily, with him) was engaged in a web of daily situations. Adam appropriated situationally differentiated spaces of interaction into a connected cluster of experiences in an overall practice of identity-formation and display. For some, the roles of Adam as both an indigenous person and a web user may have seemed conflictual; however, in all fairness, it was just another contemporary homepage and maybe not that big a deal for Adam.

Nevertheless, the dynamics between text, photographs, links, natural spaces and mental spaces influenced by the visiting experience and the social interaction between Adam and his guests were nothing short of a social practice that reminded us where we were in the world, and what values we, too, negotiated as rightfully Greenlandic and important for Adam's identity. To some extent, we were interacting in a space full of Greenlandic and non-Greenlandic boundary markers: language, physicality, culture, history, nationality, locality and kinship. Here, some guests related better than others, because they, being Greenlanders, were in-group members, while others undoubtedly felt themselves out-group members. None the less, we all understood that we were visiting a Greenlandic family representing explicitly and implicitly its degrees of affinity with Greenlandic society and the wide world.

In Mitra's (1997) analysis of a specific Usenet site, visited mainly by diasporic Indians from the subcontinent who were living abroad, he describes how discussions created boundaries: for example, knowing the Hindu scriptures, who Shahrukh Khan is, or what karNAtaka music is about, were in-group discussions catering to visitors with in-depth knowledge of Indian language, culture and society. In similar fashion, Adam and the visitors to his homepage used languages – Greenlandic, Danish and English – to direct content towards in-group or out-group visitors. At times this was a conscious act and at times it was merely a legacy of language skills and use. Thus, even though some visitors would "understand" only certain elements of Adam's space, such as his photos of people, places and houses, or the few paragraphs of English, we were all working our experiences into a larger social superstructure. Visitors with no knowledge of the Greenlandic language might well experience the language barriers in the guestbook, where many entries were in Greenlandic, as tokens of authenticity that served more as attractions than sanctions. As a social locus the experience of Adam's homepage may have felt quite "object-centered" because of its many photographs and their physical focus, but it was in fact a comprehensive dynamic of social relations positioning objects and subjects as recognizable boundary markers. The anthropologist Mark Nuttall found that Greenlanders in the small village of Kangersuatsiaq (northern Greenland) created "memoryscapes" that connoted community and sense of belonging. These were framed through mental images of local landscapes and history composed from their knowledge and remembrance of places, place names, and the events that had taken place there; and thus, by knowing, they belonged: "All give a sense of a bounded locality distinct from the memoryscape of neighboring communities" (Nutall 1992: 3).

Likewise, demonstrating knowledge of and belonging to the physical environment is fundamental to identity and sense of belonging in Greenland, where nature simply cannot be forgotten. In Dybbroe's analysis of the dynamic relations between local organization, cultural identities and their significance for a common national Greenlandic identity in a country with a mobile and moving population, she concluded that "despite mobility of residence . . . you always come from a place" (1991: 15). Today, in times of growing internet use and increased mobility (on- and offline), the argument still holds. Geography and topography remain key elements in the identities of Greenlanders. Adam's homepage may have been an objectified display and experience of the power of things, houses, mountains and icebergs, but it was nevertheless socially signified. Clifford writes: "[T]o know who you are means to know where you are" (1989: 188). Knowing is belonging. In this cultural context, a photo of Adam's village in the middle of icy nowhere accompanied by some words about his work, or his knowledge on the history of Aappilattoq, are markers to confirm Adam as a member of the community, an Aappilattormioq, and of Greenlandic society, a *Kalaaleq*. While spaces – especially wide open and, at first glance, barren spaces – are of utmost importance to Greenlanders, it is historical measure that connects them to these spaces and places, and thus to rights and self-governance. In indigenous land claim negotiations throughout the Arctic, time of occupancy has been the most prominent argument accepted by courts and commissions. Prior to settling land claims, the Inuit must prove where and how they occupy and use the land. They gather oral and written statements from local hunters; they compile maps and photographs and other images to mark their presence. They "prove" their histories through these fragments and montages. Similarly, the putting together of geographical or physical images on Adam's homepage is essentially a montage process that rearranges time and history, from personal through local to national and transnational dimensions.

So welcome, and good-bye, to Aappilattoq, Adam Grim's Family homepage. During the time from my initial visit to Adam's homepage until this essay was written, Adam's homepage has changed several times: its layout is basically the same, but much of the snow and ice have melted. Pictures from the short summer have been uploaded, with the result that the visual spaces of Aappilattoq have turned into islands surrounded by deep blue water and barren rocky hills with occasional green patches of grass and flowers. There are photos of a new grandchild on the welcome page. Pages linking and hyperlinking to his homepage are changing as well; and new entries in the guestbook are altering its meanings. The seasons have changed, the social world has changed, and cyberspace has changed too. The transforming montages on Adam's homepage identify and display his "belonging" to the multiplicity of lived and represented spaces, of physical and virtual worlds.

Notes

1   This paper has been published with the permission and help of Adam Grim, Aappilattoq, and Imina Heilmann, Upernavik.
2   In Greenlandic, Upernavik means the springtime place, and the area was used by the Inuit for seasonal hunting and living for centuries preceding its official founding by the Danish colonial power in 1772. Most Greenlanders lived an isolated life up until the 1950s, when Denmark, in the wake of anti-colonial sentiments following World War Two, decided to make Greenland a full part of Denmark together with the Faroe Islands, rather than give them independence. Modernization and social change rede-fined Greenlandic society in a short time, but with a growing number of Danes working in Greenland for high salaries and living in better-than-average housing, it became increasingly clear that differences continued to exist between Greenlanders and Danes despite common nationality. An elite of Greenlanders schooled in Denmark returned to Greenland and voiced the Greenlandic wish for self-determi-nation that led to the Greenland's Home Rule government in 1979, when Greenland became a self-governing region within the Danish Kingdom. Greenland receives a yearly subsidy from Denmark that tops its GNP with 50 percent, creating a high standard of living compared to its produce, but making Greenland dependent on Denmark. All major corporations are owned by the Home Rule, making the presence of private entrepreneurship almost non-existent.
3   The Inuit represent a diverse group of some 130,000 people living in the circumpolar Arctic regions. They are also known as Eskimo, a label considered derogatory by many Inuit (see Burch 1988).
4   The concepts of *Gemeinschaft* and *Gesellschaft* were first addressed by Tönnies in the late 1880s (see Tönnies 1955), who distinguished them to discuss rural and urban life, respectively. *Gemeinschaft* was associated with social relations in homogeneous small-scale networks, while *Gesellschaft* was more impersonal, contractual and ran parallel to the individualism of modern, urban population centres. See Pahl (1965) for further discussion of their meaning in an urban/rural perspective. The cyberspace myth has a tendency to regard cyberspace as a spearhead of the new global *Gemeinschaft*. Often referred to as the global village, this new *Gemeinschaft* supposedly brings together indi-viduals who – instead of participating in the increasingly constrained and commercialized *Gesellschafts* (associations) of modern times – now seek post-enlight-enment in the transcendent space of deterritorialized and non-commercial relationships. In contrast, however, webpages such as Adam's contradict such a clear-cut typological division of social relationships and argue that social space is much more complex, spatial and situational.
5   A recent strategy report from Greenland's national Information Technology council envisions the day when every household in Greenland will be connected to the internet by at least one computer; when networked learning will be fully integrated into the educational system and offered to those outside the educational centers of large towns; when citizens can partake in political debates via cyberspace; and when a broad sample of private and public services are accessible to all Greenlanders, be they villagers or townspeople (Grønlands IT-Råd 2000: 7). A working group Nukit will

focus on co-coordinating investments in the business sector, whereas the national ITC council will primarily focus on reaching politicians. Yet, in Greenland where people are accustomed to governmental rather than private initiative, an immediate call for action (as suggested in the report) is almost inherently deadlocked by finan-cial constraints on the government of a country where some 90 percent of the national product comes from fisheries. Whereas ITC development in many other countries relies heavily on private investment, many Greenlanders tend to look upon ITC as a service within the responsibility of the government. Thus, it was no surprise that my online pilot survey showed that most of the participants from Alaska believed that development of the internet should be promoted through private entrepreneur-ship, people in the Canadian Arctic were generally in favor of a partnership between governmental and private entrepreneurship, while most Greenlanders were in favor of developments promoted by the government (Christensen 1999).

6   Some major influences shaping Greenlandicness over the past decades include: wage and housing differentiation between Greenlanders and Danes (which favored the Danes); the introduction of self-government Home Rule in 1979; the Greenpeace anti-sealing campaigns in the 1980s; withdrawal of Greenland from EEC member-ship in 1985 (in fact the only country ever to do so); the crash of a B-52 armed with nuclear bombs close to the US Thule Airbase in a country that forbids nuclear weapons or nuclear plants on its soil in 1968; and the 1973 foundation of the Inuit Circumpolar Conference, an ethnopolitical Pan-Arctic Inuit organization gathering the voices of 130,000 Inuit/Eskimo from Alaska, Canada, Siberia and Greenland. Ever since the introduction of Home Rule, Greenlandic politicians have increasingly been voicing ideas and opinions in the area of foreign policy, an area still in the offi-cial power of the Danish government but now being contested on the way to increased independence. We can also witness a strengthening of Greenlandic iden-tity on many levels, including its internationalization. The internet adds to this ever-changing scenario.

7   It holds that, if Greenlandic society is on the periphery and dominated by the centers, we must consider that such powers relative to our frame of reference exist within Greenlandic society itself. The typical respondent for my 1998 survey was male, aged 30–35, employed, and with internet access from work, often in addition to an internet connection at home. The survey also confirmed that participants accessed the internet from larger communities. These are the signs and expressions of dominance by an elite within Greenlandic society. Over time and with increased initiatives on the part of the government, demographic trends in usage are sure to change. Historically and interestingly, however, it has been the elite who have defined Greenlandicness, called for self-determination, and been at the forefront of revitalizing the ethnopolitical symbols of Greenlandic identity. Even though the internet has without doubt increased communication between Inuit in the circumpolar Arctic, everyday use seems to follow social networks that are more national or regionally ethnic in nature. At this time, there seems to be little evidence of a pan-Arctic internet use across ethnic lines or conversely on the basis of ethnicity.

References

Publications

Berthelsen, Christian (1976) "Det at være Grønlænder: Fra en Debat i Begyndelsen af det 20. Århundrede", *Tidsskriftet Grønland* 4: 117–21.
Burch, Ernest S. Jr. (1988) *The Eskimos*. London: Macdonald Orbis.

Chandler, David (1998) *Personal Homepages and the Construction of Identities on the Web*. Paper presented at the conference Linking Theory and Practice: Issues in the Politics of Identity. University of Wales.

Christensen, Neil B. (1999) *Inuit in Cyberspace: Embedding Offline Identity and Culture Online*. MA thesis, University of Copenhagen.

Clifford, James (1989) "Notes on Travel and Theory", *Inscriptions* 5: 177–88.

Curtis, Pavel (1996) "Mudding: Social Phenomena in Text-Based Virtual Realities", in M. Stefik (ed.), *Internet Dreams: Archetypes, Myths and Metaphors*. Cambridge, MA: MIT Press, pp. 265–92.

Dybbroe, Susanne (1991) "Local Organization and Cultural Identity in Greenland in a National Perspective", *North Atlantic Studies* 3(1): 5–17.

Fienup-Riordan, Anne (1990) *Eskimo Essays: Yup'ik Lives and How We See Them*. New Brunswick: Rutgers University Press.

Grønlands IT-Råd (2000) *Vi Bygger en Nation: Grønlands Muligheder I Internet-samfundet. Forslag til en national IT-strategi*.

Hamman, Robin (1996) *Cyberorgasms: Cybersex amongst Multiple-Selves and Cyborgs in the Narrow Bandwidth Space of America Online Chat Rooms*. MA thesis, University of Essex.

Hansen, Klaus G. (1999) "Mens Vi Venter: Statusrapport over det Første År med Verdens Nordligste Internet Café I Innaarsuit. Arbejdspapir No.1414", *NORS-skrifter* No.39, Roskilde University.

Lanier, Jaron (1990) "Riding the Giant Worm to Saturn: Post-Symbolic Communication in Virtual Reality", in G. Hattinger *et al.* (eds), *Ars Electronica Vol. 2: Virtuelle Welten*. Linz: Veritas-Verlag.

Lefebvre, Henri (1991) *The Production of Space*. Oxford: Basil Blackwell.

Lillie, Jonathan J. M. (1998) *Cultural Uses of New Internet Information and Communication Technologies: Implications for US Latino Identities*. MA thesis, University of North Carolina.

Lyon, David (1997) "Cyberspace Sociality: Controversies over Computermediated Relationships", in B. Loader (ed.), *The Governance of Cyberspace*. London: Routledge, pp. 23-37.

Mitra, Ananda (1997) "Diasporic Web Sites: In-group and Out-group Discourse", *Critical Studies in Mass Communication* 14: 158–81.

North, Tim (1994) *The Internet and UseNet Global Computer Networks: An Investigation of their Culture and its Effects on New Users*. MA thesis, Curtin University, Perth.

Nuttall, Mark (1992) *Arctic Homeland: Kinship, Community and Development in Northwest Greenland*. Toronto: Toronto University Press.

Pahl, Raymond E. (1965) *Urbs in Rure. The Metropolitan Fringe in Hertfordshire*. London: London School of Economics and Political Science Geographical Papers, No. 2.

Reid, Elizabeth (1991) *Electropolis: Communication and Community on Internet Relay Chat*. BA thesis, University of Melbourne.

Rheingold, Howard (2000) *The Virtual Community: Homesteading on the Electronic Frontier*. Cambridge, MA: MIT Press.

Robins, Kevin (1995) "Cyberspace and the World We Live In", in M. Featherstone and R. Burrows (eds), *Cyberspace/Cyberbodies/Cyberpunk: Cultures of Technological Embodiment*. London: Sage, pp. 135–55.

Sejersen, Frank (1996) "Arktiske Folk som Statister og Aktører på den Globale Scene", *Stofskifte* 32: 41–56.

Tönnies, Ferdinand (1955) *Community and Association*. London: Routledge & Kegan Paul.

Turkle, Sherry (1995) *Life on the Screen: Identity in the Age of the Internet*. New York: Simon & Schuster.

Links

Administration of Cultural Affairs: http://www.kultur-upernavik.dk
Arctic Cyber Anthropology: http://home.worldonline.dk/~nbc/
Family Adam Grim's Homepage: http://iserit.greennet.gl/adamgrim/
Frederik Olsen: http://iserit.greennet.gl/utoqqaq/
Home Rule: http://www.gh.gl
Imina Heilmann: http://iserit.greennet.gl/imina/
Johnny H. Jørgensen: http://iserit.greennet.gl/johnny/
Markus Chr. Geisler: http://iserit.gl/makku/
Nicky Kristiansen's Homepage: http://iserit.greennet.gl/nickykr/
The Municipality of Upernavik: http://www.upernavik.gl
Ole Johnsen: http://iserit.greennet.gl/reolejan/
Piteraq: http://www.piteraq.gl
Prinsesse Margrethe School: http://iserit.gl/skolen/
Søren Mørch's Homepage: http://iserit.greennet.gl/tanja/
TeleGreenland: http://www.tele.gl
Upernavik Museum: http://iserit.greennet.gl/inussuk/
Upernavik Tourist Service: http://iserit.greennet.gl/turist/

Chapter 5

On line, off line and in line:

The Zapatista rebellion and the uses of technology by Indian women

Marisa Belausteguigoitia

Introduction[1]

The international circulation of the Zapatista[2] rebellion from Chiapas, Mexico, to the spectating world via the internet has become one of the most successful examples of the use of computer-mediated communications by a grassroots movement. The Zapatistas' movement gives a keen example of the internet in terms of its deployment as a "border thinking strategy", simultaneously used by many different agents, some in the mainstream and some working from below, yet all in support of movements at the margins of society. The Zapatista mobilization distinguished itself as a creative and strategic indigenous movement in large measure because it inaugurated a unique mode of organizing on line, off line and "in line" activities. In doing so, it has sparked a world-wide discussion about the meanings and implications of activism, as well as of indigenous rights.

This chapter seeks to make visible the ways in which the internet has disseminated, shaped and constructed the image and discourse of the Zapatistas and especially of the indigenous women in the Zapatista movement. Specifically, I analyze the "line" of mediators, ventriloquists, voices, resources and strategies that have been involved in the Zapatistas' struggles for equality. I further relate this to questions of representation at the limits of modernity. By "modernity" I mean the promises made by the Mexican state regarding the rights of citizenship to all Mexicans irrespective of race, class, gender or any other difference. In considering the ways in which the Zapatista movement sought to expose the government's failure to meet these promises, two questions emerge. What kind of practices are shaped, introduced, modified and interrupted by the use of the internet for an indigenous movement at the borders of modernity? What is the specific place and role of Zapatista women within the internet as a tool for communication, solidarity and dissemination of the struggle for equality and representation? This chapter offers some insights and reflections on these complex issues.

Specific context of the Zapatista movement

The Zapatistas are mainly indigenous peoples ("Indians") from the poorest zones of Chiapas, in the southern regions of Mexico and along its borders with

Guatemala. They belong to basically four original ethnic groups: Tzeltales, Tzotziles, Choles and Tojolabales, who derived from the Indian communities established in the Lacandona rainforest in the 1940s.[3] Many of these communities grew in number due to the expulsion of peasants from the farms and ranches owned by middle-class *mestizos*. Continuous displacements over the course of the twentieth century further intensified the struggle for land. In 1992, President Salinas effectively abolished the communal rights to land by enforcing a change in the Constitution and adopting a new decree that favored the privatization and commercialization of property. This series of events led up to the Zapatistas movement, but it must be understood in relation to the history and position of indigenous peoples in Mexico. As elsewhere in the New World, Indians were/are the original inhabitants of the region that later became the Mexican nation. The first fifty years following the Spanish conquest of 1521 saw over half of the indigenous population die from disease, warfare and its aftermath; and for centuries their ancestors endured hard working conditions under colonialism and post-colonial rule. Today, Indian peoples account for roughly ten percent of the Mexican population. They have been relegated not only to the geographical margins but also to the sociopolitical and economic margins, given their limited access to education, health services, sufficient employment and basic citizens' rights. Consequently, the health status of Mexico's indigenous population tends to be poor, their economic hardship rife; literacy skills are lacking and political representation has been minimal. From this perspective, it can be said that the Zapatistas, as one heterogeneous sector of indigenous peoples, were rebelling (with the aid of other indigenous and non-indigenous supporters) against five hundred years of oppression. In short, the historical legacy that still shapes Indian lives and welfare today, coupled with new forms of expulsion from communal land and the annulment of group property rights under new rules and legislation, provided the impetus for mobilization. The deciding factor – and in the eyes of the Indians, the final blow – came with the signing of the North American Free Trade Act (NAFTA) in the early 1990s. The Zapatista rebellion decisively tore the mask that veiled the Mexican state's hypocrisy towards a large majority of peasants and Indians, long alienated from both economic growth and political representation.

The Zapatista movement erupted on the first day of January 1994, the precise day that the NAFTA agreement came into effect. Officially, NAFTA represented the welcoming of Mexico – a nation where 50 percent of the population subsist below the poverty line – into the "First World" Club (that is, the Organization for Economic Co-operation and Development, or OECD). However, to a significant sector of the Indian population, it was anticipated that the new trade relations provisioned by NAFTA were poised to further marginalize indigenous farmers and producers. This was especially so given that the treaty ended import restrictions and protection on certain crops (namely corn and coffee) upon which local Indian peasant economies were based.

Accordingly, NAFTA was viewed as the latest insult in a string of government-led assaults to indigenous land rights and economic autonomy.[4]

Before adopting the strategy of militancy, Indian communities threatened by NAFTA organized a peaceful march (Xi'Nich) from the southern border to Mexico City. Silence was the response of the government towards this powerful mobilization. The famous "Basta!" ("Enough"!) headline in Mexican newspapers on the movement's opening day, that first day of the new year in 1994, was to become the first symbol representing the Zapatistas. The attitude of having endured "enough" led to the militancy, in the form of a Zapatista Declaration of War addressed to the Mexican State; war basically characterizing how many Indians came to envision their relationship to the government, given its latest "offensive" against them in the form of NAFTA. The Declaration included a list of laws deemed applicable in a state of war. These included: a law of war on taxes, law of rights and obligations of people in struggle, law of rights and obligations to the revolutionary army, a revolutionary agrarian law, a law for justice, and last but not least, a revolutionary women's law.

The movement's mediated style

What is of central importance to the Zapatista rebellion is that, from the outset, the movement represented a collaborative undertaking across race and class lines within Mexico proper, as well clearly as on a global scale, once it took form and gained status as an online campaign. While collaborative deployment of the internet as a tool to advance social agendas is not unique, of course, what is notable in the Zapatistas' case is the strategic intervention of different communities, agents and mediators working "in the flesh" as well as virtually. Within Mexico, this collaborative, embodied dimension partly stemmed from the nation's technological situation, wherein computer resources have been less available than in more developed Western countries (this was especially so at the time of the Zapatistas' movement). Internet users in Mexico typically use the internet collectively, in cyber cafés, with groups of friends and strangers queuing for access to computers. Cyberactivity represents a border technology that not only virtually connects isolated young people across the world, but also congregates them in the flesh while they group in front of the screen waiting "in line" to be "on line". It was in such a context that the movement came literally to the streets, universities and urban settings of Mexico and virtually connected them with the streets, universities and urban settings of other nations, especially in the Euro-Anglo world. In addition, the Zapatistas movement was very creative in the organization of "in the flesh" events to gather citizens from diverse social, political and cultural scenes.

In a recursive fashion, then, there was a great deal of cross-cutting and two-way feedback between local and global settings, entailing discussions mediated by computers and those taking place face-to-face. To fully appreciate the significance of these pathways and their accomplishments, we might recall that the movement was launched already in 1994, in the early days of the internet when computer-mediated communications of any kind were still quite a novelty. The movement's phenomenal networking becomes all the more remarkable when we recall the widespread illiteracy (not to mention computer illiteracy) among Indian peoples – indeed roughly 50 percent of Mexico's indigenous peoples do not even speak Spanish, the official language of governance! That the movement came to command such visibility in media spaces has largely been accredited to the key role played by the movement's leader (or non-leader, as he would prefer to be known): subcomandante Marcos.

Marcos, said to be a former graduate student, apparently belonged to an urban guerrilla movement that was badly defeated by the government during the 1970s. He moved to the Lacandona jungle in the mid-1980s and began to work with displaced communities. He was originally the military adviser of the guerrillas, but very early in the uprising Marcos proved to have exceptional communication skills. He began to "stage" press conferences masked and "adorned with a pipe and Zapata-style banderola with bullets that don't match the model of his weapon" (Peña, 1995). Gómez Peña (Peña 1995: 9) depicts his performance as follows:

> Since his first appearances in the media, Marcos appealed to the most diverse and unlikely sectors of Mexican society ... His combination of political clarity, bravado, and humility appealed to progressive politicians and activists through the world. His eclectic discourse, spiced with humor and a surprising array of references to pop culture, contemporary writers, and world news, revealed a sophisticated internationalism.

Marcos, otherwise called "el Sup" (the Sub, the one that is beneath), planned relations with the media very carefully. Garnering the attention of the international press became a priority,[5] and visibility in multiple media spaces – online as well as in newsprint – quickly became a standard feature, or guerilla tactic, of the movement. Directly as a result of the intense international presence incited through the mediation of subcomandante Marcos's now-famous communiqués via the internet[6] and the conventional media, the Mexican government agreed to negotiate a new social contract with the Zapatistas after less than one month of the uprising. Four rounds of negotiations were planned to reconsider the juridical, cultural, political and economic role of Indians within the Mexican nation. The first round, "Indigenous Rights and Cultures", ended in February 1996 with the signing of the "San Andrés Accords" by the rebels and the government. The San Andrés Accords represented basically the recognition and juridical implementation of five rights: the right of Indian communities to govern themselves autonomously, the right to be represented in the National Constitution as subjects of public right, the right to reorganize the municipalities where they reside according to their own laws of congregation, the right to ownership of lands, and – as an event considered unique in the struggle for indigenous liberation – the Accords began to reconsider the rights and demands of Indian women, an issue we consider in more detail below. Despite initial resistance from within the indigenous communities (in addition to resistance from other sectors of society and the government), the demands put forth in the Accords eventually came to be supported by a majority of Indian ethnic groups throughout the nation.

This document signified the legitimacy of Indian struggle in Mexico; in Harry Cleaver's words:

> In a very real sense, the Zapatista movement emerged as a tentative and transitionary solution to precisely the problem which confronts us everywhere: how to link up a diverse array of linguistically and culturally distinct peoples and their struggles; despite and beyond those distinctions, how to weave a variety of struggles into one struggle that never loses its multiplicity. If for no other reason, all of us who are interested in accomplishing the same goal at a wider level would do well to study carefully this microcosmic experiment that so suddenly exploded in the political firmament with the brilliance of a supernova (Cleaver 1998a).

Ultimately, the Mexican Congress rejected the San Andrés Accords (in August 2001) and approved an alternative proposal for Indian rights and culture which basically erased the capability of Indian communities to govern themselves autonomously, to be considerd subjects of public right, and to have access to land rights. After the disregard of the San Andrés Accords the Zapatistas fell silent until January 2003 (exactly 8 years after their initial uprising), when more than 20,000 Zapatistas demonstrated in San Cristóbal de Las Casas, demanding the re-instatement of the San Andrés Accords. And so the Zapatista movement continues; it also evolves, for a main speaker at this gathering was Comandante Esther, who has been one of the foremost female leaders of the Zapatistas. This speaks of a shift in the forms of representation of the Zapatistas, who increasingly include Indian women inside their leadership. In comparative terms, it is also a shift in the public visibility of indigenous women and the symbolic role that women have played in the Zapatista movement.

The situation of Zapatista women within the movement arguably has been a paradoxical one: women and their particularly agendas have been, at one and the same time, firmly central to the movement's larger mission and in certain respects peripheral to it. Indeed, the roles and image that women hold within indigenous culture have been important symbolic determinants helping to shape how the movement has framed itself and how it has been conceptualized (Rojas 1994; Stephen 1997a). In the representation of traditional culture, women are the bearers of tradition – in body (that is, in wearing traditional clothing) and in "tongue" (that is, as speakers of native Indian languages, and as less likely to be proficient in Spanish). Women's crafts and cooking, their customary dress and demeanor, their knowledge of traditional medicine, their maintenance of the arranged marriage system, their preservation of numerous traditions, etc. – all represent practices that preserve Indian ways of life. These activities make Indian women the bearers of memory and tradition. In consequence, however, the position of women – both practically and symbolically – has not favored contact with new technologies, nor necessarily with new ideas. Rather, new technologies to a large degree have appealed to contrary impulses: mobility, individuality and a predisposition towards changing habits of communication.

It is proposed, thus, that women and the "*traditio*" that they daily performed and symbolically represented played an essential role in helping to foreground the movement's appeal as a struggle for indigenous rights and lifeways. Situated in the homestead, women are constant actors in the workings of the communal property and exchange system – the very values and lifeways that the indigenous movement sought to protect. The traditional position of women might indeed be considered one "strategy" that the larger movement developed and actively deployed. Before considering the implications of this, and discussing in more depth the agendas of Zapatista women themselves, it is worthwhile to consider two other strategies that have defined the movement and contributed to its success; these are: the use of masks, and the writing of postscripts. These strategies "in the flesh" constructed the movement with a community-based identity prior to and alongside its success in cyberspace.

Masks and postscripts

Early in the eruption of the Zapatista rebellion, Mexican newspapers, journals and televised news began to show a memorable sight: Indians in military uniforms wearing ski masks. In understanding this creative strategy and its imagery, it is of note that the mask has a long history in Indian tradition and in Mexican culture, and is today common in popular culture. Mexican museums are filled with a wide array of pre-Colombian masks once used in ceremonies and war. Contemporary popular wrestlers (e.g., "Super-Barrio" [7]) are notorious because of their masks. Masks tend to show the fierce nature of the fighter while hiding the identity of the bearer. The Zapatistas inaugurated yet another use of the mask: as a device that reveals while concealing. With the act of covering their faces, they exposed and sought to deconstruct what is a common stereotype in Mexican society in regard to indigenous peoples irrespective of geographical, ethnic or political location: the notion that "all Indians look alike and are alike". In other words, the mask is a device that "performs" a prejudice based on racist thinking that homogenizes all Indians such that every Indian is a suspect, a child, an inferior. The masked strategy of Marcos and the Zapatistas essentially denounced this racist viewpoint through the enactment of an ironic image: Indians in uniform all alike, wearing "all alike" ski masks. The performance further makes clear that it is just as futile to protect the heterogeneous identities of the Indian as it is futile for the government to pretend to protect Indian rights under current conditions and through such arms of the law as NAFTA.

Clearly, in order to promote their cause for Indian rights, the Zapatista movement initially had to tackle racist prejudices concerning Indians. First and foremost the movement had to achieve visibility. Ironically here the mask played a key role, as Mexican society was confronted with the impossibility to see and hear its ultimate Other, the Indian. It could either hear the native, the voice without the body; or see the native, the body without the voice. The presence of Indian body and tongue in the same place at the same moment – such a volume of "otherness" – likely threatens reception of the Indian's message. From this perspective it can be argued that the Zapatista movement "required'" a figure and/or a venue whose voice and body (unlike those of the oft-dismissed Indian) could be seen, heard and "read" at the same time. Subcomandante Marcos – a white, educated male with a keen and witty communicative style – emerged in the site of translation and mediation to become this figure of central significance. In addition, the internet – a relatively accessible, widely-disseminated communications media – emerged in the site of translation and mediation to be a venue of central significance. Hence, the strategic intervention of two communicative devices was forged to combat racist prejudices: a charismatic leader in the form of Marcos and a charismatic technology in the form of the internet. It might be said that both Marcos and the internet perform the same tasks: to intercept the body and circulate the voice.

Early in the uprising, Marcos discussed the various uses of the mask, as is illustrated in the following postscript:

PS "From Ski Masks and other Masks."

Why all the uproar over the ski masks? Isn't Mexican culture a culture of veils? . . . I propose the following: I am disposed to take off the ski mask if Mexican society takes off the mask it uses in coveting a foreign vocation and which it put on years ago. What would happen? It's clear: Mexican civil society (excluding the Zapatistas because they know perfectly well in image, thought, word and work) would come to see, not without disillusionment, that the sub-Marcos is not a foreigner and neither is he as handsome as the 'media connection' of the PGR (Mexican Attorney General) has asserted. But not only that. On taking off its own masks Mexican civil society would come to see, with an even greater impact, that the image of itself that it had been sold is false and that the reality is much more terrible than it had imagined.

Insurgent subcomandante Marcos

In this quote, Marcos explains the Zapatista mask as a response, and a representation, of the "culture of masks" that the government has created and behind which it hides, a mask which keeps Mexican civil society from facing the truth about indigenous peoples and democracy in Mexico. The paragraph also exhibits Marcos' practice of writing "from below", from a space beneath: the postscript. Pasted below one of the communiqués delivered to the public shortly after the eruption of the Indian rebellion, the comment is a fragment, a reminder – as are all postscripts. Postscripts are residual thoughts located at the bottom of the letter, in the margins. They refer to what cannot be said in the main body of the text. As a strategy of representation developed by the Zapatistas, the postscript speaks not within and from the main body of the nation, but from the margins, from the site of Indian voices. This strategy from below represented the ways in which Marcos could be both mediator and voice, a voice well directed to perform as a mirror of the pervasive racism in Mexico. Masks and postscripts are interconnected, and both may be deployed for a similar purpose: to underline what lies below, below the mask, below the letter or below the discourse of modernity in which everybody is supposed to be treated equally by the state. There are more parallels to be drawn between the operations of internet and postscripts, between masks and unmasking.[8]

As a mask, the internet can mask or camouflage the sender, and protect the identity of the user (who can even fabricate an identity by manipulating languages and codes). Efficient in the act of ventriloquism and in the impersonation of voices, the internet represents an ideal technology to circulate the voice without the body. For the Zapatistas movement, it appears that the value of the internet as a tool for disseminating their message was inversely related to dominant Mexican prejudices against the simultaneity of voice and body of the Indian "Other". The net (like a letter) gives us the text, but does not give us the body in person; yet the presence of immediacy in answers and dialogues simulates a strong presence. Speed matters. And in the case of Zapatista cyberactivism, the speed of dissemination and of response were phenomenal and uniquely accounted for the high visibility of their campaign both in Mexico and internationally. However, the net as a form of communication offers a simulation of proximity by the interchange of body against speed (unlike a letter). Given its stream of flow of ideas and the fluidity of thoughts that would otherwise likely not be pasted in other media (letters, newspapers or television), the internet can be said to function more as a postscript than as a letter. The casual tone characteristic of online messages resembles the economy of the postscript, which runs from the "tip of the tongue" or from the "top of the head". The multivocal nature of postscripts to contain powerful messages in the guise of an afterthought also shares similarities with the internet, which gives space to alternative voices that dominant society might dismiss as "understatements". As a postscript the net may include many different voices, and geometrically empower "the cause" and direct it to multiple sites. Subcomandante Marcos has been known to paste as many as twelve postscripts on the bottom of the main letter, naming them "postscript from the postscript". In effect, then, there is always a step lower in the adventure of communication, there is always a voice or a face underneath that may be brought to the surface.

The movement's creative intervention strategies can be understood to be plays upon the deeply-embedded calculus of racism in Mexican society. According to this calculus, it is the Indian face that needs to be covered, or masked; and it is the bottom position in the social and political hierarchy that Indian peoples should "naturally" occupy. In donning masks and sending their messages via the postscripts of letters (effectively inscribing their demands from "below"), the movement exposed and moreover strategically subverted the logic of racism for the purpose of emancipating indigenous peoples from oppressive rule. In short, the Zapatista movement recognized and strategically exploited the polysemy and ambiguities of masks, postscripts and the internet. In this regard, the movement fundamentally challenged certain dominant modes of the operation of power. However, the use of cyberspace in the case of their struggles in other ways more closely resembled and preserved the global hierarchy of power relations. Here I am referring to the long "line of media-tors" (Taussig 1999) needed to extend the voices of Indians to the net, mediators both "on line" and "in line". To gain visibility and clout – indeed, in order to translate indigenous "otherness" into something more mainstream to the public opinion – the indigenous campaign required "a line of mediators". This line took shape largely in the form of non-Indians: writers, academics, artists, journalists, grassroots activists and subcomandante Marcos, himself. The "mask" and the "postscript" gained ascendancy and "took over" as successful strategies in cyberspace when numerous internet users adopted the mask as the symbol of marginality of any and all kinds. In effect, an internet collectivity was created through the adoption of the faceless Indian as a blanket symbol of the many faces of oppression that have plagued marginalized peoples everywhere. Accordingly, organizations of Algerian immigrants in France, Chicanos in the US, "Ocupas" in Madrid, peasants in Brazil, gays in San Francisco, gangs in cosmopolitan cities, students in public schools began to "wear the mask" and use language from below to support the Zapatistas campaign via the 'net. The message became: "we are all Indians"; "we all look alike"; the body is always at stake under conditions of discrimination.[9] These "masked" forms of resistance have existed not only over the net, but also in the flesh through gatherings, which had the effect of bringing together peoples in solidarity across regions of the globe. Within Mexico, too, public support crossed conventional boundaries; and mixed groups of citizens – heterogeneous with respect to race, class and gender – came to gather and show solidarity. This mixing is especially notable given the large degree of segregation that has historically characterized Mexican society.

Zapatistas' women tongues and bodies in/off/on line

Despite the multivocality of the Zapatista mask, behind it stood an Indian man, not an Indian woman. It is worthy of mention that Indian *women* actually were the first to use the economy of "the below" the letter and "below" the surface in order to represent their voices. As noted above, a Revolutionary Women's Law was the final stipulation put forth in the Zapatista Declaration of War of 1994. This last "addition" to the list called for radical changes in women's rights, changes radical less in terms of Mexican society at large, but highly so for indigenous cultures and traditional gender relations. The revolutionary women's law contained ten rights for an alternative order, including: the right for a woman to be married to a man of her choosing, the right for a woman to be part of the liberation struggle, the right for a woman to be protected from physical attack by either family or strangers, the right for a woman to command the military and to hold political office, and women's rights to education and to healthcare (especially in the area of maternal and reproductive health). These laws represent the emergence of the voices of indigenous women from below. An additional right was not specified inside these laws, but was stated repeatedly by Indian women in meetings with other mediators: the "right to rest", to have time outside of work time, to have time enough to reflect and time to think. The "right to rest" demand was not phrased inside the movement nor was it included in the Revolutionary Laws. It was located even lower, below the postscript and below the surface (Belausteguigoitia n.d.). This constitutes another one of the reasons why we rarely have indigenous women behind the screen learning how to use technologies like the internet. There is simply no time to rest, to learn, to demonstrate online. Below the letter and below the "face" of the Zapatista movement there have been mainly male Indian faces and male-authored postscripts that – notwithstanding their extraordinary communicative power – were directed mainly to unpack racism, not necessarily sexism. To the extent that indigenous women have been able to speak, it has been because outside mediators – especially Euro-American women from academic institutions, non-governmental organizations, grassroots groups and agencies with headquarters outside of Mexico – have stepped in to phrase and circulate indigenous women's demands.[10]

These organizations and agencies "participate" in the movement virtually, and in this capacity, have performed significant broadcasting and consciousness-raising roles. However, by and large, their webpages, like scores of others of their kind in support of the Zapatista cause, represent the ways in which an international cybercommunity makes sense of *what an indigenous women's struggle may represent*. The webpages are often designed more to empower the visions of Euro-American, middle class (often feminist) users, than to actively struggle for the specific demands of Indian women. Such sites tend to represent the Indian female "question" in terms to be received and understood by a cosmopolitan, disembodied audience.[11] In the absence of their own "Marcos" – their own articulate mediator devoted to their specific demands and capable of translating and concentrating their political strategies – it seems that the agendas of the Zapatista women have become spread out over a range of political causes. These may echo the more structured anti-racist discourses of the Zapatistas movement, they may relate to oppression and globalization in general, or they may resonate with feminist agendas and women's rights issues in dominant society at large, but they do not (necessarily) parlay the distinct struggles and agendas of Zapatista women or indigenous women as a unique group. It is as if the centrifugal character of cyberspace takes over, so to speak. Here, the tenuous voices of Indian women largely fall prey to appropriation, one that lacks the substantial backing of embodied activists who proved effective in rallying for the movement's "larger" cause.

So subversion has its limits. Zapatista women do not have their own complement to subcomandante Marcos. This means that they do not have a translator, ventriloquist and powerful mediation concentrated in a persona that could "unpack" and expose sexism, in the way that subcomandante Marcos unpacked and exposed racism, using the creative strategies of masks and postscripts.

Concluding thoughts

Despite the multivocality of the Zapatista mask, behind it stands an Indian man, not an Indian woman. The visibility of the indigenous Zapatista women's agenda thus had a dual, and in certain respects, canceling effect. On the one hand, it became a reified symbol for a host of women's issues, some specifically indigenous and some more universally applicable. On the other hand, this reification had the effect of detracting from the Zapatista women's immediate cause. Despite the communicative potential of the net, the voices of Indian women were trapped there in a paradox. To be "on line" and benefit from the crucial assistance of the international feminist and humanist community, Zapatista women activists needed "a line of mediators": the electronic chain of cyberactivists networking in and from organizations, universities, internet cafés and homes in support of their cause. Yet, this line served predominantly to raise consciousness regarding issues of concern in respective local contexts and/or related to broad conceptual agendas. Solidarity forged in relatively abstract, universalistic terms can, at best, only diffusely illuminate actual "in the flesh" instances of discrimination and resistance. With activists linked by virtue of a shared objection to generalized (notions of) sexism and racism, the issues that informed the immediate worlds and concerns of Zapatista women were at risk of marginalization even in the act of mobilization. Here we encounter another paradoxical inversion: the ventriloquism (in the form of masks and writing from the postscript) that so effectively worked for the larger movement was precisely the fate that threatened to engulf Zapatista women's voices, as their agendas were adopted, spoken and ultimately "ventriloquized" by others – yet in the process their unique messages were seriously splintered, and thus far largely eclipsed.

Whilst Zapatista women substantially contributed to a discourse with potential to empower women and especially marginalized women everywhere, their cause came to function more as a privileged story, as a strategic form of representation, rather than as a struggle in and of itself situated at the center of attention. It seems that more Indian women are needed to carry out their own mediation. In the absence of a "right to rest" (and hence time to gain computer skills, improve basic literacy, get online and become their own spokespersons from the margins) how can indigenous women directly benefit – in their daily lives and struggles against myriad forms and many layers of oppression – from the empowering potential of internet-linked activism and revolutionary media technologies?[12]

Notes

1   This article could not have been written without the efficient cyberethnography that Liliana Salgado helped me to carry out, and I am grateful for her assistance and her insightful conversation.
2   The name Zapatista is a derivation of the surname of Emiliano Zapata (1879–1919), the most important Indian leader of the Mexican Revolution (1910–1921). In 1911, Zapata organized the landless rural peoples of southern Mexico into a small guerilla movement. He composed the "Plan de Ayala", which called for the return of lands annexed by the *haciendas* system, and called for land and water rights for the peas-ants. In 1919, Zapata was assassinated upon the orders of Venustiano Carranza, the "first chief of the constitutional army" during the revolution. For more on Emiliano Zapata and the Zapatistas, see Stephen (2002).
3   In 1972, former president Luis Echevarría Álvarez created a "bio-reserve" in Montes Azules that "donated" these lands to their "original" bearers: 66 families belonging to the Lacandon Indian tribe. This intervention brought about the subsequent reloca-tion of more than 4000 Indian families; moreover, most settlers refused to move from what they considered their home. A long struggle for land rights ensued. Indian communities were supported to some extent by the Catholic Church, under the ideology of Liberation Theology.
4   The Zapatista rebellion has been discussed and analyzed at length. My writing here is informed by the works of many (Cleaver 1996, 1998a,b,c; Collier 1994; Clarke and Ross 1994; Soriano Hernandez 1994; Barrios Ruiz and Pons 1995; Burbach 1995; Castells 1997; Stephen 1997a,b; and the documents of the Zapatistas National Liberation Party, EZLN 1994, 1995, 1997).
5   Journalists from the *New York Times*, the *San Francisco Chronicle*, *Cambio 16*, *Le Figaro*, and *Vanity Fair* were immediately welcomed into the jungle to hold inter-views and be first-hand witnesses of the Zapatistas' creativity.
6   It is important to emphasize that the Zapatistas leadership is not officially involved in the construction of internet sites. Their modus operandi is the linking of on-line as well as in-line and off-line activities; and in this they are very outspoken in regard to the urgency for dissemination of the direct forms of oppression they are struggling with (including violence at the hands of the Mexican army). The movement has by necessity focused on events taking place in their territories and the organization of "in the flesh" resistance and mobilization. At present, there is only one computer station with internet that is known to be operated from within Indian communities. It is located in one of the settlements of displaced communities, Las Abejas, an Indian congregation of partitioned communities. One of the divisions is supported by the PRI, the oppositional party that ruled the country for more than seventy years and was overthrown from power by the democratic elections in 2000. Zapatistas refuse techonological, economic or any kind of support emanating from official parties.

Nonetheless, dozens of websites (far too numerous to count) were established on behalf of the Zapatistas cause, and dozens more sites hyperlinked. The most influential direct sites have been:

Ya Basta: one of the first sites created after the uprising. Its domain name EZLN (Zapatistas National Liberation Army) was registered with the permission of the General Committee of the Zapatistas, but (like the other sites) it is not officially constructed by the Zapatistas. The page, frequently updated, functions mainly as an information site. See http://www.ezln.org

Chiapas95 is an internet "list" culled from other online lists, such as *PeaceNet*. Chiapas95 distributes news in Spanish and English, about social struggles in the Chiapas region. Aimed at scholars and activists, it is not a discussion list; it constitutes an internet list for the redistribution of information about developments in Chiapas and Mexico, participation in cyberspace discussion, and in the work of Accion Zapatista, a local solidarity group. It has involved and contributed to research, writing and publishing on the Zapatistas situation. The Chiapas95 homepage and archives are referenced by the Latin America Network Information Center at the University of Texas, from whence it has operated, with the continued participation of Harry Cleaver, its creator and originator. See http://www.eco.utexas.edu/faculty/cleaver/chiapas95.

Zapatistas in Cyberspace: The University of Texas has also been responsible for hosting *Zapatistas in Cyberspace*, one of the most important links to many sites related with the Zapatistas in the Net. See http://www.eco.utexas.edu/faculty/cleaver/zapincyber.html

Enlace Civil (Civil Linking) created in 1996 in Mexico, is an example of the cyber-activity used to link events in the "flesh" and in the net. *Enlace Civil* was created in solidarity with the Indian peoples of several regions of Chiapas in response to their demands for translation and dissemination of information. See http://enlacecivil.org.mx

7   Super-Barrio is a social activist, who performs as a masked wrestler representing and advocating housing for the poor. He appears in the events of dispossession made through juridical orders against the poor, with the press and groups of sympathizers. He is very fat and acts, cartoon like, to be a wrestler. There are other wrestlers for justice like Fray Tormenta, the wrestler priest, and Super-Ecologista (who fights for environment rights). All of them utilize performance and media strategies to enter the political arena. For more on subcomandante Marcos as a masked social fighter see Peña (1995).

8   Taussig (1999) inverts the movement and explores the act of revealing by unmasking. Specifically, he analyzes the Zapatistas "proliferating magic" created just after state representatives "unmasked" the identity of subcomandante Marcos. Allegedly Marcos was Sebastian Guillen, born the son of a salesman in Tampico, a northern Mexican state. Authorities miscalculated that his "unmasking" would rip apart the mystic of the Zapatistas movement and thereby undermine it. Instead, the act of unmasking brought to the surface the play of masks enacted by the government, and also "played into" the dialectics of masking that has long been a part of indigenous cultural traditions and worldviews in Mexico. Taussig locates the device of mediation within the mask/*nahual* as a reference to silence and secrecy (*nahual* means "secret science"). Taussig's reading of the uses of masking/unmasking by the state and the Zapatistas underlines the dense mediations and multiple meanings operative in the strategies used by the Zapatistas.

9   T-shirts could even be bought with the legend: "Todos somos Indios." (We are all Indians). See http://www.nodo50.org

10 Mediation especially with respect to and around Zapatista women's issues has long been provided by the influential non-governmental organization *La Neta*. Working

from Mexico and internationally, it posts current information as well as "historic" archives of the Congreso Nacional Indígena, see http://laneta.apc.org. A network linking different Mexican states (notably Tehuacan, Veracruz and Michoacan) is also here worthy of mention, see http://www.pagina-web.de/ezlnenorizaba. International support has included several organizations in Italy and Spain, two countries that have been particularly active in response to the Zapatistas' call. Of note is *Ya Basta*, Italy – a comprehensive page that posts Indian women's concerns, see http://www.yabasta.it.

Previously active agencies and sites focusing on the women included *Red de Apoyo Zapatista en Madrid*, with articles from the Zapatistas journal "Rebeldia", *Plataforma de solidaridad con Chiapas de Madrid*, with a link to "mujeres zapatistas" and the sites *Zap Women* and *Creatividad Feminista*. There are numerous more agencies and sites that have posted information about Zapatista women and their struggles, but these have tended to be filtered through the particular agendas of the host site, see below.

11 To date, there are no internet sites being authored, designed, organized and administrated by Zapatista women. We find thousands of Zapatistas webpages, yet there are far fewer sites dedicated to Zapatista women, and these are not consistently updated. Posted references to Zapatista women usually give only the highlights of important events and Indian women's concerns, and they tend to circulate a fixed repertoire of images and issues. Zapatista women function more as a pretext to empower cyberpages and sites that nurture global discourses of liberation, anti-racist, anti-sexist struggles, than to actually empower their own profound cause: "the right to rest". Many of the aforementioned webpages post, for example, photographs of masked Zapatista women (including a now-famous one taken by Pedro Valtierra that shows an Indian women attacking a soldier), and photographs of "lines" of women defending their towns and families with their bodies and with sticks. The speech of Comandante Esther delivered on March 2001 before the Mexican Congress, and interviews with other female leaders (for example, Comandantes Yolanda, Ramona and Susana) are also posted on many web sites, see http://www.chiapas.indymedia.org.

12 Whilst the scenario was promising: an Indian woman giving voice to indigenous issues and indigenous women's issues to Congress in a public speech; the outcome was discouraging, with a basic dismissal of the Indians' requests. Apparently what are needed are multiple "border strategies" that may work together in complex scenarios of mediation and representation. As we have seen, the internet, as one border strategy, constitutes an irreplaceable scene for the construction of magnified forms of support that may "export" Indian discourse, but paradoxically, it also "imports" forms of misrepresentation of Indian demands. Another "border strategy" working alongside the net would be the construction of a sensitive mediation ("in line" forms of translation) for Indian women. None of these operations is sufficient if Zapatista women do not themselves gain greater control of the forms of representation that move inside the net.

Bibliography

Barrios Ruiz Walda and Pons, Leticia 1995. *Sexualidad y Religión en los Altos de Chiapas*. Tuxtla Gutiérrez: Universidad Autónoma de Chiapas, pp. 1–64.

Belausteguigoitia, Marisa (n.d.) "The Right to Rest," *development*, vol. 5, No. 45.

Burbach, Roger (1995) "Roots of the Postmodern Rebellion in Chiapas." *New Left Review* 205: 36–46.

Castells, Manuel (1997) *The Information Age: Economy, Society and Culture. Volume 2, The Power of Identity*. Malden, MA: Blackwell.

Clarke, Ben and Clifton Ross, (eds). (1994) *Voices of Fire. Communiqués and Interviews from the Zapatista National Liberation Army*. Berkeley: New Earth Publications.

Comisión de Concordia y Pacificación (COCOPA). Acuerdos de San Andrés. Available online.

Cleaver, Harry (1998b) *Zapatista: Neoliberalism, the Chiapas Uprising and Cyberspace*, Seoul: Glamuri Publishers.

Cleaver, Harry (1998c) "The Zapatista Effect: The internet and the Rise of an Alternative Political Fabric," *Journal of International Affairs* (51)2: 621–640.

Cleaver, Harry (1996) "The "Space" of Cyberspace," *Women & Performance: A Journal of Feminst Theory* (9)1: 239–248.

Collier, George A. (1994) *Basta! Land and the Zapatistas Rebellion in Chiapas*. Oakland: Food First.

Comunicación e Información de la Mujer, A.C. (1996) "Propuestas de las Mujeres Indígenas al Congreso Nacional Indígena." *Seminario "Reformas al artículo cuarto constitucional. 8–12 de octubre de 1996*.

EZLN. *Documentos y Comunicados*. (1994) Vol. 1. México: Era.

—— *Documentos y Comunicados*. Vol. 2. México: Era, 1995.

—— *Documentos y Comunicados*. Vol. 3. México: Era, 1997.

Peña, Gomez (1995) "The Subcomandante of Performance," in E. Katzenberger (ed.) *First World, Ha Ha Ha!: The Zapatista Challenge*. San Francisco: City Lights, pp. 90–91.

Rojas, Rosa (1994) *Chiapas ¿ y las mujeres qué?* México: La Correa Feminista, 1994.

Soriano Hernández, Silvia (ed.) (1994) *A propósito de la insurreción en Chiapas*, México: Asociación para el desarrollo de la Investigación Científica en Chiapas, pp. 11–99.

Stephen, Lynn (1997a) "The Zapatista opening: The Movement for Indigenous Autonomy and State Discourses on Indigenous Rights in México, 1970–1996", Journal of Latin American Anthropology, 3(1): 32.

Stephen, Lynn (1997b) *Women and Social Movements in Latin America*. Austin: University of Texas Press.

Stephen, Lynn (2002) *Zapata Lives. Histories and Cultural Politics in Southern México*. Berkeley: University of California Press.

Taussig, Michael (1999) "The disorganization of the Organization of Mimesis: The Subcomandante Unmasked," in *Defacement. Public secrecy and the labor of the negative*, California: Stanford Univeristy Press, pp. 236–248.

Chapter 6

The Meta-Native and the Militant Activist

Virtually saving the rainforest

Kyra Landzelius

Scenes and sources of conquest

At the heart of the conquest lies a jungle plot: its resources are claimed by two rival political bodies – a "Fourth World" Amazonian people and a "Third World" government. But its suspected petroleum wealth is coveted by countless more hungry bodies – foremost among them, fossil fuel-dependent "First World" consumers and their multinational market suppliers. At the heart of the resistance lies a horrifying ultimatum: the indigenous U'was' vow to commit mass suicide and violently obliterate the body politic in a desperate protest against the global appetite for energy that covets their ancestral lands. The tribe's corporeal sacrifice would, in essence, amount to a flesh-and-blood expression of the sure death to native lifeways that the U'wa assert will be the inevitable legacy an oil pipeline brings them. The conflict implodes on the geographical body of Colombia, a multi-ethnic nation divided against itself by government corruptions and democratic ambitions; leftist revolutionaries and right-wing paramilitaries; an entrenched and powerful elite, yet a growing political vitality of peoples – such as indigenous peoples – from the margins. The conflict explodes and amplifies, however, via cyberspace – teleported there by grassroots environmental activists networked through planetary telecommunications to defend the bio-bodies of natives and the eco-body of mother earth. What these bodies and their interrelations imply for an internet-based campaign to save indigenous lands, and in so doing to possibly vitalize indigenous identities, is the central topic of our discussion here.

Outline of a plot

In the spring of 1995 the semi-nomadic U'wa, a 5,000-member indigenous tribe living in the cloudforests of the Colombian Amazon, posed a horrifying ultimatum: to commit mass suicide by throwing themselves off a steep precipice if Occidental Petroleum, an American-based multinational oil company (known as "Oxy" for short), commenced plans to drill for oil on their ancestral lands. Seeking support in their struggle, the U'wa first petitioned the National Indigenous Organization of Colombia, which in turn contacted transnational environmental groups, foremost among them Rainforest Action Network and Project Underground. A little more than a year later the tribe's dilemma was orbiting cyberspace, electronically hyperlinked to a dozen grassroots organizations. Rainforest Action Network (RAN) issued coverage of the "oil invasion", the natives' crisis, the activists' agendas, and "what you – the reader – could do to help protect aboriginal territories". Thus was launched what turned out to be a lengthy, sometimes fiery, sometimes "low intensity" virtual war of words and images. As with almost any drawn-out conflict where antagonists vie to present their respective version of "the truth", this conflict has been characterized by a bevy of claims and counter-claims, accusations and counter-accusations, distorted and disputed facts, and debates about what indeed constitutes a fact. Contention has ensued over jurisdiction (concerning the rightful – legal and/or moral – ownership of subsurface mineral property); over geological knowledge (concerning the extent of oil reserves) and environmental science (concerning the kind and degree of ecosystemic impact); and over matters of an existential nature (concerning the risks to native lifeways associated with oil development).[1] A number of more elusive but potentially explosive issues also shaped the direction and terms of conflict, issues having to do with history, cultural authenticity, national duty, stewardship, entitlement, civilization, conquest, exploitation, and self-determination. The spectacle has played out against a backdrop of bodies and scenic vistas, street protests and email resistance, hyperlinks and hyper-theatrics; and, sadly, ranks pathos as well.

Befitting an epic of such proportions, there are clearly numerous twists and turns to this story, yet space prevents us from unraveling these here. Rather, we orient our discussion to what we identify as two overarching thematic fields or frames of contention, these being: contests over history, its authorship and authority; and contests regarding individual versus collective rights. We approach these frames, and the U'wa–Oxy conflict in general, with a concern to understand how underlying graphic and discursive themes "speak on" and "speak to" constructions of indigenous identity. As a construct – a condition even – of modernity, indigenous identities have long been forged into tight if counterposed relations with the respective dominant colonial/neocolonial/postcolonial political order(s) of the day. In short, what it means to be indigenous and the values placed on indigeneity have been framed in terms of modernity, and on modernity's terms. The contingency of definition in this case works both ways, however, with modernity itself staked upon the invention of the native, the primitive, the (variously noble or ignoble) "savage". Indeed many a theorist has pointed out that there are deep ideological tensions in the logics and desires of modernity, and these ambivalent and polarizing tendencies give rise to a kind of "schizophrenia" in the modernist ethos (see Taussig 1987, 1993; Torgovnick 1990; Young 1995). Clemmer (1995: 11) writes that there are "two modernities: one that exalts that which it defines as individualistic; industrially technological; factually technical; rationally secular; and cosmopolitan. And there is the other modernity that lauds that which it defines as collective and communal;

handcrafted and natural; intuitive and fatalistic; prophesied and paradoxical; local and parochial."

Following upon this thesis, I wish to explore the idea that the U'was' plight and its ensuing world wide web crusade give us a stark – perhaps even a clichéd – example of modernity's two faces and its schizophrenic dilemma. To make this suggestion is to approach the twin campaign to protect native life-ways and simultaneously save the rainforest at the millennial shift as more than "just" a simple allegory of David meets Goliath. (Although it was – in point of fact – strategically framed as such by the grassroots environmental groups that rushed to the U'was' aid and championed their cause.) Rather, to read it as more than a tale of capitalism versus resistance, aggression versus innocence, is to search behind the scenes, to "look out" for the two faces of modernity, and expressly for clues as to how they might collude, collide, crash, converge, etc. in this fable. It is to apprehend this dual campaign not only as a microcosm of modernity's intrinsic tensions, a mirror of its underlying origin myth and orga-nizing cosmologies, but to intercept this campaign as an experimental exercise that plays the myth out in a new terrain, with new actors, and according to a radically new metaphysics.

Contests over fact and fiction

Contests over the future, and who owns it, almost invariably involve contests over the past. In this matter, the U'wa–Oxy conflict proves no exception. It was the prospect of mass suicide in the present, however, that first and foremost launched the U'was' plight into the public limelight, an impending threat that earned them a cameo in an assortment of media – radio, television, newsprint, and on local, national, global scales. It was this prospect that also instigated a rather remarkable tit-for-tat tussle regarding the validity and value of history. For, as it were, the U'wa backed up their shocking declaration with an historical anecdote, to wit: they claimed that a group of tribal ancestors in the 1600s had leapt to their death as a preferred alternative to Spanish conquest and conse-quent enslavement.

Apparently, the *déjà vu* of a political suicide on their doorstep was a specter that Occidental Oil was loathe to ignore. Indeed, interestingly enough, the *déjà vu* seemed as troubling, as prestigious or as weighty a problem as the prospective suicide act itself. To make this interpretation is to try to make sense of Oxy's response to the U'was' historical account, a response that came in the form of recruitment of a Harvard University scholar to investigate the tribe's claim upon history. Upon failing to find evidence of the alleged ancestral suicide (presumably in the form of a hard text of whatever kind the scholar or Oxy may have sought), the corporation declared the U'wa to be bluffing, in effect proclaiming, or at least unambiguously implying, that they were "faking" history. Some tricky philosophical questions surface from this contest: how do we know history? who owns history? etc. But leaving aside the matter of how expert witnesses (try to) discern the actuality of an event that took place several hundred years ago in a remote region of the barely-mapped (according to Western idioms) globe and by a people far removed (then and now) from the ruling party's scribes – we might still ponder the rationale behind Oxy's quest for validation. Wrestling with its curious logic, we might point to its undeniably divinatory features, its embedded premise that implies we can somehow predict the future by verifying the past. If hard evidence could be found (or conversely if none were to be found) proving that U'wa forebears cast themselves – *en masse* and in protest – off a 500-meter precipice, could such scholarship really be deployed to conjure a tight equation between a real-world event in the distant past as a catalyst to somehow embolden, dictate, over-determine, consign, conscript, what-have-you, the actions of descendants nearly twenty generations down the line? The irony of a late-modern corporation turning to a *de facto*, if well-heeled, divination in their dealings with semi-nomadic natives should not escape us, albeit this is not to miss the significance of their crusade to uncover "the written word", which has long been a blunt tool of the civilizing mission *vis-à-vis* "the barbarian".

The dispute over historical accuracy carried some interesting connotations. We might say that it translated a contest over space (over a plot of land, of *terra firma*) into additionally a contest over time, a contest over ownership of the past. In making a repeat political suicide the dramatic and poignant epicenter of their poised resistance, the U'wa explicitly drew parallels between imperial colonialism and capitalist neocolonialism. Hereby, present-day tribal members were pulling on the clout of historical precedence in order, it seems, to buttress their current negotiating position. For Oxy's part, its move to pit textual history versus oral history was clearly rooted in the hierarchical ranking of written documents as superior to spoken testimony, and represented a not-so-veiled attempt to leverage the power of this Western stereotype in their favor. Another noteworthy implication stemming from Oxy's quest to uncover the past is that it translated a contest over historical accuracy into a contest over authenticity: namely, native authenticity. In rejecting the U'was' historical claim on a personal note backed by (the absence of) "fact", Oxy basically was alleging that the U'wa either fabricated their ancestors' actions or were at least disconnected from the truth of their ancestors' world. The effect in both cases amounted to a move to disenfranchise the tribe from its cultural past, to imply that there was no ancestral "death plunge" for them to re-enact, no legacy of resistance for them to follow, no footsteps of tradition to be taken. By implication, the petroleum giant called into question the U'was' aboriginal legitimacy and validity. Their authenticity as native peoples, no less, was put on trial and found guilty.

Viewed through the bifocals of modernity's dual and dueling passions – its discordant penchant for scientific proof, on the one hand, and for esoteric knowledge, on the other – the contest over fact and fiction appears almost a parable on the theme of civilization versus tradition. Speculating from this vantage point as to why Oxy took such pains to discredit the tribe's historical authenticity, we might surmise one motive of this move. It distanced the U'wa from their native identity and by so doing situated them "outside" of tradition (yet, paradoxically, not inside modernity either). The de-coupling from tradition might well be read as a veiled attempt to disconnect the U'wa from the image of the (innocent and potentially martyred) native and the immense public relations appeal associated with this imagery. Indeed, not only did "noble savage" symbolism constitute a fertile subtext of this saga, it moreover proved to be a powerful magnet in drawing and rallying supporters to the U'wa cause. This line of questioning brings us to the topic of the body, and to a consideration of the slippage between image and identity.

Transference between image and identity

With colonial history censoring them, and all other negotiating pathways closed to them (by government decree), the U'wa turned to the one territory, the lone weapon conspicuously in their jurisdiction: their bodies. Their threat to walk off the "Cliff of Glory" and thus re-enact the ritual suicide accredited to ancestors of bygone centuries, rendered a preference for "death with dignity" in lieu of the otherwise-anticipated slow ruin following oil encroachment. In seeking to make collective suicide a deterrent to petroleum development, the tribe ransomed the body politic as both battleground and weapon for resistance, as a provocative terrain articulating predicament and its rejoinder. The gesture essentially appointed radical martyrdom protectorate of native lifeways.

It would be difficult to overestimate the provocative sensationalism of this gesture, even (or especially?) in our image-saturated, image-starved media age – an age cogently described a "society of the spectacle" by social theorist Guy Debord (1994). The prospect of native bodies plunging to their deaths as the only escape from corporate takeover was a news item virtually guaranteed to catapult the U'wa onto/into the transnational news wires. That their cause had a staying power of more than Warhol's "fifteen minutes of fame" is almost certainly an attribute of its adoption by a number of globally-networked environmental organizations. The exceptional "commitment to self-annihilation" at the heart of the U'was' plight gave it urgency and a visibility befitting of a rallying cry that marshaled and could be marshaled by the environmental movement. Clearly, rainforest inhabitants and save-the-rainforest activists share a certain measure of ideological affinity and goals common enough to motivate the forging of instrumental alliances or at least a marriage of convenience. Rainforest Action Network, for one, organized a special "Tribal Links" campaign, making the U'wa story a centerpiece of their agenda and their website, in an early example of cyberactivism.

RAN's website provided a blow-by-blow account of the U'wa–Oxy conflict, accessible by navigating any number of links to categories of information. Some links directed the visitor to up-to-date bulletins of the latest developments, some to background history so newcomers could familiarize themselves with the conflict's opening chapters. Some links led to information about Occidental Oil (including an exposé of the company's environmental track record and its profit margins). Others led to the U'wa themselves, or at least to a re-presentation of the natives' world given coverage in a selection of U'wa myths, folktales, aphorisms and the like posted online amidst pictures. The site highlighted the main issues of contention, including debates about the estimated oil wealth; debates about the proclivity of "development" schemes to be magnets for violence, prostitution, pollution and lawless shanty-towns; debates about the ethical issues involving oil exploitation in pristine habitats that also happen to be (claimed as) someone's backyard. Site content was provided in the form of documents (e.g., the contractual agreement between Oxy and the Colombian government, who had officially approved Oxy's bid); letters (e.g., U'wa Chief KubarU'wa's Open Letter to the Colombian people detailing the tribe's opposition to the development scheme); quotes from various players (e.g., government officials, corporate representatives, indigenous peoples' organizations, U'wa leaders); and, in an interesting multiplication and recirculation between media forms, a number of articles scanned from conventional newsprint media (predominantly American, Colombian, and to a lesser extent British newspapers, with translation provided as needed). These cross-linked articles provided a portfolio of news coverage of those elements that had indeed "made it" into the news and thereby made the issue news – events such as activists' dramaturgical demonstrations on the streets of New York, Washington, London; the U'wa Chief's high-profile attendance (in full ceremonial regalia) at an Occidental shareholders' meeting in Los Angeles; geological studies and surveying at the actual site in question; and sadly, in one of the most tragic incidents to arise from this saga, the assassination of three American activists at the hands of a rebel group.[2] This chain of articles, in the form of a montage, also gave the effect of mapping the U'wa–Oxy contest so the reader could fashion a sort of mental geometry of the conflict's geopolitical shape and web of dynamics.

By far, the most striking and memorable aspect of the website relates to its graphic splendor. With a click of the mouse, visitors could download any number of photographs of the U'wa people in their natural habitat: a child drinking from a conch shell, a man smiling, a woman fetching water from a river, a man carving with a simple tool, a group of women in colorful costumes, children playing. This rich photographic essay served to introduce readers to the U'wa world – a world on the brink of possible destruction – and thereby, through the power of images and imagination, "connect" people to the U'wa cause in a graphic, emotional appeal. But these photographs arguably accomplished more. These many and captivating pictures depicting beautiful Amazonian natives in traditional attire, situated in pristine scenery amidst exotic plants and animals, arguably served to capture and condense the idyllic features and fantasy of rainforest natives, their habitats, their customs, their lives – so blessedly simple, so (seemingly) easy to fathom and dream upon.

These pictures arguably met or conjured virtually every idealized dominant (mis)conception of a "rainforest native" that percolated to Western mindsets, planted there in large measure by many a popular-culture depiction dating from Rousseau's tableaux and up to the modern-day celluloid Indian *à la* "Dances with Wolves". By selectively parading the "pretty pictures" of U'wa lives (absent a more balanced accounting), the RAN website (and that of other environmental organizations, such as Project Underground) effectively homogenized them, with the result that the photographic essay – despite its voluminous array – converged on a same symbolic singularity: fabricated in the romantic figure of a pan-native, generic native, meta-native.[3]

Thus illustrated, the meta-native – in a kind of snowballing and self-referential fashion and via imaginary fields of projection – more or less took on a life of its own. That is, it implicitly evoked what we might identify to be "noble savage" themes, to wit: natives in harmony with nature, the native "frozen" in time, the naked, innocent, childlike native, etc., and into and onto other stereotyped delimitations. Themes, moreover, that waxed inspirational: for the U'wa case/cause became a highly successful cyberspace campaign. Pan-native bodies amidst rainforest greenery but poised for self-immolation to save their homeland apparently made a perfect fit with politically-impassioned pan-activists' bodies on the streets of the metropolis: both in ideological alignment and in political solidarity to protect endangered species and endangered life-ways. We might prod further to ask just why this is so by suggesting a metonymy in play, whereby the meta-native body and the rainforest eco-body are deemed coextensive and harmonically come to represent the potential victim(s): the native as one with fauna and flora.

There are additional moments or fields of transference that we might read from website graphics. For example, to a site visitor (a netizen?) clicking through the montage, there was an obscure experience of what we might call symbolic slippage between images of exotic natives and enthusiastic street demonstrators, lush vistas and urban clamor, brilliant flowers and bright plac-ards: I am referring here to the melding of landscapes and ethnoscapes, ideoscapes and mediascapes (Appadurai 1996) of the various locales of RAN activists and U'wa activists. This digitally-induced slippage, a technological sleight-of-hand most optimally produced by computer media pyrotechnics, created a kind of graphic symphony – a symphony which engendered its own cosmology, its own translocally positioned linkages between peoples, places and performances, between power and possibilities. It simultaneously doubled as a photographic montage of "the West meets the rest", thereby embodying a performance (in microcosm) of modernity's dual face.

Stewarding the collective

The land in question, Samore, is situated in the El Cocuy National Park about 200 miles northeast of Colombia's capital city, Bogotá. In point of fact it lies outside the legal boundaries of U'wa territory. With respect to the contest discussed here, the region thus represents a border zone, a cartographic as well as politico-symbolic crossroads. By way of explaining their antagonism to petroleum prospecting, the U'wa assert that oil constitutes the "blood of mother earth" and as its vital force must remain underground *in situ*. "This oil belongs to the land, it's part of it and can't be taken out", tribal Chief KubarU'wa ordained in proffering this sentiment. The declarative implicitly raises the interrogatory whose answer has been a prerogative of those in power since time immemorial: to whom (if anyone) do the riches of the earth belong? In line for claims upon the earth's body, in this case, we have (at least) three big players, three radically different organisms: Occidental Oil Inc., the U'wa peoples, and the Colombian government.

Citing resource nationalization policy, the government holds constitutional claims upon the subsurface minerals of this 500,000-acre tract. This legal move allocates Samore's oil wealth to all citizens of Colombia; and the area comes to represent collective welfare, a bequest for the common good. The state, favoring oil "development", conceded a prospecting license to Occidental in 1992, the untoward consequences of which sparked the indigenous opposition movement. While cash constitutes the most obvious motive of government contracts with foreign petroleum industries, there are additional factors involved. Not least of these is the Colombian government's perennial challenge to demonstrate a measure of control over entrenched "problems of the interior" (namely, paramilitary insurrections, drug trafficking, and rampant lawlessness) that have dissuaded much-needed foreign investments. In fact, rebel groups bombed petroleum pipelines hundreds of times in the 1990s alone, causing spillage of several million barrels of crude oil into virgin forests and rivers and well over a billion US dollars in lost revenues. "Third World" debt relief and repayment schemes that link loan assistance to natural resource provisos have further constrained the government's position. Facing such formidable challenges to political (and environmental) order, authorities have been caught in a threefold predicament: how to police the interior, meet human rights standards, and secure outside investors. From this perspective, it is significant that the handling of Samore oil rights registered more than a domestic performance, but was seen as a test case of Colombia's geopolitical clout and eligibility for international sponsorship. The administration flagged its agenda in a jargon of progress and nationalism: jobs, revenue, "fair negotiations with indigenous pueblos", and, above all, "the interest of the Colombian people [and] the dominion of the State" were the official line. Buzzwords, in short, of the modern state – enlightened and oriented towards the collective good – supplied the rhetorical justification.

In contradistinction to the future leanings of the nation-state's designs on Samore, the U'wa purchased their entitlement in terms of the continuity between past and present. In a statement that harnessed the enduring momentum of generations, the U'wa claimed "ancestral rights we have acquired because we were born in this territory, because we are native to this land, because our forefathers and foremothers have always lived here, because when the white people came, our grandparents had been here for thousands of years". Referencing the fate of other South American tribes whose hunting, fishing and farming were jeopardized by oil production, the U'wa chief further contended that petroleum extraction would devastate their culture and "cause their physical world to implode". To decree that they have ancestral rights to the *land*, but that the oil belongs to "mother earth" – that is to say, to *no man* – is not only to dismiss all other claimants, but to deconstruct the very premise of the claim, to dethrone the precious logic of ownership. With oil ownership relegated to a matter that transcends man-made laws and plebeian ambitions, and oil itself promoted to the sacred order, we confront a competing paradigm and a face-off between worldviews. The banishment of an "earthly" protagonist in favor of earth-as-protagonist (the planet it/herself) is at once exotic, romantic even, and yet familiar; and in this protean form it readily syncretizes with counter-hegemonic trends, something along the lines of the Gaia hypothesis or New Age sentiments. While U'wa cosmology forecloses U'wa ownership on equal grounds, its corollary none the less appoints the U'wa as protectorates, assigned jurisdiction in the style of an aboriginal, managerial role. The closing sentence of their Open Letter makes this clear: "[I]n order to live in peace it is necessary both to respect the rights of all and to act in harmony with Mother Earth, we ask your help so that we, the U'wa, can continue to maintain the equilibrium of the world".

The stewardship envisioned in the U'was' testament is far from tentative; to the contrary, it is expansively communal and sufficiently opaque to theoretically include all of humankind. Despite (or perhaps because) of this (admittedly mixed) gesture of decentering while centering their position, the question of where to draw group boundaries in relation to property boundaries came to direct yet another uneasy subtext in this conflict. At issue for Occidental Oil was the question of just where the U'wa stood with regard to individual resource rights, for at one point early in the conflict the company apparently reached an agreement with a handful of U'wa to supply health and educational materials, some cash and other goods, in exchange for a license to drill. Needless to say, this deal-making amongst individuals was unequivocally rejected by tribal leaders, and denounced by rainforest dwellers and rainforest activists alike as a "cheap shot" to "divide and conquer" native will. At issue for the Colombian government, however, was the question of just where the U'wa stood with regard to collective resource rights. For the U'wa, collective orientation was at once more broad – with its expansive stewardship – and more narrow – with its delineation of U'wa (ancestrally-derived) jurisdiction, than the scale of orientation targeted by Colombia's resource nationalization policy on behalf (theoretically at least) of all the nation's citizens.

Examining this issue with respect to the two-pronged definition of modernity given above, we find the polarity between individuality and collectivity to be one of the tension points in the modernist ethos. We can again read this ethos at work in this conflict, whereby the U'was' indeterminate position was vari-ously (if inconsistently) deemed at odds with both individual and collective values, as hegemonically construed. The ensuing state of contradictions is aptly characterized, for example, by Oxy's paradoxical depiction of the U'wa. On the one hand, in its response to criticisms regarding its one-on-one negotiations with a few individual tribe members, the corporation criticized the U'wa for being *too communal*, in what (it was implied) was an antiquated and unprogres-sive, hence unmodern, way. On the other hand, in dismissing the tribe's threat of mass suicide, the corporation declared the U'wa to be *too individualistic* to actually follow through with a pan-tribal initiative such as that mandated by voluntary collective annihilation. In somewhat similar manner, the Colombian government also took issue with U'wa collectivity. With its emphasis on the entitlement of all Colombians to the nation's subsurface mineral wealth, the government (rhetorically, at least) privileged collectivity in the form of a modern citizenry. In its view, the brand of collectivity put forth in the U'was' proposed stewardship (despite its expansiveness on behalf of humankind) ulti-mately emerged as tribal and unpatriotic, and by implication unmodern. These contradictions underscore the tenacious significations that adhere to complex cultural logics, such as those apprehending individual and collective rights and responsibilities, significations that hinder simple translation between differing worldviews.

There are other ironies implicated in this clash of cultural idioms. In the act of situating themselves in the role of earth's protectorate (and being received there by activist-supporters), the U'wa tacitly assumed stewardship over the domain in question. Did their proposed stewarding of resources represent (to native and supporter alike) a gesture, by way of intention, to "save" (i.e. protect) the earth from over-exploitation? Or to "save" (i.e. deliver) the consumerist appetite from its own gluttonous ruin? Or was it to "save" (i.e. reserve) the minerals for the common good – almost sure to be eventually deter-mined by more powerful actors? These are rhetorical questions, assuredly, but the polysemy and ambiguity of the U'was' gesture, whether intended or no, may end up fronting a strategy for merely buying time – which is not to deny its significant value. It is, however, to examine the attraction of their argument, which seems to put in motion a logic whereby native peoples are entitled to their ancestral lands under an operative assumption and tacit agreement that they don't comprehensively use them! This projection too can be situated in the topos of the noble savage that hovers over this saga. Here we sense again intimations of a romance with modernity's ideal native saving modernity from itself. In being conceived free of material needs and constraints, the noble savage may represent one version of the ultimate emancipation, even a kind of enlightenment figure. Yet there may be hidden anticipations that the Native's role as protectorate of the "earth's equilibrium" – a *de facto* hands-off steward-extends up to and only until such time as said equilbruim becomes targeted for plunder; that is, until the hungry citizens of the metropolis turn to ever more remote regions to satisfy their consumption demands on the planet's "reserves". These musings lead us to consider the participatory role conceived for the U'wa, a topic to which we turn in the following discussion.

Weighing the costs of resistance

In May of 1998, three years after the U'wa pledge of mass suicide and nearly a decade into the conflict, Occidental Petroleum announced a cessation of their, and partner British Petroleum's, oil development initiatives in the Samore territory.[4] Why, we might ask – after pursuing the project so aggressively and for a period of several years, in the face of extensive critique and likely damaging publicity – did Oxy decide ultimately to call it quits? The answer, as one might expect, is manifold. Oxy attributed the decision, by and large, to a re-evaluation of the site's potential and a reorganization of corporate priorities. Oxy spokesperson Larry Meriage insisted that the company "had no intention of being on these lands without express permission". In forwarding this justification, the corporation sought to frame the issue as a domestic dispute between the U'wa and the Colombian government. Such framing not only marked a move to distance the company from "internal affairs", it also amounted to a disavowal of any possible role played by the activist campaign (a blatantly strategic move on the part of the corporation). For their part, the U'wa attributed Oxy's withdrawal to divine intervention, alleging in so many words that their prayers were answered in such a way that the oil was "hidden" from surveyors; indeed, as it turns out, exploratory drilling failed to find the expected reserves. Not surprisingly, and certainly not without a measure of truth, environmental groups viewed the withdrawal as a victory for grassroots' mobilization and its aims to police power by (at least on this occasion) curtailing the injustices of the mighty against the weak. According to Rainforest Action Network, the U'wa campaign was one of the most successful in the organization's history, and the U'wa themselves the perfect "poster child" for the organization's goals, as one RAN director of operations candidly proclaimed.[4] Given this success rate, we might pause to consider in more detail the nature of cyberactivism in general, and that involving instrumental alliances between so-called "First World" activists and "Fourth World" indigenous peoples in particular.

As noted, the RAN website introduced site visitors/readers to the U'wa–Oxy altercation through a wide array of communicative options, providing a spectrum of information in the form of excerpts from conventional newsprint, reports of corporate activity, an update of official meetings and governmental decrees, a bulletin of "latest developments" and an historical review, and numerous graphics of the U'wa in their native habitat as well as of street demonstrators in the global metropolis. The site pointedly invited readers/visitors to "get involved" in any number of ways: to petition corporate leaders, lobby politicians, donate money, join demonstrations; and through such tasks "help the U'wa avert their own self-annihilation". Involvement was readily facilitated by the website's layout itself, which posted a number of pre-edited letters addressed to Oxy's Chief Executive Officer, the Colombian Minister of Environmental Affairs, US officials, Oxy shareholders, and numerous other implicated parties. Curious and/or committed site visitors were thereby recruited as potential activists, encouraged to download and email prepackaged petitions in a relatively simple mode of engagement that we might call *push-button activism*. In likely contributing to Oxy's decision to move operations away from U'wa lands, the exercise of politico-moral outrage via the internet proved, in the case of the U'wa, to be not only effective but also convenient. Indeed, given the apparent ease of disseminating viewpoints and streamlining opposition over the world wide web, one might wonder what, if any, drawbacks might incur in dot.com resistance.

The relative infancy of the medium and the dearth of comparative studies limit our interpretive scope and our grasp of the internet's effectiveness as a tool for virtual resistance. The high profile of the U'wa struggle indicates that there are some unparalleled advantages inherent in the technology itself. Its capacity to amplify and intensify the sheer magnitude of information made available to readers/visitors changes the political playing field. As the media change, so too does the message. Among their theoretically vast advantages, virtual campaigns introduce gains in the immediacy of the event, in the currency, rapidity and multiplicity of information, in portability and, as emphasized above, in the relative simplicity of engagement on the part of activists. These qualities accommodate new possibilities in the proximity of witnessing and in the fluency of activism; and, by manipulating exposure, may help empancipate issues from hegemonic power frames. As we have seen in this case, the unique attributes of information-communications technologies have empowered new forms and expressions of opposition. We can as yet, though, only speculate about the ways in which they might constrain opposition. Paradoxically, one delimiting factor may arise from the virtual effortlessness that characterizes online lobbying itself, whereby the energetic and engaged web activist could theoretically send off a dozen or so protest letters in the course of a lunch break. Could it be that its very success might lead to a weakening of its impact, in the manner of an inflationary spiral built-in to cyberactivism? Could digitized opposition in service to grassroots ambitions come to hold less political weight, less influence or potency, as an artifact of over-use? Given its capacity to publicly amplify the cause and streamline the resistance, the internet seems the perfect political tool for a media-savvy society of the spectacle. The question still weighs in the balance, however, of whether internet with its potential equalizing access to public space can re-balance hegemonies by leveling the playing field (to wit, are we all operating under the same constraints?) or whether it will alternatively "up the ante", introducing yet another space which must be attended to, yet another battleground where hearts and minds must be won.

Matters of inflation and battlegrounds return us to that original extreme battleground/weapon first put forth in this conflict – that of native bodies poised for self-destruction – in what, on a Richter Scale of spectacles, could only be characterized as hyper-inflated. As any news editor or indeed political activist well knows, public attention is a limited good, and longevity in the limelight is measurable in nanoseconds. Given the temporality and whimsicality of the newsworthy, and the popular appetite for sensation in a competitive media playing-field, any high-stakes, high-profile, self-immolating act holds a higher publicity value and has a greater likelihood of recruiting public sympathies, if not outright support, for its cause. After all, if the U'wa had not threatened collective annihilation, if they had not been prepared to make the ultimate sacrifice, would they have made "the news"? And without making the news, would they have achieved their visibility and relative success? Sensationalism is arguably one hidden, perhaps increasing, cost of "democratic" activism of many kinds, including cyberactivism. In full recognition of the reality that they must capture the media spotlight, successful activists plan eye-catching "consciousness raising" schemes, with street demonstrations, civil disobedience, "sit-ins", picketing, militancy, and other highly dramaturgical and symbolic expressions of resistance staged in the public sphere. The U'was' dilemma and their graphic and embodied struggles toward resolution take place in a "systems world" where good causes – such not only noble but ultimately commonsensical agendas as protecting the earth's endangered habitats and species – have to compete on the terms of a media spectacle (idealism about public sphere participation notwithstanding). Notions of the "noble savage" – albeit updated, but none the less carrying much of the ideological baggage this stereotype entails (Ramos 1994) – were inevitably bound to materialize in this drama, so why not marshal them in the name of the cause? For RAN and other environmental organizations, the salience of the native body as a *happening* (or potential happening) arguably marked an *irresistible* resource in the necessarily calculated marketing of resistance. By irresistible I mean that it mobilized a romantic symbolism both too potent to be resisted (i.e. to be left under-exploited by strategists) and too clichéd to be resisted (i.e. to lay dormant in the imagination of spectators). Native bodies online were accorded a central role in the numerous graphics of U'wa peoples (in lush surroundings relaxing, celebrating, playing or engaging in low-tech tasks). This montage, it was suggested, semantically slipped into a generic, meta-native body: sign of innocence, testament to authenticity, proof of harmony betwixt man and nature.[6] Such iconography was a subtext in the campaign ethos, alongside discourses of indigenous self-determination and environmental protection. By enlisting and syncretizing the languages of empowerment and rights, outreach efforts appealed to (and co-constructed) the ideal of the influential and enlightened bourgeois individual working in concert democratically and toward a noble goal: the preservation or "deliverance" of otherwise "doomed" native cultures and environments. This allegory of deliverance over doom leads us to wonder to what extent indigenous publics must be reified (or reduced) into a version of the noble savage in order to pose a more attractive innocent to "save": a phantasy (modernity's phantasy/our phantasy) of re-placing the "wronged" in the unspoilt garden, our aboriginal home. A wish perhaps, and alas, such salvation could be so simple or so complete. In this allegorical logic we re-cognize again the dual faces of modernity: the "civilized" coddling the "traditional", individual agents rescuing besieged collectives, the globals securing the locals, etc. It is through such convergences that the U'was' cause/case has become a spectacle, straddling modernity's own internal contradictions, its ego and alter-ego.

Framed in the guise of a spectacle, however, the U'was' case/cause is subject to the kind of transience and competition that shape the politics of representation. Framed thus, causes/cases risk pivoting focus away from righteous arguments for environmental/economic justice or self-determination, and instead unwittingly collude with essentialized notions about native Others. Framed thus, too, causes/cases are vulnerable to evaporation, and poised in potential rivalry with other spectacles, especially those of like kind. Herein it is not incidental that, in withdrawing its claims on Samore, Oxy received government contracts to prospect on neighboring lands. Thus far, no indigenous groups have come forward to contest Oxy's new plans; but given that few regions of the planet are without present or descendent claimants, the possibility is great that the strategy of simply "moving downstream" will eventually resituate the problem to another indigenous group's territory, re-moved merely to another's backyard. This introduces the possibility of a slippery slope of competition between the underdogs, a vying for public recognition and support between indigenous groups themselves. To be sure, Oxy is only one of a growing number of petroleum corporations with desires and designs upon the rainforest. At any given moment – indeed, as I write – there are countless indigenous peoples worldwide adversely affected by oil development schemes. In point of fact, only a few short years after Oxy revoked its interests in Samore, another petroleum company was negotiating permission to extract oil from within present-day U'wa territory (and not just on ancestral land, as was Samore). Somewhat like a hydra, the defeat of one foe opened space for a multiplication of contenders. As the world's thirst for oil continues unabated and its quest for exploitable frontiers pushes into ever more remote regions, then conflicts (between indigenous peoples, multinational corporations, governments, activists and publics from all ranks) are likely everywhere to intensify.[7] Resistance – rarely a discrete act in any event – comes to require relentless lobbying on the part of indigenous activists asymmetrically pitted against multinational corporations with their cadre of permanent lobbyists and lawyers on retainer. Moreover, given the "limited good" of media attention, it is not inconceivable that multiple, simultaneous conflicts could tacitly, if not overtly, pit indigenous groups against each other as competitors for publicity, rivals for the title of most enigmatic poster child. In such an equation, "performative competence" might be determined in direct measure to the symbolic appeal of the noble savage, and any given group's faithful reflection thereof. To the extent that successful resistance lies in successfully garnering the "symbolic capital" of an essentialized "noble savage" image, a negative spiral could be set in motion – one likely self-defeating for the sustainability and diversity of indigeneity. Such imagery may prove a gatekeeper: disqualifiyng "nontraditional" indigenous peoples; and verily holding traditionalists to a promise to *never be modern*, to preserve (for modernist phantasies? for future exploitation?) if not necessarily their lifeways, then at least their valuable raw materials. To the extent, more-over, that indigenous rights are instrumentally bound up with environmental "rights", then indigenous peoples continue to play the unwitting role of "care-takers" of the precious and increasingly rare resources that industrial societies require and that nowadays (not incidentally, but precisely because of historical patterns of exploitation) are likely to be found in the remote regions into which many indigenous groups have been herded. And finally, to the extent that policing power requires constant vigilance and sustained activism, to keep one's guard up and keep the pressure on, then participation in acts of resistance inscribes its own form of imprisonment. This leads us to query the tyranny at the heart of participation – a tyranny that likely imposes differential costs on indigenous publics.

The tyranny of participation

The costs of indigenous activism, like all activism, are contingent on the nature of participation, its objectives, *modus operandi*, achievements and the like. As it turns out, however, indigenous participation and its appropriate identity have long posed a conundrum: just where to democratically situate indigenous peoples has proven to be a perennial issue of dissent and debate. The already-tricky matters of plurality and political representation are excessively problematized with regard to determination of the democratic roles of indigenous publics *vis-à-vis* larger dominant publics. With the aim to enrich and diversify our understanding of public-sphere participation, including taking to task theoretical tendencies to homogenize who/what is meant by "participant" (theories that typically, if somewhat naively, have assumed equal access to mean equal voice), Fraser (1990) introduced the notion of "subaltern counterpublics". By this she intends to capture the sometimes challenged and often challenging nature of participation on the part of "subaltern" citizens on/from the margins of power – minority peoples by dint of ethnicity, race, gender, sexual preference, (dis)abilities, etc. As an acutely marginalized population and category, indige-nous peoples are essentially subaltern, in their fashion; yet their alterity is of a historically and perhaps structurally different order. Given their largely indeter-minate and ambiguous political status and their paradigmatic distance *vis-à-vis* mainstream cultural epistemes, machinations, orchestrations, etc., it seems inad-equate to apprehend indigenous publics as one version of a subaltern public. Different terms of engagement arguably apply in the case of indigenous peoples. In seeking to locate U'wa activism in conjunction with the RAN environmental movement and in joint opposition to Occidental Oil, I propose the notion of "interloper" might be more fitting. Characterizing the U'wa thus as an "interloper public" attends to the way in which their cause/case (not to mention the U'wa peoples themselves) was catapulted into the global public arena (basically as a strategy of last resort), and further acknowledges the specificity and temporality of the exchange, what we might call its delimited interface with respect to the dominant order. The concept of interloper public aims, on the one hand, to be sensitive to the hegemonic constraints that more-or-less exogenous indigenous communities, such as the U'wa, operate with and under in constantly having to negotiate on power's terms. On the other hand, the concept seeks to be sensitive to indigenous peoples' aspirations to exercise a fair measure of autonomy with regard to larger governing bodies and mainstream publics, in their quests to negotiate from a position of parity as equal parties to a deal, rather than as subordinate constituencies accommodated within policies of governance.

In contributing to critical re-evaluations of the public-sphere concept, Benhabib (1992) emphasizes the need to dethrone consensus as a reified target; and takes issue with the questionable notion that consensus is (eventually, or even always desirably) reached through public-sphere deliberations. To concur with her stance as viewed though the lens of the U'wa–Oxy conflict (involving national governments and transnational activists, to boot) it is difficult to envision the shape consensus would take, how it would be reached, through what channels and on whose terms. Certain embedded ideals in Western notions of democratic participation become all the more destabilized and their normative assumptions displaced when one further takes note of the fact that the U'wa peoples' struggle against Oxy gives us a keen indication that the participatory momentum, at any instance, may well be driven first and foremost by exigencies of self-defense rather than by endeavors in self-determination. Given the potential for implicit coercion into participatory engagements, it may be necessary to dethrone participation itself, an idealized tenet of democracy that may come to embed its own tyranny. When the call to participation is a call to arms (as is not infrequently the case), then we witness a tyrannical mandate in participation – a mandate which, by dint of its cultural-historical biases, may be asymmetrically levied against indigenous peoples. To wit: indigenous interloper publics must enunciate their political agendas in borrowed idioms (i.e. in the languages of modernity) and perform them in a foreign modality (i.e. the employment of spectacles geared to ignite moral outrage). As with the U'wa experience, this may involve a marriage of convenience between Western discourses, noble savage stereotypes and sensational dramaturgies. In an image marketplace where "good causes" compete for a limited supply of populist energies, sensational activism may come to be increasingly compulsory, de rigueur, the standard menu.

Such a prospect takes on a further paradoxical bent in the case of indigenous groups who state that they ultimately seek, not inclusivity, but rather *exclusivity* (as some indigenous groups have articulated in no uncertain terms, in declaring an express desire/intention *not* to be mainstreamed, in other words to be free *of* the dominant norm). Given that participation inevitably (if unpredictably) changes activists and their world(s), indigenous groups may be at greater risk of the hidden tyrannies of participation. Driven to "public-sphere" activism largely as a last-ditch effort to save their homelands, the U'wa people now have a website of their own, one not specifically in the service of the U'wa–Oxy struggle, nor oriented to general issues of environmental degradation and/or indigenous rights; but rather one along the lines of an official group homepage. How this will impact upon their political clout, cultural values, social organization, subjectivity and agency, etc., remains to be seen. It is clear, though, that the U'wa are more prominent players on the world stage.

To the extent that participation and its tyrannies eclipse or override indigenous values and concepts, indigenous modes of being and doing, then we might say that the exogenous lifeworlds of more powerful societies come to colonize any given indigenous lifeworld. In other words, in a society of the spectacle we may well witness how a corrupted, gilded form of public sphere "participation" – a celebrated concept at the heart of democracy's "lifeworld" – might irrevocably "corrupt" the lifeworlds of cultural groups who value alternative processes of deliberation.[8] This is by no means to romanticize indigenous lifeworlds as inherently superior or preferable; it is rather to examine democratic machination and its differential costs in relation to mainstream power.[9] It is not, moreover, with the intent of dampening optimism over the possibility of justice for the underdog or of the democratic potential of a cyber public sphere, but with the aim of sharpening our critical eye on the structural and epistemic constraints of participation. Participation may well be the best (the only?) path towards representative governance in and across polities, but that should not make us naïve to the cultural-historical biases or to the asymmetric opportunity costs of the business of participation. While the tyranny of participation will likely continue to wield its differential values, there is nonetheless the consolation that the tyranny of non-participation may be greater.

Conclusion: towards thinking global

While the U'wa declared their resolve to lay their mortal bodies "on the line" to protect their homeland from oil development, it was ultimately their virtual bodies – in bucolic poses, but poised for martyrdom – that proved a decisive weapon. What ensued from the crusade to stop oil exploitation in the Amazon was a half-decade-long David-and-Goliath battle. Herein, numerous environmental and human rights groups joined forces with the indigenous U'wa in the role of righteous underdog; and Occidental Oil bedded with the Colombian government to form the mighty, but as it turned out not invincible, giant. In making claims upon a coveted plot of land deep in the rainforest (a resource – rich patch of "geospace") and in airing their claims and counter-claims over cyberspace (a relatively democratic "everyplace/noplace"), these competing players have been engaged, wittingly or no, in configuring what it means to be indigenous on a global stage in the internet age. As an interloper public, the

U'wa found/forged a forum to enunciate their message, a message which might best be summed up (in a significant twist upon a popular environmentalist slogan) as "think *local*, act *global*". The stage offered by the world wide web provided an optimal site for the emplotment and enactment of resistance campaigning, but one not without its costs, in the form of a tyranny of participation and accompanying sensationalism, image inflation, devaluation of impact, competition, and transformations of indigenous lifeways. The U'wa cause/case may well have been a perfect "poster child" for the environmental movement; yet, as we have further proposed and attempted to argue here, it might also give us a perfect poster child for the two faces of modernity, illustrating definitive and essentialist contradictions in the modernist episteme.

Notes

1 For more on this story, see Gedicks: (2001 ch. 2); for a contextual picture, see Gerlach (2003) and Escobar and Alvarez (1992). See also several reports in the journal *Cultural Survival Quarterly*, available online at www.cs.org.

2 A most tragic chapter of this story involved the murder of three Americans who had journeyed to Colombia to provide educational and public-relations support to the U'wa. Terence Freitas, a student and activist, Ingrid Washinawatok, a Native American of the Menominee peoples, and Lahee'Enae Gay, an indigenous Hawai'ian, were brutally assassinated by the leftist guerilla Revolutionary Armed Forces of Colombia (FARC), in an indefensible move to exploit the U'wa publicity for their own purposes. FARC later claimed responsibility and "apologized" for the crime.

3 This is in no way to discount the validity or authenticity of these pictures of U'wa peoples and lifeways: nor even to deny elements of "truth" in the image of the noble savage. It is, rather, to pinpoint the homogeneity of style, content, sentiment that privileged a positive slant (the rosy picture) of "rainforest" life; alongside the notable absence of other angles, including those depicting hardships (e.g., disease, strife) that the U'wa, like humans everywhere, surely must and do endure. It is, moreover, to contest the de-humanization that insistently accompanies any idealization of indigenous peoples into a romantic "postcard" image (ultimately for Western consumption). I am not necessarily accusing RAN, however, of deliberately fabricating, exploiting and/or propagating stereotypes. See discussion below.

4 This retraction followed by a year earlier the pullout of Shell Oil, a British-Dutch conglomerate and original partner in the Colombian venture. Shell was said to have sold its shares for fear of a public relations disaster following the scathing negative publicity it suffered with regard to its ventures in Nigeria, where the government had cruelly cracked-down on indigenous resistance to oil extraction, causing the deaths of possibly thousands. For various reasons, Oxy's withdrawal from Samore has been delayed, and it was three years before U'wa residents deemed the move sufficient enough for RAN to call off its campaign. However Oxy's actions clearly demonstrate an entrenched and determined interest to pursue petroleum extraction in the region at large; indeed, executives met with then-President Ernesto Samper and the Minister of Mines, Orlando Cabrales, to "exchange" Samore for new contracts in potentially crude-rich lands not claimed as part of the U'was' heritage. The U'wa victory may have been shortlived, however, given that a number of other corporations, Exetron to name one, have been aggressively in pursuit of prospecting.

5 Interview with Patrick Reinsborough of RAN, 10 June 2002.

6 These idealizations and conflations of indigenous peoples with an intrinsic environmental ethics are variations on an old theme. Hornborg (1994: 246) describes a

"conceptual symbiosis" of environmental and indigenous movements; Wade (1999: 73) calls the tendency to regard indigenous peoples "guardians of the environment" a "hall of mirrors" involving a politics of culture and biotic difference; and further notes that these projections extend into international development discourse (see also Milton 1993).

7   A proliferation of new research attests to this (see Sawyer 2004; Gedicks 2001).
8   Here we are drawing upon, and twisting, Habermas' (1987) theorizations of a life-world and a system. Habermas warns of a trend in modern societies whereby the "lifeworld", including communications in the public sphere, is at risk of being "colonized" and robbed of meaning by what he calls the "system", which works by means of bureaucracies, markets, and other institutional forms. In problematizing his argument here, I wish to query the extent to which the lifeworld of communicative rationality (as it takes shape and is normatively valued in Habermas' model) remains an artifact of Western inscriptions that – even if it were to exist in ideal form – does not automatically translate into the cultural logic and values of other societies. Hence, we might then explore the risk of dominant lifeworlds colonizing less dominant ones.
9   My critique finds parallel in the work of others who have interrogated the "rhetoric of empowerment" (see Cheater 1999) and in a related sense, "development" (Escobar 1994b; Ferguson 1994; Sen 2000). In such scenarios, we are at risk of approaching an absence at the heart of the metaphysics of presence (in the sense wherein a conceptual order is at risk of ultimately precluding that which it normally embraces) (cf. Derrida 1978).

References

Publications

Appadurai, Arjun (1996) *Modernity at Large*. Minneapolis: University of Mennesota Press.
Benhabib, Seyla (1992) *Situating the Self: Gender, Community, and Postmodernism in Contemporary Ethics*. New York: Routledge.
Cheater, Angela (ed.) (1999) *The Anthropology of Power: Empowerment and Disempowerment in Changing Structures*. London: Routledge.
Clemmer, Richard O. (1995) *Roads in the Sky: The Hopi Indians in a Century of Change*. Boulder: Westview Press.
Debord, Guy (1994) *The Society of the Spectacle*. New York: Zone Books.
Derrida, Jacques (1978) *writing and difference*. A.Bass (trans). London: Routledge & Kegan Paul.
Escobar, Arturo (1994) *Encountering Development: The Making and Unmaking of the Third World*. Princeton: Princeton University Press.
Escobar, Arturo and Alvarez, Sonia (eds) (1992) *The Making of Social Movements in Latin America: Identity, Strategy, Democracy*. Boulder: Westview Press.
Ferguson, James (1994) *The Anti-Politics machine: "Development, Depoliticization and Bureaucratic Power in Lesutho*. Minneapolis: University of Minnesota Press.
Fraser, Nancy (1990) "Rethinking the Public Sphere: A Contribution to the Critique of Actually Existing Democracy", *Social Text* 25/26: 56–80.
Gedicks, Al (2001) *ResourceRebels: Native Challenges to Mining and Oil Corporations*. Cambridge, MA: South End Press.
Gerlach, Allen (2003) *Indians. Oil and Politics; A Recent History of Ecuador*. New York: SR Books.

Habermas, Jürgen (1987) *The Theory of Communicative Action. Volume II, Lifeworld and System*. Boston: Beacon Press.

Hornborg, Alf (1994) "Environmentalism, Ethnicity and Sacred Places: Reflections on Modernity, Discourse and Power", *Canadian Review of Sociology and Anthropology*, 31(3): 245–67.

Milton, Kay (ed.) (1993) *Environmentalism: The View from Anthropology*. London: Routledge.

Ramos, Alcida Rita (1994) "The Hyperreal Indian", *Critique of Anthropology* 14(2): 153–71.

Sawyer, Susana (2004) *Crude Chronicles: Indigenous Politics, Multinational Oil, and Neoliberalism in Ecuador*. Durham, NC: Duke University Press.

Sen, Amartya (2000) *Development as Freedom*. NY: Anchor Books.

Taussig, Michael (1987) *Shamanism, Colonialism and the Wild Man: A Study in Terror and Healing*. Chicago: Chicago University Press.

——(1993) *Mimesis and Alterity: A Particular History of the Senses*. London: Routledge.

Torgovnick, Marie (1990) *Gone Primitive: Savage Intellects, Modern Lives*. Chicago: University of Chicago Press.

Wade, Peter (1999) "The Guardians of Power: Biodiversity and Multiculturality in Colombia", in A. Cheater (ed.), *The Anthropology of Power: Empowerment and Disempowerment in Changing Structures*, pp. 73-87. London: Routledge.

Young, R. (1995) *Colonial Desire: Hybridity in Theory, Culture and Race*. London: Routledge.

Links

Project Underground: www.moles.org
Rainforest Action Network: www.ran.org
U'wa Homepage: www.uwacolombia.org

Amerindian@Caribbean
Internet indigeneity in the electronic generation of Carib and Taino identities

Maximilian C. Forte

> One of the things I like best about the Internet is that millions of people whose ideas were ignored in the mainstream media can now be heard. However, one of the things I really hate about the Internet is that millions of people whose ideas were ignored in the mainstream media can now be heard.
>
> William McLaughlin, 25 May 2001: *alt.native*.

Introduction

"We are not extinct" is the *leitmotif* of most websites *by* and *for* those identifying with a Caribbean indigenous identity. This chapter addresses the electronic modes by which the contemporary "revival" of Caribbean indigeneity is generated. The ethnographic focus of this study consists of two types of groups proclaiming themselves to be engaged in "cultural revitalization": reorganized groups such as the Santa Rosa Carib Community in Trinidad, and newly-founded Taino groups based in the US. My overall concern has been to document and analyse why and how such groups are motivated to locate themselves within international indigenous networks, the ways in which these engagements have served to reshape their self-representations, and the modes by which they engage the internet in order to make connections and construct their own representations.

In much if not most of the social science literature on the cultural development of the post-Conquest Caribbean there seems to be a consensus that the indigenous has been absent or severely diminished (Forte 2001: 1–5). Neglected, however, is the current resurgence of aboriginal identities and traditions and the wider recognition that these are receiving, such as state support and recognition for bodies such as Trinidad's Santa Rosa Carib Community (SRCC). At the regional level, we can also witness the formation of the Caribbean Organization of Indigenous Peoples, and the emergence of an array of new Taino organizations composed by Puerto Ricans in the US. Moreover, there is already considerable evidence to suggest that the growth and development of Amerindian identity and traditions in one territory is significantly aided and shaped by Amerindian cultural revitalization efforts in other territories. It is from these quarters and out of these processes that a challenge to established perspectives on "Amerindian extinction" in the Caribbean has been mounted, and then disseminated almost unchallenged on the internet. Immediately, then, we are faced with a multilay-ered conflict between divergent truth claims fought along the lines of authenticity – often waged between skeptical social scientists and assertive activists, between dominant offline historiography and the online testimonies of those claiming to be surviving/descendant aboriginals. The internet allows rela-tively marginalized groups to recover a history and identity that colonialism, in large part, helped to erase or distort, and which dominant social science helped to inscribe (see Einhorn 2002).

Hence, the main questions at the center of this study revolve around the motivations, constraints, and enabling factors involved in transforming offline indigenes into what I call online N-digenes. I argue that the online, electronic assertion of "survival", by self-described "revivalist" and "restorationist" groups, occurs precisely because the offline realm places many more constraints on the dissemination of these assertions. As Cisler (1998) observed: "One of the strongest reasons for having a presence on the Internet is to provide informa-tion from a viewpoint that may not have found a voice in the mainstream media". The offline arena is dominated by established knowledge institutions (i.e. publishing houses, universities, news media, etc.) whose apparent prestige and purported legitimacy can act as an impediment to the dissemination of alternative, unorthodox or marginal perspectives. The internet allows for a significant challenge to be mounted against the veracity claims made by such institutions.

Ethnography online

Before introducing my ethnographic work and the online activities of the Santa Rosa Carib Community and the Taino groups, it is important to note that there is an offline–online nexus in the representation of Caribbean aboriginals that has resulted in a telling pattern of distinctions between groups resident in the Caribbean and those in diaspora. Three different situations with regard to any given Caribbean (or diasporic Caribbean) group's representation and activities online can be discussed. The first situation refers to groups established as territo-rially-based entities, formalized by law, with their own residential communities and their own official political structures. Examples of such groups include the Amerindian tribes in Guyana and the Caribs of Dominica. These groups are *least* represented on the internet. This is most likely due to restricted access to information technologies as a result of socioeconomic constraints; yet is possibly also due to the internet's perceived lack of relevance to these groups, who may not find the internet to be a valuable or crucial component of their political and cultural practices "on the ground".[1] In cases where these groups are repre-sented online, it is the result of cyberbrokerage or the independent efforts of non-aboriginals and/or non-Caribbean nationals. In the case of Guyana, the Amerindian Peoples' Association has a website (APA 2001), produced and maintained as a result of an initiative between the government of Guyana and the United Nations Development Program. This site has a strong political and economic focus; and is not centered on the "we are not extinct" theme, since this is not a predominant perception plaguing Guyana's Amerindians. In the case of Dominica's Carib Territory, there are at least three key vehicles through which the Caribs are represented online. Delphis Ltd. (2001a) is a Dominican website design firm that maintains Dominica's sole internet portal, called "A Virtual Dominica" (Delphis 2001b). Delphis also hosts pages on the Dominica Caribs, most notably pertaining to the *Gli-Gli* Carib Canoe Project of 1997 (Hubka 1997).[2] The Dominica Caribs are also featured on a website produced by a Dominican émigré in Canada (Riviere 2001). The other major website representing Dominica's Caribs is maintained by a German NGO, Kalinago e.V., which describes itself as consisting of "interested parties . . . committed to the preservation of the culture and traditional knowledge of the last remaining indigenous people of the Caribbean, the Caribs" (Kalinago e.V. 2001a).

The second situation with regard to online representation concerns those groups that have been recently reorganized, such as the SRCC. Although it lacks a separate land base or an autonomous political structure, the SRCC has built upon previous communal bases and has achieved some measure of state recognition and support. The SRCC embarked upon an effort to obtain a greater degree of recognition at the national level by reviving and promoting "Carib traditions" for a wider national audience. Its quest for greater exposure and validation has also taken form through efforts to ally itself with indigenous bodies abroad, including US-based Tainos. As late as 2002, SRCC members lacked any independent access to information technology or the internet. Indeed, the SRCC originally attained an online presence as part of my own collaborative cyberbrokerage (described in more detail later in the chapter). Subsequently the SRCC has also achieved online visibility via an independent Trinidadian cultural tourism site, Amerindian Trail (Marchock 2000); and as a "chapter" represented abroad by the United Confederation of Taino People based in New York (see UCTP 2001).

The third situation regarding online representations of Carib peoples refers to the many Taino groups based among Puerto Ricans in the US. Where Caribbean Amerindian websites are concerned, the online presence of the Taino dominates the internet. Most of these groups, formed in the 1990s, lack an independent, collective hold on resources. They are still very much engaged in the struggle for recognition, not just as organizations, but as *Tainos* – given the predominant perceptions that the Tainos are "extinct" in Puerto Rico (cf. Dávila 1999). I characterize these groups as "new revivalist". The dominant feature of new revivalist groups is their access to information technology and their active networking on the internet, a fact that distinguishes them from the previous two categories. In addition, in the majority of cases, these groups have their own webmasters and thus design and maintain their own websites, or have an exclusive and direct say in what is posted on their behalf. In all cases, what one sees are individuals and organizations engaged in relatively unfettered self-representation, demonstrating often-advanced internet design and networking skills.

At this point, a few words about my methodology are in order. In the case of the SRCC, the bulk of my research was conducted "on the ground" (i.e. offline) yet with online extensions. In the case of Taino groups, my research solely involved online participation and observation. At the beginning of my field-work with the SRCC, my future informants made it clear to me that they expected researchers to be of some assistance to them, not just to "come and take" (even though, in fact, previous researchers had done much to assist them). Hence, from the outset, transactionalism, pragmatism and brokerage emerged as strongly suggestive words for our relationship. It seemed to me that helping them to get online would be a way of furthering their aims for greater recognition both locally and internationally, while I, as a researcher, could gain valuable insights into their worlds and how they wish to represent themselves to others. Accordingly, I acted as a direct contributor and "co-constructor" (see Forte 1998–1999b) in the preparation of websites on behalf of my informants (SRCC 1998–2001; Los Niños del Mundo 1999–2001). To some extent I became "an insider", acting in some ways as an intern or even a consultant. This led me to create other websites as a research resource about the Caribbean, and these sites became a means of interacting with other researchers (see Forte 1998–2002, 1998–2001a, 1998–2001b). Emerging from the previous two efforts, I founded the Caribbean Amerindian Centrelink (CAC 1998–2001), a meta-site that gathers websites by or about Caribbean Amerindians under one virtual roof. It also publishes scholarly articles, essays, personal testimonies of contem-porary Tainos, and a newsletter; and is equipped with site-usage monitors to furnish a "user-model" based on traffic, linked sites, and searches. Apart from being a tool of participant observation, all of these online activities actually became a platform for furthering my offline field research goals. One of these involved observing the outcomes of what going online did for the SRCC, whose websites received several thousand visitors. In addition to an increased level of interest in the Santa Rosa Carib Community, from local journalists and students, Trinidadian expatriates, general internet users and other academic researchers, there has also been an emergence of new websites about the SRCC or sites that have begun to mention them. Another effect of how online activi-ties expanded my offline fieldwork arose with respect to the CAC meta-link, which itself became a kind of virtual "community", generating regular transac-tions and building relationships. In effect, I literally developed not just individual sites, but a web, what I have elsewhere called a "self-generated simu-lacrum of a community": that is, a network of sites, all emanating from one source, all focused on the same issues and concerns, mutually linked, and thus mutually reinforcing (Forte 2002).

Where moving online is concerned, especially via the vehicle of website development, I would argue that certain basic assumptions that have dominated our conceptions of fieldwork practice, relationships with informants, the building of rapport, issues of trust and ethics, are sometimes turned on their head or otherwise transformed in the process. I thus tend to replace notions of participant observation in this context with notions of creative observation, co-construction, and field creation. Creative observation involves the process outlined above: creating a virtual field site – a web resource – that others can then join as participants and/or observers. This is almost the reverse of traditional offline "participant observation" fieldwork, where one goes to find a community to research, one that pre-exists the ethnographer's research project, and which the ethnographer seeks to join through the mode of participant observation. In producing a website, one becomes the gatekeeper to that site, and may find oneself in the role of "key informant": questions, in other words, are no longer predominantly one-way. In online creative observation, one is in effect generating a particular set of research data, which then generates further online data that one studies.

Globalizing Caribbean aboriginals: "cultural revival" of the SRCC

The Santa Rosa Carib Community (SRCC) in the Borough of Arima, Trinidad, is a formal organization that was incorporated as a limited liability company in 1976, in order to apply for a state land grant. SRCC documents emphasize that the group's immediate needs are:

1   recognition by society and government as a legitimate cultural sector;
2   research to clarify their cultural traditions and the issue of their lands; and,
3   support from appropriate institutions in their perceived need areas.

Since the 1970s, the SRCC has come under the leadership of individuals such as President Ricardo Bharath, who progressively has steered the group in the direction of greater formalization, bureaucratization, politicization and "cultural revival".[3]

Gaining greater visibility has become a central issue for SRCC leaders in their quest to affirm their key role as valuable contributors to "the national cultural foundation". Historically, a number of factors have impeded their attempts to acquire a higher public profile in Trinidad. One of these stems from the fact that the group is concentrated locally (in Arima), rather than forming part of a national movement of re-identification with Amerindian ancestry.[4] Second, the group itself is very small, with the core of the SRCC consisting of roughly thirty people. Third, SRCC members do not stand out as physically distinctive when compared with other Trinidadians. This is critical in a society such as Trinidad to the extent that racialized notions of ethnicity have long been dominant. The long-held conviction has been that "extinction" can occur via miscegenation (see Forte 2001: 123–7, 304–8). Thus, the only "real Caribs" are the "pure Caribs" – who also happen to be "dead Caribs". Whereas the survival of Amerindians may not be the dominant narrative in Trinidad, what is more commonly or easily accepted is the notion that the society as a whole has inherited some "Amerindian cultural heritage" (Forte 2001: 280–99). SRCC leaders and spokespersons work on two fronts: to gain recognition as "true Amerindians" from other peoples and organizations whose indigenous identity is not questioned locally; and to promote themselves as the keepers of traditions which mark the "Amerindian cultural heritage" that has putatively shaped the wider "national culture" where this is seen to exist.

To a significant extent, the SRCC has achieved success in obtaining these goals. Support for Caribs tends to stem from persons who are asserting their own genealogical ties to Amerindians, and from citizens and expatriates expressing pride in the "indigenous culture of Trinidad and Tobago". Increasingly, one hears individuals asserting their Carib ancestry, both via the media and via the websites associated with the SRCC itself. The SRCC's visible association with an array of international indigenous groups who frequently exercise a presence on the ground in Trinidad helps to offset potential sanctions against individuals who locally might otherwise be seen as primarily "not pure" or "not real" Amerindians. In a nation fraught with ethnic divisions between persons of various extra-local ancestries – whether they hail from India, Africa, or the Middle East – the Caribs represent the only group that claims locality as its prime focus of loyalty. Yet, in an interesting if somewhat paradoxical turn of events, this presumed "purity" qualifies them to capture the nation's diversity: for the state, and the various parties that have held office, the Caribs have come to represent the country's ethnic diversity and national history. For a nation as heterogeneous as Trinidad, perhaps only an imaginary, abstract purity could fit the bill as an equalizer. As representatives of "the ancient bedrock" of the Trinidadian nation, they have been successful in achieving formal state recognition, as well as recognition in local school texts and the mass media.[5] At the same time, as yet another ethnic group engaged in competitive cultural display, they are financial recipients of state patronage designed to "manage diversity". The SRCC has also achieved a certain degree of political prominence, including being courted by national politicians (especially since SRCC President Bharath is himself an elected member of the Arima Borough Council for the now-ruling People's National Movement).[6] What is significant here is that there is now virtually no prominent body or individual in Trinidad society who challenges the validity of the SRCC's claims to an aboriginal history and identity. Indeed, this is indicative of the successful brokerage efforts of the SRCC and its allies and the receptivity of the society itself, owing to both new and long-established discourses for interpreting and appreciating "the indigenous presence". What is also interesting is the degree to which the language used in SRCC self-representations online is gaining increased currency offline, especially in the local news media. SRCC leaders are nonetheless keen to maximize and further their recognition within the wider society.

Cultural revival and cultural retrieval represent additional SRCC agendas. SRCC brokers define cultural retrieval as the process of rediscovering, re-learning and practicing "the ancient ways", including language, religious practices, and traditional costume. Cultural revival, as SRCC leaders use the term, entails adopting and implementing traditions learned from historical and ethnographic texts. These processes entail "cultural interchange" between themselves and other communities. Cultural interchange involves the process of acquiring indigenous traditions (that they have "lost", as Bharath says) from other Amerindian communities that are seen as still practicing them; for example, "reacquiring" from elsewhere in the Caribbean and South America traditions already in place in contemporary indigenous communities. All of this involves considerable networking on the international front. The project of articulating, enacting and displaying "Amerindian cultural heritage" has thus become fused with the search for identity-validating associations with indige-nous groups abroad.

By associating themselves with "resurgent" and "established" indigenous groups elsewhere in the Caribbean and the Americas, and by drawing on their symbolic resources, SRCC members have been able to enhance their own iden-tity and legitimacy as "indigenous" at the local level. In an outward-oriented society such as Trinidad's – which values foreign appreciation, global exposure, and international connections as prestigious forms of validation – international connections can go far towards bolstering local status. The dissemination within Trinidad of metropolitan (i.e. European and North American) and wider international valorizations of the indigenous further bolsters the value of indi-geneity at the national level. That a range of international organizations (e.g., the Organization of American States, the UN's World Intellectual Property Organization, UNESCO) and indigenous organizations (e.g., Canada's Assembly of First Nations, the Assembly of Manitoba Chiefs, and the Federation of Saskatchewan Indian Nations) have all worked with the SRCC in some capacity at some time, only serves to heighten the profile of the group within the national politics of cultural value, and the cultural politics of national value.

International exchange relationships, brokered offline and online, are thus a source of accentuated validation. As one of the SRCC brokers wrote, in telling terms: "While the members of the SRCC are striving for recognition by the nationals of Trinidad and Tobago, they are accepted by all *true Amerindians* from the Mohawk council of tribal people of Canada and the United States, to the Carib Community of Dominica" (Almarales 1994: 34, emphasis added). Almarales further emphasized: "They [SRCC members] are recognized as true Amerindian descendants outside Trinidad and Tobago" (1994: 55). In other words, their identification as indigenous is developed and defined, in part, in and through this internationalized network. The adoption (to some extent) of the customs, costumes, and ceremonial practices of North American Indians plays a role, as do personal visits (such as with the Seminole in the US). The recent adoption by the SRCC of the "First Nations" designation is another such trademark to assert this internationally-networked sense of indigeneity. The concept of cultural interchange also implies, within reasonable limits, a network where local platforms are more or less interchangeable. The principle at work seems to be that what is "indigenous" *over there* can be "indigenous" *here* and may be "indigenous" *everywhere*.

Apart from understanding what the internet is and learning how it works, "going online" posed no problems to SRCC leaders, who in fact welcomed the opportunity. As a "hi-tech" instrument that pertains to an elite, the internet can and does acquire a certain level of social prestige in Trinidad, at least as far as my informants seemed to indicate. The fact that other Caribbean Amerindian groups already had websites produced a certain "demonstration effect" as well; and the facility of having websites designed and launched on their behalf only added to the value of undertaking an online presence. In having an online presence, the SRCC would thus achieve greater visibility (see TTWD 2001) at the local level (with many Trinidadian internet users apparently keen to survey the range and types of websites representing Trinidad). This was especially the case among privileged members of the middle and upper classes with internet access and with the resources to render them prime candidates (in the eyes of SRCC brokers) as prospective patrons. For their part, SRCC members do not, as a group or as individuals, even own a computer (at the time of writing), and some currently cannot afford to have telephone connections. On the other hand, not even this helped to insulate them from the internet, as some SRCC members received "snail mail downloads" from the internet in the form of printed packages of web-based materials mailed to them from friends in the US. As I mentioned above, I acted as the SRCC's "cyber-broker". Had I not involved myself in this manner, however, I have no doubt that the SRCC would have gained an online presence eventually. Indeed, one SRCC-affiliated broker has since launched a website for a new group that emerged from the SRCC (Stollmeyer 2000).

Globalizing Caribbean aboriginals: new revival among Taino

There are parallels between the practices of the SRCC and those of the US-based Taino groups with respect to the desires of both groups for greater visibility and recognition. In contrast with my work among SRCC, much of my research with Taino groups occurred online, including participation in listservs, email interviews, and content analysis of websites. The methodological problem posed lies in the dangers inherent in reading backwards from online to offline motivations and organizations. What I can do, with some margin of "safety", is to outline here who the key actors are, the stated intentions of individuals, the idioms they use in self-representation, and the stated purposes of the organizations that they have formed. My online focus on Taino groups is not meant to imply that their existence or cultural practices only occur online. From their own websites one can see photographs of their participation in various festivals, *pow-wows*, dances, prayer meetings, family gatherings, and arts and crafts exhibitions. Of course, these are snapshots of particular moments, capturing the fleeting scenes of a day's activity. Yet, suddenly, they achieve permanence on the internet, restructured in ways that webmasters manage and edit, often with the implicit attempt of graphically inserting those shown into dominant and symbolically powerful streams of globalized representations of indigeneity.

There are at least five categories of online Taino representation and site ownership. There are personal homepages, such as Valery "Nanturey" Vargas-Stehney's (2001) *Bohio Bajacu: Taino Indian Website*, an almost "classical" personal page of the kind that was once prevalent in the early years of the internet. On that site Vargas-Stehney states, in language that is representative of that found on most Taino sites:

> My name is Nanaturey, short for Inaruri Gua Yuke Turey, (Valiant Woman from the White Earth's Sky). . . . I am India Taina Boricua, Taino Indian Woman from the Island of Boriken, from the Tribes of Canobanas and Bayamon. I have always known about my Taino roots. My family is strong with the traditions of my Ancestors.

The second category of Taino websites consists of "family" sites, often simply personal homepages writ larger. *Baramaya* (2001) is one such example of a group of families gathered to restore a chiefdom recorded in the colonial chronicles of Puerto Rico, with members coming from the purported region. Likewise, *Maisiti* (2001) describes itself as a community of Taino families dedicated to cultivating Taino family life. Taino arts and crafts websites form another category. Here one can name *Presencia Taina* (2001a, 2001b) and *Biaraku* (2001). The latter presents itself as a "Taino Cultural Interest Group", and features a range of artistic creations, sculptures, paintings and a wide array of poetry with Taino themes. In the case of *Biaraku*, as with many other sites, it is unclear who or how many people are behind the online representations. The fourth category of sites consists of those that provide what the site owners see as educational information. For example, Taino Ancestry Legacy Keepers, Inc. (TALK 2000) states that it is "a not-for-profit 501(c)(3) organization founded in 1998", whose mission is "to maintain Taino legacies by educating, informing and fostering a positive image to the general public on Taino ancestry, history, culture, historical sites and sacred ceremonial grounds by means of public forums, training sessions and conferences as well as publications and electronic means". In other words, it seeks to operate as a "Taino Education Center" online.

By far the most visibly dominant of Taino websites, the fifth category, comprises all those bodies that describe themselves as tribes, nations, confederations, or governments. The Jatibonicu Taino Tribal Nation (JTTN) is perhaps the most prominent online, in terms of traffic to its website, links to its pages from a wide array of institutions, the number of pages that it maintains, and its active online networking. The JTTN (2001) website announces its body as a "Government", and states that this . . .

> . . . tribal web site is a humble tribute to our honored Taino ancestor Cacike Orocobix (Principal Chief, Remembrance of the First Mountain) of the tribe of Jatibonicu and its Taino people. We of the Jatibonicu tribe are known as the "Great People of the Sacred High Waters".

It is difficult to ascertain the size of the group or where it is principally based (the JTTN says that is based in New Jersey and Puerto Rico). Indeed, when asked in an interview about the number of members, the head of the JTTN, Cacique (Chief) Pedro Guanikeyu Torres answered:

> We maybe number 300, 3,000 or 30,000. At this point I can only say that we are an ethnic indigenous people that number in the thousands and that we are still growing as people are still returning back into the Taino family circle.
> (Vázquez 2001)

Primarily, the JTTN seems motivated to gain recognition of Taino survival, and formal recognition of itself as a representative body from "our common Governments in Puerto Rico and in the United States" (see Vázquez 2001). The JTTN testifies to having received the recognition of the state of New Jersey, as well as producing certificates conferred by the US Census Bureau indicating, apparently, forms of indirect or implicit recognition (JTTN 2001).

Another example of a site self-described as a confederated, or tribal, body is the United Confederation of Taino People (see UCTP 2001). Based in New York, the UCTP was formed in 1993 as an attempt to unite the disparate and often competing Taino groups, and is headed by Roberto "Mucaro" Borrero. On its site, the UCTP does not indicate its membership size, but does list several chapters across the Caribbean region and Hawai'i. Backed by a letter from SRCC President Bharath the UCTP also represents Trinidad's SRCC abroad. The UCTP has also become active on a number of fronts: in anti-globalization protests; in an online and offline campaign to obtain the revocation of the 1493 Papal Bull *Inter Caetera*;[7] and, in various ceremonies held in New York to commemorate the annual United Nations International Day for the World's Indigenous People.

In a manner that parallels the Trinidad SRCC's quest for greater public association with indigenous groups abroad, Taino groups have also been active in the internationalizing aspect of the revival of Caribbean indigeneity. As Dávila (1999: 25) explains, Taino groups and associations "have tended to conceptualize themselves not so much in nationalist as in diasporic terms". In addition, Dávila found that most of the Taino revivalists were either born or raised in the US, with most residing there, and it was in the US that "most of the Tainos recouped their indigenous identity" (1999: 19). The Native American movement played a key role, in ways that parallel the Canadian First Nations presence in the Caribbean. Many of today's US-based Tainos had experiences working on Native American publications, serving as translators to Central and South American indigenous delegations to the United Nations, and/or participating in Native American *pow-wows* and other activities (Dávila 1999: 19). Taino organizations have also received the backing of Canada's Assembly of First Nations in their campaign to have colonial-era decrees promulgated by the Spanish Crown "to protect the indigenes of Hispaniola" accepted today as valid treaties by the United Nations (see Barreiro and Laraque 1998).

"We are not extinct" is, as I flagged at the outset, the leitmotif of most Taino websites. To "prove" biological survival is therefore a critical agenda of many of these sites. Accordingly, a number of these sites (JTTN 2001; TALK 2000; Vázquez 2001) report or reproduce published DNA studies (conducted by Juan Carlos Martínez Cruzado at the University of Puerto Rico) that suggest the genetic continuity of Tainos in Puerto Rico. Numerous Taino websites further argue the case for Taino cultural survival, suggesting that Amerindian communities survived in remote mountain regions of Puerto Rico and Cuba, mixed into the rural peasant populations known as *jíbaros* and *guajiros* respectively. Some may speak of the survival of Amerindian customs (the making of *cassava* bread, for example), or about Amerindian stories told by grandmothers; others simply emphasize their self-knowledge of Taino as being the result of spiritual revelations. Hence, Vargas-Stehney (2001) declares "We The Taino Are Still Here" (also JTTN 2001 and TALK 2000). Similarly, *Biaraku* (2001) argues:

> In spite of the myth of "extinction", we, the descendants of the Taino people, have managed to survive despite all odds. Although most of us are of mixed origins, many of us retain the knowledge of our indigenous identity as a family legacy, others are striving to reclaim it, and others are still unaware of their Taino heritage. A heritage that encompasses more than place names and derived vocabulary, but a distinct a way of life that has meaning for us in the present time.

José "TureyCu" Lopez (2001) of the Turabo Aymaco tribe ("those survivors and their descendants of the [1492] massacre" [TTAT 2001; cf. Torres 1996a]) writes:

> I have been blessed with the high honor of restoring and breathing rebirth into the ancient Native American Taino Tribe of Aymaco, Borinken (Puerto Rico). Many will still declare that the Native American Taino Tribes of the Caribbean are extinct, but I, many scholars and others who know the real facts, know that this is a falsehood, perpetrated by those who do not want to see our Native American people once again thrive.

In a similar fashion, Pedro Torres (1996b) of the Jatibonicu Taino Tribal Nation writes:

We as a Taino people must start writing to anyone who is presently authoring articles of misinformation about the extinction of our Taino people and to correct those who are promoting this kind of misinformation about our Nation. It is the responsibility of a people to justly defend their Taino national sovereignty. In this way putting to rest once and for all the false rumors that we as a people are extinct.

These perspectives on "Taino survival" are being echoed and amplified across other, non-Taino, websites, as in the case of Richard Vázquez's (2001) article in *About.com*, a fairly reputable and popular web-based information resource. Vázquez tells readers in bold print, "the Caribbean Taino Indians have been considered extinct for hundreds of years, yet they have always been with us", and then adds:

> History books and encyclopedias still refer to the Taino/Arawak people as the first tribe to be decimated by colonialism. It would be more appropriate to say that this was the first tribe to be "told" they were extinct. . . . While their governments and temples fell, the people remained and continued to influence our culture – and ancestry.

Beyond assertions of survival, continuity or reawakening, there is also a pronounced tendency among Taino websites (as for the Santa Rosa Carib Community) to immediately structure self-representation along the lines established in the dominant discourses of North American Indian bodies. This graphically demonstrates the processes whereby newly established Taino groups read and sift through various globalized ideas, images and symbolic resources in order to define their indigeneity as "First Nations", which is itself a North American trope of indigeneity. The internet allows Taino groups to project what they see as distinctly Taino and Caribbean aspects of Caribbean culture, especially in terms of iconography and material culture. The internet may even help to strengthen the association between certain items and icons with "Taino identity", in a manner that renders them emblematic of "authentic" Taino identity. Yet, apart from their actual residence in the US, there are two interrelated forces accounting for the tendency of Taino groups to structure their online representations in terms evocative of politicized forms of North American indigeneity. One is the fact that North American modes of representing indigeneity have achieved a certain prestige, respectability and worldwide exposure. The second is the need to make "Taino identity" communicable and intelligible to a wider online public that may well be unfamiliar with Caribbean Amerindian histories and cultures.

In order to insert themselves within more globalized and specifically North American patterns for representing indigeneity, and to gain direct and indirect recognition and legitimacy in the process, a number of Taino internet specialists have been active in garnering online forms of recognition for Taino groups. The outcomes of such online networking can be seen in various examples. One method is for Taino groups to be incorporated in listings of Native American websites. In a letter to United Native America (UNA 2000), Torres of the Jatibonicu Taino Tribal Nation states (in reference to a petition for a US national Native American holiday):

> I believe that your petition does not cover the Taino Native American Indian people of the United States territory of Puerto Rico. We are the original people who greeted Christopher Columbus on October 12, 1492. Your petition covers the United States, Alaska and Hawaii and does not include the United States territory of Puerto Rico. Please add the US Territory of Puerto Rico to your petition as we who are Taino are also Native Americans.

The founder of UNA answered, seemingly without reservations: "I fully agree with your request to add the Taino Indian Nation of Puerto Rico to the holiday petition."[8] In addition to outside networking and recognition, there is a network of interlinked, mutually referring, Taino websites that now build on each other's online presence. In the case of these Taino networks on the internet, we can delineate patterns of association and commonality. Via regular exchange (electronic newsletters, email petitions, mailing lists, listservs, newsgroups, message boards, chatrooms, and individual email messages) these sites build common interests (e.g., affirming Taino survival, seeking recognition as Tainos). They do so through related content (essays on Taino history and culture, archaeological sites, language resources, etc.), shared perspectives and symbols (petroglyphic icons, *zemis*,[9] animal figures seen as sacred symbols in Taino cosmology). By cross-referencing, the granting of awards, hyperlinks, webrings and the like, they form boundaries of mutual advantage. As a result, the legitimacy of each site is bolstered by the fact that other such sites exist as well – rendering any one Taino site less of a "one-click wonder".[10]

Online *N-digenes*: electronically generated "revival"

There is a dynamic relationship between the offline and the online dimensions of cultural practice. Online practices of self-representation are a vital facet of offline politics, shaped by them and shaping them in their turn. While realities are being constructed and disseminated on the internet that have not yet taken root on the ground – i.e. a sovereign Taino government – it is important to recognize the possibility of "real-life facts on the ground" being reshaped and informed by electronically-generated realities.

It is certainly the case that internet practice is of value to those who have undertaken it. Indeed, as their engagement with the internet is not a "given" that we can take for granted, the fact that it occurs must indicate that it is viewed by activists and brokers as a valuable and potentially efficacious medium compared with previously more restricted modes of self-representation. Many of the groups and individuals in question try to achieve online that which is substantially more difficult to achieve offline: that is, wider dissemination and greater recognition of the contemporary presence of Caribbean indigenes. It is also possible that what is asserted online is a hypercorrection for that which is under represented offline. The internet is a medium that enables heavy presentation – for example, many of the Taino sites are heavy in terms of beautification and elaborate appearance: large and vibrant graphics heavy with depictions of "traditional wear" and various forms of plumage, petroglyphic symbols, "mood music" (chants, songs, nature sounds) and, sky and starlight backgrounds in some cases. As has been widely observed in other areas of internet culture, "individuals are disembodied and, in theory, unbound by the body's constraints" (Doheny-Farina 1996: 65). Individuals can also "multiply" themselves in "virtual" terms, masking their actual membership numbers. Doheny-Farina thus argues, perhaps too strongly, "the World Wide Web. . . . is primarily a graphics delivery system, a presentation medium masked as an interactive network. Deliberative rhetoric is defeated every time by image" (1996: 79).

This raises issues concerning invention, aboriginality, and the internet. Of course, *every* construction involving the internet implies a certain degree of "inventiveness" given the relative novelty of the form, process, and purpose of the communication. Also, the immediate context of identity construction on the internet is, necessarily, very modern. Digital representation of aboriginality as an invention approximates, in my view, Hobsbawm's (1983) notion of "invention of tradition", in so far as it involves a rapidly instituted construction that is meant to fit within a putatively long and pre-existing tradition, an approach that, despite its many critics, is not premised on notions of "falsity" as such but on history and contemporaneity. What contemporary Taino and SRCC activists are doing is to invent new modes for representing survival and propounding perspectives that have been marginal or not widely accepted previously.

My argument suggests that, in helping to promote the visibility of peoples long believed to have been extinct, or ignored for being minorities, the internet also helps to *embody* groups facing difficulties in gaining offline acceptance as

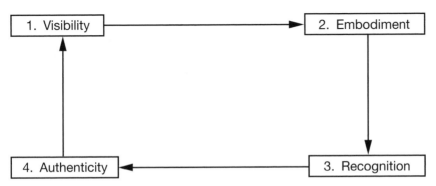

Figure 7.1 The 'V.E.R.A. city loop' of Electronic 'Revival'

"indigenous". It simultaneously facilitates mutual online and offline recognition between these groups, thereby lending further authority and authenticity to any given group in its respective offline context(s). In other words, and as depicted in Figure 7.1, I examine the processes by which the "veracity" of Caribbean Amerindian indigeneity is sought and attained by electronic means of promotion. This involves a loop of processes that I call the V.E.R.A.city loop: that is, online visibility helping to virtually embody groups who might not otherwise be noticed or distinguished and who – given this virtualized visibility and embodiment – subsequently gain recognition from prospective allies and brokers. Depending upon the reputation of one's ally, the fact of being recognized itself adds authenticity to a particular, previously under-recognized group's claim to be "real Tainos" or "real Caribs". I see this as a loop in the sense that the process reinforces and continually repeats itself.

Conclusions: Caribbean aboriginality and internet indigeneity

My aim in this chapter has been to describe and analyze the means and processes by which Caribbean indigenes have been transformed into N-digenes. My expectation is that the internet will soon become (if it is not already the case) the frontline in the assertion of the survival and/or revival of Caribbean Amerindian identities, for most of the territories in question. As socially marginal groups whose historical authenticity is questioned by some, or held in the hands of academics, the internet invites them to create new and powerful modes of attesting to their history and "reclaiming" their identity.

The internet itself also plays an increasingly central role in enabling the global diffusion of ideas of indigeneity. The question of "globalized indigeneity", to the extent that one can meaningfully speak of this, represents an important paradox of indigeneity: seemingly free-floating whilst emphasizing local rootedness. I suggest that the globalized spread of motifs, practices, products, ideologies, cosmologies, organizations, media and support networks of indigeneity, especially on the internet, have led to the construction of indigeneity as a macro phenomenon, lifted from the confines of any one location, and seemingly applicable to any other location. At this level, we are then speaking of an indigenous macro-community that is trans-local and constitutes a virtual meta-indigeneity. Indeed we might speak of a "virtual" indigeneity as in the sense of "being both related to and increasingly 'disconnected' from its formal referent" (Geschiere and Meyer 1998: 606) – that "formal referent" previously seen as confined to distinct physical localities. We may thus be able to speak of interchangeable "local platforms" and adaptable globalized meanings, motifs, and so forth, ultimately leading to a situation where the network is the indigene. In this regard, it is important to underscore the extent to which the symbols and discourses of indigenous groups in one part of the world can and do impact upon the symbols and discourses of indigenous groups in another part of the world, especially on the internet.

On the other hand, this transmission and transference is not one that is multilateral in the case of Caribbean indigeneity, where North American Indian labels, motifs and representations influence contemporary articulations of Caribbean indigeneity rather than *vice versa*. Amongst the indigenous population of the Americas as a whole, there is a differential level of representation on the internet, with North America clearly leading South America in terms of the number of sites pertaining to the indigenous peoples of the respective continents. That indigenous websites pertaining to the Caribbean are beginning to outnumber those for South America is, clearly, a phenomenon that is deserving of continued research and interpretation. Clearly, realities are being forged on the internet that do not neatly correspond to those "on the ground", and yet they may reshape and even overtake those realities in the not too distant future. Studying these new realities requires new research methods. In my own work, this has led me to engage in online field creation, which has in turn fostered opportunities for "creative observation". A transformation in the role of the ethnographer and in the setting of the ethnography, creative observation entails different research relationships and processes. This is not fake ethnography, or a mere reduction of ethnography to discourse or text analysis, but an expansion of ethnography into new realms of interaction.

Notes

1 Finding explanations for this can be complicated. In the case of the Dominica Caribs, thanks to the efforts of various NGOs, representative bodies have in fact achieved some limited access to information technology, yet the evidence suggests that this is being underutilized nevertheless. A German NGO remarked: "We continue to be dissatisfied with the level of contact with the Caribs. Despite all the advanced technological developments that aid communication this has remained a sticking point. Letter, fax, and email exchange are often one-sided and can be drawn out over months. Despite new technology we continue to rely as before on personal contact" (Kalinago e.V. 2001b).

2 This involved a much-publicized journey from Dominica to the Orinoco River, relinking Carib communities along the way (see Forte 1998–1999a).

3 For more details on the history of this organization, please see Forte (2001; 1998–2002).

4 Statistical breakdowns of Trinidad and Tobago's multi-ethnic population show 39.5 percent as "African", 40.3 percent as "East Indian", 18.4 percent as "mixed", 0.6 percent as "European", and 1 percent as "other" (USDoS 1998).

5 This is detailed in chapter 5 of Forte (2001) as well as in Forte (1998–2002).

6 The PNM was in office from independence in 1962 to 1986, again from 1991 to 1995, and once more from 2001.

7 The 1493 Papal Bull *Inter Caetera*, or "solemn edict" issued by the Pope, established an (arbitrary) north–south meridian dividing the globe into western and eastern halves, and partitioned these to Spain and Portugal, respectively. The edict essentially granted these mercantile powers full rights of conquest throughout "New World" territories, including subjugation of non-Christian "pagan" natives. Since at least the early 1970s, numerous indigenous rights groups have petitioned the Vatican to revoke the Bull.

8 Further examples include: a *Native American Timeline* and a page of *Hopi Links Native American Resources*, both of which list the JTTN as well as the UCTP (see Watson 2001; Hopi 2001); and an *Indian Nations* list (Rocha 2001) and a listing of *USA Tribal Governments* (see NSCIA 2001), which both name the JTTN.
9 Usually carved from wood or stone and not much bigger than can be held in a hand, these are seen as containing spirits and are often associated with shamans and chiefs, sometimes depicting skeletal yet fertile representations of shamans.
10 Of course, there is no gainsaying that Taino organizations have become almost notorious in some circles for their intense rivalry and frequent bickering. Some of the Taino websites (e.g., Vargas-Stehney 2001; TTAT 2001; JTTN 2001) explicitly refer to these intra-Taino conflicts, and in some cases we can also witness online forms of schism exemplified by the existence of two separate groups and sites under the title of *Presencia Taina* (2001a, 2001b).

References

Almarales, Beryl (1994) *The Santa Rosa Carib Community from 1974–1993.* Bachelor's thesis, University of the West Indies, St Augustine, Trinidad.
Amerindian Peoples' Association (APA) (2001) *Amerindian Peoples' Association: Guyana.* Georgetown, Guyana: Sustainable Development Networking Programme. Available online: http://www.sdnp.org.gy/apa/
Baramaya (2001) *Baramaya: A Brief History.* New York: Baramaya. Available online: http://baramaya-taino.com/new_page_3.htm
Barreiro, José and Laraque, Marie-Helene (1998) "Canada First Nations Back Taino Treaty", *Native Americas Magazine*: Hemispheric Digest, Winter. Available online: http://nativeamericas.aip.cornell.edu/win98/win98hd.html#anchor293412
Biaraku (2001) *Biaraku: 'First People of a Sacred Place'.* Available online: http://members.aol.com/staino/intro.html
Caribbean Amerindian Centrelink (CAC) (1998–2001) *Caribbean Amerindian Centrelink.* Arima, Trinidad, and Adelaide, Australia: CAC. Available online: http://www.centrelink.org
Ciboney (2001) *Ciboney Tribe: Siboneyes de la Florida.* Kendall, FL: Jorge Luis Salt. Available online: http://www.ciboneytribe.org
Cisler, Steve (1998) "The Internet and Indigenous Groups", *Cultural Survival Quarterly.* Available online: http://cs.org/publications/CSQ/csqinternet.html#Cisler
Cultural Survival Quarterly (1998) *The Internet and Indigenous Groups.* Available online: http://cs.org/publications/CSQ/csqinternet.html
Dávila, Arlene (1999) "Local/Diasporic Tainos: Towards a Cultural Politics of Memory, Reality and Imagery", in G. Haslip-Viera (ed.), *Taíno Revival: Critical Perspectives on Puerto Rican Identity and Cultural Politics.* New York: Centro de Estudios Puertorriqueños, Hunter College, City University of New York, pp. 11–29.
Delphis (2001a) *Delphis Ltd.: Website Design, Development and Promotion.* Roseau, Dominica: Delphis. Available online: http://www.delphis.dm/dolphin.htm
——(2001b) *A Virtual Dominica.* Roseau, Dominica: Delphis. Available online: http://www.delphis.dm/home.htm
Dodge, Martin (2001) *An Atlas of Cyberspaces.* Available online: http://www.cybergeography.org/atlas/geographic.html
Doheny-Farina, Steven (1996) *The Wired Neighborhood.* New Haven, CT: Yale University Press.

Einhorn, Arthur (2002) "Out of Pandora's Closet: A Commentary on Racism, Identity, and Cultural Revival", *The CAC Review* 3(5). Available online: http://www.centre-link.org/Jun2002.html

Forte, Maximilian C. (1998–1999a) "The International Indigene: Regional and Global Integration of Caribbean Amerindian Communities", *Issues in Caribbean Amerindian Studies* 1(1). Available online: http://www.centrelink.org/II.html

——(1998–1999b) "From Smoke Ceremonies to Cyberspace: Globalized Indigeneity, Multi-Sited Research, and the Internet", *Issues in Caribbean Amerindian Studies* 1(1). Available online: http://www.centrelink.org/Internet.html.

——(1998–2001a) *A University of Adelaide Anthropological Field Project on Trinidad's Self-Identified Amerindian Descendants, 1998–1999.* Arima, Trinidad: Maximilian C. Forte. Available online: http://members.theglobe.com/mcforte/default.html

——(1998–2001b) *Gateway to the Caribs of Trinidad and Tobago.* Arima, Trinidad: Maximilian C. Forte. Available online: http://members.tripod.com/Trinidad_Tobago_CARIB/Carib.htm

——(1998–2002) *The First Nations of Trinidad and Tobago.* Arima, Trinidad: Maximilian C. Forte. Available online: http://www.centrelink.org/fntt/index.html

——(2001) *Re-engineering Indigeneity: Cultural Brokerage, the Political Economy of Tradition and the Santa Rosa Carib Community of Arima, Trinidad and Tobago.* PhD dissertation, Adelaide University.

——(2002) "'We are not Extinct': The Revival of Carib and Taino Identities, the Internet, and the Transformation of Offline Indigenes into Online 'N-digenes'", *Sincronía: Una Revista Electrónica De Estudios Culturales.*

Geschiere, Peter and Meyer, Birgit (1998) "Globalization and Identity: Dialectics of Flow and Closure", *Development and Change* 29: 601–15.

Hobsbawm, Eric J. (1983) "Introduction: Inventing Traditions", in E. Hobsbawm and T. Ranger (eds), *The Invention of Tradition.* Cambridge: Cambridge University Press, pp. 1–14.

Hopi (2001) *Native American Resources.* Available online: http://fraktali.849pm.com/text/hopi/nativelinks.html

Hubka, Renee (1997) *'Gli Gli': The Carib Canoe Project.* Roseau, Dominica: Delphis. Available online: http://www.delphis.dm/gligli/index.html

Jatibonicu Taino Tribal Nation (JTTN) (2001) *Government of the Jatibonicu Taino Tribal Nation of Boriken.* Vineland, NJ: JTTN. Available online: http://www.taino-tribe.org/jati-boni.html

Kalinago e.V. (2001a) *Kalinago e.V.: Association for the Promotion of the Last Indigenous People of the Caribbean (Verein zur Förderung des letzten indigenen Volkes der Karibik).* Frankfurt: Kalinago e.V. Available online: http://www.kalinago.org/english/index.html

—— (2001b) *Kalinago e.V. in its Third Year.* Frankfurt: Kalinago e.V. Available online: http://www.kalinago.org/english/text/kalinago3year.htm

Lopez, José "TureyCu" (2001) *Press Release, August 2000.* New York: Taino Turabo Aymaco Tribe. Available online: http://www.indio.net/aymaco/page2.htm

Los Niños del Mundo (1999–2001) *Cristo Adonis' Los Niños del Mundo: Trinidad Parang Website.* Arima, Trinidad: Cristo Adonis' Los Niños del Mundo. Available online: http://www.freeyellow.com/members6/trinidadtobagoparang/shaman.html

Maisiti (2001) *Maisiti Yukayeke of the Taino Tribe.* New York: Indio.net. Available online: http://www.indio.net/maisiti/

Marchock, Ryan (2000) *AmerindianTrail.com: Welcome to Trinidad and Tobago*. Unpublished manuscript.

National Spinal Cord Injury Association (NSCIA) (2001) *USA Tribal Governments*. Bethesda, MD: NSCIA. Available online: http://www.spinalcord.org/chapters/native_american_governments.htm

Presencia Taina (2001a) *Atihuibancex: Mountain Wind Group*. New York: Presencia Taina. Available online: http://www.presenciataina.net

——(2001b) *Atihuibancex: Mountain Wind Group*. New York: Roger Hernandez. Available online: http://www.presenciataina.org

Ramirez, Gladys Nieves (2001a) "Con Herencia Indígena 62 percent de los Boricuas", *El Nuevo Día* (Puerto Rico), 4 May 2001. Available online: http://www.endi.com/locales/html/p58c03m5.asp

——(2001b) "Misioneros de la cultura taína", *El Nuevo Día* (Puerto Rico), 4 May 2001. Available online: http://www.endi.com/locales/html/p58b03m5.asp

Riviere, Raglan Eugene (2001) *The Caribs of Dominica*. Ottawa: Raglan E. Riviere. Available online: http://www.geocities.com/Athens/Agora/3820/carib.html

Rocha, Victor (2001) *Indian Nations*. Victor Rocha Communications, LLC. Available online: http://pechanga.net/indian_nations.htm

Santa Rosa Carib Community (SRCC) (1998–2001) *The Santa Rosa Carib Community*. Arima, Trinidad: SRCC and Maximilian C. Forte. Available online: http://SRCC1CaribCommunity.tripod.com/

Stollmeyer, John (2000) *Kairi Tukuienyo Karinya*. Port of Spain, Trinidad: Turtle Island Children. Available online: http://www.angelfire.com/id/kairi/tukuienyo.html

Taino Ancestry Legacy Keepers (TALK) (2000) *Taino Ancestry Legacy Keepers, Inc.* New York: Indio.net. Available online: http://www.indio.net/talk/index.html

Taino Turabo Aymaco Tribe (TTAT) (2001) *The Native American Indian Taino Turabo Aymaco Tribe of Boriken*. New York: José "TureyCu" Lopez. Available online: http://www.indio.net/aymaco/index.html

Torres, Pedro (1996a) *The Historical Roots of a Nation*. Vineland, NJ: Jatibonicu Taino Tribal Nation. Available online: http://www.hartford-hwp.com/Taino/docs/Tnation.html

——(1996b): "Chief Torres of Arawak Indian Descent Denies Claims of Genocide", message to Prof. Bob Corbett from Pedro Torres. Available online: http://www.webster.edu/~corbetre/haiti/history/precolumbian/genocide.htm

Trinidad and Tobago Web Directory (TTWD) (2001) *Native People of Trinidad and Tobago: The Trinidad and Tobago Web Directory, Society and Culture*. Port of Spain, Trinidad: Search.co.tt. Available online: http://www.search.co.tt/dir/native/

United Confederation of Taino People (UCTP) (2001) *The United Confederation of Taino People (UCTP) – Honoring Caribbean Indigenous Peoples: Past, Present and Future*. New York: Indigenouspeople.org. Available online: http://www.indigenous-people.org/natlit/uctp/

United Native America (UNA) (2000) E-mail exchange between Pedro Torres of the Jatibonicu Taino Tribal Nation and Mike Graham of United Native America, regarding Native American bodies listed on the petition for a Native American Holiday. United Native America. Available online: http://www.unitednativeamerica.com/ah1a.htm

United States Department of State (USDoS) (1998) *Background Notes: Trinidad and Tobago*. Washington D.C.: United States Department of State, Bureau of Inter-American Affairs. Available online: http://www.state.gov/www/background_notes/trinidad_tobago_0398_bgn.html

Vargas-Stehney, Valery "Nanturey" (2001) *Bohio Bajacu: Taino Indian Website*: Valery "Nanaturey" Vargas-Stehney. Available online: http://www.angelfire.com/ct/taino/index.html

Vázquez, Richard L. (2001) *The Taino Survival*. Las Culturas.com. Available online: http://www.lasculturas.com/aa/aa100900a.php

Watson, Robert A. (2001) *Native American Timeline*. Raw.communications. Available online: http://www.channel-e-philadelphia.com/natresources.html

Chapter 8

Debating Language and Identity Online

Tongans on the net

Helen Lee

Introduction

An important theme in discussions of globalization has been the tension between its supposedly homogenizing influences and the reassertion and revitalization of cultural identity that occur in response to this process. My concern in this chapter is to explore this issue of cultural identity from the perspective of its links with language. Manuel Castells has argued that, in the context of globalization, "language, the direct expression of culture, becomes the trench of cultural resistance, the last bastion of self-control, the refuge of identifiable meaning" (cited in Warschauer 2000: 155). By focusing on diasporic Tongans' presence in cyberspace I will examine the language/identity intersection through two quite different yet interconnected issues: first, the ways in which language use is contested in negotiations surrounding cultural identity; and second, the role of computer-mediated communication in giving voice to the silenced. My aim is to interrogate the assumption that cultural identity necessarily must be connected to a particular language, and to explore the complex relationship between language and "culture".

The Tongans who have a presence in cyberspace are primarily those living in "Western" nations, particularly the US, New Zealand and Australia. They are mainly adolescents and young adults, who were either born overseas or migrated with their families as young children, and for the most part are urban-dwelling and have access to computers through work, educational institutions, or home. Thus, they are predominantly the children of the migrants who left Tonga seeking better opportunities for themselves and their families. Tonga is an archipelago of coral atolls and volcanic islands in the western Pacific Ocean. Never formally colonized, Tonga was a British protectorate from 1900 to 1970. It is a complexly hierarchical society ruled by a king, but with a Westminster-style Parliament, some members of which are hereditary "nobles". Tonga's economy remains largely reliant on agricultural exports and foreign aid, and, most crucially, on remittances from Tongans now living overseas. Large-scale migration by Tongans began in the late 1960s and declined in the 1980s, as the main host nations tightened their immigration policies, which thus made it increasingly difficult for Tongans to immigrate except through family reunification programs. There are no accurate figures showing the number of Tongans now living abroad, but if Tongans born overseas (and "part-Tongans") are included, my estimation is that there are around 100,000 – approximately the number of people remaining in Tonga.

"Ethnic groups", language, and the world wide web

In considering the issue of global communications for ethnic groups online, Elkins argues that virtual groups "have the potential to be just as fundamental to the identities of some people as the existing ethnic communities whose existence we have taken for granted for decades or even centuries" (1997: 141). Although Elkins does not specifically address the issue of language and the internet,[1] his arguments assume that "virtual ethnic communities" will communicate in their own languages. Yet the connection between language and identity in forms of global communications such as the internet is not so simple; in fact, it has been widely assumed that English is, and will remain, the dominant "unofficial global language" of the world wide web (Mitra and Cohen 1999: 189). Discussions of languages other than English have focused on issues such as inequalities of access to computer-mediated communications, and the problems of using particular scripts. However, sites in languages other than English have increased rapidly, so that by August 2000 they constituted fully 31 percent of webpages, and these "other" languages were being used on the internet by 43 percent of users (Abbott 2001: 107). Of course, the issue of unequal access remains; and Abbott reminds us that only about 5.4 percent of the world's population are internet users, with 44 percent of these being in the USA and Canada alone. Such figures tend to be read with the assumption that these users in "Western" nations are "Westerners" conversing in English – but many of these users are in fact from a wide range of migrant, refugee and ethnic groups, and are using many different languages. Some authors acknowledge that the dominance of English on the internet is over, and that the number of non-English sites is continuing to rise and may soon overtake those in English (Crystal 2001: 3). Crystal notes that he has found over 1,000 languages represented on the internet, adding:

> I would guess that about a quarter of the world's languages have some sort of internet presence . . . [however] until a critical mass of internet penetration in a country builds up, and a corresponding mass of content exists in the local language, the motivation to switch from English-language sites will be limited to those for whom issues of identity outweigh issues of information.
>
> (Crystal 2001: 3)

Again, the use of non-English languages within English-speaking nations is ignored. With the tendency in the cyberspace literature to maintain the old "the West versus the Rest" distinction, sites that transcend national borders and undermine this distinction have been generally neglected. In fact, a vast number of people in the "West" are accessing many different kinds of sites in languages other than English, from information-oriented sites for expatriates, to discussion forums, to personal homepages, to online media, and so on.

Many aspects of such sites are worthy of study; my own interest here[2] is their role in the construction and enhancement of collective identities. There is a small but growing body of work in this area, such as the study of Goan sites which beginning in the mid-1990s have been established by diasporic Goan peoples from their small state on the west coast of India (Gomes 2001). Gomes reveals these sites play an important role in the assertion and expression of Goan identity for participants. Sites appealing to dispersed peoples, such as Goans, also facilitate new forms of transnational connections as people within the home countries gain access to computers and the world wide web and begin to participate in discussions, share news and information, and otherwise communicate with the diasporic population. Another study, which looks at Trinidadian participation on the internet, makes the important point that, rather than constructing new identities through their cyberspace encounters, dispersed groups such as ethnic diasporas "hold to older senses of self and place" (Miller and Slater 2001: 85). Miller and Slater describe how Trinidadian participants make the internet "a Trini place, a place where they could be Trini and perform being Trini" (2000: 85). Thus, they are simultaneously representing Trinidad, and constructing representations of it. The participants use English and patois, "the latter written with complete orthographic and syntactic regularity", and at times both, "mixed in highly conscious and playful ways" depending on "context, matters at hand, displays of status or cultural capital and so on" (Miller and Slater 2000: 91). Through this they use language to create "a specifically Trinidadian Internet space" (Miller and Slater 2000: 94).

While Gomes, and Miller and Slater, focus on the use of the internet to assert identity and create particular cultural (cyber)spaces, the issue of language revitalization is also salient. Warschauer observes that speakers of many languages "have already started to make use of the Internet's capacity to connect isolated groups of small numbers of speakers and to allow low-cost archiving and publishing as a way to promote language maintenance and revitalization" (2000: 157). Using the example of Hawai'ian sites in which participants can explore and express their Hawai'ian identities, he shows that such sites can be valuable for individuals who have found it difficult to do this in "real life". He points to the potential of the internet to revitalize minority languages: "defense of language means defense of community, autonomy, and power ... People will struggle to maintain their language when they see it as not only an important part of their grandparents' past, but also of their own future" (Warschauer 2000: 166). Further, he argues, language is "a powerful and flexible medium for assertion of identity against cultural homogenization", and the internet provides "opportunities for those who challenge English-language hegemony" (Warschauer 2000: 167–8). The issues surrounding language and its maintenance or revitalization via the internet are not simple, however, particularly when language becomes a tool for the assertion of status, or for evaluations of "authenticity". The complexities of these issues have been debated by Tongans themselves since they first gained a presence in cyberspace, and continue to be highly contentious.

Tongans on the net

The first internet site to be established by a Tongan was *Tonga Online*, set up in 1995 by Taholo Kami, at the time a student at a US university, as a way to make contact with other Tongans. Linked to this site was the *Kava Bowl* (KB), an online discussion forum, which I followed from early 1996 to late 1998 (see Morton 1999, 2001). Using the visual image of a *kumete*, or *kava* bowl, the forum sought to emulate the informal discussions that take place throughout the Pacific, as men sit and drink kava, talking and singing, often from evening until early morning. Of course, in the virtual case, anyone who can access the site can join the discussions, and at any time: this was indicative of the way communications on the *KB* actually differed significantly, in some respects, from those in "real life".

Although most participants on the *KB* were young, and resident (at least temporarily) in Western nations, there also were many older Tongan participants as well as some non-Tongans. The latter usually were people who had spent some time working in Tonga, were married (or formerly married) to a Tongan, or for some other reason had a particular interest in Tonga and its people. A few of these non-Tongans became very active on the *KB*, as participants and as part of the "KB Admin" who monitored the forum. Tongans of many ages, levels of education and forms of occupation participated, and several older Tongan men were frequent posters whose opinions appeared to be highly valued by the other participants. The *Kava Bowl* proved to be tremendously popular, and by early 1998 was receiving over half a million "hits" per month. Originally a single-discussion forum, it was later split into different forums for purposes such as greetings and announcements, discussion of issues, poetry and creative writing, and so on. However, the *KB* was frequently disrupted by technical problems in 1999 and 2000 and often was not functioning at all; it now seems unlikely to be restored. When the *KB* was unavailable, some regular participants moved to other Tongan and Pacific sites, such as the *Tongan History Association Forum* (until that, too, ceased to function) and the *Polynesian Cafe*.[3] More recently they have turned to new sites, such as *Planet Tonga*, which will be discussed later in this chapter.

Elkins argues that "the technologies which make feasible these new virtual communities will allow existing dispersed ethnic communities to find new means of support, persistence, and governance" (1997: 141). Given the kinds of "virtual communities" Tongans have formed, I doubt whether the latter question of newfound governance could be the case for them, but computer-mediated communication certainly appears to be facilitating the support and persistence to which Elkins refers. Forums like the *KB* have already demonstrated that they can serve to overcome the difficulties posed by geographic dispersal, at least for those who have access to the necessary technology.[4] I have argued elsewhere that transnational ties between the diaspora and Tonga have been in decline, but the emergence of Tongan internet sites (based in Tonga and overseas) might encourage a resurgence of such ties, as well as build and strengthen increasing ties across the diaspora (Lee 2004). In its heyday, the *KB* formed an extension of the existing Tongan diasporic global community, rather than existing simply as a "virtual community". Much of the information shared was about events and people offline, and to some extent the discussions were influenced by Tongan cultural values and behavioral norms. However, as will become clear, the *KB* was also an arena in which these values and norms could be challenged, often by people who would be constrained from doing so in "real life".

Increasingly, links between the diaspora and Tonga are being constructed through email and the internet. Young people who have not had direct contact with relatives in Tonga, and know little about the islands, can now use the various Tongan-oriented sites to access news and information about Tonga, and some are communicating with family members via email. Within Tonga there is strong support for information technologies on the part of the royal family; and funds raised overseas (for example, by ex-students' associations) are now often directed toward establishing computing facilities in even the most remote schools. However, issues of unequal access in Tonga are still significant, with relatively few Tongans being able to afford the high cost of internet connection. In any case, the unreliability of an electricity system prone to power cuts, and ongoing difficulties with servers, mean that access to email and internet communications are often temporarily shut down.

Since *Tonga Online* appeared on the world wide web, many other Tonga-oriented sites have been established by individuals and groups in the diaspora and, to a more limited extent, in Tonga itself. The majority use English as their sole or primary language, and many are designed to appeal to both Tongans and potential visitors to Tonga, offering a wide range of information, current news, and links to related sites. As more diasporic Tongans become computer literate, individual and family homepages are proliferating, most of which proudly identify the owners as Tongan. Moreover, the design of the Tonga-oriented sites has become increasingly sophisticated over the years, and users of the discussion forums have become more familiar with the conventions of computer-mediated communications (e.g., in the use of common abbreviations, acronyms, emoticons, and nicknames). In a survey of the *KB* in 1996 I found 74 percent of posters used their real names (Morton 2001), yet by 2001 very few real names were being used in forums and chatrooms linked to Tongan sites.

Planet Tonga, a site established by Tongan university students in the US early in 2001, is a carefully structured and complex site with 24 separate forums. It, like the others, provides, an array of information, opinions, news, links, and so on.[5] Although the site is vastly different from the *KB* in organization and appearance, it is interesting that the contents of the posts are very similar, as are the proportions of types of post. As on the *KB*, there are serious discussions of current events and issues of interest, but lighthearted exchanges are by far the most common – much like the banter that young people typically exchange in "real-life" situations. The most striking difference between the *KB* and *Planet Tonga* (*PT*) is the predominant use of the Tongan language in the latter. According to PT's webmaster, "the intended audience is anyone who has a vested interest in Tonga" (personal communication, email 4 June 2001); however it would be difficult for someone without fluency in Tongan to follow most discussions and participate fully.

Another site to appear in 2001 was the *Tongan Youth Forum*. Much simpler in design than *Planet Tonga*, it is a single-discussion forum with links to other Tongan and a few religious sites. As its name indicates, it is aimed at young people, and its welcome statement reads: "Tongan Youth recognizes the difficulties that our younger generation encounter at school and their current environments. Therefore, in an attempt to alleviates [sic] these difficulties, we provide this forum to enable discussions and hopefully brings [sic] resolution for these problems." Again, there is a remarkable similarity in the content of the messages compared to the *KB*, and as with the *KB* the predominant language is English.

Language and identity

Although the majority of posts on the *KB* were in English, the issue of language was a pervading theme, particularly its connection to cultural identity. There were many conversations and comments on this topic: a typical example is a post about the importance of young people holding on to Tongan culture, which argues: "the key is to maintain the Tongan language among our people" (25 November 1997). On the *Tongan Youth Forum* (20 June 2001) the same concerns are being expressed:

> i have encountered more tongan young adults and youngsters who are unable to speak their "native" tongue than i would care to meet . . . i fear that this rapidly growing generation of tongans will have no connection to the culture through the avenue we know as language (in this case, the tongan language). what then? will they still be tongan because their roots are embedded in tonga? most definitely, in my perspective, but it will not be the same, no? because if the language is not understood or easily transmittable to them, then what else within the tongan culture is lacking in their life?

Language is an emotional and highly contentious issue for Tongans, and these posts allude to the fact that it has also become a generational issue, since the majority of fluent Tongan speakers outside Tonga are "first-generation" migrants, while their children and grandchildren have much lower rates of fluency. Even the young people who learn some Tongan are considered incompetent speakers, if their pronunciation is poor or their vocabulary limited, and if they have not grasped the intricacies such as the flowery language of speechmaking or the different levels of language used to address chiefs and royalty.

Young people's lack of fluency is partly the result of the decision made by many parents not to teach their children Tongan. One of the primary aims of migration has been to provide children with a good education, and many parents have considered fluency in English to be essential for educational success. Yet even parents who wanted their children to learn Tongan found it difficult, given the children's constant exposure to English at school, through the media and in the wider community. Those who have poor or nonexistent Tongan language skills often become deeply frustrated by the constraints this places on their interactions with fluent members of their kin group, church, and the Tongan "community". When they are at times regarded as not being "real" or "true" Tongans because of their lack of fluency, it can be difficult for them to feel securely Tongan. In my study of Tongans in Melbourne, while 80.6 percent of individuals could speak English very well, only 52.5 percent spoke Tongan very well, and 32.8 percent spoke Tongan not well or not at all (Lee 2003). Many Tongans overseas now converse with one another in English, even those whose first language was Tongan.

Pushing against this trend, there is an active group of younger Tongans who are becoming increasingly vocal (both online and offline) about the importance of language for identity. Typically they represent the better-educated youth who have grown up bilingual and who have a deep appreciation for their fluency in both Tongan and English. They are well aware that many young Tongans are becoming alienated from their "cultural heritage", and they believe this can be linked to problems like delinquency, drug use, dropping-out of high school, and so on. One example of the activities of these advocates can be found at the site *Planet Tonga*, which includes a *Tonga Language Journal* "created to help maintain and enhance the use of our native language". Here, Tongans are encouraged to post writings in Tongan, such as poems and speeches, and to respond to postings on a discussion forum.[6] Tevita Ka'ili, who was involved in establishing *Planet Tonga*, reasoned that "one of the best ways to revitalize and enrich a language is to create a publishing place and a written literary tradition (native speakers writing poems, songs, stories, speeches, essays)" (personal communication, email 4 June 2001). He explained that the name of the language journal – *Tefua 'a Vaka Lautala*, which translates as "the gathering of the boats of Lautala" – is meant to imply "the gathering of many skilled individuals to embark on a difficult work". This language journal and its associated forum sparked interesting discussions, almost entirely in Tongan and covering various topics. For example, in the autumn of 1998, a heated discussion ensued about the use of Tongan versus English on the *KB*.[7] One poster argued that reading the Tongan messages "helps me with my attempts of learning and retaining a language of which I only used to know the kapekape [swear words] and 'Malo e lelei' [greetings], etc. When I come across something I don't understand, I look up my Tongan dictionary or ask for help". Likewise, another post in this thread stated:

> I appreciate the Tongan posts because then I get to measure my shabby Tongan to it and IMPROVE it. Why can't all you non-Tongan speaking TONGANS learn how to speak Tongan? Our language is the backbone of our culture, not English-the coloniser's language. Learn to be bilingual . . . it's a shame you don't know your own language.

A message from a non-Tongan complaining about the use of the Tongan language led a Tongan man in the US to implore the "virtual guest" to "please adapt to our language and customs". Another response to the initial post, from a Tongan in New Zealand, read: "The call for English is understandable but you forget there are also Tongans who would appreciate exchanging views or pleasantries in Tongan – not to be exclusive but to revel in the unique use of our language. There are not too many forums where this sort of exchange can take place so why not on the KB?"[8]

Inclusivity versus exclusivity

The recurring question of just who the KB should be for – how inclusive or exclusive it should be – centered around the issue of language. For the most part, it was assumed that the major issue was whether the forum should be primarily for Tongans – and therefore use the Tongan language – or whether it should be more widely accessible – and therefore use English. Differing visions of the possibilities of cyberspace emerged, with some participants envisioning sites like the KB as the means to represent Tongans to "outsiders", while others were more concerned with generating communication between dispersed Tongans. The willingness of some bilingual Tongans to have KB posts in English, for a non-Tongan "audience", to some extent reflects their view of their role in "real life" as representing Tongan culture to the host society; other bilingual Tongans who are more influenced by postcolonial critiques of "the West" regard discussions in Tongan as vital expressions of cultural identity. The first of these positions was expressed by a Tongan man living in the US, who (on 10 February 1998) wrote:

> This is like those of us Polys [Polynesians] who speak our language in the presence of those who do not speak it. It is rude, inconsiderate, and arrogant. At least in this forum one could translate into English what one writes. There are so few of us speaking our language but there are millions of English speakers around the world who could benefit from our input.

Why limit your contribution to a few hundreds (???) and deny millions who would come here to learn what we're all about? The more we write in English the better people will understand our trials and struggles. . . . The Internet is for "sharing." We cannot share our thoughts, our culture, and what we are so proud of if we are only talking amongst ourselves.

A response to his post (on 10 February 1998) by another US-based Tongan took the opposite view:

This forum was created by a Pacific Islander primarily for Pacific Islanders. While I welcome non-Pacific Islanders, I do not want them insisting that we speak English . . . part of "reaching as many netters" as possible is exposing them to our beautiful written language. If a reader needs a translation, the reader should unilaterally go out and get a translation.

It is interesting to note that the second poster referred to Pacific Islanders; there was a common slippage in *KB* discussions between the terms "Tongans" and "Pacific Islanders" (and similar terms such as "Polys" or "Polynesians") which ignored the language differences between these groups. The "pan-ethnic" terms were commonly used to assert a strong sense of solidarity with other Islanders, yet, even allowing for the similarities between some Pacific languages, it can safely be assumed that many non-Tongan Pacific Islander participants would not be able to read posts in Tongan. Assertions of inclusivity of identity thus neglected the exclusivity created by language use!

KB participants who argued for the use of the Tongan language often pointed out that older Tongans with poor English were excluded from participating in *KB* discussions. One young woman said her parents felt excluded, and (on 10 February 1998) retorted angrily to the non-Tongan who complained about posts in Tongan:

YOU are NOT the one that is being segregated or left out! IT'S OUR PARENTS!! We are missing the knowledge and wisdom of all Tongan parents because we have unconsciously left them out of our cyberspace world. . . . By asking us not to speak Tongan, is the same as asking us not to be Tongans (which WE ARE). Isn't that why you visited our forum? If you are interested in Tongans, then you also need to take interest in their language. If you notice the name of this Forum, it's called "KAVABOWL." Kava is a Tongan word and Bowl is an English word. Tongan and English. The Tongan word is first and foremost, English secondary. And that's how you should expect to find topics written. If it's in English you're welcome to read and respond. If it's in Tongan, then it does not pertain to you because you are NOT Tongan and you would not understand its meaning anyways!!!!?

Others were less concerned with exclusion than with identity maintenance, as with the poster who (on 10 February 1998) described language as "the main tool" for perpetuating culture and advocated the occasional use of Tongan as "a cultural reality check". Awareness that non-Tongans participated in and "lurked" on the *KB* led some posters to use the Tongan language to address remarks only to Tongan speakers. In addition, while many participants who posted in English expressed controversial opinions on a whole range of issues, some preferred to discuss sensitive issues in Tongan and thus limit their "audience". For example, one long post (on 22 August 1996), arguing that Tongans overseas needed to "let go" of some of their cultural values and practices in order to succeed in their jobs, strategically switched back and forth between Tongan and English. The post began in English: "There is something that has been bothering me for quite some time now. This is regarding our Tongan community overseas." The writer then switched to using Tongan for any potentially controversial comments, but ended the message in English with the explanation: "Sorry for going back and forth from Tongan to English but I feel it to be a very touchy subject, that I don't want any hard feelings and what not." However, there were considerable differences in what posters considered sensitive issues, and there did not appear to be any topics that participants were unwilling to discuss in English.

What is striking about many of these posts is that they ignore the crucial fact that today so many Tongans, particularly young people, do not speak, read or write Tongan. Many posts on the *KB* were confessions by people who did not know Tongan, who expressed their regret and frustration about this, and who described being ridiculed and rejected by Tongan speakers. Parents also contributed, expressing their own frustration in trying to ensure their children spoke Tongan. The forum was used not just to describe their feelings and experiences, and receive often sympathetic responses, but also as a way to ask other Tongans to make allowances for those unable to use Tongan fluently. One post (on 16 April 1997) was from a Tongan raised in the US, aged 30, who could "barely speak Tongan . . . I get frustrated and embarrassed when I do try to speak and people mimic my Western accent and mock my ignorance". Another (on 3 March 1997) pled for fellow Tongans to "build up our people by TEACHING instead of CONDEMNING". It would be difficult for young Tongans to say any of these things in "real life", given the barriers to such communication imposed by the hierarchical social structure and associated values such as respect and humility emphasized in Tongan culture (Morton 1996). As I argue below, the *KB* and similar sites provide a rare opportunity for such sentiments to be articulated.

Tonglish

The strong presence of young Tongans on the *KB* was revealed not only in the content of the discussions, but also in the kinds of language used in many posts. In order to claim at least a modicum of "authenticity", those who could speak some Tongan included what they could, particularly commonly-used terms and phrases, such as the expressions *"ofa atu"* ("love to you") and *"faka'apa'apa atu"* ("respect to you") at the end of messages. Tongan versions of English words were also used, as in "*Amelika*" for America. Bonnie Urciuoli observes that those who are not "full speakers" of a language still use what they do know to create a sense of belonging, and often use their limited language ability in innovative ways (1995: 530). This also can be seen in the use of an interesting combination of Tongan and English, known as "Tonglish", in which both languages were combined. This has also been used on *Planet Tonga*, and the following post (on 31 May 2001) exemplifies the creative and complex constructions that might be involved: "Sup NoKalo. . . . fefe hake. . . . well we're nettin' from da kiwi land of white cloud. NZ all da way. . . . Very nice to hear from our peepz around da world especially moutolu mei he fonua lahi koena. . . . Much ofa atuz".[9] As this message shows, "Tonglish" also incorporates the variations of English that many young Tongans overseas have adopted, such as rap, gang and street talk, and/or "black English" (i.e. Ebonics). As such it is an important statement of hybridized identity. Many young people value this ability to play with languages, particularly when an obvious ease with Tongan is cleverly combined with forms of English fashionable among youth in the dominant culture. However, these variants of English were not welcomed by all *KB* participants, as in the following message (posted on 14 October 1997) by "Tongan Pride":

> As I scroll through the *KB* on a daily basis, I find myself perturbed, most of the time annoyed with a lot of the language that goes on in here. Is it me or is our future generation of Tongan/Americans becoming obsessed with "street talk"? I find it hard to believe that most of these individuals use "slang" with their parents, in school, or at their jobs. . . . Remember, talk conveys more than just your intelligence. It says a lot about who you are, what kind of background you come from, and will gain you respect in this very dominated world where we are the minorities. I can understand Tongan slang, but the "props, yo, wuzz," etc. is weird. The ability to communicate effectively will impact more than you think.

To some extent, arguments about the appropriate use of English reflect cross-generational differences, but they also expose attitudinal differences amongst young people, partly related to different socio-economic backgrounds. The heated discussions about the word "nigger" and its many variants (e.g., niggas, n****z, nigg@) demonstrated this most starkly. Over a period of several months a number of messages criticized some people on the forum who referred to each other using this term. Some responses defended its use, as in those by "GHETTO PRODUCT NIGG@" and "NIGGA 4 LIFE!!!!", and the poster who wrote:

> We peeps out in Killa Cali [California] may act Black and dress like it but when it comes down to our culture we REPRESENT our POLYNESIAN

ROOTS so you betta chickty check yo self on that point and don't PLAYA HATE on killa CALI FOLKS cause we ain't even tryin to HATE on ya (25 March 1998).

Conversely, a series of defensive posts countered with the title "proud to be Ebonics free!!!" One message in this series ended by stating emphatically: "Niggaz are for blacks. Islanders are for polynesians . . . there's no polynesian pride to be a nigga!" (25 March 1998). Other posts reminded participants of the Tongan values of respect and humility, and urged posters to uphold these, not only in order to maintain "the Tongan way", but also to present Tongans as favorably as possible to anyone accessing the site. In seeking to manage heated discussions, the *Kava Bowl* administrators supported censorship, stating that they reserved the right to delete posts that contained abusive language or personal attacks, and any posts that showed "total disregard for the conservative sensibilities held by the largest portion of the 'population' in *KB*" (20 February 1998). In similar fashion, *Planet Tonga* posts a statement of "Rules and Agreement" that restricts vulgar language and defamatory comments. However, unlike the *KB*, *PT* states that it does "not actively monitor the contents" of messages posted, thus placing responsibility more squarely upon the participants. Finally, it is of note that the *iTonga* forum actually closed down due to abusive and inappropriate language.

These discussions reveal highly divergent constructions of "Polynesian", reflecting equally divergent experiences of growing up overseas. Yet identifying as Polynesian remains important to all of the participants; through this and many other discussions the very grounds of Tongan (and, more broadly, Polynesian) identity were being contested and negotiated. Language became the pivotal issue in many of these discussions, as the equation between identity and particular forms of language use was debated.

Giving voice to the silenced?

These debates about language use on Tongan internet sites raise important issues about the roles of these kinds of "ethnic virtual communities": to what extent do they offer possibilities for reconstructions of identity, for challenges to the status quo of "real-life" communities, and how much are they simply extensions of those communities and the kinds of social relations they encompass? Or do these computer-mediated forms of communication, particularly their relative anonymity, merely allow for the open discussion of issues and opinions that are also present – but "taboo" and largely unspoken – offline?

As their statement about censorship reveals, the *KB* administrators certainly made concessions to the "conservative sensibilities" of some participants, and explicitly portrayed this as maintaining "Polynesian culture and tradition". Yet the discussions were allowed to go far beyond the limits of such sensibilities in many respects, and the *KB* enabled existing undercurrents to surface for all to see. Commoners were able to express criticisms of the power structures within Tonga: the monarchy, the government, the nobility, and the church. More broadly, the hierarchical values and social structuring of Tongan society (at home and abroad) were questioned. Diasporic Tongans could express their resentments about their treatment in their host societies. Women could complain about men drinking too much kava and neglecting their families, and gender relations more generally could be critiqued. Topics that are rarely discussed openly by Tongans could be broached: child abuse and domestic violence, homosexuality, abortion, teenage sexuality, and so on.

In the vigorous debates that ensued when such topics were raised, a whole spectrum of perspectives would emerge, revealing immensely wide-ranging views, not just of the topic at hand but also of the more fundamental issues of what it means to be Tongan and how Tongans should position themselves in relation to host societies. While some participants were deeply shocked and offended to see such topics openly discussed, the majority relished the opportunity to present their opinions and experiences. Young people were given a voice through the *KB* and other sites in a way they had not experienced within their own families and communities. They could criticize everything from the King of Tonga to their parents' child-rearing practices; they could describe their experiences and feelings, and share their problems. The role played by the *KB* in this regard was acknowledged many times by participants. One wrote (on 12 January 1998):

> The kavabowl helps give us cultural identity and unity; especially to the second-generation students outside of Tonga. We learn from each other and seek for those examples to emulate within our own culture. We have an opportunity for some of the things we are too afraid to discuss with our parents or leaders. The kavabowl has been the means for our finding answers and reflecting on very important decisions for our lives.

Tongan youth often experience a significant disjuncture between the "outside world" of school and non-Tongan peers, and their Tongan homes and communities, and it is clear that some turn to discussion forums to find ways to deal with this, even if only by finding others who share their difficulties.

Identity issues figured largely in their discussions and, as we have seen, the language they used expressed their identities and challenged the widely shared notions of what it means to be Tongan. Many proudly asserted their Tongan identities, defying those who would deny them authenticity because of their lack of language abilities and knowledge of "the Tongan way". Many of those young people who aired their views on the *KB* did so in English; for many it was their only language, and while their lack of Tongan, combined with their youth, would normally create a double barrier to the expression of such views, the *KB* circumvented both. For them, and for the other users of the site, language ability was not a barrier in posting messages. It was reading messages that caused problems for those who were not bilingual, and those without good knowledge of English would have had limited access to the discussions. On *Planet Tonga* this has been reversed, and individuals with little or no Tongan are now the ones who are less able to fully participate. *Planet Tonga* does not prevent participation in English, but one has to wonder whether the dominant use of Tongan is also serving to silence some of the young Tongans who participated so eagerly in the English-language *KB* discussions. On the other hand, it could be argued that the predominance of Tongan in *PT* discussions means that, overall, young participants are able to communicate their messages to a wider cross-section of the Tongan "community", including those with poor English. Unlike the *KB* there seems to be little input from non-Tongans at *PT* – the high proportion of posts in Tongan seems to preclude this, making it more exclusively Tongan than *KB* ever was. The plethora of Tongan and other Pacific sites gives young people a wide choice of forums in which to participate, and sites such as the *Tongan Youth Forum* continue to cater to those with poor Tongan language ability.

The various discussion forums seem to be reflecting a growing division amongst young, diasporic Tongans, between those who speak Tongan and those who do not. The former tend to be accepted as "authentically" Tongan by the older generations, and those who are bilingual and well-educated are emerging as the new "elite" within the diasporic populations. They are respected for their language skills and knowledge of Tongan etiquette, as well as their ability to succeed in the host societies. Some express a distinctly post-colonial critique of historical and contemporary relations between Tongan and "Western" societies, while also challenging some aspects of the Tongan way. The internet is but one way of disseminating their views.[10] At the same time, young people who do not speak Tongan are becoming increasingly marginalized and disaffected, even when they want to identify as Tongan, and, ironically, even when their lack of Tongan is due to their parents' desire for them to succeed overseas. These are the young people for whom the pan-ethnic identifications of Polynesian and Pacific Islander are more appealing, and who are more likely to turn to English-language forums, including the more generally "Pacific" forums. One of the difficulties with cyberspace as a field of investigation is that, when a "virtual community" such as the *KB* simply ceases to exist, it is impossible to trace what happens to its members. Some familiar nicknames from the *KB* now appear on *Planet Tonga* and the *Tongan Youth Forum* (and appear to be the same people), but the rest of the "KBers" have either moved to other sites or are no longer online (or have changed names). Similarly, while the project of language revitalization which is central to the aims of *Planet Tonga* is laudable, its impact cannot be gauged, except anecdotally. We cannot accurately measure the "real-world" impact of such discussion forums or even how many individuals participate in them. Nevertheless, the forums themselves provide tremendously valuable insights – into the contested nature of cultural identity and its relationship to language, for example. Cyberspace is a "field" in which anyone with access to a computer

and internet connection can gain a voice, and forums like the Tongan examples I have discussed here can add completely new dimensions to our
understanding of those who, in "real life", are so much less free to speak.

Language issues are clearly becoming central concerns in the debates about
cultural identity occurring within and between groups, as well as being critical
to self-perceptions, and this is reflected in the kinds of internet discussions I
have considered here, which deal with inclusivity and exclusivity, authenticity
and inauthenticity, censorship and freedom of expression. Some of those participating in Tongan internet sites would wholeheartedly agree with Castells that
language is "the direct expression of culture" and the ultimate means of
retaining identity in the face of globalization. Others, however, would reflect on
their own experiences and their attempts to assert their identities despite their
lack of competence in Tongan, and they would argue that it is not so simple.
Language and "culture" have a complex and often confusing relationship which,
for young people, like those in the Tongan diaspora, can add to the challenges
inherent in the process of identity construction.

Notes

1   Elkins is concerned mainly with the creation of "virtual ethnic communities"
     through telecommunications, i.e. through television programs with global coverage
     that can be targeted to specific language and ethnic groups. However, he also
     mentions email and the internet as facilitating "personal interaction with other
     members of the community throughout the world" (1997: 148).
2   My research on Tongan participation on the internet was part of a broader project
     on the Tongan diaspora, focusing on young people and the construction of cultural
     identities (see Lee 2003). This project was funded from January 1995 to June 1996
     by a Postdoctoral Fellowship at the University of Melbourne, held in the Gender
     Studies Research Unit, Department of History. Further funding was granted by the
     Australian Research Council in the form of a Postdoctoral Fellowship held in the
     School of Sociology, Politics and Anthropology (now the School of Social Sciences)
     at La Trobe University, from July 1996 to June 1999. My involvement with the
     Tongan History Association (THA) extended my interests in Tongan participation
     on the internet, when I was the moderator of the THA discussion forum, linked to
     the Kava Bowl site, from 1998 to 2000. Neither forum is currently active online. I
     have also followed with interest the emergence of numerous other Tongan sites, and
     I am grateful to the site owners for their permission to research these sites.
3   Although I am focusing here on participation in internet discussion forums, Tongans
     have also explored other means of computer-mediated communication, often in associ-
     ation with such forums. For example, two email discussion lists were set up on *Tonga
     Online*, which were active for relatively short periods; later e-groups were used, also by
     Tonga Online. Today it has an email discussion group claiming to have 600 members.
     For a while, a site based in Tonga, *Tongatapu* on the Net, generated a newsletter that
     was sent to an email list, summarizing current news from Tonga and the diaspora.
4   The issue of access is pertinent, and of course it is impossible to gauge accurately
     how many Tongans actually use these sites, or share and receive information via
     people who do. The *KB* was reaching the heights of its popularity while I was
     conducting my fieldwork in Melbourne, and I was impressed by how quickly word of
     it had spread. Many young people I spoke with had accessed the *KB* or other
     Tongan-oriented internet sites. However, in this paper I do not assume that all, or

even a majority, of Tongans have access to the technology and skills required to participate regularly in discussion forums like the KB.

5 Included on the Planet Tonga site are a "spotlight" section that describes the accomplishments of Tongans, a collection of current news articles about Tonga or diasporic Tongans, featured articles by Tongans, an online phonebook listing Tongans worldwide, and announcements about a range of events such as anniversaries, weddings, graduations, and festivals. The layout for the forums is far more sophisticated than was the KB layout, with information about how many topics have been raised, how many posts, who started the topic (by nickname), when the latest post was made, and who moderates each forum. There is also a separate page listing all posts for the current day, which bulletin board they are posted on, and the author's (nick)name.

6 An interesting feature of Tongans' use of cyberspace is the use of Tongan words for English terms: I have seen "cyberspace" translated into Tongan, "*i taumama'o*" (literally: very high and distant); and Tevita Ka'ili observed that the word "*paenga*" has been used for "forum". He explains: "*Paenga* is a mat on which the game of *lafo* (a disc-throwing game) is played. The word '*paenga*' is hardly used in Tonga because the game of *lafo* is rarely played by Tongans. The word '*lafo*' is used metaphorically to mean the tossing of ideas . . . Here, we can see how the word '*paenga*' has emerged to mean forum. In this sense, paenga is the mat for tossing of ideas. This is a unique Tongan translation of the word forum . . . The word '*leke*' has also been resurrected to refer to forum or chatroom. *Leke* is an old Tongan word for 'room' in the Tongan *fale* [house]" (personal communication, email 4 June 2001).

7 In addition to the discussion forum, the KB had four "chatrooms" in which participants could communicate synchronically. My observations of these suggested that Tongan was used more often in the chatrooms than on the forum. However, the content of the conversations was much less serious and, as these conversations were "viewed" by far fewer people and were not archived, I decided to focus on the discussion forum.

8 One problem with the use of the Tongan language in computer-mediated communication is its reliance on macrons, accent marks that indicate the pronunciation of a word and thereby distinguish it (and its meaning) from words with similar characters. Given that macrons are cumbersome to formulate using basic software and tend to travel poorly over networks, their absence in online texts can significantly alter the meaning of words.

9 "*Sup NoKalo*" is a greeting to another poster, using his/her nickname (as in, "what's up, *NoKalo?*"), "*fefe hake*" is a common Tongan greeting ("how are you?"), "our *peepz*" refers to other Tongans ("*peepz*" is slang for "people"), "*moutolu mei he fonua lahi koena*" means "all of you from the big country [in this case, America]", and finally "*ofa atuz*" is a version of "*ofa atu*", or "love to you".

10 See Franklin (2001). In Lee (2003) I examine other means which young people are using to express their views, such as art, creative writing, and so on.

References

Publications

Abbott, Jason (2001) "Democracy@internet.asia? The Challenges to the Emancipatory Potential of the Net: Lessons from China and Malaysia", *Third World Quarterly* 22(1): 99–114.

Crystal, David (2001) "Weaving a Web of Linguistic Diversity: The Global English Debate", *The Guardian Weekly* 25–31 January, 164(5): 3.

Elkins, David (1997) "Globalization, Telecommunication, and Virtual Ethnic Communities", *International Political Science Review* 18: 139–52.

Franklin, Marianne (2001) *The Internet and Postcolonial Politics of Representation: Pacific Traversals*. Doctoral dissertation, University of Amsterdam.

Gomes, Alberto (2001) "Going Goan on the Goa-Net: Computer-Mediated Communication and Goan Diaspora", *Social Analysis* 45(1): 53–80.

Jones, Steve (ed.) (1999) *Doing Internet Research: Critical Issues and Methods for Examining the Net*. Thousand Oaks, CA: Sage.

Ka'ili, David, and 'Anapesi Ka'ili (1999) "Can We Become Tongan Without Speaking Tongan?", *Moana* 4: 15.

Mitra, Ananda and Cohen, Elisia (1999) "Analyzing the Web: Directions and Challenges", in S. Jones (ed.), *Doing Internet Research: Critical Issues and Methods for Examining the Net*. Thousand Oaks, CA: Sage, pp. 179–202.

Miller, Daniel and Slater, Don (2001) *The Internet: An Ethnographic Approach*. Oxford: Berg.

Lee, Helen Morton (2002) *Between Two Shores: Tongans Overseas*. Honolulu: University of Hawai'i Press.

——(Forthcoming) "All Tongans are Connected: Tongan Transnationalism", in V. Lockwood (ed.), *Pacific Island Societies in a Global World*. Englewood Cliffs, NJ: Prentice Hall.

Morton, Helen (1996) *Becoming Tongan: An Ethnography of Childhood*. Honolulu: University of Hawai'i Press.

——(1999) "Islanders in Space: Tongans Online", in R. King and J. Connell (ed.), *Small Worlds, Global Lives: Islanders and Migration*. London: Pinter, pp. 235–53.

——(2001) "I is for Identity: What's in a Name?", *Social Analysis* 45(1): 69–82.

Urciuoli, Bonnie (1995) "Language and Borders", *Annual Review of Anthropology* 24: 525–46.

Warschauer, Mark (2000) "Language, Identity, and the Internet", in B. Kolko, L. Nakamura and G. Rodman (eds), *Race in Cyberspace*. New York: Routledge, pp. 151–170.

Links

Planet Tonga. http://planet-tonga.com
Tonga Online. http://www.tongaonline.com
Tongan Youth Forum. http://www.voy.com/17898/

Chapter 9

Deterritorialized People in Hyberspace
Creating and debating Harari identity over the internet

Camilla Gibb

Introduction[1]

In 1991, Ethiopians abroad celebrated as revolutionary forces toppled the socialist dictatorship that had ruled their country of origin for nearly two decades. This regime, known as the *Dergue*, will be remembered by many Ethiopians and foreign observers as a reign of terror during which the government committed gross systematic and wide-scale human rights abuses.[2] Not only did the atrocities committed by the *Dergue* throughout the 1970s and 1980s create massive internal displacement, but hundreds of thousands of Ethiopians were scattered worldwide in search of refuge. In less than two decades, a global diaspora was created of people from a country with no previous history of emigration.

Diaspora, the idea of people who imagine themselves as a nation outside of a homeland, is a phenomenon implying movement – not only dispersal, but often that of an idealized return.[3] Until recently, Ethiopians living outside the country were considered to be living in exile, an undesirable and involuntary state of homelessness that could only be rectified by returning. In the Ethiopian case, the possibility of return became an option in 1991. The majority of those living in exile, however, did not seize upon that opportunity. This has forced the creation of an identity that acknowledges the permanence of diaspora, and demands the establishment of borders which define a community in global terms.

In this chapter I explore aspects of this negotiation amongst members of one Ethiopian community: the Harari, a community of Muslim Ethiopians originally from the city of Harar. The Harari are today a dispersed community, with one third of their population now scattered across the globe. With the launching of a Harari email discussion forum and several websites devoted to their history, language and culture, Hararis are using the internet as a space within which the widest number of people from the community living abroad can "meet" to debate and create a new global identity. Ironically, however, this conversation tends to exclude Hararis in Ethiopia (who lack access to the new information-communications technologies) and most elders living abroad (who are generally not conversant in English and/or in the technological language required to participate). Elders are well aware of what is communicated, though, as emails are regularly shared, translated and debated within families and community associations in different cities.

In the deterritorialized space of cyberspace, where time and space are compressed and constructions are detached from any local reference, a limited number of Hararis are invoking a new language of nationhood in order to give shape to a now-dispersed community. This is an example of how new media can provide a forum for the creation of national identity outside national borders, and how those with access to this technology are the ones most active in that discussion. This exploration of the use of new media offers insight into the ways in which transnational and, more broadly, trans-temporal and trans-spatial processes are involved in redefining community relations and identities amongst dispersed peoples in a postmodern world. Some scholars have called such identities transmigrant or transnational rather than emigrant, in order to suggest that identities are multiply constituted and lived across borders.[4] These identities may, in fact, be further complicated by the creation of an additional border or dimension – a virtual reality within which aspects of community and culture are simultaneously being defined.

Harari homeland and history

The Harari homeland is not the country of Ethiopia: it is the small walled city of Harar in the eastern highlands. Harar was founded as early as the ninth century, and the walled interior was built in the sixteenth century as a defensive measure. The city has been legendary among Ethiopians and adventurous European travelers.[5] Hararis governed what was an independent Muslim city state and a center of commerce and Islamic scholarship for several centuries. As a population, they stood in a privileged position with respect to the neigh-bouring populations of Oromo, Somali, Argobba and Afar. Hararis owned the fertile farmland around the city, monopolized trade in the marketplace, and converted neighboring populations to Islam. While they were able to fend off successive attempts at invasion by warring factions of Oromo over the centuries, in 1887 the Harari army (which included both Hararis and enculturated Oromo) was ultimately defeated by the Amharas. The Amhara army (of Abyssinian Christian highlanders) annexed Harar in their campaign of territo-rial expansion, incorporating it into the country we know today as Ethiopia. As Hararis consider their city and its inhabitants to have been occupied and annexed by these colonizing Amharas, they have long maintained that their identity is distinct.[6]

During the twentieth century the Harari minority lived under two successive Amhara dictatorships: an imperial state established by King Menelik and latterly headed by Africa's longest reigning leader, Haile Selassie; and the socialist dictatorship known as the Dergue, which emerged from the bloody revolution which overthrew the imperial regime in 1974. Over the course of this time, Christian nationalists dominated Ethiopian politics, despite the fact that somewhere in the order of 60 percent of the country's residents were acknowledged to be Muslim (as suggested by a 1994 census under the new democratic government). In the attempt to unify and bring under central control the disparate peoples of Ethiopia, the language of the Amharas was adopted as the national language and Ethiopian Orthodox Christianity as the official religion of the state. Under Haile Selassie's rule (1930–1974), government propaganda, asserting that Ethiopia was a Christian island in a Muslim sea, was used to solicit support from the United States against the "Muslim threat". The *Dergue* military dictatorship which seized power from Emperor Selassie in 1974 none the less continued its policy of enforced linguistic, religious and cultural conversion, exercising brutal and oppressive measures designed to suppress ethnic difference (see Kinfe 1994: 155, 157).

Since the overthrow of the *Dergue* in 1991, Ethiopia has adopted a democratic constitution, which nominally guarantees basic human rights including the right to freedom of expression in ethno-cultural and religious terms.[7] The government elected in 1995 proposed to restructure the country along ethnic lines, dividing the country into nine ethnic regions, which were granted the right to self-determination (up to and including the right to secession). It was on this basis that Eritrea gained independence from Ethiopia in 1993, after thirty years of protracted struggle, though border disputes continue to this day. It was on this basis too that Harar became the smallest of these newly-defined autonomous regions. In this new era, after more than a century of foreign rule, Hararis have been granted the right to govern their city again. While the Hararis have seen dramatic changes over recent decades, they remain an affluent and exclusive community, and now have administrative control over a region where they are far outnumbered by resident Oromo and Amhara populations. This suggests a situation more complicated than a macro-political perspective (like that given above, which divides the country neatly into the oppressors and the oppressed). While national rule was indeed Amhara, the hierarchies of power in local sites were complexly stratified and often reflected long-standing historical patterns.

The historical pattern for Hararis found them at the apex of what Waldron described as a "pyramid of ethnic stratification" (Waldron 1974: 6), referring to a centuries-long dominance over both agriculture and trade. In the early twentieth century, when the French railway linking the capital city to the coast through nearby Dire Dawa was built, the city of Harar declined in importance as a primary trading center. Nearly all Hararis moved into commerce (in order to capitalize on the cheap influx of new foreign goods that came by way of Dire Dawa), and they rented their farmland to Oromo tenants in a kind of feudalist arrangement where Hararis constituted a wealthy landed class. On coming to power in the mid-1970s the Dergue sought to abolish private property and collectivize farmland. This socialist rule had dramatic repercussions on the Harari: politically (including the execution of significant numbers of Harari involved in resistance movements); and economically (by undermining their relative economic prestige over neighboring populations). However, in many cases the Harari managed to retain control over their land through creative arrangements with their Oromo tenants, and through subdividing their land within families into the ten-hectare plots which individuals were permitted to own. Hararis have long been skilled traders, popularly likening themselves to the Jews of America, and continued to dominate the markets of Harar. During the years of oppression and because of their relative affluence, a larger percentage of Hararis were able to secure passage abroad than was the case for members of many other populations. Those abroad sent back substantial remittances to their families, which have continued to support the historical pattern of marked differentials in wealth between Hararis and their neighbors.

Today, as a wealthy, highly literate and exclusively urban community, Hararis have come to be better represented proportionately in the new central government than any other ethnic group. The right to rule their city was won through vocal assertions of their previous autonomy. With popular party slogans like "The history of Harar is not the history of Ethiopia", their representative party, the Harari National League, has been able to demand recognition of the former autonomy of the city state.

Harari diaspora and the imperative of return

The first extensive ethnographic work on the Hararis was undertaken in the early 1970s, before the *Dergue* regime began to deny foreign researchers access to most parts of the country. At that time, the community was described as a "one-city culture" – with the vast majority of the population living within the city walls and sharing something they described as a moral commitment to remaining there, and, in particular, to defending the city from outside forces (Waldron 1974). Over the two decades from the 1970s to the 1990s, approximately two-thirds of the community left Harar, however: one-third took up residence in larger Ethiopian cities, and the other third sought political asylum abroad. Most eventually settled in Europe, North America and Australia, and sought citizenship in foreign lands. The establishment of these communities abroad has continued to attract Harari in the post-dictatorship era. Migration thus presents a new historical option for the younger generation of Ethiopian Hararis, seeking educational and/or economic prospects, or to be reunited with family. Today, Hararis in diaspora are concentrated in the major urban centers of Toronto, Washington, Dallas, Houston, Atlanta, Los Angeles and Sydney. Only one third of the total population of Hararis remains in the original city.

Nevertheless, while Hararis have become dispersed around the globe, they still call themselves the Ge 'usu, literally "the people of the city of Harar". This highly emotive and place-referential language is used to refer to many aspects of their culture. Yet, in describing their current dispersal, they also see themselves as *butugne 'usu* (dispersed or scattered people) or *baqannga* (refugees – from the verb for flight, escape or evacuation during wartime). As much as they are sons and daughters of the city, Hararis are sons and daughters of transnational passage and a global diaspora. Where the notion of exile is associated with a temporary foreign residence, community-building becomes a diasporic process. Thus, we might ask: What transformations of identity occur when the people of the city leave the city? If Ge 'usu identity refers to a specific place, how is identity recreated in multiple sites, and in whose terms and what language? How is this place embodied, abstracted or widened to encompass a global arena?

Whereas most scholarship on diasporic communities emphasizes the sense of collectivity which dispersed peoples work to achieve, a newly-formed diaspora like the Harari serves to illustrate the generational differences between members and the consequent tensions which occur as a community resettles in multiple sites. "The empowering paradox of diaspora", states Clifford (1994: 322), "is that dwelling here assumes a solidarity and connection with there". In fact, whereas Clifford rightly critiques the assumption that there is a common "there" or "axis of origin and return", equally as problematic is the implicit assumption of a solidarity and connection "here". The diasporic and Western-world orientation of a significant percentage of Harari youth threatens to sever cultural continuity and contact with the city of origin that is their homeland. While a long-established diaspora might share a common cross-generational orientation to a homeland most have never known, a situation involving a parent generation (that flees the homeland as refugees) and their children (who have no memory of the homeland) creates very different cross-generational orientations. Events at "home" necessarily impact upon diasporic identities, yet impact differently in the case of first-generation migrants than in the case of their children. In the early stages of diaspora formation, then, it is likely that generational and gendered differences create tensions that determine what will be shared among subsequent diasporic generations (see Gibb 1999a; Gibb and Rothenberg 2000).

In many diasporic cases, the idea of repatriation to the homeland is phrased as conditional, dependent upon a change in the circumstances which led to dispersal, and often attached (in the collective imagination) to a political or spiritual event such as the establishment of a separate state, the overthrow of a dictatorship, the cessation of war, or, for the more eschatologically oriented, the day of resurrection or the afterlife. Since most Ethiopians who fled their country did so as a result of direct or indirect persecution by the Dergue, the fall of this regime and the installation of a democratic government marked (at that time) the realization of the condition upon which the idea of return was premised. Few Ethiopians have actually returned home, though; and thus the worldwide dispersal of Ethiopians must be recognized as having a permanence, even though repatriation is (for many) now possible. For the Harari, the sentiment "when there is democracy in Ethiopia [we will return]" is being re-articulated as a question of whether or not lasting peace and democracy is ever possible in Ethiopia. The thought of having to give up material gains acquired abroad undoubtedly informs much of this new questioning. Cross-generation differences in attitudes toward repatriation also assert a critical influence. Ethiopian Harari youth in the diaspora – the first generation of Hararis to grow up outside Ethiopia – tend to identify more with the contexts in which the majority of them have been raised than with the distant homeland most left as young children. When repatriation is discussed, it is framed by their experiences in and perceptions of their current environment and not simply by reflections upon a remembered homeland.

For people whose diasporic identities have to some extent been defined in terms of the notion of eventual return to the homeland from which they were (and are) exiled, rejecting the possibility of return once return is made possible inevitably results in a reconsideration of one's place, and one's people, in the world. As Clifford (1994: 307) notes, "Peoples whose sense of identity is centrally defined by collective histories of displacement and violent loss cannot be 'cured' by merging into a new national community". When return home is not possible, resisting merger may be easier: at a distance, home can be idealized and exile considered temporary. With the reopening of space and the creation of the option of return, the language of exile necessarily transforms into the new language of diaspora, and identities are redefined in light of this.

Connecting nation within diaspora

As we have seen, rates of repatriation have been particularly low among Hararis. Aside from a small number of middle-aged men who returned to Harar from exile in the early years to take up positions of leadership in the new administration, most returns "home" have been in the form of visits, particularly for family and/or investment purposes.[8] Connections between the homeland and the diaspora also take the form of correspondence and remittances, as well as traffic in marriage partners. As an endogamous community, Hararis maintain a strict preference for marriage within the group.[9] Arranged marriages were particularly important during the early years of diaspora when the gender ratio was highly imbalanced (given that the first wave of emigrants were predominantly young men). Today, arranged marriages between Hararis are not uncommon and are seen as one way of perpetuating Harari language and culture in the diaspora. In this matter, there remains a preference for marriage to women and girls from the city, as they are seen to embody the homeland. By patrolling its borders in this way, the Harari community tacitly seeks to ensure its survival.

For Hararis living in the diaspora, contact with other Hararis takes place through various networks, including those based on kinship, cultural festivals, sports (such as soccer competitions) and communication. The fastest and easiest mode of communication has proven to be *Harari-Net* (*H-net*), the Harari email discussion list established in 1996. *H-net* brings together Hararis who might otherwise never have the opportunity to interact. Thus it transcends traditional associations, which are primarily based on kinship and physical proximity. The research presented here is based upon my studies of *H-net*, and also includes multi-sited ethnographic work among the Hararis (see Marcus 1995), involving three years of field research in the city of Harar and in Toronto (where nearly 10 percent of Hararis – the largest concentration living outside of Ethiopia – has come to reside). My field research in Toronto has drawn upon complementary sets of relations: participant observation with both individual families and the Harari community association, and my parallel involvement in discussions taking place on *Harari-Net*. Membership of *H-net* requires nomination by one or more Harari "brothers" or "sisters", which means that to a large extent this virtual community is founded on real-world connections. I was allowed access to this closed and moderated list, otherwise exclusively subscribed to by Hararis. Some of the methodological concerns which might be legitimately raised relating to the anonymity of this kind of exchange are mediated by the fact that I, as well as most of the subscribers, know many of the *H-net* members in person. Indeed, people frequently elaborate on discussions raised on *H-net* when they meet face to face.

The majority of *H-net* subscribers are young men resident in North America. Communication is dominated by Harari teenagers and young adults, many of whom grew up outside Ethiopia – for example, in Somalia, Saudi Arabia and Italy, before coming to the West – and who might thus have been born in the first country of their parents' exile and arrived in North America speaking Arabic or Italian. For many *H-net* members, then, Harar represents something of a mythological homeland, which they do not remember or have never even visited. Return to this place is thus rarely interpreted literally among members of this generation. As Tololyan notes, "it makes more sense to think of diasporan or diasporic existence as not necessarily involving a physical return but rather a re-turn, a repeated turning to the concept and/or the reality of the homeland", an orientation which may be manifest in symbolic, ritual or religious rather than physical terms (Tololyan 1996: 14–15). While this might be true in the case of Jews of the Western diaspora to which Tololyan refers, the parents of the *H-net* generation of Hararis generally still speak of return in literal terms. Their children too, as I discuss here, may invoke return as a literal, physical notion at certain times when they feel insecure about their future in North America.

While there is today this increased contact between Hararis in the homeland and abroad, contact via internet technologies is still largely a matter of exchanges between Hararis in diaspora. This state of affairs allows Hararis in diaspora to construct, circulate and consume images of the homeland over the internet. Because, as Appadurai (1995) notes, "the homeland is partly invented, existing only in the imagination of the deterritorialized groups", the internet is one place where that imagination can speak in visual, textual and interactive terms. It provides an environment in which young, literate and technologically savvy Hararis become in some senses responsible for the communication and creation of their culture in diaspora. The loosening of ties between people and place has fundamentally altered the basis of cultural reproduction in this case. Elders in the community, who have hitherto been responsible for transmitting knowledge of Harari history, religion and culture, are largely excluded from this form of inter-diasporic communication, although many are often informed by their children about the discussions which take place online. Young Hararis who have had no physical relationship with the actual city of Harar are thus engaged in redefining community and identity in the global and largely impersonal arena of cyberspace – a space that largely excludes both elders in the diaspora and Hararis in the homeland.

Precisely what this global identity of Harariness is, though – particularly for the youth of a scattered people whose contact with the homeland has been limited and whose experiences between there and here have been so varied – is unclear. What has been most consistent, perhaps, is the sustained or even increased commitment to Islam in the North American context. For many Hararis, religious identity, rather than national or ethnic identity, has become the most salient point of reference in the diaspora. Many have found in Islam an ideological framework through which to cope with the upheaval of recent decades, and through which to establish new relations in the non-Muslim countries in which they have resettled. In Toronto, for instance, many Hararis (particularly men in their late twenties and thirties) have told me that they have become "more Muslim" since being in Canada. In being part of a larger Muslim community, or *umma*, Hararis become situated in a wider ideological framework and social network from which they can derive support.

For those Hararis who tend to identify first and foremost as Muslims in this context, specific historical knowledge about the city becomes less relevant than the history of Islam (with which most Harari children are taught to be familiar). However, if Hararis are "simply" Muslims, the relevance and meaning of the term "Harari" appears to be unclear to some members of the community. In pondering this, one young man posted the following message on *H-net* entitled WHO AM I? "I've just got one brief question", he wrote. "What makes a Harari . . . Harari???" (signed Wafa, age 18, Texas). The discussion this question generated proved that there was no immediate, obvious or unanimous answer. Until this point, discussion on the net had assumed a shared identity. Wafa was, in all innocence, asking precisely what was shared. "You have to be, believe, feel and understand what it is to be Harari to be Harari" was someone's circular reply. "I subscribe to *H-net* because I am a Harari" was someone else's equally tautological answer. "If I were simply a Muslim, I would only subscribe to Islam-Net, if I identified as an Arab it would be Arab-Net, or as an African, African-Net. As it is, I subscribe to *Harari-Net*". Farhan, a regular contributor and vehement Harari nationalist, posed a similar question in response to Wafa:

> Harar is just the capital city of the Emirate of Harar. You can choose to live anywhere you like. The question is, are you Harari or will you change your ethnicity when you move?

Farhan's answer assumes that there is something constant about Harari identity over time and space. Remaining Harari is in some senses a commitment to the embodiment of place. While the debates which have ensued on *H-net* played with various criteria, primarily linguistic and cultural, and acknowledged both blood lines and assimilation as means of connection to the community, what appeared to be central was the notion of allegiance. One subscriber defined this as "a strong – not superficial – belief that you belong to the Harari Nation". Critical to the Harari understanding of nationhood is kinship: as a nation they are *ahli* (family) and all Hararis are related to each other, as many Harari proverbs assert.

Ahmed, an *H-net* contributor, wrote:

> If we organize ourselves we will be winners – we will attain our goal – we will be one of the recognized nations which has historical background, which has identity, which has its own religion, culture and tradition in the universe.

Other discussants tended to agree with Ahmed's assumption that, through nationhood, identity can be recognizable and permanent. They conceptualized Harar as a nation both historically and in contemporary terms. Its historical appeal was to a glorious and exalted past in which the city stood at the center of an autonomous Muslim state governed by a Harari elite. Today, it enjoys a democratic present in which the Hararis have been granted the right to self-govern the region they historically have dominated. Like other instances of diaspora, where eventually "the concept of homeland is overlaid by the national idea", Hararis have "come to view themselves as members of one nation that is spread across different states" (Tololyan 1996: 14). This illustrates how the concept of nationhood is largely problematic in a world where populations are not bounded by national borders. The condition of dispersal has provoked this particular discussion of Harari nationalism. Whereas Hararis in Harar refer to themselves as a community, a people, or a tribe, young Hararis in the diaspora have begun asserting Harariness as nationality. Somewhat ironically, in order to do so, they must make constant reference to the motherland and discuss what their obligations to it should be. The form of this allegiance, the issue of repatriation, and the experience of Hararis as Muslim Africans in the diaspora, are complexly intertwined – as discussions on *H-net* suggest.

Harari identity in the world at large

Hararis who have grown up in North America describe themselves as "bicultural" and are in many respects more American or Canadian than Ethiopian or Harari. These youth have less romantic, or rather differently conceived, ideals than their parents about their homeland. For example, one of the first questions many youth asked me upon my return from thirteen months of fieldwork in

Harar, was how I could stand the desperately unhygienic conditions, the lack of adequate water, the flies, cockroaches, rats and hyenas, and the lack of modern conveniences which they associate with a city they see as dirty, crowded and "third-world". Still, although many of them might condemn it as third-world, they do not perceive Harar as a hostile, racist world – terms often leveled by Hararis in North America against the government and citizens of the United States. Voiced in the language of racism, and raised on a media which has demonized Muslims – from the Iran-Contra affair, to the Lockerbie bombing, the *fatwa* issued against Salman Rushdie, Saddam Hussein's "mother of all battles", and most recently and most grandly the terrorist ring headed by Osama bin Laden held responsible for the 9-11 terrorist acts – Harari youth in the United States are well aware that as Muslims they are popularly associated with America's post-cold-war public enemy number one.

Whereas members of their parents' generation see return to Harar as a moral imperative, the discussion of repatriation among youth on *H-net* is voiced primarily as a response to the perceived anti-Muslim sentiment in the United States and, by extension and association, in Canada. Return is thus informed less by changes at "home" which are needed to make this option possible, and more by geopolitical events which make the idea of returning "home" (i.e. to a perceived sympathetic climate) an appealing option. These concerns played themselves out dramatically in 2000 through an ongoing discussion about the New Year millennium shift, popularly dubbed Y2K; and they have undoubtedly intensified since the US "war on terror" following the terrorist destruction of American buildings, including the World Trade Center in New York City. With respect to the Y2K shift, the discussions on *H-net* throughout 1999 captured in heightened form the general anxiety concerning a potential impending millennial computer crisis (in retrospect, an imagined crisis that never materialized, but one that many experts and lay people alike predicted and feared would happen at the time). A couple of *H-net* members, prophesying total pandemonium in the year 2000, had already begun in 1998 urgently to encourage Hararis to return home. As one participant, Mohammed, wrote:

> Our chance of survival is greater there. Ethiopia will not be as affected as the US. Of course the impact will be there. Shortage of gasoline and consumer goods will (happen) everywhere . . . Harar is less dependent on electricity, and there is no water and wastewater treatment plants and no chemical plants to worry about. If you acquire land, you could start farming, raising cattle and chickens. All we need to survive is food, water, shelter, and clothing. The rest is luxury and materialism.

In his text, a new romance of the homeland is put forth, with appeals to a return to a simple agricultural existence (ignoring the fact that Hararis, although historically farmers and traders, stopped working the land over a century ago). It idealizes an environment which many young Hararis otherwise imagine as an undesirable place to live. Other *H-net* participants identified additional "advantages" to living in Harar, including "a sewer system which won't fail (because there isn't one)", and "Y2K compliant cooking equipment" (in other words, a fireplace).

H-net members expressed the sentiment that, if Y2K was going to impoverish everyone in North America, then it was better to be poor among your own people. Yet what was mainly at issue was not the fear of the breakdown of infrastructure and the supply of essential resources, but social breakdown as well. As one wrote:

> I would not recommend that you stay in this country. The US is a place that is highly charged with racial tension. With the economic disparities that already exist, when further exacerbated by Y2K induced poverty the whole place could erupt into Balkan style warfare.... There is talk of National Guards being deployed in some states due to Y2K. What is the consequence of that to you? I would only remind you of what the Canadian special forces did to Somalis in Somalia.

Another member added:

> I was watching C-SPAN [a televised news program] last night. The State Department at the CIA were giving a briefing to the Senate subcommittee on Y2K. The issue raised was the possibility of terrorism in the U.S. during the Y2K crisis. And of course I hope we all know who is meant by these terrorists. Whenever there is a problem in the west they always look for a scapegoat. I happened to watch the 700 Club one night. It is a Christian ministry station. They were also discussing Y2K and terrorism. However, unlike the CIA they named who they thought were the potential terrorists, and lo and behold it was us ("the Muslims").

Related to this was the Muslim attitude that millennial anxiety is a Christian superstition: the Muslim calendar, after all, begins 622 years after the Christian calendar (with the *Hijra*, the flight of the Prophet Mohammed and his followers from Mecca to Medina). But while Hararis use the *Hijri* calendar for the purposes of fasting and commemorating other Islamic events, this was false comfort for those who live in the West and those who rely on Western technology based on the Gregorian calendar. Using Islam as a counter-argument, several members responded with appeals to religious faith (or fatalism, depending on your perspective) with sentiments like "Nothing will happen to us that Allah has not willed", or likening this to the punishment God inflicted during Noah's lifetime upon those who disobeyed him. Being Muslim might be a problem in a racist America, but Islam is still salvation.

The *H-net* correspondent Mohammed ended one of his frequent postings on this subject with the following postscript: "In my humble view I believe this is the time . . . *Gey waldow gey giba', tey saribey waraba yagba 'ba"*. This line is from the chorus of an old Harari wedding song and translates as: "Child of Harar, return to Harar. Let the hyena live in the black mountain". The lines are understood to be a call for Hararis to return to where they belong, to their rightful place in the city of Harar. The city is juxtaposed with the black mountain; the hyena is juxtaposed with the child of the city. The black mountain is not a specific place, but an untamed wilderness, a metaphor for all the distant and alien places beyond the city. As an urban population, the place of the Hararis is in the city. The world outside the city wall is inhabited by threatening creatures – hyenas and outsiders. Relations with these outsiders must be carefully negotiated through political, economic and ceremonial means.

The verse above has come to serve as something of an allegory, a narrative device that alludes to historical circumstances and can also refer to the current dispersal of the *Ge waldach*, the children of Harar. Flight and exile from the city are likened to the *Hijra*, which the Prophet Mohammed and his followers were forced to make in order to escape persecution in Medina for their religious beliefs. The journey many Hararis have been forced to undertake has been a migratory passage over landscapes that have symbolic and moral meanings. Arrival in non-Muslim countries demands the creation of Muslim space, creating a separate social and moral universe within dominant society (see Metcalf 1996). The verse also encapsulates the imperative for Hararis to reside in Harar. As one Harari stated: "Anywhere that is not Harar is considered 'Tey Sari' – a place not fit for Hararis to inhabit". The obligation to honor this call is regarded as the "last will of the ancestors". When this is impossible, as in the case of those forced to flee as refugees, the duty is, in the words of one young Harari man, "to contribute everything we can afford to strengthen and enhance the interests of our people in Harar". One of these obligations is to protect and defend the city: to wage *jihad*, holy war, and be willing to die in defense of Islam. In the wake of a possible Y2K crisis, as one *H-net* participant wrote, "it is potentially possible that any kind of warmongers could invade Harar and destroy it. Protecting Harar could be one incentive to make you think of going back". In this comment, the notion that the rightful Harari place is back in the city of Harar is adapted in response to a new context of racism and perceived racism against Muslims (and against Africans in general).

Defining what is foreign, and maintaining boundaries around the group in such a way as to prevent foreign infiltration, are both issues with which Hararis have long had to contend. This is even truer in the diaspora, where the Harari population cannot rely on the continued occupation of a place to support their claims to exercise power greater than their numbers might warrant. In the diaspora, alliances with other Muslims create a sense of belonging to a much wider and more effective community – the *umma*, or brotherhood of Islam. For Muslim minorities everywhere, the interpretation of [Islamic] concepts provides the basis for establishing principles by which Muslim life can be maintained in non-Muslim contexts (see Voll 1991: 205). Generational differences are reflected in these trends, and in Harari conceptions about both their homeland and their lands of diaspora. Romance about the homeland among elders is based on a nostalgia that their children do not and cannot share. This nostalgia refers to the social rather than environmental aspects of Harar. Many older Hararis miss the tight sense of community and obligatory support made possible in the concentrated space of Harar, with neighbors and extended family residing in close proximity. Imagining the homeland in romantic terms is easier for them because, as Tololyan (1996: 29) states, first-generation emigrants "bear the homeland's and nation's marks in body and speech and soul". Parents literally embody the cultural signifiers – from the circumcised genitalia of women, to the mother tongue, to national dress – that their children opt not to carry. When members of the younger generation do adopt signifiers they tend to choose transnational symbols of Islam (e.g., the veil and modest dress) – recognizable currency in North America that connects them to the broader community of believers. Having grown up here, their associations are not nearly as exclusively Harari as those of their parents, and their relationships to other Muslims are emphasized.

Balancing essentialisms

Eickelman and Piscatori (1990: xiv) write that "Muslims seem effortlessly to juggle local and multiple identities – villager, tribesman, woman, citizen – with the broader identity of believer and to legitimize them all by reference to the idiom of the cosmopolitan community of believers (*umma*)". While I question the effortlessness of this balancing act, this idea of "juggling" has relevance if updated to a context where sites of identity represent battlegrounds within which there are limits (as well as advantages) to Muslim expression. Such was the case for Hararis in the "officially" Christian Ethiopia, and is the case today for diasporic Hararis who form a religious minority in North America. Through Muslim discourse, Hararis can simultaneously orient themselves in multiple landscapes. As part of the broader *umma* of Muslims worldwide, they can make allies to defend against racism. They adopt *jihad*, not only as the fight against forces that seek to demonize their religion and its followers, but also with respect to the homeland, in terms of defending their holy city of origin, known as *medinat-al-awlia* (the city of saints). The imperative of return is articulated in a culturally-specific discourse calling the children of the city to return from the black mountain, and this is framed by broader Muslim principles. The romance of former autonomy and glory is not, however, a sufficient basis upon which to construct a new state in what is a complex, ethnically heterogeneous locale.[10]

Interestingly, while young Hararis in the diaspora conjure the ideal of Harar as a nation, it is at the level of nation-states (Ethiopian, American and Canadian) that reconciling multiple identities appears to be problematic. Among Hararis, return is still phrased in terms of origin; that is to say, "home" is Harar, rather than the spiritual heartland of Mecca, or even the nation-state of Ethiopia writ large.

This is not to deny that some Harari on certain occasions invoke a larger identity of "Ethiopian-ness". Such a practice further underscores their adeptness at juggling; and (it seems largely for the sake of convenience), reflecting the convention to identify origin in national terms (e.g., population statistics privilege national origin over sub-national or ethnic origin or religious orientation) and the fact that the designation "Harari" is for the most part unknown to anyone not of Ethiopian background. "But for those of you proud of being Ethiopian", writes Farhan, "do you know how we became Ethiopian? Do you know [the Amhara King] Menelik? Do you know Chelenko [the infamous battle at which Harari autonomy was lost]?" Many Harari children born in the diaspora have, in fact, never heard of either. The Chelenko battle, used to support the current claims to Harari authority in Ethiopia, is the one historical episode most often referred to on *H-net*. Historical references like this one are being evoked in discussions on *H-net* to frame questions about how to build a new Harari nation. In their identity as "long-distance nationalists" (to borrow a phrase from Anderson [1983: 12]) *H-net* members engage in regular debates about the homeland (e.g., discussing how the economy of Harar should be revived; whether the Harari should employ their own currency, as they did in earlier times; whether there should be an independent Harari army, as there once was).

Such discussions both legitimize and are empowered by the discourse of Harari nationhood. This discourse – which invokes a specific localized place and tangible reference point – is, ironically, largely being generated and debated in the deterritorialized space of hyperspace. Through the internet a place may be relocated in virtual reality and a community constituted around a deterritorialized point of reference. Community ties amongst dispersed people may thus be redefined as networks of overlapping relationships, many of which have virtual dimensions, and many of which may be defined by youth whose contact with their place of origin is actually limited. Contemporary identity, then, may not only be a hybrid, transnational or transmigrant formulation, but a phenomenon related to the creation of a virtual form of cultural and community existence, one that is exportable across, or despite, the apparent limitations of time and space.

Notes

1 My research in Canada has been made possible by a Postdoctoral Research Fellowship from the Social Sciences and Humanities Research Council of Canada. Fieldwork in Harar and follow-up were supported by the Harold Hyam Wingate Foundation, and by supplementary grants from the Emslie Horniman Fund of the Royal Anthropological Institute, and the Lienhardt Fund at the University of Oxford.
2 "*Dergue*" is Amharic for council, and refers to the Provisional Military Council which ruled the country between 1974 and 1991 and was latterly led by Mengistu Haile Mariam. For details of the atrocities committed under the *Dergue*, see de Waal (1991).
3 The strictest definition, as Khachig Tololyan notes, is that shaped by the Jewish paradigm, wherein "the desire to return to the homeland is considered a necessary part of the definition of 'diaspora'" (1996: 14). See also Kearney (1995: 553) and Safran (1991: 83–4). For a discussion of diaspora in the Ethiopian context, see Sorenson (1992).

4 For a discussion of transnational identities, see Glick-Schiller *et al.* (1992, 1995). For the argument on the restructurings of space and time under globalization see Harvey (1989); for the relationship between identity and these space/time processes, see Kearney (1995: 553).

5 The most famous of these was Sir Richard Burton, who in 1854 was the first non-Muslim to enter the city. In his book, *First Footsteps in East Africa: or, An Exploration of Harar*, he calls the city "forbidden" and "under a guardian spell" and writes that it is "the ancient metropolis of a once mighty race, the only permanent settlement in Eastern Africa, the reported seat of Muslim learning, a walled city of stone houses, possessing its independent chief, its peculiar population, its unknown language, its own coinage, the emporium of the coffee trade, (and) the head-quarters of slavery" (1987: xxvi; see also Bardey 1897).

6 There are many ethnic groups within Ethiopia: the Oromo (the largest single ethnic group in the country), Amhara, Gurage, Argobba, Eritreans and Tigrayans, to name a few. The complex inter-group history has been detailed elsewhere (Caulk 1971, 1972, 1977; Hassen 1980, 1990; Zewde 1991).

7 The extent of the new government's commitment to democracy has, however, been subject to question since its inception. Major political parties such as the Oromo Liberation Front (representing the majority of Oromos in the country) boycotted the 1995 elections, suggesting that the current government is not truly representative of the diversity in the country. The current regime has also been criticized for reversing its stance on the freedom of the press and for continued aggression against Oromo nationalists.

8 For example, while I was in Harar, I met a Harari Canadian businessman who was there to identify investment opportunities for a consortium of 50 Harari businessmen in North America. At the time, they were considering purchasing a gravel quarry. In 1998, though, they began construction of a modern shopping complex just outside the city wall, where imported goods such as televisions and computers, goods previously not available in the area, are now being sold.

9 Despite a strict pretence to endogamy and ethnic exclusivity, members of other populations, notably Oromo and Somali, can and sometimes do "become" Harari through a recognized process known as *Ge limaad* (learning the way of the city), or, rather, the way of life of its people. This involves adopting the language and cultural and religious practices of the Harari, and being integrated socially through kinship, friendship, and membership in a community observance association. As Harariness has long been associated with class-based prestige, enculturation is often considered desirable by Oromo and Somali who have lived in the urban Harari environment for generations, have already adopted many aspects of Harari culture, and have strong social ties with Hararis. For a detailed discussion of the subject of arranged marriages see Gibb (2001).

10 Nor, for that matter, does the creation of an essentialist nationhood which uses territorial claims to assert identity as ancient and homogenous peoples (see Gibb 1999b; see also Appadurai 1995, Anderson 1983, Glick-Schiller *et al.* 1992).

References

Anderson, Benedict (1983) *Imagined Communities: Reflections on the Origin and Spread of Nationalism*. London: Verso.

Appadurai, Arjun (1995) "The Production of Locality", in R. Fardon (ed.), *Counterworks: Managing the Diversity of Knowledge*. London: Routledge, pp. 204–25.

Bardey, Alfred (1897) "Notes sur le Harrar", *Bulletin de Geographie Historique et Descriptive*, 130–80.

Burton, Richard (1987) *First Footsteps in East Africa: or, An Exploration of Harar*. New York: Dover.

Caulk, Richard (1971) "The Occupation of Harar: January 1887", *Journal of Ethiopian Studies* IX(2): 1–19.

——(1972) "Religion and the State in 19th Century Ethiopia", *Journal of Ethiopian Studies* X(1): 3–20.

——(1977) "Harar Town and its Neighbours in the Nineteenth Century", *Journal of African History* XVIII(3): 369–86.

Clifford, James (1994) "Diasporas", *Cultural Anthropology* 9(3): 302–38.

de Waal, Alex (1991) *Evil Days: 30 Years of War and Famine in Ethiopia*. London: Human Rights Watch.

Eickelman, Dale and Piscatori, James (1990) "Social Theory in the Study of Muslim Societies", in D. Eickelman and J. Piscatori (eds), *Muslim Travellers: Pilgrimage, Migration and the Religious Imagination*. New York: Routledge, pp. 3–28.

Gibb, Camilla (1999a) "Religious Identification in Transnational Contexts: Being and Becoming Muslim in Ethiopia and Canada", *Diaspora: A Journal of Transnational Studies* 7(2): pp. 247–67.

——(1999b) "*Baraka* Without Borders: Integrating Communities in the City of Saints", *The Journal of Religion in Africa* XXVII(I): 88–108.

——(2001) "Manufacturing Place and the Embodiment of Tradition: Muslim Africans in a Deterritorialized World", in C. Rothenburg and G. Currie (eds), *Feminist (Re)visions: of the subject*. Maryland: Lexington Books.

Gibb, Camilla and Rothenburg, Celia (2000) "Believing Women: Harari and Palestinian Women at Home and in the Diaspora", *Journal of Muslim Minority Affairs* 20(2): 243–59.

Glick-Schiller, Nina, Basch, Laura and Blanc-Szanton, Cristina. (eds) (1992) *Towards a Transnational Perspective on Migration*. New York: New York Academy of Sciences.

——(1995) "From Immigrant to Transmigrant: Theorizing Transnational Migration", *Anthropological Quarterly* 48–63.

Harvey, David (1989) *The Urban Experience*. Baltimore: Johns Hopkins University Press.

Hassen, Mohammed (1980) "Menelik's Conquest of Harar, 1887, and its Effect on the Political Organization of the Surrounding Oromos up to 1900", in D. Donham and W. James (eds), *Working Papers on Society and History in Imperial Ethiopia: The Southern Periphery from the 1880s to 1974*. Cambridge: Cambridge University Press, pp. 227–46.

——(1990) *The Oromo of Ethiopia: A History 1570–1860*. Cambridge: Cambridge University Press, African Studies Series No. 66.

Kearney, Michael (1995) "The Local and the Global: The Anthropology of Globalization and Transnationalism", *Annual Review of Anthropology* 24: 547–65.

Kinfe, Abraham (1994) *Ethiopia: From Bullets to the Ballot Box*. Lawrenceville, NJ: Red Sea Press.

Marcus, George (1995) "Ethnography in/of the World System: The Emergence of Multi-Sited Ethnography", *Annual Review of Anthropology* 24: 95–117.

Metcalf, Barbara (1996) "Introduction: Sacred Words, Sanctioned Practice, New Communities", in B. Metcalf (ed.), *Making Muslim Space in North America and Europe*. Berkeley: University of California Press, pp. 1–30.

Safran, William (1991) "Diasporas in Modern Societies: Myths of Homeland and Return", *Diaspora: A Journal of Transnational Studies* 1(1): 83–9.

Sorenson, John (1992) "Essence and Contingency in the Construction of Nationhood: Transformations of Identity in Ethiopia and Its Diasporas", *Diaspora: A Journal of Transnational Studies* 2(2): 201–28.

Tololyan, Khachig (1996) "Rethinking Diaspora(s): Stateless Power in the Transnational Moment", *Diaspora: A Journal of Transnational Studies* 5(1): 3–6.

Voll, John O. (1991) "Islamic Issues for Muslims in the United States", in Y. Haddad (ed.), *The Muslims of America*. New York: Oxford University Press, pp. 205–16.

Waldron, Sidney (1974) *Social Organization and Social Control in the Walled City of Harar, Ethiopia*. Doctoral dissertation, New York: Columbia University Press.

Zewde, Bahru (1991) *A History of Modern Ethiopia 1855–1974*. London: James Curry.

Chapter 10

Negotiating Nationhood on the Net

The case of the Turcomans and Assyrians of Iraq

Hala Fattah

Introduction

A central argument has swirled around the contours of the Iraqi nation from its inception in the 1920s until the present day. Briefly stated, it pits the legitimacy of Iraq as a nation-state against that of a whole host of different "national" communities, all of them settled within the borders of the modern state. The claim has been made that Iraq has never cohered into a nation because successive governments have prevented the assimilation and integration of "the multiple histories of Iraqis" into "a single narrative of state power" (Tripp 2000: 4–7). Even though this theory holds true for most periods of Iraq's formation, its singular focus on a narrow clique of Sunni officers (Sunnis, the majority faith in Islam but a numerical minority in Iraq) and Baath officials (Baath, the former ruling party in Iraq) misreads much of Iraqi history. To a large extent, the argument is more of a Western construct than an indigenous formulation. Nevertheless, it gains currency when set against the constant violence and rapid change accompanying state centralization. Still, those who have propounded the "illegitimacy" thesis have failed to understand that even state-centered ideology is not monolithic and has its ebbs and flows, and that in certain periods (such as under the monarchy), Iraqis did indeed forge solid ties of marriage, commercial partnerships, and social relationships across ethnic and sectarian lines (Batatu 1978: 47–50). Even though this reality failed to make an impact on the particularistic Sunni Arab vision espoused by various Iraqi governments, the notion of Iraq as an enduring and viable nation built upon the energies and talents of its diverse citizenry has made deep inroads. A vibrant Iraqi nationalism exists today, even if it is conceptualized differently from that of the past.

This said, it is obvious that Iraqi nationalism appeals to certain groups more than others. For instance, various observers have noted that, over the last 80 years, *some* of the Kurds have been somewhat more ambivalent about their Iraqi identity than other communities in the country. While there are many historic reasons for this situation, I will not dwell on these in this chapter. Rather, I am more interested in the different ways in which social groups both inside and outside of Iraq are reformulating their ties to Iraq, even as the country passes through one of the severest tests in its history. Nowhere is this re-affiliation or re-identification with Iraq more apparent than on the world wide web, where a significant process of re-negotiating history, ethnicity and religion is visibly gathering momentum on dozens of "Iraqi" websites. There, the thrashing out of particularistic interpretations of history, culture and politics intersects with the growth of identity projections by national and "pre-national" groups, all of which have their own websites. This article is concerned with the sites of two important social groupings in Iraq, namely, the Turcomans and the Assyrians. According to the Declaration of Principles pronounced at the First Turcoman Congress in Irbil (northern Iraq) in October 1997, the Iraqi Turcomans (both Sunnis and Shi'a) migrated from Central Asia to today's Turkmenistan, eventually arriving in Iraq in the twelfth century. Nowadays, the Sunni Turcomans speak a form of Turkish that corresponds to that of the Turks of Istanbul, while the Shi'a speak an Azeri-influenced Turkish dialect (see Nissman 1999). The Turcoman homeland is basically in northern Iraq, from Tel'A'far in the north to Mandali in the South. The Assyrians, on the other hand, are a Christian people, following four different rites: that of the Apostolic and Catholic Assyrians (the Church of the East), Assyrian Orthodox, Chaldean Catholics and Protestants. In Iraq, the Assyrians also live in the north, specifically in the "Assyrian Triangle" between the Lower Zab and Tigris rivers.

The Turcomans and Assyrians are important elements in an identity debate that continues to find echoes up to the present day. The contention of this writer is that one of the key issues in this debate on Iraqi identity is how best to make use of a particular community's history in the battle to re-envision a collectivity's "place" on the national agenda, even as that agenda is constantly shifting due to forces largely outside of the country's control. Perhaps most interesting of all is the way that these communities consistantly have sought to maneuver – at times relinquish – at times underscore – their ties with Iraq the state, especially as constituted in the recent past, attempting to insinuate themselves in the ongoing dialogue of remaking the Iraqi nation of the future.

A word of caution: even though minority groups' sites resort to the necessary fiction that their claim to history is "objective", interpretations of the past are necessarily self-serving, as any reading of Benedict Anderson's *Imagined Communities* makes clear (Anderson 1991: 1–7). My purpose is not to tear down historical interpretations by resorting to a static and fixed past, but to see how these interpretations are used to justify a minority group's vision of inclusion/ exclusion in a reformulated Iraqi state. Proceeding from the premise that "identity and community are to a significant degree constructed and subject to invention and reimagination" (Hudson 2000), I am interested in finding out how these two social groups are attempting to overcome their political marginalization by means of the rational representation of their past and future. As Hoerder (2000: 226) points out with regard to the nation/state distinction, nations or cultural groups "assert special group rights against other groups which define themselves as nations, [but] the democratic state . . . is theorized as neutral and thus as treating each and every person as equal, regardless of culture, ethnicity, religion, color of skin, gender, class or position in the life cycle". How then are the Turcomans and Assyrians actively reshaping their national identities by manipulating history, ethnicity and information? And how are they confronting the reality of a democratically-challenged state?

Finally, since the internet is not available to everyone, it is important to ask where Iraqi sites are located in the "real" world. After the first Gulf War, Iraqi Kurdistan became a "safe haven", ostensibly guaranteed by the UN but in reality coming under the protection of the US and the UK. After a large number of NGOs and UN personnel entered the region to pursue the twin goals of the rehabilitation and reconstruction of Kurdistan's war-torn infrastructure, Iraqi Kurdistan found itself in an advantageous position, at least with respect to the rest of the country. As of early 2000, the Kurdish region was wired to "more than 20 satellite-linked centers for telephone, fax and Internet", even as its three universities are also connected to the world wide web.[1] On the other hand, and as a result of the continuing state of disrepair of the telecommunications sector, which was badly damaged during the Gulf War, south-central Iraq only acquired access to the internet recently. In December 2001 it was calculated that Iraq's only email service, www.uruklink.net, counted just 225 subscribers.[2] Because of this situation, the majority of cyber groups online have emerged from the greater Iraqi diaspora. A large proportion of these are situated in North America, and represent exiles, refugees and political dissidents whose broader agendas include social justice, political freedom, greater cultural rights and more representative government. The Turcoman and Assyrian websites reviewed in this article are most definitely the expression of the Iraqi diaspora; none that I have looked at are hosted in Iraq proper or Iraqi Kurdistan.

Ethnicity and sectarian affiliation: a selective view of Iraqi sites on the net

Among the most sophisticated sites about Iraq on the internet are several that refuse to openly call themselves Iraqi. Because of their history of tortuous relations with the Iraqi state (particularly with Saddam Hussein's recently-toppled Baath regime that had held power for 34 years), Assyrian websites have tended to marginalize their national connections to Iraq, and have promoted a quasi-separatist agenda that bypasses the state but accentuates the long cultural and historic roots of the community in the region. On the other hand, most Turcoman sites are adamant about their Iraqi-ness, but equally ambivalent about their connections to the Iraqi state. However, while the web has allowed both communities infinite freedom to actualize their national potential (if only in the virtual world), certain constraints inhibit both communities' attempts at further self-actualization online. Because Iraq still harbors a sizeable Turcoman and Assyrian population caught between government strategies and US designs (an issue discussed in more detail below), a clear realization seems to prevail among activists on the web that neither community is entirely free to redesign its national agenda. Certain limitations most definitely take over when co-religionists or co-ethnics are leading precarious lives in the home country. Coupled with a genuine feeling that Iraq is indeed *one* of the national homes of both Turcomans and Assyrians, this residual connection to an idea of Iraq inevitably colors the interpretation of their community's history, and paradoxically reinforces their Iraqi identity in the process.

Of the many "northern" Iraqi communities that have contributed their share to the makeup of the country, two of the most significant in historical legacy, cultural involvement and socio-political longevity are the Turcomans and Assyrians. Ties of cooperation, as well as a history of conflict, may well intrude on their associations with each other, and yet there is a certain symmetry in viewing these two communities as a unity. One of the most interesting facets that characterize these groups is their transnational reach coupled with their local focus. For instance, the wider Turcoman "nation" spreads out from Iraq into Syria, Azerbaijan and Turkey, while Assyrians are to be found in Iraq, Syria, Turkey, Iran and Lebanon. Both communities are the self-proclaimed heirs of two remarkable civilizations that left their imprint on the region for centuries to come, of which their descendants are justifiably proud. On the other hand, there is a specificity to the Turcoman and Assyrian experience in Iraq that is directly related to their long affinity with the country. This is why any analysis of the negotiation strategies of these communities with the Iraqi state entails a re-examination of the way transnationalism affects particularistic identity in each specific case (see Anderson 1998).

A post-Gulf War history of the Turcomans and Assyrians in Iraq

Prior to the Gulf War of 1991, Iraq's northern communities, including the Assyrians and Turcomans, lived under a sovereign and highly centralized state. Although the cultural as well as sociopolitical rights of Iraq's national groups have not traditionally been accorded the respect they deserve, neither under the monarchy (which came to an end in 1958) nor under the republican regimes that followed it, for the Turcomans and Assyrians, at least, little changed after the Gulf War. As was mentioned above, after the war the United Nations created a "safe haven" for Kurds and other national groups in the northern part of the country. The Turcoman and Assyrian communities, as well, of course, as the Kurds, were divided between two separate zones, one living above the 36th parallel (i.e. the "safe haven", which was set up ostensibly to protect the Kurds and others from threats by the Iraqi government) and one below, dominated by the Iraqi regime. An autonomous Kurdistan Regional Government (KRG) was created in 1992 and a power-sharing agreement was signed between the two most powerful Kurdish parties, the KDP (Kurdistan Democratic Party) and the PUK (Patriotic Union of Kurdistan). The agreement broke down soon after signing, however, and internecine fighting between the two Kurdish parties became an off-and-on current of a larger war. These hostilities threatened not only to disrupt the nation-building efforts of the once-united Kurdish leadership in northern Iraq but to thwart as well the collective well-being of the other national groups under the larger federal structure set up in Kurdistan (Gunter 1996). Of these, the Turcomans and Assyrians seemingly had the most cause to worry.

Variously accused of harboring pro-Turkish tendencies or of acting as Turkish agents in Kurdistan by their enemies, the Turcoman population in northern Iraq has generally borne the brunt of their leadership's ambitions. Although criticism has surfaced of Kurdish attempts to manipulate the Turcomans' rights to their native language and traditions, a number of Turcoman parties vowed nevertheless to cooperate with the Kurdistan Regional Government (KRG) in their federal experiment. The only hold-out was the Iraqi Turkmen Front, a coalition of several Turcoman parties in northern Iraq which had adamantly refused to join the KRG. Viewed as a mouthpiece for Turkish claims on Iraq, the Front has been criticized for its obstructionist views by Turcomans and Kurds alike (Radio Free Europe 2002). This has not prevented the Turkish government from openly reiterating its view that an Autonomous Zone for Iraqi Turcomans be established, along the lines of the KRG; nor for one of its most fervent supporters, Jamal Shan, of the Iraqi Turkoman National Party, to call for "a homeland in northern Bet-Nahrain with the city of Kirkuk as its center".[3]

Just as dissatisfied as the Turcomans by the post-Gulf War arrangements in northern Iraq, the Assyrians have let it be known that they, too, want satisfaction of their principal demands. On 14 December 2001, for example, the Assyrian International News Agency made the following accusations online:

> [T]he Assyrian community in the northern UN Safe Haven have faced a terror campaign by the Kurdish paramilitary organizations occupying Assyrian areas. Although Assyrians have successfully fought for greater political expression and for the formation of Assyrian language schools in northern Iraq, Assyrian organizations as well as human rights organizations such as Amnesty International have documented extensive abuses against Assyrians including assassinations of Assyrian political leaders and extensive land expropriations. . . . Since the Gulf War, most of the 200 Assyrian villages razed by the government have been illegally occupied by Kurdish tribes tied to the ruling paramilitary parties while another 50 villages have been occupied in whole or in part by Kurds. These 250 villages must be returned to their rightful Assyrian owners.

Turcomans in cyberspace

To understand how these conflicting agendas are worked out online, it is important to take stock of some of the most notable websites of either community.

Most Turcoman (or Turkmen) sites are in the Turkish language, whether hosted by Iraqi, Syrian, Azeri or Turkish groups on the net (although a few have Arabic and English sections as well). With respect to Iraqi Turcomans, it is clear that the connection with Turkey shapes the community's historical view of the world, and nowhere more so than on the web. Virtually all the Turcoman sites I surveyed dated the community's origin to the ninth century AD, when one of the Abbasid Caliphs in Baghdad recruited Turkish soldiers to staff his army. Eventually these same troops became the force behind the throne, and even overthrew one Caliph and replaced him with another. The website of the Turkmen Peoples' Party, one of the Iraqi Turcoman political groupings, is particularly interesting in the way it Turkifies every invasion force, occupation army and government after the Turkic-speaking Mongols ransacked Iraq in the thirteenth century. This Turco-centric angle is so pervasive that the Turkish soldiery of the Persian Shah are given more importance than the Persian occupation of Baghdad itself, while the Ottoman Empire's reconquest and control of Iraq are subsumed into the wider narrative of "Turkish" expansion without a thought given to the multi-ethnic plurality and diversity that made up the Ottoman experience. Finally, more astounding still, and completely unsupported by historical facts, is the claim that "The Turks have ruled Iraq from 833 to 1924".

The Iraqi Turcomans' focus on Turkey is, of course, conditioned by two factors: Turkey's "big brother" role in northern Iraq after the Gulf War; and the reality of regional politics. In the wake of Iraq's defeat in the war, the Turkish Republic has seized upon what it considers to be a golden opportunity to advance its interests in northern Iraq by re-energizing its support for Iraqi Turcoman groups, trying to stave off the specter of a potential Kurdish state and bolstering Iraq's territorial integrity in the face of Iran – Turkey's rival in the region.[4] The Iraqi Turcomans' emphasis on Turkey's position in northern Iraq is also complemented by the realization that regional alliances, of both a formal and an informal kind, must be initiated among the many Turkish-language groups in neighboring countries, such as in Syria, Iran, Armenia, Azerbaijan and Turkey itself, in order to provide a counterweight to the Iraqi Turcomans' political isolation.

It is the Iraqi Turcomans' attempt to strike an equitable balance between these transnational proclivities and their community's wholesale identification with Iraq as their country of origin that provides a dilemma that has yet to be solved satisfactorily. For while all the Turcoman websites I looked at unequivocally back a unified Iraq, characterized by democracy, human rights, freedom and a multi-parliamentary system, these same sites also refer back to the historical injustices committed against the Turcomans from as early as 1924 onwards. The ambivalence towards the Iraqi state is manifested in a number of ways. For instance, the community historically was assimilated faster than other minorities in the country, in part because most of its members were Sunni Muslim and Turcophile, two advantages that allowed Turcomans easy access and integration into the post-Ottoman Sunni elite. As early as 1921, and definitely by 1947,

Iraqi Turcomans had begun moving to Baghdad and other cities in Iraq, and had begun the process of acculturating into an Arab environment (Longrigg 1953: 9, 381). Yet most websites skirt the issue of voluntary assimilation altogether (perhaps because it dilutes a Turcoman political platform?). Instead, their ire was reserved for Iraqi government attempts (under Saddam) from about 1970 onwards to forcibly deport Turcomans from their ancestral homeland in the north of the country to locations further south at an accelerated pace.[5] The Iraqi government was also criticized for defaulting on language and cultural rights, for political assassinations of prominent Turcoman politicians and army officers, and for favoritism to other minorities in Iraq.

And yet there is hope that, in the post-Baath era, the three-million-strong (by their own count) Turcoman community will once again regain its position in society. This is apparent from the relations its members have forged with other non-Arab minorities in the north such as the Kurds. For despite fierce contestation over Kirkuk, the city claimed by Turcomans as well as Kurds, the Turcomans have moved towards acceptance of a future federal arrangement for Iraq, in which indigenous communities have a chance to preserve their autonomy in a decentralized state system (Selahaddin 2000). The interesting thing to note about the Turcomans is that, as the most assimilated minority in northern Iraq, they seem to feel that they have no other agenda but to stay where they are and to defend themselves against the encroachment of the Iraqi state. Short of a Turkish invasion of northern Iraq that might set off a chain of events in which the Iraqi Turcomans would then revert to the "mother" country (at present a remote possibility), the Turcomans have no intention of declaring independence from Iraq. As their websites make very clear, the Turcomans have a long history of attachment to the country that goes well beyond a resigned acceptance of their socio-political situation in a once-dictatorial state. Jamal Shan, of the Iraqi Turkoman National Party, put it this way:

> We, in the Iraqi Turkoman National Party, work in accordance with three fundamental principles. The first is the preservation of Iraqi national terri-torial integrity. The second is the need for all the citizens of Iraq to exercise their legitimate national rights on an equal basis. And the third is that the Turkomans run the administration of their region, Turkomaneli, with Kirkuk as its center in whatever form. Thus our people will have the benefit of their full national rights. None of the questions or problems of the peoples of Iraq can be solved without the participation of the Turkomans. What is worth noting is the international support for our people's cause, the support that we have demanded for the victory of our people and all the peoples of Iraq in accordance with legitimacy and equity.[6]

The Turcomans value the fact that Iraq as a whole, and especially the northern part of the country, is the established homeland from which their fathers and forefathers spread out all over the country, and they are justifiably proud of their achievements in the making of the country, and its traditions. Were it not for the depredations visited upon them by Iraqi governments of past and the present, the Turcomans quite conceivably would have no qualms about returning to Iraq, to live alongside other minorities in a state that guaranteed their civic, socio-cultural, political and economic rights. And while all diasporic communities subscribe to the myth of "return", the Turcomans may be the one Iraqi group that will actually fulfill it.

Assyrians on the net

In comparison to the paucity of Turcoman sites on the web, there is a veritable plethora of Assyrian cyber-communities, quite a number of which are hosted by various Assyrian groups in North America, Europe and Australia. Indeed, the *San Jose Mercury News* reported in its 2 September 2001 edition that, "persecuted and displaced from their ancestral home in the Middle East, Assyrians are finding a virtual homeland in cyberspace". A typical website is that of the Assyrian International News Agency (AINA), which sets down the Assyrian credo, in all of its bold simplicity, in this way: "Assyrians are not Arabs. Assyrians, including Chaldeans and Syriacs [of which Maronites are a branch], are the indigenous Christian people of Mesopotamia and have a history, spanning seven thousand years, that predates the Arab conquest of the region". While this is the view held by the majority of Assyrians around the world, it is none the less the equivalent of throwing down the gauntlet to non-Assyrian Iraqis. By not equating themselves with an Arab civilization that "Arabized" the majority of Iraq's native population, and by pointedly referring to Iraq as Mesopotamia even after 80-odd years of its establishment as a nation-state, most non-Assyrian Iraqi Arabs would consider AINA's views to be somewhat anachronistic, if not apolitical and narrowly nationalistic. Paradoxically, AINA's portrayal of Assyrian "civilization [as] the foundation of Arab civilization" rings true with many Assyrians today, even as it continues to rankle with Arabs wherever they are. Indeed, the fall-out from the Assyrians' insistence that they are just who they say they are took on such grave dimensions that, on 5 October 2001, AINA lodged an online protest against the Arab American Institute, the *Chicago Tribune*, and several other groups in the US, categorically rejecting the labeling of Assyrians as "Arab".[7]

This theme is picked up by other Assyrian websites. One site that tries to bypass polemics and offer a perspective on the current situation of Assyrian Iraqis is that of the Assyrian Democratic Movement, or Zowaa, a highly interesting mix of political activism, historical narrative and visionary pragmatics. As the premier site of Iraqi Assyrians, Zowaa focuses on the development of Assyrian activism in the country, and relates the history of oppression, assassinations, deportation and exile familiar to most Assyrian Iraqis. But as Zowaa's representative in the US and Canada, Lincoln Malik, makes clear:

[T]hese massacres represent only part of [Assyrian] history, albeit its most painful part. We must look at history comprehensively and with purpose. Selective renditions of history may help win an argument in a coffee shop, but are not useful for serious political deliberations. To be relevant, the discussion must focus on the ideas and strategies offered our people in the current historical era. Abstract discussions of what may have been, or ought to be, will not deliver our people from their current national dilemma.[8]

Speaking for Zowaa, Malik asserts that Assyrians are the indigenous people of Iraq, and neither a national nor an ethnic, religious or linguistic minority. As such, their rights in Bet-Nahrain, the Assyrian homeland (most of which is in northern Iraq, but it also extends to Syria, Iran and Turkey) are guaranteed by the UN Declaration of Rights of Indigenous Peoples and have the full weight of international law behind them. There is an implication in the text that other national groups, such as the Turcomans, do not qualify for such a distinction. Because of their peculiar historic circumstances, Assyrians refuse to become assimilated and will never accept forced "Arabization" by the regime, and yet they are "loyal Iraqis. . . . who love their country, and will join the struggle to save it from the hated dictatorship. In this [the Assyrians] are allied with the broad masses of the Iraqi people from the Kurdish north to the Shia Arab south". Therefore, everything must be done to protect and preserve the Assyrian community still in Iraq, "under the banner of democracy in Iraq, and affirmation of [the Assyrian] national existence in [their] homeland".

Zowaa's insistence that cultural rights cannot stand alone, and must be buttressed by political and civil liberties finds wide echo among other Assyrian political parties. For instance, the Assyrian International News Agency insisted on the fact that:

Assyrians, including Chaldeans and Syriacs, are one indigenous ethnic group is self-evident, but constitutional recognition of this fact is by no means a trivial metaphysical concept, and carries profound implications. All other rights, whether they be political or cultural, are founded first and foremost on constitutional recognition. With official constitutional recognition, other Assyrian concerns can be appropriately legally and politically addressed, including greater cultural expression, religious freedom, teaching of the Assyrian language, and preservation of historically Assyrian lands. Even the fundamental issue of the return of expropriated Assyrian villages begins first with official constitutional recognition.[9]

Another party, the Assyrian Democratic Organization, or Mtakasta, which claims a deeper affinity with Assyrians in Syria, holds similar beliefs. Ironically, a wide rift has developed between Mtakasta and Zowaa, which it accuses of high-handedness, excessive secrecy and ill-advised political alliances with various Iraqi Kurdish factions. But both Mtakasta and Zowaa are adamant that a political solution to Assyrian rights must be found within the greater Iraqi (or, in Mtakasta's case, Syrian) nation. This is because the vision of a supra-Assyrian nation endowed with cultural, religious and linguistic privileges, and functioning as a collective standard to which all Assyrians should aspire, is a useful panacea for the Assyrian diaspora, but is untenable as a realistic alternative.

Finally, among the most interesting sites on the web is that of the *Journal of Assyrian Academic Studies* (*JAAS*), the only scholarly publication devoted entirely to "serious research about the culture of the Assyrians, from and after the time it survived the demise of empire".[10] The premise of the journal is itself intriguing, and it speaks to the dispersal of Assyrian communities all over the world. Briefly stated, JAAS believes that it is high time for scholars to move away from the study of Assyrian civilization in antiquity, and legends of the "fall", to a study of Assyrians in the modern world, especially in the diaspora. As a leading Assyrian specialist states on the front page of *JAAS* put it, "confusion [exists] between the annihilation of the Assyrian political system [i.e. Assyria in Antiquity] and the annihilation of the Assyrian people", by which the professor is of course referring to the history of oppression of the Assyrian people by various regimes, Iraqi, Iranian and Turkish, from the beginning of the twentieth century onwards.

In two fascinating reviews in a recent issue of *JAAS* of the Saudi anthropologist Madawi Al-Rasheed's book, *Iraqi Assyrian Christians in London: The Construction of Ethnicity* (1998), a number of additional points are made with respect to the realities of Assyrian diasporic existence in the UK and elsewhere. While one reviewer gently takes Al-Rasheed to task for daring to question the idea that present-day Assyrians are the direct descendants of the Assyrians of old, and launches into a physiognomic investigation that ends up in the Assyrian section of the Louvre Museum in Paris (!), another criticizes her for conflating the five recognized "Assyrian" denominations with the Church of the East (the Assyrian National Church). Throughout the reviews, the reader is continually made aware of the "ever-morphing" spectacle of Assyrians forgetting parts of their historical existence and over-inflating others, even as they include some Assyrian denominations and proceed to forget others. Finally, in view of the strong statements made by Assyrian political parties on the web, it is interesting to note the scholarly consensus on present-day Assyrians in London as being virtually apolitical, and so conservative as to be reclusive in all matters except religion and language.

Buzz words: identity, human rights and freedom of expression in the chats

Other than official proclamations on party-affiliated websites, where can the attentive net-surfer go to gauge popular perceptions of Turcoman or Assyrian reality? One of the best, and certainly more entertaining, ways to understand what the virtual generation is grappling with, is to check out the chatrooms. In a recent exchange on the *Assyrian Forum*,[11] an Australian named Rob posted a rather provocative message asking for help in buying "a woman from Mesopotamia (blue eyes, black hair, virgin, in good health)". Whether facetious or not, Rob's message was seen as racist and objectionable by a number of site users, and he was immediately bombarded with a slew of disparaging answers. One reader replied:

> I think an Assyrian woman would not be suitable for a man of your cosmopolitan taste. I do have a chicken for sale, with very large drumsticks. Interested?

And another instantly retorted:

> Maybe we can help you in buying a wife, but to get an idea of the market value, can you tell us your mom's price first? Where did your dad find your mom? On e-Bay?

From the viewpoint of the concerned Third-World activist, the ignorance exhibited towards Assyrians, Turcomans or any other Middle Eastern national group by "your average Joe" is more or less viewed as a given, and is no less intense on the web as it is in everyday life. Assyrians, in particular, face another hazard: as Christians, they feel they are essentially part of "the West", and yet the West misunderstands them, and insists on lumping them together with other less "civilized" minorities. It must be noted that the notion of Assyrian exceptionalism that permeates all sites devoted to Assyrian history or culture is an integral part of every national group's ethos, particularly those striving to make their mark in national politics. After all, a reified (or perhaps, rarified) view of a particular cultural group's history and civilization is the *sine qua non* of any self-respecting social and political grouping. For that reason, constructing a civilization online has its pitfalls, because the exploration of a specific identity and history on a global scale cannot be for a culture's devotees alone. Ultimately, for any society to thrive and expand on the net, new audiences must be brought within the familiar ambit, even though awareness of other groups and ethnicities percolates slowly on the web.

Rob's query also had the effect of stirring opinions on another catch-all term, "Mesopotamia". While one reader noted that the term had been appropriated by many Iraqi communities (so that it had become almost generic shorthand for pre-modern Iraq) and did not necessarily refer to the Assyrians as a whole (therefore attempting to stave off the massive onslaught on Rob's cynical statement by Assyrians rushing to rescue female honor?), the word does have religious, historic and ideological connotations that Assyrians associate with their existence in Iraq prior to the Arab conquests of the Fertile Crescent. This confusion is only natural; a young Iraqi Assyrian who may have studied in Iraqi schools and only left the country recently would no doubt have assimilated the notion, very prevalent in Iraqi textbooks of the seventies and eighties, that modern Iraq is the direct recipient of the many diverse civilizations of *Bayn al-nahrayn* (Mesopotamia in Arabic). A diaspora Assyrian, on the other hand, more in touch with the symbols and signs that permeate the Assyrian ideological renaissance on the net, would have instantly associated Mesopotamia with the borderless Bet-Nahrain, the Assyrian homeland of old, and taken immediate umbrage.

This difference also pervades the Assyrians' dilemma with regard to the symbols of Iraqi authority. Like all Iraqis, Assyrians have distinctive and very personal views with regard to the country's leadership. And, much like their countrymen (and countrywomen) all over the globe, they have long harboured concerns that a strike against Iraq was in the offing. In late 2002 (before the conception of Operation Iraqi Freedom – the so-called "second Gulf War"), the *Assyrian Forum* carried an interesting discussion about ideas for bombing Iraq. One reader expressed himself in the following manner:

> [B]ear in mind that the notion of attacking Iraq/Assyro-Babylonia is not because the nation possesses weapons of mass destruction, which the West provided (to the Iraqi leadership) in the first place, or because of the dictatorial regime of Mr. Hussein, because there are plenty of dictators in the Middle East and the West has also created them. No. . . . No, the call to attack Iraq is coming from those who are (intent) on scoring another (act of) revenge after Operation Babylon in 1982 [i.e. Israel].

This was immediately shouted down by other posts, one of which made the case that Iraqis should demand a refund because their leadership had not lived up to their expectations! Over and above the tangible apprehension for Assyrians in Iraq, however, a number of posts have also taken to exploring the situation of Assyrians in other parts of the world. The editors of *Zinda*, an Assyrian online magazine, for instance, alerted their magazine's readership to the double-standards employed against Iranian Assyrians in Vienna, normally one of the refugee collection points in Europe. According to the magazine, Iranian Assyrians, who had usually sought and received permission to emigrate to the US in past years, were now being refused the opportunity to join their compatriots in America. As a result of the pressures exerted on Austria and other European governments by President Khatami of Iran (who has commented that "Christians are relatively satisfied with the extent of freedoms granted them in Iran"), as well as the concern of many Assyrian political groups that the decline of native Christians in the Middle East was causing an exodus that could not be arrested, Assyrian émigrés were being left in limbo. Stranded by these different pressures and with nowhere to go, Iranian Assyrians have been left in dire straits in Austria, a situation that *Zinda's* editors were adamant could be ameliorated if Assyrians were indeed granted their full rights in Iran, thus reversing the drain of Assyrian refugees to the West.

Chat groups are an important addition to the more official party-sponsored websites because they present a diversity of views. Using the anonymity that is their most characteristic feature, subscribers to online forums can be candid about their likes and dislikes, and revel in their freedom to be as different as they wish. While Turcoman discussion groups are not as prevalent as Assyrian ones, they are growing, for there is nothing as exhilarating as letting off steam in cyberspace. This is especially the case with Iraqis who have grown up believing that freedom of expression is for other people, and that their closed societies back home were the norm, not the exception.

A summation: the use (and abuse) of history on the net

Reference has already been made to Turcoman claims of a continuous Turkish political presence in the whole of Iraq "from 833 to 1924", an assertion far too metaphorical to be historically accurate. Other groups in the region make a similar reinterpretation of history. In an official letter to the Arab American Institute, asking it to stop identifying Assyrians and Maronites as Arabs, the Coalition of American Assyrians and Maronites (CAM) laid stress on several issues, all of them relating to the distinctive histories claimed by different peoples in the Arab/Middle East region. CAM asserted: that Assyrians and Maronites are ethnically distinct from Arabs while Assyrians also are different on the linguistic front; that both Assyrians and Maronites diverge from the rest of the native peoples in the region by virtue of their Christianity; that Assyrians are the indigenous peoples of northern Iraq, southeast Turkey, northeast Syria and northwest Iran, while Maronites are the indigenous peoples of Lebanon; and finally – and this is the clincher – that Assyrians and their civilizations, and the Phoenicians of Lebanon, span seven thousand years and pre-date the Arab conquest of the region.[12]

It goes without saying that both the Turcoman and Assyrian visions of religious–linguistic–cultural differences and sweeping historical pretensions are made possible by the freedom and, to a certain extent, the anonymity of the net. But freedom and anonymity quite often function as obstacles to the larger Turcoman and Assyrian projects of regaining a political foothold in Iraq on more equitable terms than before. While recourse to the greater Assyrian Empire or pan-Turkism is a necessary marker in identity politics, making possible the further in-gathering of diasporic communities in cyberspace around a central ideology of cultural inclusiveness and pride of place, the more pragmatic Turcoman and Assyrian political leadership does not accord history as privileged a position as political survival or, indeed, as national regeneration. For instance, Ninos Gaboro, the head of Mtakasto (the Assyrian Democratic Organization) is on record as supporting the following positions:

That [the Assyrian leadership] concentrate on minimizing dispersion of our peoples, especially in the Middle East [and] that [the leadership] actively involve the educated segment of our society in the decision-making process and every other political and economic aspect of our lives.

In order to do so, Mtakasto believes that the most urgent objectives in Syria, Iraq and wherever Assyrians are settled, are to:

> Secure [Assyrians'] national existence;Awaken and develop our national identity;Support unity among various denominations andWork for the recognition of Assyrian national existence in the Middle East, all of which are legitimate rights.[13]

Similarly, Zowaa (the Assyrian Democratic Movement) is for the strict enforcement of human rights for Assyrians in Iraq because "Assyrians . . . do not have an ancestral homeland outside of Iraq", Thus, in both parties' appeals for a reliable survival mechanism to protect Assyrians, whether in Iraq or Syria, the notion of a wider Assyrian nation independent of, and oblivious to, any successor regime that comes after "the fall" is circumscribed out of necessity and pragmatic considerations.

Conclusion

After the Gulf War and deep into its sequel, the "illegitimacy" thesis, that depicts Iraq as another Yugoslavia breaking into ethnic or sectarian enclaves of Sunnis, Shi'ites and Kurds, is being put to severe test. Inevitably, in its narrow delimitations, this thesis perpetuates false dichotomies that regulate other Iraqi ethnic and religious communities to an obscurity which they most certainly do not deserve. Perhaps because neither the Turcomans nor the Assyrians fit readily into the US strategic vision for Iraq (unlike the Kurds and the Shi'a), both groups must fight for their existence using unconventional tools. Of these, the internet is the most versatile. At once virtual meeting place, ethnicity index, cultural club and political barometer, the internet brings diasporic communities together and shakes them up into a heady mixture. What emerges is a field of dreams that achieves its greatest actualization on the world wide web. By allowing the convergence of dozens of sites on greater Turkmenistan and Assyria to project the histories of indigenous peoples, and their collective visions of the future, the internet makes possible the renegotiation of identities and nationalities that had long been relegated to the backwater of exile. Unlike the facile generalizations implicit in the "illegitimacy" thesis that posits Iraqi nationalism as a brittle phenomenon held together by coercion, Turcoman and Assyrian websites are fully agreed on their Iraqiness, but seek to define it on their own terms. Because both communities view Iraq as their homeland, and the Turcoman and Assyrian populations still settled in the country as tangible proof of their civilizational heritage as well as their future promise, neither community thinks of questioning their Iraqi nationhood. None the less, by means of their online agendas for cultural and political regeneration, and their re-imbued visions of citizenship in Iraq, Turcoman and Assyrian cyberactivists are putting Iraq, and the world, on notice of their programs and intentions, and so beginning a vital and necessary dialogue regarding the question of their long-awaited "return" to their homeland.

Notes

1   As noted in a BBC report: *Wired World of Iraqi Kurds*, 15 August 2001.
2   As noted in the CNN report: *Internet in Iraq: Limited, Appreciated*, 16 December 2001.
3   The demand for a Turcoman Safe Haven was relayed by a reporter to Massoud Barazani, the then leader of the Kurdish Democratic Party, on the televised show, "*Liqa' al-yawm*" broadcast on the Al-Jazeera satellite TV station, 19 February 2002. The quote from Jamal Shan comes from a report in the Assyrian online magazine, *Zinda*.
4   See http://www.foreignpolicy.org.tr/ing/books/oguzlu_09.html.
5   Discussed on the website *Iraqi Turkman Front*.
6   As cited in *Zinda*, http://www.zindamagazine.com/magazine/index.php.
7   At a conference on Iraq at Villanova University, Pa., in 1988, which I was fortunate to attend, the Vicar General of U.S. Chaldeans, Monsignor Sarhad Jammo, made the comment that Assyrians were "Iraqis, not Arabs". An Egyptian Professor in the audience immediately got up from his seat to challenge the assertion, but failed to make headway with the clergyman.
8   Posted on the website of the Assyrian Democratic Movement.
9   Citation from the Assyrian International News Agency website.
10 Citation from *Journal of Assyrian Academic Studies* online.
11 A discussion list sponsored by Assyria Online, see www.aina.org/aol.
12 Posted on the website of the Assyrian International News Agency.
13 Posted on the website of the Assyrian Democratic Movement.

References

Publications

Al-Rasheed, Madawi (1998) *Iraqi Assyrian Christians in London: The Construction of Ethnicity*. Ceredigion, UK: Edwin Mellen Press.
Anderson, Benedict (1991) *Imagined Communities: Reflections on the Origins and Spread of Nationalism*. London: Verso.
Anderson, Jon W. (1998) "Transnational Media and Regionalism", *Transnational Broadcasting Studies*, No.1, Fall.
Batatu, Hanna (1978) *The Old Social Classes and the New Revolutionary Movements of Iraq*. Princeton: Princeton University Press.
Gunter, Michael M. (1996) "The KDP–PUK Conflict in Northern Iraq" *Middle East Journal*, 50(2): 225-241.
Hoerder, Dirk (2000) "Negotiating Nations: Exclusions, Networks, Inclusions", *Histoire Sociale/Social History* Vol. XXXIII: 226.
Hudson, Michael C. (2000) "*Creative Destruction": Information Technology and the Political Culture Revolution in the Arab World*". Paper presented at the Conference on Transnationalism, Royal Institute for Inter-Faith Studies, Amman, Jordan, 19–21 June.

Longrigg, Stephen Helmsley (1953) *Iraq, 1900 to 1950*. London, New York and Toronto: Oxford University Press.

Nissman, David (1999) *The Iraqi Turkomans: Who They Are and What They Want*. Radio Free Europe/Radio Liberty 2(5), March.

Radio Free Europe (2002) *Radio Liberty Iraq Report* (5)1, 11 January.

Selahaddin (2000) "PDK is Running away from the Kurds", *Kurdish Observer*, 26 November. Available online: www.kurdishobserver.com/2000/11/26/hab01.html

Tripp, Charles (2000) *A History of Iraq*. Cambridge: Cambridge University Press.

Links

Assyrian International News Agency. www.aina.org

Iraqi Turkman Front. www.turkmencephesi.org

Journal of Assyrian Academic Studies. www.jaas.org

Mtakasto (Assyrian Democratic Organization). www.atour.com

Turkmen People Party. www.angelfire.com/tn/halk/

Zinda (Assyrian online magazine). www.zindamagazine.com

Zowaa (Assyrian Democratic Movement). www.zowaa.org

Chapter 11

Discussion Lists and Public Policy on iGhana

Chimps and feral activists

John Philip Schaefer

Introduction: Internet Ghana

In late 1999 a crisis was building in Ghana – not an economic crisis, nor a political one, but one of representation, the representation of Ghana on the internet. On one side, Ghana's diasporic elite. On the other side, Ghana's domestic political establishment, US activists, and their captive chimpanzees. This is a story of how internet discussion lists influenced public policy in Ghana.

This chapter argues that iGhana is a virtual nation, existing on the internet and imagined in the minds of its citizens, the people who participate in its maintenance, especially by discussing topics on the internet. None of the netizens have used the term iGhana, but I like to think that iGhana ("Internet Ghana") holds resonance as a heuristic device that refers to myriad social practices and communicative spaces coalescing around diverse internet users interested in things Ghanaian. iGhana's existence is directly related to the existence of Ghana, a postcolonial nation (see Chatterjee 1993) in west Africa that is as much an "imagined community" (Anderson 1983) as any other (cyber)nation. It can be presumed that at least some Ghanaians were present online from the early 1980s as members of European and American academic and corporate circles. Perhaps one of the best-known examples of such pioneers is Nii Quaynor, a former research scientist at Digital Equipment Corporation in the US. Quaynor founded the first internet service provider (ISP) in West Africa, and was, as of 2002, the only person on the board of Directors of the Internet Corporation for Assigned Names and Numbers (ICANN) from an African country.[1] Another pioneer of iGhana is Francis Akoto, a Ghanaian working in the high-tech industry in Finland, who consistently has maintained a Ghana homepage for many years. According to the site's history, Akoto developed the site in 1993 or 1994 on the server of the University of Tampere in Finland.[2] I found it in 1996. Born and raised in Ghana, I left at age 16 to go to the United States for schooling; and to combat homesickness at college I surfed the web for news from Ghana soon after I got online. In 1998 Akoto built into his site a discussion forum, *Say It Loud*, to compete with *Ghana Forum*, an older discussion list that had begun as a listserve, before being replicated on the web. The two discussion lists languished until late in 1999, when traffic increased greatly. To keep up with this growth, Akoto transferred *Say It Loud* to a new, commercial server and hired a web developer.

In this chapter I discuss the two sites, *Ghana Forum* and *Say It Loud*, where members of the Ghanaian diasporic opposition community meet and debate with members of the domestic political community and interested others. I contend that these sites represent two expressions of iGhana; and that they work through fields of representation that exist both textually and spatially. Many of the debates on these sites implicitly concerned questions of how (i)Ghana should be represented. In tracing the threads of political discourse in locations or sites not bound by physical geography, I here follow one of the most entertaining and hotly contested threads: a conflict about an attempted chimpanzee repatriation campaign. I also briefly analyse broader topics, such as how language, class, and the internet are implicated in both expressly positive and complexly ambivalent ways to represent what it means to be Ghanaian.

Two paths converging and diverging: *Ghana Forum* and *Say It Loud*

One can infer (from language and discussion content, and through user self-identification) that *Ghana Forum* predominantly was populated by well-educated, middle- and upper-class Ghanaian diasporic professionals living and working in North America, Europe and Australia. It was later joined by upper-class and upper-middle-class Ghanaians resident in Ghana. Members of Parliament, diplomats, corporate executives, and at least one presidential candidate posted to the *Ghana Forum*. According to members of *Ghana Forum*, it was a more sober and responsible discussion list than *Say It Loud*. The latter was a news site for overseas Ghanaians and a general site for anyone interested in Ghanaian culture, history or politics. *Say It Loud* was the more popular of the two lists, in both senses of the word. *Say It Loud* tended to have much higher traffic than did *Ghana Forum*;[3] and its contributors appeared to hail from the lower-middle and lower classes, as revealed in their less-polished English and opinions. The language was more radical, debates more heated, vitriol, more personal on *Say It Loud*. Akoto appears to have relished the reputation it acquired, advertising on his site that "It's Hot, But It Doesn't Burn".

The two forums tended to feed off one another, however. The same message was often posted to each of the forums, and frequent references were made to discussions on the other forum. In one exchange the Dutch webmaster of Akoto's website consulted H. Kwesi, a leading figure on *Ghana Forum*, and playfully suggested that Kwesi might direct recent "weird contributors" and "worse lunatics" on *Ghana Forum* to "another forum", presumably his own *Say It Loud* (*Ghana Forum*, 7 January 2000). Kwesi replied:

> It seems to me that the two forums have different target markets: [*Say It Loud*] seems to be going for the "mass market", while *Ghana Forum* appears

content with being a "niche" competitor. . . . In any case, you're both providing an invaluable service for the Ghanaian community. Keep it up and thanks for being here – and there.

The forums represented two classes of diasporic Ghanaian society. On one hand, there were the urbane, reasonable professionals – emigrant doctors, lawyers and academics – who discussed topics rationally, from evidence. They often appeared embarrassed by the "other" Ghana. Some protested when "illiterates" posted on the forum, complaining that the use of heterodox spelling and creative punctuation presented a poor face to the world. They characterized this other group as hot-headed and reactionary: the working-class taxi-drivers; the janitors and the peddlers of trinkets; economic refugees who, although performing menial labor in the crowded cities of the Eurocenter, still often saved enough to return to Ghana considerably financially better off than they were when they left. Their language was of the type caricatured (and lauded) by the Ghanaian linguistics professor, Kwesi Yankah, in his famous popular column "Woes of a Kwatriot": they spoke "no big English".[4]

The chimpanzee opposition

The chimp saga began in October 1999 when Friends of Animals (FOA), based in New York, and Primarily Primates, from Texas, presented a plan to the Ghana government to relocate to Ghana chimpanzees that came from circuses, zoos and the US National Air and Space agency (NASA). Though native to Ghana, chimpanzees were believed to have become extinct there until a small community was discovered in 1998 in the Western Region. The plan was to lease an island on Lake Volta in eastern Ghana, relocate the chimpanzees there, and then build a game park for ecotourism. The activists represented their intention as being fourtold: 1) liberate the animals from captivity; 2) atone for past "mining" of African wildlife by zoos and carnivals; 3) revive the Ghanaian wildlife population; and 4) develop Ghana's tourist industry so that the cost of keeping the chimps would not burden the Ghanaian economy, but might contribute to it.

Ghana was at the time nearing the twentieth year of a political scene dominated by the larger-than-life Jerry Rawlings, who first seized power in 1979 during a popular uprising. He immediately established a military tribunal under the Armed Forces Revolutionary Council, which proceeded to execute many former leaders of Ghana, including all previous heads of state. Elections were held, and a civilian government ruled until the end of 1981, when Rawlings again overthrew the government in a military coup. After an initial period of Cuban-inspired socialism, Rawlings' regime of the Provisional National Defense Council (PNDC) introduced the kind of structural adjustment policy reforms mandated by the International Monetary Fund. In so doing, he aligned himself with capitalist economic initiatives and hence with Western nation-states.

These policies continued after the return to civilian rule in 1992, with Rawlings re-elected president in 1996. The chimpanzee debate took place in a political context thus characterized by a putative democracy and free press, under a liberal center-left civilian government, but with continued fears of political instability and arbitrary decision-making. In this climate, the fact that FOA proposed that the chimp repatriation scheme be established in the Volta Region along the eastern border with Togo was not likely to be interpreted as politically neutral. Rawlings' mother was a member of the Ewe ethnic group, which is the dominant group in the Volta Region. Given a long-standing (albeit widely discounted, with evidence) general impression that this region received preferential treatment from the PNDC and it's successor regime, the NDC (National Democratic Congress) the chimp scheme was taken as further evidence of favoritism.

The independent newspaper, *The Ghanaian Chronicle*, broke the chimp story when it became known that Valerie Sackey, the British widow of a Ghanaian businessman and a long-time advisor to Rawlings, was involved in the planning. The mention of Sackey's name in connection with the plan further animated the opposition. After the story broke the director of FOA, Priscilla Feral, posted the proposed plan on *Say It Loud*, and thereby launched an involved and often acrimonious debate waged mostly on the two forums. The goals seemed laudable at best; but at worst the plan was perceived to be part of a government scheme to increase power. In addition, or alternatively, it was taken to represent an extension of colonialist domination or postcolonial racism: evidence that Africa was regarded as a dumping-ground for Western rejects and the natural home of beasts "returned" to their animalistic continent. Such accusations were indeed introduced into the online debate. Opposition to the plan clustered around discourses of epidemiology, racism and invasion, and was further charged with historical as well as contemporary political issues.

Feral agency and the civilizing mission

This debate was characterized by a great deal of acrimonious language, especially on *Say It Loud*. Given the definition of the word "feral" it is perhaps not too surprising that numerous unkind comments surfaced regarding Patricia Feral's surname. "Feral" describes the state of domesticated animals that have returned to the wild. They are widely seen as dangerous and capable of uncontrolled destruction, like European rabbits introduced to Australia or pigs to Hawai'i, or the feral dogs who, in March 2001, killed a child playing in a park in the mid-western USA. Crosby (1986) argues that the expansion of European flora and fauna into colonies in the temperate zones was an inherent feature of colonialism, but such plants and animals can also be seen as failures of the civilizing mission of animal husbandry, spurning their owners and biting the hand that feeds them. Now often considered the mistakes of colonial-era experiments, many such animals were non-native and could be viewed as alien invaders that took too successfully to the new worlds of colonial discovery.

In the world of the internet, rumors about the chimp repatriation scheme and its "Feral" leader flew thick and fast. Some forum posters expressed concern that the criticism of Patricia Feral bordered on the abusive, and several posts around this time attempted to temper the rhetoric and to apologize to Feral. This question of abusive language was apparent in one of the melodrama's sub-plots: the fact that people posting to the list repeatedly misspelled Feral's name. Her name was often spelled "Ferai", and mistaken members of the list tried on numerous occasions to correct their fellow netizens' spelling from Feral to Ferai. Believing themselves to have callously coined the surname Feral, some iGhanaians exhibited hypercorrection, entreating other forumers to stop using it. When these doubters on *Say It Loud* were reassured by members in the know that her name was indeed Feral, their suspicions were only magnified. Terence, a forumer on *Say It Loud* (*Say It Loud*, 11 February 1999) wrote:

> The name "Feral" kept bothering me as one associated with animals. So I looked up her supposedly last name in the English dictionary and guess what I found? The word "feral" means an animal that was domesticated which is released back into the wild. Just like her proposal with these burger[5] chimps. I think she is using a made up name to hide behind. Such deviousness!!! Friends, she may not only be a liar, but hiding behind a fake name that has a hidden meaning as well.

In focusing on the issue of "feral", the discussions confronted the perception (on the part of many iGhanaians) that the chimp relocation scheme implied that Africa was itself "feral" and regressive in terms of the "civilizing" heights of European colonialism. In this view, the scheme marked a postcolonial extension of the civilizing mission. The scheme's advocate was accordingly derided as "the Feral", and FOA as "the chimp squad". In "Beware the Feral's Chimp Squad" (*Say It Loud*, 11 April 1999), one poster wrote:

> Evidence is mounting that the Feral has employed a Chimp Squad of agents who are attempting to infiltrate this forum with disinformation and to confuse the issue about these burger chimps. A word to the wise is in order whenever you see a posting that might attempt to argue in favor of this diabolical organization – the Friends of Animals (but Enemies of Humans!).

In the opposition to the chimp scheme, we witness an inversion of the notion of ferality. Under this logic, the chimps were not feral in the US, where they were cloistered in zoos, circuses and laboratories, but it was feared they would become feral when they "returned" to Ghana. Once in Ghana they might get off the island and spread their diseases, or whatever mutations might have occurred from their exposure to radiation and other experiments, among the wild chimpanzees, or other animal (including human) populations of Ghana.

The importance of disease discourse in the direction and tenor of the debate is considered next.

Epidemiology and invasion

Fears about disease and infection were foremost among the criticisms levied by opponents to the chimp scheme. FOA initially proposed that the chimps had been rescued or bought from research institutions and military contractors, and might have been subject to medical experiments. *Ghana Forum* posters imme-diately inferred that the chimps had been infected with HIV or cancers, and articulated fears that the animals might bring infections into Ghana. Kofi, a *Ghana Forum* poster and *Say It Loud* contributor, alleged (*Say It Loud*, 28 November 1999) that he had privileged Ghanaian contacts in laboratories in the Washington D.C. area claiming evidence that the chimps were infected:

> We have people who work at NIH [National Institutes of Health]. . . . who affirm our fears. Just recently, residents in Reston, Virginia, a D.C. suburb were up in arms because some animals at a lab used for all kinds of sickly experiments had fled into the neighborhood. . . . Feral's animals were "rescued" from labs.{..}. Would you say that such animals do not harbor the viruses of their research?

iGhanaians also labelled what they considered to be the dumping of old, diseased, contaminated chimps in Ghana as just another instance of an American attempt to avoid dealing with its own problems. In this argument, they recalled the legacy of Africa being exploited as a dumping ground for toxic waste, contaminated food, used clothes, worn out cars, and other commodities rejected by Westernized countries. For example, Kwabena wrote (*Say It Loud*, 21 October 1999):

> Thank you for providing information that outlines FOA's paternalistic thinking, colonialist typologizing, and atomistic prejudice. Whatever humanitarian tinge there is, it is based on a carefully crafted bureaucratic double-speak: fruitless exercise in semantics embellished for the unwary. . . . The fact that your organization has all these high-sounding objectives does not mean that Ghanaians should just accept them. Time was when we accepted such concocted humanitarian garbage. . . . Western countries hide behind these so-called international organizations to perpetuate unspeak-able atrocities on Africans and propaganda about Africa.

The idea of infectious Africa as a continent of mysterious and deadly diseases has a long legacy, one that is rooted in fact for the European colonialist. During nineteenth-century colonial expeditions, Ghana, and indeed the whole coast of west Africa, was described by Europeans as the "White Man's Graveyard" on

the basis of the high mortalities suffered by colonial administrators – missionaries, soldiers, businessmen – who commonly lasted a few months or less. In a
direct inheritance from colonial stereotypes, Western science and media still
perpetuate the notion that European and US tourists who visit the continent
will fall prey to myriad diseases for which they have no defenses. Interestingly,
at the base of these arguments, the emphasis has been put on the vile and
contagious nature of Africa as the dark continent, rather than on the relative
weakness of the foreigners' immune systems. This imagery continues to describe
Africa as an ultimate, primal source of disease. All visitors to the region are
warned of "infectious Africa" by Western physicians with their requirements to
submit to a battery of pre-travel inoculations and prophylactic measures.

With regard to the real and conceptual relationship between disease and
tourism, we should here recall that tourism was one of the four incentives FOA
put forth in support of the chimp relocation scheme. It can be suggested that
forumers implicitly perceived a discourse of economic exploitation, cultural
exchange, sexuality, and metaphors of contagion mixed with representations of
Africa and the African diaspora. Here I make reference to the work of
Browning (1998), who has studied how AIDS and the African diaspora are
both equated with a pandemic through the employment of scientific metaphors
of contagion made even more threatening. Xenophobia is defended in the name
of public health when people join capital in the transnational flows facilitated
by late modernity. Browning's insight reveals that "economic imbalances, in
conjunction with the flow of media images, necessarily destabilize sexual
exchanges, creating intimacies precisely at the points most strenuously marked
as Other" (1998: 9). In the case of the chimp relocation scheme, rhetorics of
ecotourism and development (and the economic imbalances they would
purportedly redress) maintained a narrative that the chimpanzees could not
infect Africa, since this was, after all, their "homeland". In refuting this narrative, a rupture or disjuncture was forced by iGhanaians, who reasserted their
agency and faced down opponents through the odd intimacy of the internet.

"Back to Africa, Sort Of": issues of race and power

Arguments about the chimp repatriation scheme also coalesced around discussions of colonialism, geopolitics and the "Back to Africa" movement of the late
nineteenth/early twentieth centuries. "Back to Africa, Sort Of" was the title of a
Say It Loud discussion thread that made explicit reference to the relocation
movement in which formerly enslaved Africans from New World regions (US
and the Caribbean) were encouraged to return "back" to Africa. The ideology
and historical dynamics of this movement were complex: for example, it viewed
out-migration from "white" countries as deliverance from racism, but it was
seized upon as well by white separatists who saw in Back to Africa a solution to
the "negro problem". None the less, it did result in several thousand people
"returning" to Africa.[6] The "Back to Africa, Sort Of" discussion drew a line

between "returning" chimpanzees to a present-day Ghana, and the historical idea of returning African-Americans to a generic Africa. A racist subtext to the FOA resettlement scheme was clearly perceived by some forum posters who chose to parody the scheme as a kind of solution to the "chimpanzee problem". In playing with this analogy, they were perhaps also exposing the ultimate futility of past repatriation experiments with respect to things and beings "African".

At the moment, face-to-face encounters between Ghanaians and African-Americans largely take place through tourism. Of note here is the heritage tourism that the Ghanaian government has been promoting, particularly with regard to the slave forts of past centuries (where slaves were rounded up before being loaded on ships to the New World). These coastal forts are presently being turned into tourist sites. Bruner (1996) discusses the ambivalence surrounding these forts, which hold different significance for African-American heritage tourists – who see them as sites of enslavement and exile – than they do for Ghanaians, who see them as historical monuments and festival sites. As a child in Ghana in the 1980s' I repeatedly heard the rumor that, when a prominent African-American visited Africa and viewed the poverty, he stated "I thank God that my granddaddy got on that boat".[7] We inferred from this that some African-Americans believed their past experiences of enslavement and oppression were preferable to living in present-day Africa. This attitude continues to rankle among many Ghanaians.

Allegations of racism circulated in the context of the chimpanzee relocation scheme. Patricia Feral defended FOA against the charge by noting that its Washington D.C. office employed a number of African-Americans. This statement clearly underestimated the sensitivity of issues of economics and race, both globally and locally. Some forum posters claimed that Feral was on the defensive, and characterized her statement as dissimulation designed to detract from more dubious motives. Some also mused upon the probability that the jobs for African-Americans in her office were – like the proposed 40 tourism jobs that would be created in Ghana – at the low end of the pay scale. This raised the question of employment, domestic politics and power: key issues for peoples in diaspora. For example, when FOA proposed to send paramilitary equipment to aid gamekeepers in the proposed park, forum posters seized upon the potential for abuse by regimes in power. Given that Ghana suffered from at least five coups d'état between 1966 and 1981, military takeovers seem never to be far from people's minds. Thus, some posters envisioned a new source for military equipment, as well as the specter of a "chimp army" – soldiers armed through the proposed park's resources – with the potential to overthrow or support a regime. Complicating matters further was the view, held by some iGhanaians and reflected in their rhetoric, that the chimp relocation scheme represented a kind of "incursion" that would infiltrate Ghana and play into domestic political power games. The rhetoric of some forum posters itself took a militaristic turn, as in the completely over-the-top response of J.W., who wrote (*Say It Loud*, 11 April 1999):

> Blowing the projected chimps to smithereens is the last resort being planned by loyalists in Ghana if project is implemented. . . . Please inundate your folks back home as to the nature of this evil project and its impending doom to the country.

In short, iGhanaians argued against incursion from the animal rights activists and looked upon their project of aid and development with suspicion. This included regarding the project as either some kind of postcolonial guilty conscience, a neo-colonial hegemony, or both. In doing so, iGhanaians may have appeared to be advocating a primordial, autochthonous purity for the nation-state. Moreover, and ironically, similar claims of national "purity" have also been made by members of the political elite back home in Ghana, even as Ghana itself is coming increasingly under the control of international aid and development agencies. Hence, the situation of the virtual nation iGhana finds Ghanaians negotiating a power bid – filtered through the internet – between an opposition diasporic elite and a domestic political elite. It is important to note, however, that this diasporic political elite did not represent a uniform voice or some kind of monolithic entity. Rather, all political persuasions were represented on iGhana. They all seemed to share, none the less, a great deal of ambivalence in regard to Ghana's two "pure" political lineages: the socialist Nkrumahist tradition, and the bourgeois-conservative Danquah–Busia tradition. Contemporary political parties tend to define themselves in relation to these two lineages (Pellow and Chazan 1986). Rawlings' National Democratic Congress (NDC) is widely viewed as the representative of the center-left (and would be considered Nkrumahist socialist were it not for its erosion of the welfare state following upon neo-liberal World Bank policies). The center-right Danquah–Busia tradition is clearly represented by the New Patriotic Party (NPP). On iGhana, NDC-type rhetoric about saving social welfare was front and center. Just as broadly circulating, however, were NPP-led opposition calls for "positive change".

Such cultural hybridity is nothing new in diaspora (Lavie and Swedenburg 1996: 9); although it might have different implications in the age of internet, given the anonymity of identities online. Indeterminacy with regard to identity on the internet might thus further complicate the already-strained conditions in play in a diasporic population's use of popular media, where emigrants characteristically maintain multiple relationships across borders and within borderlands (Naficy 1993). In the case of the discussion forums used by diasporic Ghanaians (as evidenced by the chimp relocation scheme and many other issues under debate) there were multiple cross-border relationships – all ultimately with relevance to questions of "homeland". At this point, it would be appropriate to entertain a discussion of some of the characteristics and identities of iGhana as a space and as a text. Then we can turn to a final word about the implications of iGhana for the chimp relocation scheme and its fate.

iGhanaians: diasporic identity and virtual nations

Working towards an understanding of iGhana as a virtual nation necessitates consideration of the qualities of a nation, in the contemporary geographical-political and social senses of the term. Attempts to establish the links between space, identity and culture, and nation (let alone e-nation) have been fraught with difficulty. One of the more influential discussions of the development of modern nations and their accompanying nationalism is Anderson's (1983) thesis that printed matter was the first and most enduring capitalist expression of the nation. According to Anderson, nations are imagined political communities – limited and sovereign – and the rise of Western nation-states has been through capitalism, especially what he terms "print-capitalism": the emerging state use of print media to promote a national identity intended to replace and oppose antiquated identities. In the service of nationalism, print-capitalism creates "print-languages", unified communication fields on the national level that standardize and fix linguistic forms from the dominant dialects. Nations are delimited, in that borders are not supposed to overlap, and ideally each nation is free to exert power in its own region. By invoking their sovereignty, nations posit themselves as the final authority in administering their economies, territories and citizens; and they retain as their supreme goal their self-preservation.

Appadurai (1996) expands and updates Anderson's thesis to include "electronic capitalism". The emphasis of this new technology remains that of producing and encouraging identification with the nation, but through different media and thus with some different effects. Radio and television – the electronic media – do not need a literate audience, merely a consuming one, and thus lend themselves better to mass mobilization within non-literate contexts. With the arrival of the internet, electronic capitalism has itself undergone transformation. The governmental policies that regulated radio and television programming, although by no means absent on the internet, are to some extent occluded by the ease of access, the anonimity of the user and the difficulties of monitoring the uses of the technology. Nevertheless, the egalitarian nature of radio broadcast is countered by the high cost of computers and the preferential nature of access to telecommunications. Literacy is again required, and a computer literacy is now prerequisite. There is thus a digital divide that challenges the role of electronic capitalism in the formation of an imagined community of the nation-state.

In considering the rise of nationalism globally, Stoler (1995) critiques Anderson's emphasis on nationalism's supposedly linear progression through time and its spatial origin in Europe. She convincingly argues that the modernity of Europe often developed simultaneously in the colonies. The colonies, like the "Third World" of the present, can be considered "laboratories of modernity"[8] or sites of experimentation in new techniques and technologies. One area of experimentation in iGhana (if not necessarily yet within Ghana) has been in bridging the digital divide. I suggest that iGhanaians accomplished this bridge

by combining old media with new media; that is, combining print and electronic modes of communication and information exchange.

Another important point about the nation is the idea that each nation "has"
its citizens. Citizens in cyberspace, however, tend to be "notoriously anonymous", so to speak. On some occasions and in certain forums, these netizens
define themselves, however rudimentarily (Markham 1998), but the majority
are identified only through their online nicknames and whatever contextual
clues are available. The indeterminacy of identity over the internet has tended
to be cast in positive terms: a *New Yorker* cartoon from the early 1990s quipped
that "On the Internet, nobody knows you're a dog" (Steiner 1993). Some
researchers, however, have claimed that there is a growing sense of ambivalence
among internet users about online anonymity.[9] Virtual nations are patterned on
existing nations, yet with different modes of interaction and representation.
Policing and surveillance none the less still occur. For example, if a troublesome
or unruly forum poster maintains a consistent alias, the moderator can limit
participation or even expel the poster from the list. Posters at *Ghana Forum* and
Say It Loud petitioned the webmaster on occasion to ban certain posters, but,
given the nature of these forums, this was difficult to achieve.[10] Even when a
netizen continues to post under different aliases, his or her "identity" to some
extent may be transparent to the other participant-members of a discussion
forum, particularly in the case of a small group with a relatively consistent
participant base. This was the case concerning the poster(s) known as Jake/
Young Bajan on *Ghana Forum*. When I first joined iGhana in 1999 some of the
most protracted arguments were being started or intensified by Jake. Jake
appeared to be a white, middle-class American from the southern United States
who was interested in Africa and race; and he later admitted to posting
provocative articles under several aliases. The indeterminacy of Jake's "identity"
can be said to have posed a nuisance when Jake continued to post after having
been invited to leave. Jake threatened to leave, returned a few times, and then
disappeared at the same time that Young Bajan began posting. Young Bajan
claimed to be Bahaman but sounded so suspiciously like Jake in his favorite
topics and provocative stances to some of the other posters that they began
calling him JYB ("Jake/Young Bajan"). This example suggests that it may not
readily be possible to hide identity in certain small and "tight" virtual communities, where idiomatic and/or discursive characteristics might be clues to
identity. The most successful means for bringing about the departure of
unwanted "would-be Ghanaians" (the term was first used to describe the
chimps!) was isolation from and hostility on the part of the regular posters.

One other feature of the nation-state that we should consider here is the
matter of real (that is to say, geophysical) space. Established characteristics of
nation-states include their limited, clearly demarcated borders; in contrast,
virtual communities have differently defined borders, even an absence of borders.
Cyberspace has been described as no bigger – and no smaller – than the human
imagination. Casting the internet as space is itself a metaphoric refiguring,

defined through recourse to more familiar modes of representation. Morse discusses the "nonspace of the mind": the virtual world of the networked computer "in which" (or through which) people interact with varying degrees of personhood (1998: 179–81). iGhana, like other virtual nations, faces challenges in formulating its reality with respect to space and population. In seeking to understand e-nations, however, it is necessary to go beyond the dichotomies of real versus virtual spaces. Soja's discussions on space and place (1996) might be useful in this regard. Soja adopts Lefebvre's trialectic model of perceived, conceived and lived space, which he recasts as Firstspace, Secondspace and Thirdspace. The first, perceived space, is the space of the practice of a society's conscious, material existence. Conceived space, in contrast, combines authoritative representations of space with the relations of production and the control over knowledge. The third, the synthetic space of representation and lived experience, is conceptualized as a space for othering that transcends dichotomous thinking (Soja 1996: 64–70). Like all nations, iGhana has simultaneous ties to all three spaces: the everyday practices of Ghanaians in Ghana and outside; the real controls and economic considerations involved in maintaining a website; and the lived experiences that are played out when netizens interact on and through websites. However, iGhana's ties to Firstspace and Secondspace seem to recede in comparison to the extensive representational power of an online universe. Perhaps Soja's concept of othering can help us to re-think cyberspace, not merely as some "other" space but, *pace* Soja, as some way "'other than' the established way of thinking spatially" (Soja 1996: 163).[11]

iGhana and other virtual nations that are tied to a "3-D" country draw on the history, society and unique structures of feeling or attitudes that obtain in "real" nation counterparts. As netizens of a virtual nation, iGhanaians have contested and constantly redefined identities. Citizenship was a frequent topic on discussion forums, despite or perhaps primarily because of the deterritorializing experiences of many diasporic Ghanaians. From these discussions it can be discerned that the majority of iGhanaians were exiled – economically, politically, or in other ways – from Ghana, and others were born or became naturalized citizens of Western countries. I would argue that the topic of citizenship was so popular because many iGhanaians have sustained a relationship to Ghanaian identity. Diasporic Ghanaians tend to maintain deep emotional ties to their homeland of Ghana; and they may have a heightened sensitivity regarding Ghana's marginal place in the world system. Questions of citizenship and anonymity demand greater discussion than is possible here, but clearly citizenship and belonging in online communities are decided by members, not by official governing bodies. Moreover, we must permit that at least some iGhanaians may never have been, or no longer were, "Ghanaian" at all, thus their most immediate common indigeneity was to the internet.[12]

In contrast to the question of a real Ghana versus a simulacrum in the form of iGhana, it is of interest to mention other forms of truly and solely virtual nations that have been pioneered on the internet. One such infamous "non-territorial entity" is the Republic of Lomar. After learning of the site via *Ghana Forum*, I visited Lomar and became a legal citizen of Lomar by signing up online.[13] I can now apply for a Lomar passport and driver's license. In one sense, it's perfectly meaningless, since no such country exists. But in another sense, it is not meaningless; and the people who set it up insist that it is not a hoax. In April 2001, the website claimed that Lomar was a "virtual republic" seeking to establish sovereignty. Yet, in March 2002, the site argued emphatically that Lomar was not a "micronation" (a quasi-legitimate designation of the Google search directory), but was rather a human rights organization: the Republic of Lomar Foundation. Further along this line, by May 2002 the Republic of Lomar had transformed into both "a nonprofit non-governmental organization" (NGO) and a passport-issuing "quasi-state". Lomar currently focuses on "diplomatic representation of the oppressed and unrepresented" via the promotion of "a complementary non-territorial approach to citizenship".[14] Accordingly, it asserts that it exists "to issue passports and other necessary documents to refugees, stateless, and undocumented individuals". The complications surrounding Lomar's historical self-creation derive in part from attempts (in the site's early days) by some unsavory individuals to cheat desperate refugees by selling them Lomar passports. There are numerous other "micronations" on the internet, some of which claim a more tangible or acquisitive relationship to territory. The Kingdoms of Elgaland and Vargaland, for example, lay claim to all "no person's land" that exists or has existed between international boundaries, as well as all areas "up to a width of 10 nautical miles" outside the territorial waters of all nations.[15] Arguably, these many "virtual communities" reflect the diversity of expressions of and in cyberspace. It is to the issue of the expressions and culture of virtual nations that I now turn.

One of the trickiest questions involving the nation-state is the question of the relationship between culture and space. Forum posters on both *Say It Loud* and *Ghana Forum* were clearly participants in cyberspace, but this is not to imply that they were members of an homogenous cyberculture. In other words, cyberculture should not be equated or conflated with "cyberspace"; and in emphasizing this some authors have chosen to use the plural of cybercultures (Bell 2001). This approach counters research that has tended to refer to cyberspace as an homogeneous space where the internet is envisioned as a virtual reality separate from "real" life (following the fiction of William Gibson, 1984).[16] In this view, the typical cyberpunk is a young, suburban American who spends his days and nights online. He knows all about programming and web development. Wearing a virtual reality headset, he writes killer apps in Linux and Java, surfs the web on a T1 line, hacks sites, downloads MP3s, creates alternative worlds in MUDs and MOOs, and otherwise lives online. The jargon is intentional – since cyberpunks are from another culture, they should speak another language. This stereotype is not representative of the experiences of most users of networked computers (DiMaggio *et al.* 2001), nevertheless, its theme has suffered many conceptual studies of the internet.

Opposition and resolution

As noted, the chimp relocation plan sparked a power bid between an opposition diasporic elite and a domestic political elite. This power bid must be contextualized within the contemporary political climate, both translocal and domestic. When Rawlings' regime, despite its history of autocratic rule, relinquished control over the political structure in 1993, democracy and a free press allowed a return of the civil society that had flourished in previous periods. Throughout the 1990s private newspapers proliferated, led by *The Ghanaian Chronicle*. The success of the *Chronicle*, along with its online counterpart, was a most telling turn of events, because it kept diasporic members of the opposition immediately apprised of Ghanaian political developments while enabling writers to respond quickly to the issues of the day. In addition to press liberalization, Ghana during the 1990s underwent liberalization of the airwaves, which resulted in 40 private FM radio stations broadcasting in the major cities by the year 2000. According to Friedman (2001), the FM stations played a decisive role in the 2000 election. Another decisive role, however, was played by the internet. The internet allowed the immediate relay of information from Ghana to the cities of the metropole, affording diasporic Ghanaians timely responses. Due to the relatively democratic and open nature of discussion lists, many more Ghanaians were able to participate in the debate, enabling non-elite members of the diasporic community to express their opinions, although how much attention was paid to their opinions is up for conjecture. The point here is that private capital, mobilized toward print, electronic, and internet media, produced not only a virtual community but enabled a political movement.

I hesitate to argue that the tenor of the 2000 election was determined by the chimpanzee contest. Rather, the same factors that had been driving the impetus of Ghanaian civil society for several years were implicated in the virtual debate, and these included trade liberalization, increasing press freedom, and privatization of the airwaves in addition to internet access. Friedman (2001: A-27) notes that "the FM [radio stations were] all run by young Ghanaians who were either educated or had worked in the West" (possibly since 1998, and if so with exposure to the internet, and thus to *Say It Loud* and *Ghana Forum*). The chimp saga was a harbinger of the opposition's tools in the 2000 election, which included not only forays into print and broadcast media, but the deployment of cybertechnology as well. The opposition bridged the digital divide, not by seeking ways to exploit the full panoply of internet resources, but rather by employing those aspects of the internet deemed most useful to their ends. Yes, global interconnectivity is possible, but in this case theoretically unlimited interconnectivity was, in actuality, pragmatically limited and refocused toward a common goal.

After approximately three months of debate, research and lobbying, the NDC-dominated Parliament decided to cancel the chimp relocation program. This was perceived as a victory by opposition iGhanaians, who engaged their antagonists on their own terms and in their own space. If the space of a "speech act" can be extended to online communication, then in a Bakhtinian sense we might say that they achieved agency through dialogue with the activists (Bakhtin, cited in Bhabha 1993: 189). January 2000 marked the end of the chimp saga. Twelve months later, in January 2001, John Kufuor of the opposition was sworn in after winning a hard-fought presidential election, ending 21 years of Rawlings's domination over Ghanaian politics.

Notes

1 ICANN, the internet's "technical coordination body", wields more power over the internet than nearly any other institution, see http://www.icann.org/.
2 See http://www.ghanaweb.com/GhanaHomePage/aboutus.php.
3 Although still technically in existence, Ghana Forum was largely inactive in 2002.
4 Yankah's observations of underclass Ghanaians' "broken vernacular" in the column is all the more telling (though no less humorous) because he was critiquing the misuse of "big English" by Rawlings-era politicians (see below) speaking "very good English to very vernacular ears" (1996: 2). Yankah's column ran from the mid-1980s until the early 1990s in the Ghanaian weekly *The Mirror*.
5 *Burger* or *boga* (pronounced bawga) is a term in Ghanaian English related to the German *burgher* or French *bourgeois*. According to Kirby (1998: 38) the word refers to "any flashy wheeler-dealer, uniform of gold chains, baggy trousers and driving a late model BMW or small 'Benz.' Now often associated with drugs".
6 The movement began in earnest with the American Colonization Society (1817–1912), the group that founded Liberia and "relocated" 15,000 African-Americans there by 1890 (Redkey 1969: 74). Another "relocation" scheme involved a trip to what is now Ghana led by an astute but shadowy man from the region, Chief Alfred C. Sam, who led several hundred Oklahomans to Galveston in 1914, where he bought a ship and sailed to the African "gold coast" with 60 African-Americans on board. When the ship arrived in Africa, Sam disappeared; and the majority of the passengers returned to the United States (Redkey 1969: 292; Stein 1986: 111). Marcus Garvey, the person most often associated with the Back to Africa movement, was a Jamaican populist who founded the Universal Negro Improvement Association (UNIA) in New York in 1917. Garvey's movement grew quickly, but he hit his nadir in 1922 when he met with a Ku Klux Klan leader in a misguided attempt to court popular white opinion in the US South (Vincent 1971: 191). This association of Garvey with "Back to Africa" is overwhelming despite the fact that few African-Americans emigrated through his efforts. One of Garvey's associates later claimed that the UNIA was not a Back to Africa movement but rather a movement "to redeem Africa" (quoted in Stein 1986: 109; see also Vincent 1971).
7 The quote has been attributed to the boxer Muhammad Ali by Dinesh D'Souza (http://www.dartreview.com/issues/10.15.01/multiculturalism.html) or to a member of Ali's entourage, after the 1974 *Rumble in the Jungle* with George Foreman in Mobutu's Zaire. For a recent restatement, see Richburg 1997: xiv.
8 For further discussion of modernity, consult the engagement between Dilip Gaonkar (1999) and Timothy Mitchell (2000) over "alternative modernities".
9 For example, in her online research, anthropologist Kathryn Wickens requires not only online but "3D" or real-life identification of prospective members by established community members (November 2000, personal communication). See http://www.framerate.net/kate/index.html.
10 Relative to other internet sites, *Ghana Forum* and *Say It Loud* have been characterized by an absence of official gatekeeping, and virtually none from the nation-state

of Ghana. This is partly a result of the two forums' domain place on the internet, which was outside the scope of the top-level domain of .gh, for Ghana. This top-level domain, as well as Ghana's international web portal, were under the exclusive control of Nii Quaynor, whom the *Boston Globe* named "maybe the most influential [geek] in all of Africa" (Bray 2001). Quaynor, deemed by Uimonen (2001:53-59) an "Internet pioneer" of the developing world, developed west Africa's first internet service provider in 1996/1997 (Uimonen 2001: 57). In a 2001 attempt to curb what he called "freeloading" of the type done by *Ghanaweb.com* and *Ghanaforum.com*, Quaynor began limiting the speed and convenience of access by Ghanaian ISPs to international sites. *Say It Loud* and Ghana Forum continued to be hosted on internationally based servers, which afforded their webmasters control over their sites (within the limits of the governments in which their servers were based). According to Bray (2001), a proposed undersea cable will provide Ghana with direct internet access through Telkom South Africa.
11 I am indebted to Kyra Landzelius for some of this discussion.
12 The discussions that centered around citizenship raised intriguing questions about identity and representation that are largely beyond the scope of this essay, yet raise key questions. For instance, when one iGhanaian identifies herself as an African-American woman in Washington D.C., who hopes to visit Ghana one day, or when another iGhanaian admits that he is a white South African in Australia who has never been to west Africa, how should we as researchers deal with these identities and self-representations?
13 See http://www.republic-of-lomar.org/. Other micronations are listed at http://directory.google.com/Top/Society/Issues/Secession/Micronations/.
14 At http://www.republic-of-lomar.org/information/introduction.htm, accessed 14 May 2002.
15 At http://www.it.kth.se/KREV.
16 Many such analyses of cyberculture were based on the uses of networked computers from the 1970s to the mid-1990s (Morse 1998), before the internet became popular and messy. After 1995, computer design and marketing began to center on home internet access, and other views of the Internet have emerged. However, much research, has been limited to studies of semi-professional and middle-class users. The characteristics exhibited by users of Multi-User Domains (MUDs), object-oriented MUDs (MOOs) Instant messaging computer programs, I seek you, ICQ and Internet Relay Chat IRC chat applications include decontextualized identity-constructions, escapist and addictive use patterns, role-playing, and other radical social patterns.
17 Markham (1998) studies female-only discussions lists. Miller and Slater (2001) examine the place of the internet in Trinidad and *vice versa*.

References

Publications

Anderson, Benedict (1983) *Imagined Communities*. London: Verso.
Appadurai, Arjun (1996) *Modernity at Large: Cultural Dimensions of Globalization*. Minneapolis: University of Minnesota Press.
Bell, David (2001) *An Introduction to Cybercultures*. London: Routledge.
Bhabha, Homi K. (1993) "The Postcolonial and the Postmodern: The Question of Agency", in S. During (ed.), *The Cultural Studies Reader*, 2nd edition. London: Routledge, pp 189–208.
Bray, Hiawatha (2001) "Critics Don't Deter Internet Visionary", *Boston Globe*, 24 July 2001. Available online at www.boston.com/globe/nation/packages/wiring_africa/part 3_bar1.htm.

Browning, Barbara (1998) *Infectious Rhythm: Metaphors of Contagion and the Spread of African Culture*. London: Routledge.
Bruner, Edward M. (1996) "Tourism in Ghana: The Representation of Slavery and the Return of the Black Diaspora", *American Anthropologist* 98(2): 290–304.
Chatterjee, Partha (1993) *The Nation and Its Fragments: Colonial and Postcolonial Histories*. Princeton: Princeton University Press.
Crosby, Alfred W. (1986) *Ecological Imperialism: The Biological Expansion of Europe, 900–1900*. Cambridge: Cambridge University Press.
DiMaggio, Paul, Hargittai, Eszter, Newman, W. Russell, and Robinson, John P. (2001) "Social Implications of the Internet", *Annual Review of Sociology* 27: 307–36.
Friedman, Thomas (2001) "Low-Tech Democracy", *New York Times*, 17 May: A-27.
Gaonkar, Dilip (1999) "On Alternative Modernities", *Public Culture* 11(1): 153–74.
Gibson, William (1984) *Neuromancer*. New York: Ace.
Kirby, Jon P. (1998) *A North American's Guide to Ghanaian English*. Tamale, Northern Region: Tamale Institute of Cross-Cultural Studies.
Lavie, Smadar and Swedenburg, Ted (1996) *Displacement, Diaspora and Geographies of Identity*. Durham, NC, and London: Duke University Press.
Markham, Annette N. (1998) *Life Online: Researching Real Experience in Virtual Space*. Walnut Creek, CA: AltaMira Press.
Miller, Daniel and Slater, Don (2001) *The Internet: An Ethnographic Approach*. Oxford: Berg.
Mitchell, Timothy (2000) "The Stage of Modernity", in T. Mitchell (ed.), *Questions of Modernity*. Minneapolis: University of Minnesota Press. pp. 1–34.
Morse, Margaret (1998) *Virtualities: Television, Media Art, and Cyberculture*. Bloomington: Indiana University Press.
Naficy, Hamid (1993) *The Making of Exile Cultures: Iranian Television in Los Angeles*. Minneapolis: University of Minnesota Press.
Pellow, Deborah and Chazan, Naomi (1986) *Ghana: Coping with Uncertainty*. Boulder CO: Westview Press.
Redkey, Edwin S. (1969) *Black Exodus: Black Nationalist and Back-to-Africa Movements, 1890–1910*. New Haven: Yale University Press.
Richburg, Keith B. (1997) *Out of America: A Black Man Confronts Africa*. New York: Basicbooks.
Soja, Edward W. (1996) *Thirdspace: Journeys to Los Angeles and Other Real-and-Imagined Places*. Oxford and Cambridge, MA: Blackwell.
Stein, Judith (1986) *The World of Marcus Garvey: Race and Class in Modern Society*. Baton Rouge: Louisiana State University Press.
Steiner, Peter (1993) "On the Internet, nobody knows you're a dog", cartoon, *The New Yorker* 69:20 (5 July): 61.
Stoler, Ann Laura (1995) *Race and the Education of Desire: Foucault's History of Sexuality and the Colonial Order of Things*. Durham, NC: Duke University Press.
Uimonen, Paula (2001) "Transnational.Dynamics@Development.Net: Internet, Modernization and Globalization", *Stockholm Studies in Social Anthropology* 49. Stockholm: Amqvist and Wiksell International.
Vincent, Theodore G. (1971) *Black Power and the Garvey Movement*. Berkeley, CA: Ramparts Press.
Yankah, Kwesi (1996) *Woes of a Kwatriot (1990–91): No Big English*. Accra: Anansesem.

Links

Friends of Animals. http://www.friendsofanimals.org/
Ghana Forum. http://www.ghanaforum.com/forum/
Ghana Home Page. http://www.ghanaweb.com/
Ghanaian Chronicle online edition. http://www.ghanaian-chronicle.com/

Chapter 12

The Transformation of Discourse Online

Toward a holistic diagnosis of the nature of social inequality in Burundi

Rose M. Kadende-Kaiser

Introduction

The civil war in Burundi that began in October 1993 has triggered a proliferation of diverse views and opinions regarding the nature of the ethnic conflict and the strategies necessary for conflict resolution (Gahama 1999; Sumu 2001; Ndarubagiye 1996). The internet has served as an interesting resource in this process. Issues concerning social inequality, ethnicity and approaches to peace have all been explored and debated via electronic news updates as well as online discussions. This chapter explores the perspectives of two such online discussion groups or bulletin boards: *Burundi Youth Council*, accessible at www.burundiyouth.com; and *Burundinet* which is no longer accessible online.[1] In both of these discussion groups, Hutu and Tutsi Burundians residing in the diaspora have been engaging in a diagnosis of the roots of conflict in Burundi in order to determine the most appropriate mechanisms for peaceful conflict transformation.

Burundinet (*B-net*) was most active during the early years of post-1993 violence; and had several hundred members by the middle of its second year (the only time a membership record was provided). Most of these member-participants lived in the diaspora, thus relatively few *B-netters* were actually living in Burundi at the time that *B-net* was active. By contrast, the majority of participants on *Burundi Youth Council* (BYC), which emerged seven years into the war, reside in Burundi; although the most active members are still primarily those living in the West, where internet is more easily accessible. Many such members are refugees or have the equivalent of a temporary protected status in their countries of residence (e.g., to pursue university education or occupations). Based on thematic areas of interest that the network interactants focus on, *Burundinet* and BYC exhibit a number of divergent features.

In comparing the contents of these two newsgroups, I argue that there is a transformation of discourse online. Indeed, while both *B-net* and BYC are engaged in discussing appropriate mechanisms for ending ethnic violence, their diagnoses of the roots of Burundi problems are quite different. In general, they approach the question of social inequality differently. For *B-netters*, social inequality was perceived as an issue of group ethnic identity. On this forum, it was commonplace to blame the ethnic "other" for the problems facing Burundi. At times, individual *Burundinet* users had to be reminded to "abide by the network rules", or join another network. In contrast, for participants on BYC, social inequality is seen as part of a larger picture that includes other aspects of identity as well. This transformation of discourse online could be interpreted with skepticism that BYC is trying to avoid, instead of confront, problems associated with the question of ethnicity in Burundi. However, as the rules of engagement on their website explain, the BYC site managers are aware that debates related to ethnicity often end up in a stalemate, and can easily escalate into "cyberwars". To avoid this, and to promote productive discussions, BYC's executive committee has posted a set of rules, or netiquette, aimed at encouraging interactions across ethnic lines. This netiquette is grounded in their belief that a holistic approach would enable Burundians of all ethnic backgrounds to address shared concerns as well as differences.

Background on ethnicity and ethnic conflict in Burundi

Before the advent of German (1896–1916) and Belgian colonialism (1916–1962), Burundi was under the leadership of the Ganwa monarchy for approximately four centuries (fifteenth century through 1965). Ethnicity was a fluid process whereby Hutu and Tutsi experienced identity shifts depending on the tasks they were expected to perform in service to the monarchy. As Ress explains, by the nineteenth century "the royal court had evolved an elaborate system of rewards and responsibilities . . . allotted to various influential lineages and clans" (1992: 39). Clan differentiation diminished the relevance of ethnicity as a rigid marker of primordial identity.

During the early years of German and Belgian colonial rule, fluidity gave way to a gradual rigidification of identity, with an emphasis on the institutionalization of Hutu/Tutsi differences. Explicit roles were assigned for each ethnic group. According to Lemarchand, a "distorted" colonial depiction represented Burundi society in terms of an "ethnic pyramid", with the minority Tutsi "holding the commanding heights of power" over the majority Hutu farmers and the numerically small, hunter-gatherer Twa (Lemarchand 1974: 8). It further transformed the traditional, decentralized monarchy in Burundi into a highly centralized and efficient bureaucratic order that resembled the Belgian constitutional monarchy. This process increased the exclusion of Hutu in traditional governance, while select Tutsi clans gained political and economic dominance in the country. By the time of independence in 1962, the Ganwa King Mwambutsa IV, who had clearly sided with the colonialists, had also lost popular support.

With the end of the monarchy in sight, struggles for power between leaders of Hutu and Tutsi origin marked the beginning of an interethnic mistrust. This turned into violence around the independence period and in subsequent years as assassinations and other oppressive measures were taken to silence opposition. According to some sources, as many as two hundred thousand Burundians, the majority of whom were Hutu men, were killed in 1972 alone. The civil war that started in 1993 continues to take the lives of hundreds of thousands more. Today, the majority of the victims are Hutu and Tutsi civilians caught between a predominantly Tutsi army and the majority of Hutu militias, or "rebel groups". Approximately 15 percent of the Burundi population has been living in displacement, both internally and outside the country since 1993 (see, e.g., Sabimbona online at www.unifem.undp.org/public/landrights). None the less, the two groups continue to speak the same language, Kirundi, and share similar cultural practices, and until 1993 they lived together in the same hills, mountains or neighborhoods, attended the same church services and conducted their businesses through the same markets. The forced separation in the aftermath of the civil war is part of the enigma that Burundians, in the country and the diaspora, are still trying to come to terms with as they explore alternative approaches to conflict transformation.

Research methodology: accessing data online

Data collection for this study has involved observing the internet discussion groups of *Burundinet* and *Burundi Youth Council*, and identifying the issues of most concern to member-participants. In the case of *Burundinet*, personal email addresses were often available, thus giving me direct contact with individual B-net users for "interview" purposes. However, this option was not available for most *Burundi Youth Council* users, and as a result I directed questions to the entire membership through the main BYC address or through a board member. Alongside questions about access to messages and the ownership of online data, the issue of online identity becomes critical in doing virtual ethnography. Here, I have proceeded with an assumption that most of the BYC interactants are Burundians or have a strong affinity to Burundi. Markers like multi-lingual fluency (such as the use of Kirundi, French and English in the same message) or a specific reference to a social and political background in Burundi, indicate that the sender is familiar with the cultural history of the country and is most likely a Burundian.

While the data collection for my research on *B-net* remained virtual during the two years that I was involved in the project, an interaction between the virtual and the real worlds for BYC has allowed me to gain further insights into the nature of the organization as an internet community. My introduction to BYC came about from a chance face-to-face meeting with a member, who gave me first-hand information on BYC's interests and the organization's perspectives on the Burundi conflict. I have been a member since March 2001. I had the opportunity to attend the first BYC Peace Summit that was held in Washington D.C. in late summer of 2001. This important step moves beyond the virtual BYC, wherein leaders aspire to meetings in Africa in order to substantially increase the participation by Burundians "back home". Such face-to-face meetings are arguably critical to help bridge spatial and ideological gaps created in the construction of identity in Burundi today.

Burundinet

As noted above, *Burundinet* was most active during the early years of post-1993 violence. At a time when Burundi was involved in a civil war between the Hutu and Tutsi ethnic groups, *B-net* served as a multiethnic forum of internet communication which enabled Burundians in the diaspora to create a virtual community, albeit one imbued with diverse visions and agendas regarding appropriate mechanisms for conflict resolution. The network also facilitated the discussion of strategies that would contribute to a more peaceful cohabitation across the ethnic line in post-conflict Burundi (Kadende-Kaiser 2000: 142).

The bulk of *Burundinet* messages reflected on the impact of ethnicity in Burundian struggles for democratic rule. Perspectives that documented other forms of group identity and intergroup tensions often appeared in comparative perspective with ethnicity. Three factors may explain why *B-net* members felt so consumed with the issue of ethnicity. First, the network was created during the early years of the ethnic violence, a time when most Burundians, Hutu and Tutsi alike, were still grieving the loss of life due to the 1993 ethnic violence. Second, ethnicity has thus far been the only form of identification that has directly fueled inter-group violence. Finally, Burundians have rarely had the opportunity openly to discuss their feelings about the endemic ethnic violence and the impact this has had on their own lives. Therefore, *B-net* served as a vehicle through which ethnic differences could be articulated online for those in the diaspora, away from the threat and actualization of violence that prevailed during that time in Burundi.

Based on my analyses of *B-net* discussions, I suggest that three predominant perspectives on the causes of ethnic violence and its resolutions emerged online. I label these the regionalist, nationalist, and universalist standpoints. From a regional standpoint, *B-net* messages focused on the "locus of power" (Lukes 1996) in reference to the southern region of Bururi, the region of origin for the country's first three presidents who ruled from 1966–93 and then again from 1996 to the present (the incumbent president at the time of the elections in June 1993 returned to power in a military coup in July 1996). On *B-net*, Bururi was deemed the center of economic and political stability at the expense of the rest of the country, which was labeled the "third world" (Author G, 25 January 1996). Indeed, geographic locality did play a role, as certain regions of the country became infamous for their ethnic cleansing. One *B-netter* establishes this link as he reflects on an eyewitness account of violence:

> I remember from those days in 1993 from an eyewitness that the army had closed off Bururi from the rest of the country in order to protect this partic-
> ular province. . . . It is not unlogic [sic], when you know that within the

Tutsi community the Bururians never liked the "Northerns" [sic] and were never very keen to go too fast to help them. They knew and expected Hutus would raise their vengeance against these Tutsi (who were never involved in coups d'états) and this solved the problem of Tutsi opposition against Bururi.

This narrative not only helps to establish a link between ethnic and intra-Tutsi differences, but it also brings to light the intricacies of how regionalism and clan exclusivity limited the national, cross-ethnic legitimacy of the political system.

Among *B-netters* who adopted the nationalist standpoint, true democracy existed in pre-colonial Burundi when "our ancestors" were least concerned about ethnic differences and more interested in the consolidation of the Burundi nation. A lack of documented history on Hutu–Tutsi conflict prior to the colonialists' arrival is taken as proof that interethnic violence is a recent phenomenon. It is also interpreted to mean that it is reversible, not as entrenched as many seem to believe. Hence, from those holding a nationalist perspective, *B-netters* are invited to "look historically at the relationship between their Hutu and Tutsi ancestors" if they are interested in coming to terms with their "so-called differences", as one B-netter wrote (Author E, 8 September 1995). Reconstructing (online) the pre-colonial legacy that brought Hutu and Tutsi together in a coalition against foreign invasion thus became a unifying theme. In general, an outsider was presented as the common enemy, such as Rumaliza, the Arab slave-trader who invaded Burundi during the nineteenth century and who is mentioned in major Burundi history books as well as in several *B-net* messages (Author Q, 11 March 1996):

> When Rumaliza made it to the shores of Lake Tanganyika, to capture some slaves, do you think it was only the Hutu, the Tutsi or the Twa who fought for national integrity and that of its people? When it came time to fighting against the colonial invasion, everyone was there.

This message highlights the idea that the strength of pre-colonial Burundi lay in its dominant interethnic coalition and that this joint interest in national unity must be revived.

B-net participants who adopted a universalistic standpoint tended to present Burundi as a country currently at a "low point" in its history. This perspective suggested that, if *B-netters* considered Burundi not as an isolated case but in comparative terms with other countries that have suffered violent civil turmoil as well as colonial invasions and subsequent internal divisions, they would realize that Burundi could eventually transcend its current difficulties. Several topics were addressed in this category. For example, rather than reflecting on the problematic nature of the Burundi army (with a Tutsi majority that assaulted Hutu civilians), proponents of the universalistic approach focus on what they see as inherent tensions between national armies and opponents among the civilian populations during times of violent conflict. One B-netter summarizes this point when he suggests that:

> I have no trust in any army, regardless of its origin. The Rwandan example (to help you) shows that clearly Hutus are capable of similar crimes [as the ones committed by the Tutsi army in Burundi], just like the Americans in Vietnam, the Serbs and Croats, the Belgians in their colonies as well as the French, in short anyone who holds an army and sees oneself as invincible.

Burundinet messages with a universalistic outlook also highlighted the impact of transnational forces such as colonialism on the current state of affairs in many nations of the world. As with the nationalist perspective, the assumption is that a "return" to a pre-colonial Burundi would bring back a harmonious relationship between Hutu and Tutsi by enabling them to be equal political partners. One message that captures this attitude is here worth citing at length, from a B-netter who pointed out:

> After the arrival of the colonizer, the Tutsi saw his status elevated . . . to the level of his [colonial] master. He lacks nothing more than the color of the skin in order to occupy his position! *Divide et Impera.* First Act. Next, and I am perhaps jumping some steps here, it is the turn of the king, who becomes nothing but a "marrionetter," when Harroy (the brave) was in the process of remodeling the history of Rwanda and Burundi. The king, who is now bored and has no real power, finds himself a hobby. He becomes a "twisteur" and is thinking already of [moving to] Geneva. Second Act. Then comes the wave of decolonization, with Rwagasore, the PDC and others. This son of the king [who] decides to work for the independence of his country under the republican umbrella, must have annoyed and surprised the "pourvoyeur" of civilization. Besides, he is married to a Hutu. An open-minded person indeed. Unfortunately, he is put to jail (in Bururi), but he wins after all. Then comes the ultimate solution. Someone pays Kageorgis for the scrupulous job that would benefit the sons of Baranyanka. Third Act. *Divide et Impera.* And I personally believe that Burundi missed a pacific and democratic evolution during this period.

This historical account brings to light several key actors and agents of colonialism. It makes mention of the colonial plan for a *Divide et Impera* policy that led to the assassination of Prince Louis Rwagasore, the son of King Mwambutsa IV, by a Greek businessman named Kageorgis on the shores of Lake Tanganyika on 13 October 1961. Burundi became independent on 1 July 1962, and Rwagasore is still perceived by many Burundians as the hero of independence. The message also recognizes that the colonialists as well as Rwagasore's rivals (such as the sons of Baranyanka, who were accused of master-minding the plot to assassinate him) became the identifiable winners. Burundi lost at this point a credible replacement for Rwagasore, as well as the capacity to achieve independence without resorting to violent power struggles. The King had clearly sold out to the colonizers and was already engaged in getting ready for a fresh start in Switzerland. The country has since endured various moments of interethnic conflict. Violent plots that are often engineered at the top level of leadership against political opponents end up trickling down into civilian populations through various channels, as manipulative struggles for leadership continue to involve constituents on each side of the ethnic divide. In short, the universalistic standpoint held that the Burundi case should not be analysed as distinctive. Instead, it felt that by placing the Burundi case in "proper" perspective, it would appear as a less isolated and perhaps less hopeless one.

In summarizing the online discourse on *Burundinet*, it is clear that, despite its explosive potential, ethnicity received a great deal of attention. Ideological differences varied constantly depending on whether a pro-Hutu or pro-Tutsi stand was taken. Representations of interethnic relations often perpetuated a binary opposition in which one group was held to be the oppressor and the other the oppressed. Such ethnically-biased topics prevented many from accepting the credibility of the perspective of the "other" side, and discussions in this context frequently ended up in a stalemate. Messages were often judged on the basis of their bias (or neutrality) towards one or the other ethnic group, and assumptions were made about the sender's ethnic background. Reactions to such messages were either sympathetic or they expressed outrage over a complete disregard for the pain of the other side. Deep frustrations could be sensed as many were still trying to cope with the traumas of violence. Some on *Burundinet* were among the most serious victims of the war, having lost entire families during the early phases of conflict. The nature of such discussions eventually forced some members to resign or refrain from active involvement in *B-net* discussions. Indeed, complaints were raised over and over again regarding ethnic partiality and unproductive interactions, as well as the nature of individual ethnic group suffering.

Regardless of these stumbling blocks or the different interpretations circulating on B-net, the Burundi saying that *"ibuye riserutse ntiriba ricishe isuka"* (when a stone sticks out of the ground it can no longer destroy the hoe) is fitting to contextualize the significance of this online forum. The saying speaks to the importance of dialogue: bringing different tales of truth to light is an important step towards conflict resolution. Disagreements – like those expressed online with regard to the roots of ethnic violence – are still necessary before a frank dialogue can begin. I thus consider the discussions that were initiated on *Burundinet* to be productive, not only because they allowed Burundians to articulate their differences in a physically safe (virtual) environment, but also because, without being aware of what the "other" thinks about his/her status, ethnic or otherwise, a movement towards resolving ideological differences that have turned into endemic violence in Burundi will be hard to achieve.

Burundi Youth Council

The second online discussion group under consideration in this chapter, *Burundi Youth Council* (BYC), was launched in October 2000, when its three founding members, two Tutsi and a Hutu, turned their email exchanges about the nature of the Burundi conflict into a bulletin board. As they exchanged perspectives on conflict resolution they discovered that, despite their ethnic differences, there were several points of agreement between them, and they subsequently decided to launch an open discussion about practical mechanisms for facilitating cross-ethnic dialogue. The ultimate goal was to create a space where Burundians could start moving away from a process of mutual hatred and victimization based on ethnicity. The group continued to expand and by the end of the first year they had reached approximately 700 members.

At the time of BYC's initiation, several pacifist groups were already engaged in projects aimed at assisting Burundians in post-conflict peace-building efforts and reconstruction (see Hara 1999, for example). Although BYC was not necessarily inspired by these international efforts, one can argue for the importance of time in healing and reconciliation. The fact that in general BYC members are relatively younger than members of *Burundinet* is also meaningful; obviously they were even younger when the war started in 1993. This age gap might account for the different approaches to the issue of inter-group conflict. In contrast to the dominant discourse that favored ethnicity on *B-net*, and probably in an attempt to detonate ethnicity's explosive potential, BYC's executive committee from the outset has strongly discouraged messages that express a strong bi-partisanship. When such messages appear, they are quickly removed from the site in order to prevent access by and reactions from subsequent readers. BYC approaches to understanding the nature of social inequality in Burundi seek to look beyond ethnicity.

The members of this network are guided by a shared interest in reconstruction – physical, mental and ideological – to serve as the common ground from which they can devise alternative methods of conflict transformation. Activism on behalf of Burundi youth is clearly defined on the BYC website in five major statements that also serve as the code of conduct:

> The site seeks to promote whatever unites the Burundi youth.
> Nothing is gained when we reinforce the spiral of hatred and violence that has destroyed the Burundi of our elders.
> A message sender should strive for whatever enriches others by sharing with them ideas that are progressive and non-divisive in nature.
> A sender should never encourage ethnic, regional, and political hatred.
> A sender should respect the site's neutrality and should never post any message that reflects political bi-partisanship.

BYC ground-rules are there to serve as guiding principles towards a goal of mutual enrichment, transcending difference and embracing diversity. As noted, inter-group hatred rooted in ethnicity, political bi-partisanship and regionalism are forbidden. The question of mixed heritage (for youth whose parents are of Hutu and Tutsi ethnic backgrounds), and the implications of this mixed identity on youth well-being and development, are also discussed. BYC also seeks to engage future governments to include youth in the enhancement of peaceful developments in the country. Moreover, by raising funds for youth development programs, BYC is working to enhance youth opportunities and self-esteem. Since youth development has never been a priority in previous governance, activism by the youth is thus geared towards ensuring that future government policies will take notice of their needs and concerns. Finally, by creating this space, albeit a virtual one, the Burundi youth both at home and in the diaspora strive to remain actively involved in a critical evaluation of the existing social-cultural and political structures in the country.

BYC goals are not only being enacted online: as an executive member expressed to me in an interview, the organization is engaged in "doing everything to make sure that there will be more opportunities for us to meet physically". Raising the funds necessary to enable BYC members to meet is therefore one of their aims. The executive member also explained to me why BYC members attached such importance to social issues that had no direct bearing on the ethnic question, at a time when ethnic violence was still taking place in the country:

> Politicians have for many years claimed to represent the views and perspectives of the majority of Burundi citizens. The radio and television are media of the government and are not open to criticism. The internet allows us to challenge the dominant perspective that analyses the Burundi conflict by focusing only on ethnicity. All of a sudden, we realized that we could voice our opinion in a safe environment and not worry about government censorship.

It is this freedom of expression that indeed attracts many BYC members. While recognizing that ethnicity remains problematic within Burundi, my interviewee argued that "it would not be as big a deal if politicians had not used [ethnicity] as a tool to seek empowerment. So, what we have decided to do is to shift our attention to other issues of survival." The issues circulating on the BYC bulletin boards are nonetheless heated topics that potentially challenge Burundi cultural traditions. Prominent among the controversial discussions are gender issues like the role of women in politics, the prevalence of domestic violence in Burundi society, abortion and teenage pregnancy, as well as issues concerning sexual orientation. I now turn to a more detailed discussion of these topics with respect to Burundi culture.

The importance of women in the Burundi domestic sphere is expressed in a traditional saying "*nyamuhusha itunga ahusha umugore*" (one who has missed out on a good wife is also parted from riches). In Burundi, women are generally revered for their contributions to the household, for their procreative capacity (especially those who bear male children), and their overall devotion to family wellbeing. Beyond this, however, women wield little power.

They have far less education and economic opportunities than do men, and are subject to different laws that discriminate against them even within the family. Even in today's world, it is the task of rural women to make weekly or daily trips to the market; to fetch firewood for cooking purposes; to sow, weed and harvest. Given their limited access to positions of power, few women have control over what happens to them in times of conflict. As war wages, women live in constant fear of rape or other attacks upon themselves or their daughters. War widows become further victimized in a culture that disinherits women, where to lose a son or a husband means to lose economic security.

Discussions taking place on the BYC bulletin board have begun to address the particular issue of women's struggles, and the discriminations they have uniquely suffered. The gender-related themes and calls for action that have emerged online include the establishment of laws to eradicate wife-beating and violence against women, determining ways to transform tradition in favor of women's rights, and questions related to the establishment of a more equitable education system across gender and class. In addition, laws protective of individual human rights such as those related to abortion and sexual orientation have been proposed. Of particular interest to BYC's youth policy is the place of women in Burundi society and the importance of establishing a more equitable structure that gives women a prominent role in the politics of development in the country. Members of the BYC executive committee, who often post opinions about the topics raised online, expressed their position with regard to the status of women in Burundi (*Burundiyouth.com*: "Women's place in society", initiated on 27 April 2001):

> One of BYC's concerns is women issues. That's why we have a committee working on the matter. If you want to help them, write to burundiyouth@hotmail.com, and we will put you in touch with the Responsible [or the person in charge of the committee]. Also we invite you to make some research on some laws that are pending in the National Assembly regarding women on their rights to own ITONGO [the family plot].

While this message was written as a rejoinder to a previous posting, the sender also introduced a new topic, bringing to the members' attention women's land rights. The addition of the land issue serves as another indication that the BYC initiators are interested in tackling a wide range of issues related to gender inequality in Burundi. They are also interested in identifying appropriate mechanisms for redressing existing tensions. In this regard, some BYC participants have argued that a link exists between the exclusion of women in major decision-making organs of government and the government's ineptitude at peace-building. One BYC user established this link when she asked (Burundiyouth: "Women's place in society", initiated on 27 April 2001):

So why are women in our country not involved in the decision making of bringing back peace in our beloved country, is it that they don't have any opinions? I don't think so. I think it's just because they are not given any chance to talk, to express their opinions. We have very intelligent women in our country but they have just not been given the chance to speak up. An example is in this community, i think you can all agree that there are many intelligent girls that you could never have known if there was not BYC that permits us to speak out, congratulations to all the girls on this community.

This message goes on to identify the root of the problem in a cultural tradition that does not encourage women's active involvement in public life. For this author, change will occur only once women stand up for their rights, and once men cooperate with women, instead of seeking to monopolize the decision-making apparatus. By taking a holistic approach that includes gender as a crucial component in this search for appropriate mechanisms for reducing social tensions and inequality in Burundi, BYC users are bringing to the surface cultural elements and social structures that have hindered efforts at conflict resolution. As a BYC board member admits, when he states (*Burundiyouth.com*: "BYC and gender equality", 24 February 2001):

> [O]ur view is that women are the pillar of a society and that they deserve the same chances as men, they are also in a good position to promote peace and reconciliation and to prepare the future generations to tolerance. The discrimination against women is a serious problem that should be treated as seriously as other forms of discrimination. Here BYC is making an appeal to open the debate of how we can improve the conditions of the women in Burundi.

While women are increasingly being recognized as instrumental players in facilitating peaceful resolution of conflict[2] they are still rarely accorded space to articulate their perspectives. Arguably, BYC provides one such forum for women to express their voice, and for both sexes to debate gender issues.

Another issue that has attracted attention is that of domestic violence. In one instance, a BYC board member posted a news report about a Burundian woman activist who organized the first national conference in Burundi on the theme of violence against women. Many network members expressed pride in this initiative. They also called for the creation and implementation of legal rights and protection for abused women. Here is how one net member expressed these concerns:

> Violence exists in our communities. We all know a physically or morally abused woman, either in our families or in our neighbourhoods . . . but few people talk about it. Thanx to BYC for showing their support to the

women. My call goes to all the young men and women out there: we always meet on this forum to discuss many issues but when it comes to women, people seem to be out of words. We might not find a solution to all the problems Burundian youth faces, but the least we can do is stand up and say THIS IS WRONG. Women should not be beaten up, raped, morally abused and we keep quiet thinking that it will not happen to us but sooner or later the victim will be a close friend, a daughter, a sister . . . Let's all say "*battre les femmes, plus jamais ça*" (violence against women, never again) and of course PREACH IT AND ACT ON IT.

Indeed, acting to eradicate domestic violence remains a key challenge, as existing research on abused women within the community continues to demonstrate (see, for example: Allard 1991; Bannister 1993; Heise 1994; French *et al.* 1998). Many Burundian women have remained silent, afraid to denounce acts of violence committed against them. Based on the number of online responses, however, one realizes that significant recognition is starting to be accorded these issues by *BYC* users.

The topics of abortion and teenage pregnancy (which are relatively recent phenomena in Burundi) have also generated a wide range of debate on the *BYC* site. Although there is a clear divide between those supportive of abortion rights and those who oppose them, many *BYC* posters nonetheless acknowledged the difficulty involved in the decision to abort: that the woman was caught "between a rock and a hard place". The following response is illustrative:

> She [the woman] has not created life, certainly right . . . So I do not support abortion (except in rape cases or when giving birth causes a threat to the mother). I cannot however impose my views on anyone! Especially not Girls, coz I am not one!

While expressing a personal opinion, this message also seeks to remain non-judgmental, and to allow room for a woman's freedom of choice. The issue of abortion – one of the most controversial topics in the modern world even where women's rights have achieved a relatively high level of recognition and success – has thus also found its way onto the *Burundi Youth Council* bulletin board. Here, it is not only being recognized as a serious practical matter for Burundian women, it has entered into larger discussions concerning traditional culture and Western individual rights discourses.

Another controversy being debated on *BYC* is the issue of sexual orientation. Some *BYC* members have expressed the viewpoint that human rights cannot be achieved while the rights of homosexuals (and other marginalized peoples) are denied. Their messages, based in the belief that homosexuality is natural and pan-cultural, call for it to be illegal to discriminate against gays and lesbians in Burundi society. Some members, however, consider homosexuality to be "un-Burundian behavior": indicative of assimilation and a loss of the traditional morality characteristic of Burundian cultural heritage. One BYC user asks: "could any one explain to me why young Burundians out of the country . . . are turning to be gays and Lesbians? What's the hell is going on?????????"

In challenging such assumptions, another member states (*Burundiyouth.com*: "Discussion about young Burundians 'turning' gay and lesbian", 29 April 2001):

> I think you've been walking with blinders on! That's obviously why you think it's an American-learned way of thinking – living. . . . As other many Africans like to say: "homosexuality is a white man thing!" It's wrong! Gay people are everywhere . . . out or closeted, effeminates or straight acting.

If indeed more Burundians are now "coming out of the closet", it is likely because fear of discrimination is reduced in the Western countries where many Burundians in the diaspora currently reside. The following message (signed with a pseudonym) is indicative of the fact that online interaction may allow for more expressive freedom, but only to a degree:

> Until BYC can guarantee my physical safety, the unconditional love of my family and friends, AND my job, I will be known as the lesbian Nuru who is half Kenyan and half American. Make me a guarantee and I'll come prancing out – perhaps even in Ikirundi.

These concerns that individual users could become targets of attacks online and/or rejected in the "real world" serve as testimonies that online discussions are not bulletproof spaces of interaction. Nevertheless, more information about the nature and impact of social inequality in Burundi has been provided online by Burundians in the diaspora than would otherwise be exchanged face-to-face or in official representations of social relations in Burundi.

In considering overall trends in BYC discussions, my data concur with the opinion of a BYC executive member. When I interviewed him he stated that what has emerged on BYC is an "ideological" split between the "liberal" and the "conservatives". The first group represents those who are open and willing to discuss any issues. They aim to identify barriers to the achievement of human rights for all in Burundi society, including the development of new policies that will take into account marginalized members. Ultimately, in their view, the ethnic question should be addressed within a larger context of tolerance. The "conservative" group, while still supportive of an approach that seeks to look beyond ethnicity in analyses of social inequality in Burundi, nonetheless wants to limit the types of issues raised online. For this group, alternative social behaviors (like homosexuality, teenage pregnancy and abortion) are a clear proof that Burundi social structures are in the process of disintegrating. They believe that what constitutes and should guide the soul of every "true" Burundian can be lost through radical liberalism. This group suggests that a line be drawn between freedom of expression, on the one hand, and cultural relativism based on recognition of the specificity of Burundi cultural traditions, on the other. Failure to do so, in their opinion, will result in cultural alienation and assimilation. Liberal and conservative views on the BYC site provide the foundation upon which concerns with digital democracy can be problematized.

The public sphere: problematizing democratic principles online

If the internet is a democratic and safe medium of communication, then it should be conducive to opening lines of communication across, for example, class, gender and ethnic barriers. Yet, in comparing *Burundinet* and BYC, I was intrigued by one notable difference: while *B-netters* were engaged in heated debates about ethnicity, they tended to give their email addresses, whereas BYC participants tended to choose to remain anonymous (many choosing a pseudonym that masked even gender as well as ethnicity). My first interview question then was: why is it that most BYC users seek to hide their identity, starting with their real names? The answers to this question were often framed in terms of fear (of exposure, betrayal, rejection), or insecurity about consequences. Possible discrimination based on gender differences, sexual orientation, and political views in the real world, constitute ample reasons for members to want to conceal certain elements of their multiple identities.

This leads to another question, related to the first: can we still trust that democratic principles are being promoted online when those involved in the discussion process do not even feel comfortable identifying themselves? And if we can, then to what extent does the internet promote democratic principles? The argument can be made that, so long as online users still fear that honesty and openness are going to turn against them, then this "micro-public sphere" that BYC represents is not as democratic as the executive committee would like it to be. For purposes of deciphering the practice of democracy and the safety of online discussions, hiding behind a nickname and keeping individual email addresses inaccessible has a double effect. There is an element of "illusive" safety that many internet users appreciate: the ability to express multiple identities, to shift identities, indeed the mutability of identities (Jones 1995: 31; see also: Palmer 1995; Dubrovsky *et al.* 1991; Walther *et al.* 1994) as well as the potential for keeping individual net users protected from possible online attacks or "flames" (Lea *et al.* 1992). It is in this light that Spears and Lea (1994) question assumptions about virtual safety and the "equalization phenomenon" (Dubrovsky *et al.* 1991: 122) of computer-mediated communication. They contend that computer-mediated communication has the potential to enhance the sense of anonymity, hence creating an environment that is conducive to the statement of "one's true mind and authentic self" (Spears and Lea 1994: 430). Yet they also warn that, "if power and influence are not outside, but are at least partly encoded within us, it becomes far less easy to argue that the source of power is necessarily displaced or diluted by the distanciation, isolation, and anonymity characteristic of [online communications]" (Spears and Lea 1994: 437). While I concur that virtual safety confers certain advantages and is conducive to the creation of virtual identities, I argue that, far from being released from the pressures of the real world, BYC web users and messages conveyed on the BYC website continue to reflect on the historical and cultural reality in Burundi and its impact on the users' lives today. After all, this search for a virtual space of freedom and fantasy would become irrelevant had the actual physical space of gender interactions been fair and open to the achievement of human potential for men and women. Hence, virtual space cannot fully mask the virtues and vices of the real world but is often a replica of it. Nonetheless, BYC users take advantage of this virtual space as best they can, as they seek to lay the groundwork for "real-world" democracy, nurtured online.

Research on digital democracy provides a broad range of references that document the extent to which information technologies can influence "practices that are presumed to be democratic" (Hacker and Van Dijk 2000: 1). For some theorists, democratic principles require the establishment of a "public sphere" that gives citizens the freedom to engage in open debates about matters that are crucial to the development of representative public institutions. Seeking to establish the genealogy of the "public sphere", Keane (2000: 70) notes that in "the modern prominence of the public sphere the language of 'the public', 'public virtue' and 'public opinion' was a weapon in support of 'liberty of the press' and other publicly shared freedoms". Malina (1999) refers to the potential of the public sphere, as envisaged by Habermas (1989), as an arena for democracy. However, Malina (1999: 25) reminds us that the initial European version of the "public" sphere was undemocratic, consisting of "the eighteenth-century European bourgeoisie, a group of privileged and powerful men engaged in 'face-to-face' communicative action in critical judgment of public authority". This elite openly discussed political issues in a space set apart from the state.

Studies of the public sphere constitute an interesting vantage point from which to decipher what *Burundinet* and *BYC* represent. Membership of both these internet newsgroups includes Hutu and Tutsi groups of the Burundian diaspora, and these are the same groups that have been involved in ethnic fighting since October 1993. There are several factors that contribute to enhancing democratic engagements on the internet, and members of these two newsgroups have illustrated the potential of internet communication as they articulate issues of concern to them. While the main objectives for both have been to discuss conflict resolution in Burundi, I argue that, since their diagnoses are different, so are their proposed recommendations. *Burundinet* focused mainly on identifying the "evil-doers", who in most cases were assumed to be members of the "other" ethnic group. BYC has challenged the dominant discourse according to which Burundi society and conflict are only to be characterized in terms of ethnicity. Instead, BYC members are more interested in determining other social ills that, when compounded, lead to victimization at many different levels, ethnic and otherwise.

As the "practice of politics does not escape public notice" (Malina 1999: 30), BYC serves as an alternative forum of communication, a virtual space where Burundian youth feel somewhat comfortable questioning existing policies in the country by contributing, albeit virtually and for the most part anonymously, to current debates in the politics of national reconstruction. Among other achievements, the BYC site allows different groups that have been marginalized in political discourse in Burundi to be represented. In this context, BYC is a "micro-public sphere" that functions like "bottom-up small scale locales in which citizens forge their identities, often in opposition to top-down 'imperializing' powers bent on regulating, redefining or extinguishing ('or stationing') public life at the local level" (Fiske, in Keane 2000: 77). Through participation in this electronic communication group (where government censorship is absent or at worst limited), debates about taboo topics can also be aired. Criticisms about the role of the political leadership, past and present, in the creation or reinforcement of social divisions can be raised. As issues are raised, it becomes clear that cultural traditions that condone discrimination against various sectors of Burundi society are being challenged online. It is in this context that active BYC members hope to transform existing divisions and rebuild fractured communities. Laying out the ground rules for the establishment of a more peaceful Burundi is not left to the discretion of politicians. BYC members believe that peace will return only when the population has come to terms with the effects of the war on their lives, and when the people have voluntarily determined that survival will depend less on difference, ethnic or otherwise, and more on establishing common ground. They believe that, once they have identified shared concerns, they can then act on assuring that the livelihood of each social group is not jeopardized when ethnicity is prioritized over other forms of individual and group identity.

BYC represents a case where one can argue for the potential of the internet to construct and reconstruct meaning, hence providing individuals with the opportunity to transform mainstream cultural texts into alternative texts (Gersch 1998: 312). Ultimately, its success will depend on the extent to which this dialectic between an engagement in exploring "alternative modes of identity, subjectivity, sexuality, and politics offered within the realm of interactive technology" (O'Farrell and Vallone 1999: 148) will transpire in the "real world". Taking into account BYC recommendations and views has the potential to facilitate the development of new policies, with new voices and new actors. Only then can women also contribute as equal partners in national reconstruction and development. Only then can we hope for a transformation of Burundi society towards lasting conflict resolution.

Notes

1   There is today a Burundinet newsgroup affiliated with a major opposition party in Burundi. This has no relation to the *Burundinet* I discuss in this paper and of which I was a member until the end of 1997.

2   See Maundi (2003), for example, as he reflects on the instrumental role played by the United Nations Development Fund for Women (UNIFEM) in developing strategies that made it possible for Burundi women to attend later rounds of negotiation in Arusha, Tanzania during the later part of the process.

References

Allard, Sharon Angella (1991) "Rethinking the Battered Woman Syndrome: A Black Feminist Perspective", *UCLA Women's Law Journal* 1(1): 191–208.

Bannister, Shelley A. (1993) "Battered Women Who Kill Their Abusers: Their Courtroom Battles", in R. Muraskin and T. Alleman (eds), *It's A Crime: Women and Justice* Engelwood Cliffs, NJ: Regents/Prentice Hall.

Chretien, Jean-Pierre, Guichaoua, A. and Le Jeune, G. (1989) *La Crise d'Aout 1988 au Burundi*. Paris: Centre de Recherche Africaines.

Dubrovsky, Vitaly J., Kiesler, Sara and Beheruz, N. Sethna (1991) "The Equalization Phenomenon: Status Effects in Computer-Mediated and Face-to-Face Decision-Making Groups", *Human-Computer Interaction* 6: 119–46.

French, Stanley G., Teays, Wanda and Purdy, Laura M. (1998) *Violence Against Women: Philosophical Perspectives*. Ithaca: Cornell University Press.

Gahama, Joseph (1999) "Burundi", in A. Adedeji (ed.), *Comprehending and Mastering African Conflicts: The Search for Sustainable Peace and Good Governance*. London: Zed Books (in association with the African Centre for Development and Strategic Studies, Ijebu-Ode, Nigeria).

Gersch, Beate (1998) "Gender at the Crossroads: The Internet as Cultural Texts", *Journal of Communication Inquiry* 22(3): 306–21.

Habermas, Jürgen (1989) *The Structural Transformation of the Public Sphere: An Inquiry into a Category of Bourgeois Society*. Cambridge, MA: MIT Press.

Hacker, Kenneth L. and Van Dijk, Jan (2000) *Digital Democracy: Issues of Theory and Practice*. London: Sage.

Hara, Fabienne (1999) "Burundi: A Case of Parallel Diplomacy", in C. Chester A. Crocker *et al.* (eds), *Herding Cats: Multiparty Mediation in a Complex World*. Washington D.C.: United States Institute of Peace Press, pp. 135–58.

Heise, Lori L. (1994) "Gender-Based Abuse: The Global Epidemic", in A. J. Dan (ed.), *Reframing Women's Health: Multidisciplinary Research and Practice*. Thousand Oaks, CA: Sage, pp. 233–52.

Jones, Stephen, G. (1995) *Cybersociety: Computer-Mediated Communication and Community*. Thousand Oaks, CA: Sage.

Kadende-Kaiser, Rose M. (2000) "Interpreting Language and Cultural Discourse: Internet Communication Among Burundians in the Diaspora", *Africa Today* 47(2): 121–50.

Keane, John (2000) "Structural Transformation of the Public Sphere", in Kenneth L. Hacker and J. van Dijk (eds), *Digital Democracy: Issues of Theory and Practice*. London: Sage, pp. 70–89.

Lea, Martin, O'Shea, Tim, Fung, Pat and Spears, Russell (1992) "'Flaming' in Computer Mediated Communication: Observations Explanations, Implications", in Martin Lea (ed.), *Context of Computer-Mediated Communication*. New York: Harvester Wheatsheaf, pp. 89–112.

Lemarchand, Rene (1974) "Selective Genocide in Burundi", Minority Rights Group Report, No. 20.

——(1994) *Burundi: Ethnic Conflict and Genocide*. Washington D.C.: The Woodrow Wilson Center.

Lukes, Stephen (1996) *Power*. Oxford: Basil Blackwell.

Malina, Anna (1999) "Perspectives on Citizen Democratisation and Alienation in the Virtual Sphere", in B. N. Hague and B. Loader (eds), *Digital Democracy: Discourse and Decision Making in the Information Age*. London: Routledge, pp.23–38.

Melady, Thomas (1974) *Burundi: The Tragic Years*. New York: Orbis Books.

Maundi, Mohammed Omar (2003) "Preventing Conflict Escalation in Burundi" in C.H. Sriram and K. Wermester (eds) *From Promise to Practice: Strengthening UN Capacities for the Prevention of Violent Conflict*. Boulder: Lynne Reiner Publishers, pp. 327–50.

Ndarubagiye, Léonce (1996) *Burundi: The Origins of the Hutu–Tutsi Conflict*. No publisher indicated.

Nindorera, Louise-Marie (1993) "Hutuland et Tutsiland?", *Panafrika*, 24 November.

O'Farrell, Mary Ann and Vallone, Lynne (1999) *Virtual Gender: Fantasies of Subjectivity and Embodiment*. Michigan: University of Michigan Press.

Palmer, Mark T. (1995) "Interpersonal Communication and Virtual Reality: Mediating Interpersonal Relationships", in F. Biocca and M. R. Levy, *Communication in the Age of Virtual Reality*. Hillsdale, NJ: Laurence Erlbaum, pp. 277–99.

Ress, David (1992) *The Burundi Ethnic Massacres: 1988*. San Francisco: Mellon Research University Press.

Spears, Russell, and Lea, Martin (1994) "Panacea or Panopticon? The Hidden Power in Computer-Mediated Communication", *Communication Research* 21(4): 427–59.

Sumu, Cyriaque (2001) *Burundi: Non à la decomposition*. Montreal: Bureau régional pour l'Afrique Centrale.

Walther, Joseph B., Anderson, Jeffrey F. and Park, David W. (1994) "Interpersonal Effects in Computer-Mediated Interaction: A Meta-Analysis of Social and Antisocial Communication", *Communication Research* 21(4): 460–87.

Chapter 13

Ch(c0de): Virtual occupations, encrypted identities, and the Al-Aqsa intifada

William C. Taggart

Indigenous claims and conflicts

It is just after noon in Ramallah. Friday prayers have just ended and there is a crowd growing in the city's center, a traffic circle punctuated with what looks like a giant iron flower, known in Ramallah as the Manarah. Roads disappear in every direction, spreading out from the circle. Groups of young men with flags from each of the Palestine resistance organizations begin to march up these streets towards the Manarah. Hamas is the loudest group, and, as they get closer, I can hear the slogans they are chanting: "Down with America. Down with the CIA. Down with Israel". When the center fills up, each group makes a circle around the Manarah. The Hamas group burns an effigy of an Apache helicopter, used so often by Israel in "targeted assasinations" of Hamas activists. The groups then march out from the Manarah, go a couple of blocks, make a turn and return to the city center. Leaders of Fatah walk arm-in-arm at the front. The PFLP (Popular Front for the Liberation of Palestine), Islamic Jihad and Hamas follow. As we walk through one of Ramallah's side streets I see a young girl standing on the sidewalk. She is probably no more than four or five years old. She is smiling and clapping, and I watch her as she tries to mouth the words to the slogans. It looks like a parade.

The groups reassemble around the Manarah and begin to march to the Israeli checkpoint on the outskirts of town. After about a mile we take a right turn. I notice young boys wrapping *khafiyyas* around their heads. One boy wraps a Hamas flag around his body. After another block we are at the top of a small hill. We take a left and begin down the hill. At the "end" of the road I can see a large area of blackened pavement. This is the clash site, the "playground" for these young boys. We get closer to the clash site and the adults drop away. A father grabs his children and takes them to cover, behind walls and buildings on either side of the street. The boys move forward. The clash begins. Israeli defense forces are stationed in jeeps in front of us. I take cover behind a huge cement block in the middle of the street, used to block traffic. The boys take several different positions and begin to throw rocks and roll burning tires. The Israelis fire back from their jeeps with rubber bullets. I see one boy shot in the eye, another in the leg. After about half an hour watching the Palestinian boys and Israel soldiers

exchange rocks for rubber bullets, I hear a child's voice calling out: "*Bouza!*
Bouza!" Ice cream. The boy is selling ice cream. I give him a *shekel* and take the
ice cream, which is actually more like a popsicle. Crouching behind the cement
block, I eat the flavored ice and wait for the next shot.

In Islamabad, Pakistan, Macwiz has just returned home. He goes to his
room, cluttered with wires and "boxes" (i.e. computers). He dials up his ISP
and logs into his IRC chatroom. Someone has sent him a new script. Mac
smiles. His friend came through after all. Mac begins to rummage around his
room for a CD. After a couple of minutes, he finds it. Tupac. He puts it on, and
the sounds of East Coast rap thump through the room. Mac loves Tupac. He
listens:

> Hey Mister! It's time for me to explain that I'm the rebel
> Cold as the devil
> Straight from the underground, the rebel, a lower level . . .
> They won't be happy till I'm banned
> The most dangerous weapon: an educated black man
> So point blank in your face, pump up the bass
> and join the human race
> (*2Pacalypse Now.* 1992. BMG, Jive, Silvertone)

Mac surveys a list of "targets" that he compiled last night. Each of these websites
has a particular "bug" (i.e. a vulnerability) that his new piece of code will
exploit. He checks the script again and points it at his target. Executing the
code, Mac leans back in his chair, smiling to himself. The script worked. Visitors
to this site will now see a message from Mac himself: "Support the Freedom
Movement . . . SAVE KASHMIR AND PALESTINE!" Mac laughs under his
breath. "One down and five more to go. It is going to be a long night."[1]

The Second or Al-Aqsa Intifada, which began after former Israeli politician
Ariel Sharon's now-infamous visit to the Dome of the Rock in the Old City of
Jerusalem, has had profound global consequences. One of these is the emergence of global cyberactivism and cyber-resistance carried out on behalf of both
Israelis and Palestinians. The focus of this chapter is on a particular sort of
cyberactivist: "script kiddies" and "hackers" who deface websites by exploiting
vulnerabilities in operating systems and web applications. These "defacements"
replace the original front page of a website with images and texts of the
attacker's choosing. These images and texts can be provocative, insidious, and
at times humorous. In this chapter, I argue that the script kiddies and hackers
often have double motives. First and foremost, defacement is a way to gain prestige and status within hacker/defacer underground communities. Second,
defacement is a way to articulate political convictions and to have their agendas
aired in public forums.

The parallels between the street-level resisters of Palestine and the global,
networked defacers who support them are truly striking. The members of both

groups are generally young: half of those killed in the Al-Aqsa Intifada are boys under 16. By the same token, most defacers are teenagers: the youngest I interviewed was 14, the oldest, 24. Members of both groups share the double motivation noted above: they earn bragging points within their respective communities, while at the same time feeling like they are doing something politically useful. Nonetheless, in both cases, the actions of the groups are largely symbolic. Throwing a rock at an Israeli tank does nothing to the tank. Defacing an Arab or Israeli website does little damage to the site in the long run. And finally, it can be said that both groups are "marginalized", albeit in different ways. Many Palestinian families were displaced upon the formation of the state of Israel. Likewise hackers and their script kiddie offspring – arguably the original occupants of cyberspace – are now largely invisible, crowded out by the hegemony of global capital. The actions of both hackers and rock throwers push hegemony back, at least for a moment.

With respect to the issue of indigeneity, it is further of note that both sides in the Palestinian–Israeli conflict claim that they are the "indigenous" occupants of historic Palestine. Jews appeal to the mythopoetic "promised land". Palestinians march through the streets of the West Bank and Gaza, led by old men carrying the keys to the homes from which they were dispossessed in 1948 on the establishment of the Jewish homeland. In this conflict, both sides claim exclusive victim status. A defacement by the pro-Palestinian group The World's Fantabulous Defacers (WFD 2001) illustrates this point:

> 1947, All of what is now modern Israel was Palestine. Out of seemingly nowhere, ultra-nationalistic Jews came out of nowhere, butchered and killed thousands upon thousands of Muslim and Christian Palestinians in order to steal the authority. Babies were beheaded. Children's throats were slit. 500 Palestinian villages were wiped off the map. Hundreds of Mosques and Churches were eradicated. Over 5 Million Palestinians were thrown out of their homes and forced to live in refugee camps in Gaza, West Bank, and neighboring countries. And for 50+ years, the Palestinian people have been indiscriminately treated as 2nd Class Citizens, denied not only the land that is rightfully theirs, but also the basic human rights of common society. This . . . is the great injustice of the Middle East . . . The Western Media will never tell you this because it is run by the very people who support, fund, and foster these inhumane atrocities . . .

This version of history is directly challenged by many Israelis, who argue that the land was promised to them by God, and point out that Jews have a long history in Palestine: they did not "come out of nowhere" as the WFD asserts. They also argue that the Holocaust was a far greater obscenity than the displacement of the Palestinians, and that establishing an independent Jewish homeland was necessary in order to prevent another Holocaust from occurring in the future. These competing notions of indigeneity and history are, at present, wholly irreconcilable for the vast majority of the Palestinian and Israeli public.

It may be useful at this point to revisit the meaning of the word "indigenous" and pursue its relevance to the topic at hand. The word "indigenous" is defined in *Webster's Dictionary* as "having originated in and being produced, growing, or living naturally in a particular region or environment". This definition typically indicates people living in physical environments, usually bounded by certain geographical constructs (e.g., the Bedouin, the Inuit, Native Americans, Australian aborigines, etc.) and unified by language and culture. However, if we problematize this definition we may extend the concept of indigeneity into new types of spaces, including "virtual" ones. Doing so, we can draw parallels between hackers and other indigenous peoples, in this case Palestinians and/or Israelis. I argue that, because hackers built the internet and devised its protocols, they are its orginal inhabitants and therefore "indigenous" to cyberspace. Hackers, working in conjunction with the Department of Defense, created the ARPAnet, the predecessor to the modern internet. They devised the TCP/IP protocols which "create" virtual spaces. They brought into being UNIX and Linux, without which the internet would not be possible. Hackers created and maintained the first "online communities", which were largely free from the institutions of government and corporate power. One such aboriginal site in the development of hacker culture was the artificial intelligence (AI) lab at MIT (see Levy 1984). Richard Stallman, an AI pioneer who joined the MIT Lab in 1971, was enthusiastic about the hacker paradise the Lab had come to represent, with its Hacker Ethic (to wit: that information in all its forms must be free; thus computer systems must remain open and equally accessible). However, by 1983, Stallman felt that the Ethic had largely been betrayed, and that the original "anarchic atmosphere" had become "polluted". Up to this time, the copying and sharing of files had been encouraged, and computers had little, if any, security. With a new generation of programmers taking control of the Lab, measures were instituted that reflected a respect for "propietary" code and security. In his own words, Stallman felt like the last of his kind: "I read a book the other day. It's called *Ishi, the Last Yahi*. It's a book about the last survivor of a tribe of Indians, initially with his family, and then they died out one by one . . . I'm the last survivor of a dead culture, and I really don't belong in this world anymore" (quoted in Levy 1984: 434). As it turns out, hacker culture did not die (due at least in part to Stallman's participation in the open-source "movement"), but the shift away from the anarchic computer culture that Stallman bemoaned was to be permanent. It is hard to imagine today any major computer system running without passwords, for instance. Hacker culture today survives only in the background, and only occasionally is the mainstream reminded of its existence.

It should be stated that the term hacker itself is a sign of contestation. It has been adopted as a blanket term for a counter-establishment ethos; for example, Nelson (1996) uses the concept of "hacker" in its broadest sense, denoting a

242 William C. Taggart

person who stretches the limits of existing systems, be they digital or otherwise. Some in the world of information systems use the term only to describe those individuals, expert programmers and obsessive tinkerers who push the boundaries of code in positive and productive ways. Individuals who break into computer systems and cause harm are, in contrast, deemed "crackers". The mainstream media and the public at-large often misunderstand hacker and defacer communities, painting them as malicious techno-geeks, romanticized electronic cowboys, or – worse – "cyber-terrorists". They are to be feared; they are the savages of the electronic frontier. Even the academic literature has mainly served to reiterate common misconceptions of hacking as illicit activity (cf. Taylor 1999). Interestingly, these views are directly at odds with how most hackers see themselves. The editor of the popular *Hacker Quarterly* defines the "spirit" of hacking thus: "What hackers do is figure out technology and experiment with it in ways many people never imagined. They also have a strong desire to share this information with others" (Goldstein 2001). My research with web vandals on both sides of the Palestinian–Israeli conflict found similar attitudes. The hackers and defacers I interviewed (following my informants, I use both terms) envisioned themselves as members of hacker culture. However, while in fact most hackers do not commit illegal or illicit acts, the hackers I discuss here largely have and will continue to commit illegal acts, although the true danger they represent is arguably exaggerated.

After all, in the Palestinian–Israeli conflict, website defacement is largely a sideshow to what is a physical and psychological conflict over land, religion and identity. And although the actions of defacers may seem incendiary, they are largely regarded by those involved in the conflict to be almost irrelevant when compared to the very real cycle of violence and anger that has consumed the peoples of Israel and Palestine since 1948 with the founding of the modern state of Israel. Angry rhetoric and provocative images have been features of political discourse in the region for decades, so propaganda from pro-Palestinian and pro-Israeli website defacers is nothing new and is often met with shrugs, knowing grunts, and sighs: people have seen this before. I have had many opportunities to show some of these images and texts to Palestinians, although I have had to be careful when showing pro-Israeli propaganda in public internet cafés in Ramallah, as it easily could have gotten me into major trouble with the Mukhabarat (the secret police). Without exception, the immediate response to these images has been an anxious silence. For example, when I showed several pro-Israeli defacements to the owner of a well-maintained internet café close to the city center, he too looked with the characteristic silence I had grown to expect. But upon being presented with a then-recent defacement of *www.al-aqsa.org* – a Palestinian activist site defaced with a pro-Zionist message – he blurted out "those bastards!" and then retreated into his silence. Perhaps the image that draws the strongest reaction in my experience is featured in a defacement of Palestine's Ministry of Education, which was vandalized by an unknown attacker near the beginning of the Al-Aqsa Intifada. The image features a pig in

Arab dress writing the Qur'an. On the side of the pig is written the name Muhammed. This blatantly offensive cartoon is characteristically met with the same reaction by a group of Palestinians and Muslims: a prolonged gasp and then, stunned silence.

In stark contrast, defacements of Yasser Arafat's image generally evoked a lighter reception. For example, on the bottom of the same page (the one I shared with my "informants") there was a graphic of Arafat's face pasted on the body of a baby orangutan. In contrast to the anger or indignation that most hacking elicited, this caricature was nearly always met with laughter, as Palestinians themselves often "poked fun" at their septuagenarian leader. Far from violating taboos, this hacked image basically resonated with the contemporary political humor. In his day, Arafat jokes were commonly heard on the streets of Palestine: indeed, an inflated plastic Arafat (used as a punching bag) was a popular toy found in the Occupied Territories.

Defacement and defacers

There are countless websites devoted to activist causes in connection with the Al-Aqsa Intifada and the Palestinian–Israeli conflict. *Palestineremembered.com* is the "Home of All Ethnically Cleansed Palestinians" and provides maps detailing the accumulation of land by early Israeli settlers in the post-World War II era. *Womeningreen.org* is the website for "Women for Israel's Tomorrow" and presents viewers with a far-right, absolutist form of Israeli Zionism. *Electronicintifada.net* is a resource guide "for countering myth, distortion and spin from the Israeli war machine". There are literally hundreds of such sites covering the range of Palestinian and Israeli opinions. In addition, there are email lists, Usenet groups, and other forums related to both Palestinian and Israeli cyberactivism. These sites make prime targets for hackers and defacers. For example, the website of the American–Israel Public Affairs Committee (AIPAC) was subject to an attack by a Pakistani hacker, Dr. Nuker, the founder of the Pakistan Hacking Club. Dr. Nuker defaced the site with pro-Palestinian propaganda and stole credit card information from the server, posting the credit card numbers of contributors on the world wide web. This is perhaps the single most malicious attack among all of the defacements that I have examined: the stealing of credit card numbers goes well beyond mere vandalism.

In the wake of the Al-Aqsa Intifada, hundreds of websites have been defaced in support of both the Palestinians and the Israelis. The groups performing these acts can be divided according to their sympathies. Notable pro-Palestinian groups and individuals include (but are not limited to) the *World's Fantabulous Defacers* (the WFD), the *SilverLords* (one of the most prolific defacing groups in the world according to *www.alldas.org*, with over a thousand websites attacked so far), *GForce Pakistan*, and *LinuxLover*. Pro-Israeli groups include the *m0sad team* and *InfernoZ*. Each defacing group is translocal in character and each possesses unique transnational characteristics. From my correspondence with these groups I have discovered that the "real-space" locus of the pro-Palestinian groups is urban Pakistan, their sympathy for the plight of the Palestinians apparently being grafted onto their earlier support for Kashmiri separatists. The pro-Israeli groups are primarily Russian Jews and Russian immigrants to Israel, 800,000 of whom have emigrated to Israel over the past decade. For these Russian Jews in particular, finding and asserting their "native" identity as belongers, albeit recent arrivals, within the ethnically-plural (and ethnically-hierarchical) state of Israel presents certain challenges, challenges which might be met, in part, through ultra-nationalistic activities such as the defacement of Arab and Palestinian sites.

All of these groups post their defacements in English, even though some members of these groups (especially the Russian-oriented pro-Israeli ones) are not at all fluent in English, as I discovered while conducting email interviews. My feeble attempts at communicating with *InfernoZ* in computer-translated Russian were a miserable failure, but luckily I was put in touch with the *m0sad team*, named after Israel's famed intelligence service, Mossad, and the most active of all the pro-Israeli groups. Much to my delight, the *m0sad team*'s members were able to respond to my queries in English, although it was somewhat broken. All of the pro-Palestinian defacers I interviewed were fluent in English. The fact that English is currently the lingua franca of these groups raises a number of important questions regarding homogeneity and globalization, questions that cannot be fully discussed here. However, the use of English by these groups acknowledges its status as a prime facilitator of global cultural flow; defacements in Urdu or Russian could and would limit the target audiences.

One characteristic seemingly shared by members of these groups is their youth and their male gender. Most of the members of the defacer groups I studied were in their late teens, but I was surprised to learn that the Pro-Israeli defacer InfernoZ was a mere fourteen-year-old Russian kid. In the hacker/defacer underground, children as young as seven or eight have been known to find and use malicious scripts written by others. These script kiddies are often viewed with disdain by "real" or "elite" hackers, who see their actions as lacking in sophistication and skill. However, many "elite" hackers – by their own admission – began their careers by repeating the exploits of others, only later developing their skills to the point where they could create and use original hacks.

Website defacers use unconventional methodologies to promote their social agenda, and thus represent a special case for those studying online activism. At this point, a few words about my own methodology are in order. I used a number of different data collection methods for my online fieldwork, combining email, real-time Internet Relay Chatting (IRC), and the similar application ICQ (I Seek You) that allows users to see who is logged on at any given time. I also perused digital archives, in particular studying archived defacements as collected by the "mirroring" sites *attrition.org* and *alldas.org*, and paying special attention to defacements related to Palestine and Israel. The second step in this process was to contact each defacer or defacer group through their posted email address and begin dialogues with them. Email remains my primary means of data collection, for several reasons. Writing email allows me to formulate questions and responses in a calculated and sensitive way. Furthermore, recording "conversations" through email is an easy process, whereas it is usually difficult to record "chats" with informants on the various technologies that these groups and individuals use, most commonly ICQ and mIRC (modified Internet Relay Chat). Email has its peculiarities, however. One problem with emailing such groups is that, when sending queries to one of the addresses posted on a defacement, I would often get replies from several individuals writing collaboratively, or from different individuals each time I sent mail. This complicated the process of establishing rapport with my subjects. For the purpose of establishing rapport I found "live" chatting to be superior to email, given that the spontaneity of chatting on IRC lends itself to more "authentic", less formal conversations, and allows a sense of trust to develop.[2]

Of all the defacers I have interviewed, I remain the closest to Macwiz of the group *SilverLords*. Macwiz is an eager and responsive informant, and always the first person I turn to when I have a question about defacement and defacing. He is an intelligent and complex eighteen-year-old living (I am told) in Islamabad. During the summer of 2001, I spent many days in Mac's mIRC channel, exchanging stories and, above all, listening. In one conversation, Macwiz complained to me that he had little time to hack as he was busy preparing for his college entrance exams. Mac's political thinking is somewhat hybrid and dissonant: while much of it is nominally "Western", he also appeals to the forces of global Islamic unity. For example, after the terrorist attacks on the World Trade Center and the Pentagon in September of 2001, he told me that at first he was shocked, but later thought that perhaps America "deserved" it because of its support for Israel. However, he also told me that he had donated $50 to the American Red Cross for their victim relief effort and insisted that he "cared about the victims". In confronting the plurality of worlds in which Macwiz moves and creates meaning, it is of relevance to turn our attention to the hybrid elements of hacker culture and the diverse influences which shape it.

The culture of hackers

My research with pro-Palestinian and pro-Israeli hackers calls into question the relationships between resistance movements and art and artists, and the spaces they inhabit. Like the graffiti artists of the West Bank and Gaza, website defacers work to establish ideological borders and expose enemies and rivals. Such practices of constructing identity are not unique to the Middle East or South Asia, but are mirrored in the murals, graffiti and public works of art to be found in conflict zones in Northern Ireland and Mexico, for example, and in the graffiti of urban centers everywhere. In her ethnography of gangs and hip-hop graffiti in Los Angeles, Phillips (1999) builds upon Armando Silva's seven distinct characteristics of graffiti that set it apart from other media forms: marginality, anonymity, spontaneity, setting (elements of space, design and color), speed, precariousness (the use of cheap, easy-to-obtain materials) and *fugacidad* (the fleeting nature or ephemerality of the marks). Website defacements share many of these same characteristics. There are differences, however. While graffiti artists typically use spray paint, website defacers use UNIX, C, HTML and JavaScript. Both graffiti and website defacements are ephemeral, yet web defacements usually last a maximum of a few hours, whereas graffiti typically lasts a while longer. Despite the similarities between their art, the artists creating street graffiti and those creating hacked websites differ in important ways. Defacers are generally not familiar with each other through the sharing of a local space/place. They seldom meet physically, and their communication via text-based email and chat applications is bounded by the (limiting) sensory experiences of electronic communication. Within "virtual" communities the face-to-face neighborhood dynamics of graffiti production are absent. Nevertheless, defacers have established idioms of conduct and linguistic cues for expressing cameraderie and/or contempt. For instance, "Greetz" are given to those individuals and groups with which they align themselves; "Fuckz" are given to opponents as defacers taunt their rivals. Such attributions, written into many defaces, serve almost as a kind of genealogy of these marginalized groups and (meta)groups and remind one of record liner notes and the content of some hip-hop music, where rappers give "props" and "shout out" to their friends in the scene, and also deride their enemies. Like rappers, these defacers see themselves as confronting the hegemonic discourses of everyday life and their (oppressed) positions. This may be one of the reasons why Macwiz (and many others like him) gravitates towards rap music: he may feel that the lyrics of oppression and resistance common to rap in particular speak to his situation.

On any given day, dozens of websites worldwide are defaced, and these defaces are then posted on defacement mirrors. These mirrors provide a more-or-less permanent space to exhibit the exploits of the defacers and their messages, which characteristically have an ephemeral lifespan on the targeted websites (as, once discovered, they are generally removed within a matter of hours). In addition to giving defacements a longer web-life, these mirrors also function as important places of community for hackers and defacers. For the past several years, participants in the "game" of defacing websites were concentrated in two virtual oases, *attrition.org* and its defacement mirror, along with its twin site, *alldas.org*. These sites sat in the center of the global hacker/defacer underground and were fascinating places in which to eavesdrop on global popular discourse. Hitlerites, Pakistani nationalists, radical environmentalists and anti-capitalists, anarchists, and those playing the game simply for the challenge and the opportunity to demonstrate their knowledge and skill – all found a (virtual) watering hole at these sites. However, in May of 2000, *attrition.org* shut down its defacement mirror, due to a marked increase in defacement activity. The volunteers who maintained the site could no longer keep up with the volume of hacked sites pouring into their in-boxes at a rate of 100+ reports daily. As a non-profit organization, the webmasters of *attrition.org* simply could not afford to divert the required time and attention away from their day-jobs and everyday lives. As they put in a communiqué entitled "EVOLUTION", they had "done their time". With *attrition.org* no longer current, *alldas.org* is currently the only major site left to catalog defacements. If and when alldas.org goes down (and it has been known to be offline for as long as a month at a time, due to denial-of-service attacks) then the public manifestation of the hacker/defacer community evaporates.

In considering hacker culture, it is of interest that the pro-Palestinian and pro-Israeli defacers whom I interviewed expressed little animosity toward the defacers working the opposite side of the conflict; at least, that is how they represented themselves in the interview context. There seems to be a level of mutual respect between these defacing groups despite their political differences. When speaking of the opposition *m0sad* team (the premier pro-Israeli defacer group), n00gie, a hacker from the sophisticated and very active pro-Palestinian *World's Fantabulous Defacers* (WFD), told me that he had started out much like the members of the *m0sad team*, performing relatively unsophisticated, low-level hacks at a young age. Given the rhetorical severity of his groups' defacements, I had imagined that n00gie would condemn the m0sad team. Instead, he identified with them and did not necessarily indict them as opponents. Likewise, *m0sad team* defacers spoke of the WFD in much the same sympathetic tone. The explanation for such attitudes lies, I believe, in the nature of these groups and the larger community to which they belong – that of the hacker/defacer underground.

The Green Line in reality and virtuality

The Al-Aqsa uprising in Israel and the Occupied Territories (the West Bank and Gaza Strip) generated processes that engaged both state and anti-state actors. One of the major themes of this study is the difference in perception and action across border zones. How individuals think, act, and feel about uprisings depends largely upon which side of the Green Line they are from – the line the divide that has separated the West Bank from Israel – they are from. "Inside" the Green Line (i.e. in the Occupied Territories, which historically tended to be more-or-less closed to the "outside world"), local knowledge and "bread-and-butter" politics generally have been at the forefront of public and personal perceptions. Here, more attention is paid to local politics and group affiliation: whether one is associated with Hamas or with Fatah, with the PFLP (Popular Front for the Liberation of Palestine) or with Islamic Jihad – such alignments are more apt to determine one's ideological orientations and political objectives. "Outside" the Green Line (i.e. in other Palestinian regions and in Israel), internationally-mediated discourses and images (such as CNN, BBC and increasingly Al-Jazeera) have been more likely to shape Palestinian opinion. Here, the Palestinians driven from their homes in 1948 and/or in 1967 have focused attention on issues surrounding Israeli withdrawal from the West Bank and Gaza; and especially on the emotionally-fraught and politically-explosive question of repatriation for some of the three million Palestinian refugees. Political affiliation is less likely to be a divisive matter or an overriding concern "outside" the Green Line; this is so throughout most of neighboring Jordan, which historically has banned Palestinian political groups and restricted their operations within its borders. The situation varies in Syria and Lebanon, however, where (in the refugee camps and some of the cities) Palestinian groups have been allowed to operate with (relative) impunity. Such local–global differences in the weight accorded to matters of political affiliation are not unique to the Palestinians, certainly. It is a widely held notion that there are major differences between the politics of Jewish groups within Israel and those on the outside, which tend to be more conservative. In Israel itself, there is a high level of political complexity, laid out on a continuum that stretches from the dovelike Gush Shalom (Peace Now) to the far right (and now banned) Kach party. Jewish organizations outside Israel, and especially in the United States, tend to gloss over these differences in favor of blanket support for Israel. The "bread and butter" politics of the Likud, Shas, or Labor parties are dissimulated into voices of unanimity and broad-based US support for Israel. These global–local differences become evident when one takes up the study of acts of defacement committed by actors both inside and outside the Green Line and Israel.

These differences are evident in the defacements that hackers leave behind. Pro-Israeli defacer groups within Israel accurately reflect internal Israeli discourse. Israeli groups often list the names and pictures of the Israeli dead in defacements, thereby personalizing the conflict. One defacement, which occupied the façade of Saudi Arabia's Ministry of Health, displayed all the pictures and names of the Israeli dead, lit by virtual candlelight. Another showed photos of those killed in the Dolphinarium suicide bombing in Tel Aviv, where twenty-one Israelis, mostly young immigrants from Russia, were killed while queuing outside a discotheque. It was at first unclear who had actually created the defacement, the only clue being a rather mysterious (not to mention poorly spelled) inscription: "Was Hacked By 14 years old kid, The Survivers in the Sucide Bombing Will Revange! Stop the terror in israel!!!" I came across this defacement in mid-June 2001 when it was posted on *alldas.org.* only a short time after the actual event. At the time, I was soon to leave the United States to continue my fieldwork in the West Bank. Seeking information, I emailed a member of the *m0sad team* defacing group, which is largely composed of immigrant Russian teenagers to Israel, as I felt certain that he could shed some light on the recent event, since the bombing had been directed towards the Russian-Israeli community. His return email informed me that one of the members of his group had almost been killed in the explosion. I was stunned at the thought; and knowing that within days I was about to go to the center of the conflict, I was anxious.

A few days and thousands of miles later, I stepped out of a taxi in the West Bank town of Ramallah and was immediately confronted with dozens of posters in the city center featuring the eerie, smiling image of Hassan Hutri, his body wrapped in explosives. Hutri, a Palestinian refugee from one of Jordan's many refugee camps, was the person who annihilated himself along with those outside the Dolphinarium disco. In Palestine he was considered, at least by some, to be a hero and a martyr. At that moment, the global had became local for me, and somehow the bridge between international website defacers and actors "on the ground" in Palestine and Israel became clear. Posting pictures of martyrs is a common practice in Ramallah, and together with factional graffiti in red, black and blue, these posters are one of the most distinctive features of the city's streets. They are everywhere: images of young men and old men, often posed with a copy of the Qur'an in one hand and in the other a Kalashnokov – the weapon of choice among Palestine's resistance move-ments that is commonly seen on the streets of Palestine's *de facto* capital, slung across the backs of young, non-uniformed men from one of the Palestinian National Authority's thirteen police forces. Often the martyr's image is grafted onto an image of the Dome of the Rock, perhaps the most important symbol to Palestinian fighters, and the spot where the current uprising began. This cultural practice of confronting people with the names and faces of the dead is one that has carried over into the realm of cyberspace and is a revealing clue in determining the "encrypted" backgrounds and identities of the defacers in my study.

Virtual occupations

Now only information has real cost.
And it cannot be guarded by armed squad
or even by the government special forces. One
man can destroy a whole company with one click.
Remember about it . . .

(m0sad team 2001).

Any discussion of website defacement must deal with the defacements them-selves and the responses to the words and images they project. These defacements are revealing for what they say about the nature of the Palestinian–Israeli conflict and those people involved with it, both in the physical center of the conflict and at the cyberspatial periphery. The dialectics of global and local difference are especially interesting. To this end, I will briefly describe and analyze several defacements that are representative of those posted during the year 2001, in conjunction with the Al-Aqsa Intifada.

The images and texts of the defacements reflect these groups' respective engage-ment with competing mediascapes constructed around ideologies of post-diasporic nationalism (in the case of the Israeli and Russian defacers) and global Islamic unity (in the case of the pro-Palestinian defacers). The Russian-Israeli defacers disrupt Islamic websites and therefore disrupt these public, online faces of resistance. For example, a pro-Israeli group altered the *hamas.org* website, making a porn site appear in place of the normal Hamas site. The spiritual leader of Hamas, Sheikh Ahmad Yassin, responded by accusing Israeli intelligence forces of being behind the attack, stating: "They are trying to disfigure the image of Islam and the Muslims" (BBC News 2001). It was never clear who actually altered the Hamas site, but my research would suggest that it was not, in fact, Israeli intelligence; more likely it was the work of Russian-Israeli teenagers.

Pro-Palestinian defacers have typically attacked Israeli and pro-Israeli sites in defense of their Muslim brothers. *The World's Fantabulous Defacers* were responsible for defacing Ariel Sharon's website only four days before the Israeli election of 2001, in which Sharon was elected prime minister in a landslide victory. It was widely reported by Israeli radio and the BBC that the defacement was carried out by Hezbollah. However, this appears to be completely erroneous: defacers almost always leave "calling cards" in the form of email addresses where they can be reached. When I reached the WFD, I learned that they were mainly young Pakistanis, but also had members somewhere in Europe. They supported Hezbollah for its efforts against Israeli occupiers in south Lebanon, but they were not Hezbollah members themselves. These mistakes in attribution are common in mainstream media coverage of "hacktivist" activity, and have contributed to the widespread proliferation of cyberfolklore. When I was in Ramallah during the summer of 2001, disruptions of internet access were often blamed on "the Jews" in a kind of nebulous, conspiratorial way. While it is true that some Israelis have at times attacked Palestinian internet service providers, it is no doubt untrue that hackers are responsible for every creeping page-load that Palestinians experience. By the same token it is often wrongly claimed by Israelis that Palestinians are deeply involved in the Palestinian–Israeli cyber–conflict: during my research I have not encountered a single Palestinian hacker or website defacer. From my experience, Palestinian teenagers using computers are more interested in listening to music, corresponding with friends, and looking at pornography than they are in committing acts of resistance against the Israeli state. For young men in Palestine, the internet is a welcome escape from the brutality of war and occupation. Resistance is (literally) only a stone's throw away, it needn't be sought in cyberspace. Yet outside of Palestine, those who support the Palestinian cause have little chance to do anything substantial to directly influence the situation; and I believe it is the frustration that results from this helplessness that in part motivates young people throughout the Islamic world to lash out against the Israeli state and those who oppose the cause of Palestinian self-determination.

In *WFD's* defacement of Sharon's website, the defacers "left behind", among other images and texts, a satirical letter purportedly from Sharon, and notable for its stridency, cynicism and confrontational stance:

> We here in Israel believe that all Palestinians are terrorists. Even the babies, so we behead them all too. I myself enjoy this very much. In fact, the only reason I can continue to commit these brutal crimes is because the Western and American media portrays me, Ariel Sharon, as a loving, grandpa-type figure.

The good-old folks at the *American New York Times* and *Washington Post* love me and Israel more than they love their own country. They continue to deceive the American people as more and more American money comes pouring into my government's hands. Muahahahahah!

We, Israel, are a Nation, a State, and a People who desire the utter and complete genocide of the Palestinian people and we are closer than ever to accomplishing that goal. With the trust of the lords of the American mass media, such as CNN, we have continued to manipulate the American people into believing our lies. Ha ha ha, how naive they are!

Our Israeli forces have murdered 390 Palestinians and wounded another 18,000, while they have only killed 48 of our Israeli people. And yet the Americans think that we are the victims, and that they are the terrorists, when in reality we are the terrorists!

So finally, I say to you this. With an experienced leadership in murdering and butchering Palestinians and telling the whole world that we are the victims of their violence, we will succeed in our ultimate Zionist goals of rebuilding the Kingdom of David, and ruling the entire world from Jerusalem.

I ask for your trust and support in our quest to destroy the Palestinian people once and for all.

With blessings.

A. Sharon

(*WFD* Note: But Sharon, by God, you will never achieve this inhumane goal . . . You will be stopped. No matter how much power you have, no matter how much tanks, artillery, and planes you have, no matter what the World Bank and IMF do for you . . . Israel, you will lose . . . Reckoning will come.)

It would be useful at this point to compare the above letter left by the *WFD* to a defacement by the pro-Israeli *m0sad team*:

A Peace accord is not made with a person, but with a nation.
Unfortunately, we know the Palestinian "nation" all too well.
We came to know them when a young Palestinian cut the throat of an
Israeli soldier or when a mob murdered and mutilated the bodies of soldiers
in Ramallah.
We came to know them when they got near a car of a border checkpoint
station worker and sprayed the car with bullets from a short range.
We came to known them when a crowd of children ran towards Israeli
vehicles, their hands full of stones and Molotov cocktails, in order to kill or
at least wound people they don't know, as long as they were Jewish.
We came to known them when they sent terrorists to blow themselves up
and kill children and women with themselves.
Arafat and his people, the Palestinians, for years have woven a fabric of
hatred. This hatred lies without any mercy or humanity, without any
distinction between a religious or a secular Jew, between a Right wing to

the most extreme Left wing supporter.
The Palestinians' one and only goal is obvious – the extermination of the
Israeli nation.
Arafat is NOT a partner for peace. The Palestinian people are NOT part-
ners for peace.

The events and ideas expressed in the *m0sad team* text suggest that the author
lives within Israel, whereas the *WFD*'s "letter" contains hints that its writer(s)
live outside the Green Line and are responding to different representations of the
conflict. For example, the m0sad team makes reference to political diversity in
Israel. The slogans of the *m0sad team* are familiar to anyone who regularly reads
Israeli newspapers. "Arafat is NOT a partner for peace" was a commonly heard
refrain among Israeli right-wingers. As for the *WFD*, few in the Occupied
Territories feel that all Israelis and Jews are genocidal monsters (but they do
consider Sharon himself to be an agent of genocide due to his complicity in the
1982 Sabra and Shatilla massacres in Lebanon).[3] Most Palestinians recognize that
Israelis are "there to stay"; and that the most important cause of suffering from the
Palestinians at the hands of the Israelis is not indiscriminate violence perpetrated
by the Israeli army and settlers, but the oppressive system of incarceration/occupa-
tion that splits families, disrupts commerce, and humiliates its victims.

The words and images contained in such defaces mirror the common stereotypes of the conflict made by each side. Those taking a pro-Israeli stance, for
instance, have asserted that the Israelis desire peace and security above all else,
whereas pro-Palestinians argued that violence is an expression of resistance
against the tyrannical occupation. The statements of defacers hold closely to
conventional political lines; their stances, however, are amplified in tone and
explicitly designed to shock and offend the opposition. One pro-Palestinian
defacement, for instance, features a cartoon character urinating on an Israeli flag.
One pro-Israeli defacement features the proclamation "We will destroy the
Arabs", a common refrain heard on the streets of Israel, especially in the aftermath of Palestinian attacks. Such acts represent not only a resistance to opposing
viewpoints, however, but also to the hegemony of corporate-controlled media
and the state. Even large institutions can be affected by the actions committed
by a few determined teenagers: I spoke with one UN representative in Palestine
who insisted that the UN website for her department be hosted by an American
server, not a Palestinian server, for fear of "cyber-terrorism". In the media, these
defacements create media vectors (or coverage) of their own, allowing those
engaging in them a modicum of voice and agency. The actors in this conflict
therefore are media *participants* and not merely passive consumers.

Conclusion

The encrypted identities of the actors in this ongoing struggle for voice and
agency and the heteroglossic nuances of the global–local dialectics permeating

this conflict are compelling examples of the challenges ethnographers face when going online. Given that conflicts that begin on the ground are increasingly moving into and across the coded spaces of the internet, it is imperative, therefore, that a social nomadology of technology be articulated, for, without it, it will be impossible to understand the relationship between individuals and larger social forces, phenomena, and powers in cyberspace. Website defacers offer a new way to imagine the spaces of the world wide web that emphasize activism and interactivity over passivity and reliance on centralized sources of information. Thus cyberspace is becoming a site not only for the reproduction of modernist social and political forces, it is becoming an arena in which new and old ways of living can be imagined and re-imagined.

Notes

1   This is a fictionalized account based on ethnographic data (interviews and "chats" with Macwiz).
2   Much has been written about identity in cyberspace and the problems that arise for ethnographers (see, e.g., Stone 1995 and Turkle 1995). However, my subjects differ somewhat in that I have had no face-to-face interactions with hacker individuals and/or groups, who actively protect their identities for fear of prosecution. The online dimension of this ethnographic project is therefore inherently unstable. I must trust that these individuals are who they say they are; if they aren't, then this project is elaborately disinformative. I do not know the real names and identities of my informants, who could face severe penalties if apprehended. I am left with hybrid, complex and often encrypted identities that strain legibility. What can be learned from these encryptions is a theme of this study, and presents me with compounded methodological concerns.
3   In June 2001, a group of twenty-three Lebanese and Palestinians filed a complaint against Ariel Sharon in the Belgian courts, which have implemented a set of universal jurisdiction laws, allowing Belgium to prosecute people living abroad accused of crimes under international law. The complaint alleged that Sharon was complicit in the 1982 Sabra and Shatila massacres in Lebanon, carried out by Lebanese Phalangists under Israeli Defense Forces supervision. In 1983, the official Israeli Commission of Inquiry into the Events at the Refugee Camps in Beirut concluded that Minister of Defence Ariel Sharon had "disregarded the danger of acts of vengeance and bloodshed by Phalangists . . . failed to take this danger into account when he decided to have the Phalangists enter the camps . . . [and had not ordered] appropriate measures for preventing or reducing the danger of massacre as a condition for the Phalangists' entry into the camps" (Amnesty International 2001). However, Israel made no serious reprimands of Sharon. Another angle to the case came in the autumn of 2002, when a leading witness for the prosecution, was assassinated two days after publically stating that he had incriminating evidence against Sharon and was willing to testify for the prosecution. Israel has never seriously reprimanded Sharon.

References

Amnesty International (2001) "Amnesty International Urges Investigation of Ariel Sharon". Available online: www.web.amnesty.org.

BBC News (2001) "Hamas Hit By Porn Attack". Available online: news.bbc.co.uk/hi/english/world/middle_east/newsid_1207000/1207551.stm

Goldstein, Emmanuel (2001) "Questions", *2600: The Hacker Quarterly*. New York.

InfernoZ (2001) Interview, personal correspondence (email), 11 and 13 April.

Levy, Steven (1984) *Hackers*. New York: Dell.

m0sad team (2001) Interview, personal correspondence (email), 12 and 15 April.

n00gie (2001) Interview, ICQ. 17 April.

Nelson, Diane M. (1996) "Maya Hackers and the Cyberspatialized Nation-State: Modernity, Ethnostalgia, and a Lizard Queen in Guatemala", *Cultural Anthropology* 11(3): 287–308.

Phillips, Susan A. (1999) *Wallbangin': Gangs and Graffiti in L.A.* Chicago: University of Chicago Press.

SilverLords (2001) Interview, personal correspondence (email), 12 and 13 April.

Stone, Roseanne Allucquere (1995) *The War of Desire and Technology at the Close of the Mechanical Age*. Cambridge, MA: MIT Press.

Taylor, Paul (1999) *Hackers*. New York: Routledge Press.

Turkle, Sherry (1995) *Life On the Screen: Identity in the Age of the Internet*. New York: Simon and Schuster.

Chapter 14

Internet Counter Counter-Insurgency

TamilNet.com and ethnic conflict in Sri Lanka[1]

Mark Whitaker

Introduction

On 31 December 2003 I was in Colombo, Sri Lanka's capital city, waiting to get my hair cut, when I picked up a newspaper and read that S. Pathmanathan, the Government Agent of Sri Lanka's war-torn Northern Province, was issuing a very spirited statement. In an official letter that somehow made its way immediately into all of Sri Lanka's major national newspapers, Pathmanathan was claiming that the "pro-rebel" news website, *TamilNet.com*, had completely misquoted him when it reported his saying – rather loudly – at a public meeting in Chavakacheri (a northern Tamil town previously flattened by Sri Lanka's civil war) that "the Sri Lankan government hasn't spent a cent on rehabilitation in the Northern Peninsula in the last two years". The political and, as it were, spatial context of Pathmanathan's concern was, I imagined, as immediately obvious to all Sri Lankan newspaper readers as it was to me. Sri Lanka's eighteen-year-long civil war had been tentatively paused two years earlier by the signing of a ceasefire agreement between the Sri Lankan government (a government permanently dominated by Sri Lanka's Sinhala speaking and largely Buddhist majority) and the Liberation Tigers of Tamil Eelam, the ruthless, militarily efficient insurgent army that had long been seeking to create a separate state for Sri Lanka's Tamil minority in the island nation's northern and eastern provinces.[2] Everyone knew, however, that the ceasefire agreement was a frail reed upon which to build a peace, and that the weight of any single broken promise by either side regarding (among many other things) the distribution of rehabilitation money might be enough to bring everything crashing down. It was quite understandable, therefore, that Pathmanathan should be upset.

Of additional interest to me, however, since I am curious about the role of the internet in Sri Lanka's ethnic conflict, was what this story suggested about the status that *TamilNet.com* and a few other internet sites currently hold in Sri Lanka's hotly contested public sphere. Why should S. Pathmanathan, a relatively senior public official, feel it necessary to refute a story appearing in a "pro-rebel" website? To what audience was he speaking? For that matter, why should this exchange be important enough for most newspapers to carry it on their front page? Of more immediate interest to me, though, was how

TamilNet.com would respond to the aspersions Pathmanathan had cast upon its factual reliability. Over twenty years of research in Sri Lanka – much of it spent in the eastern, rural, predominantly Tamil, Batticaloa District – provided a direction for my queries. So I hurried over to the house of Dharmeratnam Sivaram, *TamilNet.com's* editor, and a man whom I have known since 1982 when he was a young university student, and I waved my rolled-up newspaper at him.[3] "Hey", I said, "this doesn't look good, does it?"

As he had just risen after a hard night of journalistic socializing, Sivaram cast a baleful eye at my wrinkled and now woefully unreadable exhibit, while readjusting his sarong.

"Young man", he intoned – he sometimes calls me "young man', though neither of us is young any more and I am several years older (and fatter and grayer) than he – "what has been done to your hair"?

"Never mind my hair".

"No, it looks good. You look younger. You look, in fact", he squinted at me further, "too young".

"The story"?

He smiled a hard smile.

"Just wait".

The next day, while accompanying my wife and I on an audiotape buying expedition (two anthropologists and a journalist can go through quite a lot of audiotape), Sivaram was approached by an exhausted – looking, rather intense young man bearing all the tell-tale marks of a long bus journey. He carried a battered little box containing two audiotapes. He was, in fact, one of Sivaram's reporters, just down from Jaffna on the overnight bus.

"So this is everything?" said Sivaram, cocking an eye.

"Everything," said the man, who then, rather mysteriously, disappeared.

That night, sitting at his laptop, Sivaram composed a response to Pathmanathan based on transcripts of the audiotapes of his remarks in Chavakacheri. He then appended audioclips of those remarks to the story so that readers could, by simply clicking on an icon, actually hear Pathmanathan say what he had just denied that he had said. Satisfied, he uploaded the response to *TamilNet.com*.

"Isn't that rather gilding the lily?"

"Young man," said Sivaram, patiently, "you didn't think I would print a politician's remarks without having a tape to back me up? That is elementary journalism."

It is certainly easy, in one way, to point to *TamilNet.com* as a good, even a classic example of "indigenous cyberactivism". *TamilNet.com* is a news site on the world wide web initially organized in 1995 by a group of Sri Lankan Tamil expatriates in North America and Europe – middle-aged men, mostly engineers and computer scientists, who left Sri Lanka years before (along with, roughly, 700,000 other Tamils) as a result of the war (Fuglerud 1999: 1). Its public purpose, as stated on its virtual masthead, was "reporting to the world on Tamil affairs". Its more political aim – or one of them, anyway – was to counter what its creators perceived as the indifference and hostility of the Western press toward the Sri Lankan Tamil nationalist independence movement. At first a bit of a disappointment – no "hits" to speak of – it was reorganized in 1996 from Sri Lanka by Dharmeratnam Sivaram, a famous Sri Lankan Tamil columnist, into a Sri Lankan Tamil internet news agency with its own string of reporters. After that it rapidly became *de rigueur* reading, not just for Tamil expatriates but also for any member of government or the press (both in Sri Lanka and abroad) responsible for following, influencing or directing Sri Lankan affairs. Soon international news agencies such as the BBC, Reuters and AP, and major Indian newspapers such as *The Hindu*, all regularly cited or credited *TamilNet.com* stories in their reports, albeit with accompanying cautions about the "pro-rebel" nature of the site. Similarly, all the Sri Lankan national dailies – Sinhala, Tamil, and English – regularly used its reports, though generally accompanied by even harsher condemnations of the source (Whitaker 2004b: 492).

So, by any measure, *TamilNet.com* must be considered a spectacularly successful indigenous cyberactivist site. Its intervention – or, better, its insinuation – of a Tamil nationalist perspective into the hitherto tight web of national and international newspaper and news agency coverage of Sri Lanka in the mid-nineties was a direct challenge to the various hegemonic forces, Sri Lankan and international, that largely controlled non-Sri Lankan Tamil public debate about and knowledge of the communal conflict there. Or, putting this another way (and, I think, more accurately), *TamilNet.com* successfully added another public, its own "indigenous" one, to the hitherto too constrained and "hegemonic" public sphere within which too few people (all too often, mainly national and international elites) were already surrounding, debating, and considering Sri Lanka. The basic aim of this chapter, then, is to narrate, ethnographically, the story of just how the creators of *TamilNet.com* accomplished this subversive intrusion.

But telling this story is complicated (and made, I believe, more interesting) by the necessity of also explaining two important facts. First, *TamilNet.com's* intricate and dangerous Sri Lankan and international political context involves a long-running, hot contest between two competing nationalisms (i.e. between two visions of how and for whom Sri Lanka should work, one Tamil and one Sinhala) occurring within a still larger arena of geopolitical competition between regional and international powers (i.e. most recently, India and the United States, and also, at the present time, within the circumstances of the US "War on Terror"). This socio-political tableau, I think, might best be characterized, at all its levels, by using Antonio Gramsci's rather dour model of "hegemony". By "hegemony", it should be remembered, Gramsci, writing as both a practical politician and an imprisoned insurgent, meant a kind of political struggle that is, for the most part, continuous, asymmetrically dialogic, Machiavellian, and (thus, though this is often left out by people who invoke Gramsci) *always* backed up by real or potential violence (Gramsci 1971: 125–9; Crehan 2002: 146).

With regard to this last fact, the intricate interplay in Sri Lanka between contemporary and competing "technologies" of insurgency and counter-insurgency – the well developed and much exported cultural systems created for both fighting and suppressing what professional military theorists call, somewhat ingenuously, "low intensity wars" – is the most relevant feature. It is relevant, to be explicit, to the tune of at least 100,000 (mostly non-combatant) deaths over nineteen years of conflict.[4] Even now, during periods of official ceasefire, individuals die almost every day, particularly in Sri Lanka's Batticaloa District, in a violent, *sub-rosa* jockeying for position between the government and the Liberation Tigers of Tamil Eelan LTTE. This kind of "shadow war" (to use Dharmeratnam Sivaram's phrase) is often found in states involved in the deadly politics of insurgency and counter-insurgency. It is mindfulness about the delicacy of this ongoing, teetering balance between a fragile peace and the potential for more war that clogs Sri Lanka's public arenas with its toughest hegemonic barriers to free and open discussion – for both the Sri Lankan government and the LTTE have cautioned about threats to solidarity, have corralled "organic" intellectuals, have exercised direct and indirect control over media, and have practiced outright violence in order to enforce discursive conformity within what is, in effect, their two competing public spheres. With regard to public discourse of any sort, then, the central thing to note about Sri Lanka's Gramscian political and geopolitical context is that it is rather tightly constrained. Henceforth, for the purposes of this paper, I shall refer to this aspect of Sri Lanka's political landscape as its "Gramscian hegemonic context".

In contrast to all this, however, there is another political landscape, and our second fact: the quite different context operating on the internet, a much less constrained and less violence-laden "virtual" arena in which there are fewer barriers to participation. Here, as I have discussed in an earlier paper (Whitaker 2004b), the most important feature is the relative cheapness with which anyone possessing a computer and a link to the internet can create and upload professional-looking, and thus "marketable", content, despite the otherwise constraining "market logic" built into many parts of the internet's underlying technology. This relative openness of the internet is precisely what allows *TamilNet.com* for $2000 a month to compete for people's attention on an equal footing with international news agencies and the Sri Lankan government which is spending, or is capable of spending, very much more.[5] And it is precisely this openness that has led at least one interesting theorist, O'Baoill, to assert that the internet is best characterized by invoking Jürgen Habermas' normative model of the properly constituted "public sphere" – that is to say, his model of the kind of ideal, perfect, public sphere where real "communicative action" (i.e. effective, rational, political discussion) can take place (O'Baoill 2000).

O'Baoill's argument, somewhat arbitrarily expanded here by me for descriptive purposes, works something like this: Habermas' normative model requires three preconditions: 1) universal access (i.e. anyone can play); 2) rational debate (i.e. anything can be discussed till a consensus is reached); and 3) disregard of rank (i.e. the ranks of the players in any public controversy are ignored or unknown) (O'Baoill 2000: 4; Habermas 1992: 449). Now while Habermas' own historical discussions (which, in some ways, are rather Gramscian: see Habermas 1989) of actual, mostly European public spheres make it quite clear that such preconditions are unlikely to be found wherever state systems, driven by their "functional" needs, have "colonized" the "lifeworld" of daily discourse by means of media manipulation, consumer advertising, and, I would add, sheer muscle – for, as Taussig has famously noted (1987: 5), fear trumps discourse and tends to shut it down – this is clearly not true online. For the internet, by contrast and for now (at least in regard to contemporary Sri Lanka), appears to satisfy to an amazing degree all three features of Habermas' normative model. That is: 1) the internet is open to anyone who can afford a computer and a link to the internet – and while the cost of such access is not trivial, especially for largely cash-poor Sri Lankans, it is certainly far less prohibitively costly than, say, obtaining a printing press or a radio station; 2) filtering devices notwithstanding, anything can, indeed, be discussed on the internet (though "consensus" is more doubtful); and 3) "rank" (and gender – see Haraway 1996) is very difficult to discern on the internet given the use of relatively universal mark-up languages (like HTML), which allow all sites to look equally professional. The internet, then, in some ways does indeed look like the "radical-democratic" public sphere that Habermas' model was seeking to create (Habermas 1992: 444). Henceforth, for the purposes of this chapter, I shall refer to this aspect of the internet's political landscape as its "normative Habermasian context".

Leaving aside the issue of whether O'Baoill's claim is ultimately convincing or not (especially given the way I have shamelessly exaggerated it), I would none the less argue that characterizing the internet this way is usefully suggestive. Why? Because, heuristically (or ethno*graphic*ally), the real contrast between the internet's relative openness – and, hence, its Habermasian normative proclivities – and the gritty, even sanguinary, Gramscian landscape of battling hegemonies that currently surrounds Sri Lanka, needs to be highlighted. For ultimately, I would argue, the best explanation of *TamilNet.com*'s (and the internet's) unusual importance in Sri Lankan public discourse is found in the interaction *between* these two quite distinct and even incoherent "Gramscian" and "Habermasian" political contexts – an interaction that was (to a certain extent) strategically recognized and utilized by *TamilNet.com*'s creators as they were constructing the site. But to make their story clear we need to consider each of these political contexts in turn. Let us start, then, with Sri Lanka's "Gramscian" ethnic conflict and the geopolitical complications it has entailed.

War, counter-insurgency doctrine, and cyber-insurgency: Sri Lanka's "Gramscian" ethnic conflict

The war began in 1983. An ambush set up by the LTTE killed thirteen soldiers and led to the most bloody anti-Tamil riots in Sri Lankan history – riots that some have suggested were pre-planned by the Sri Lankan government as a kind of "final solution" to the Tamil problem (Wilson 2000: 113). Estimates vary, but it is known that thousands of Tamil people were killed, over 100,000 homes and businesses were destroyed, and 178,000 fled abroad, many to Tamil Nadu, sparking the interest of the government in Delhi, and beginning a diaspora that would grow to around 700,000 by the mid-1990s (Whitaker 2004a: 411). After the riots, in a mutual drawing of lines in the sand, large numbers of Tamil youths rushed to join a wildly proliferating number of separatist groups[6] while the government, for its part, quickly passed the Sixth Amendment to the Constitution which demanded an oath of allegiance to a unitary state, thereby effectively removing all Tamil representation in Parliament. The disjunction of Sri Lankan discourse into distinct Tamil and Sinhala public spheres was, therefore, complete; in a sense there really was nothing left to do but fight.

The war raged for nineteen years, with brief breaks in the fighting in 1987, 1990 and 1994, before sputtering to an inconclusive (but longer-lasting) pause in 2001. Geopolitical circumstances surrounding the conflict, however, led to some frankly weird interludes in this supposedly internal and purely "ethnic" struggle as the external context slowly evolved from the Cold War to the "War on Terror". For example, initially, the Tamil separatist groups were supported with weapons and training by India – with India hoping, most likely, for a kind of East Pakistan-like resolution of Sri Lanka's difficulties in favor of India's regional ambitions (Gunaratna 1993). It was here that Tamil militants were first exposed to standard counter-insurgency doctrine in the form of the British training manuals used by the Indian army (Whitaker 1997: 203), manuals which emphasized – as the American manuals still do – the need to complement military force with various forms of civic coercion and persuasion. This educational and military cooperation between India and the militants ended in 1987, however, when the Jayawardena government signed an accord with India that allowed an Indian Peace Keeping Force (IPKF) to occupy the north and east for the purpose of overseeing devolutionary elections. But this, in turn, quickly developed into a war between the IPKF and the LTTE, a war in which the LTTE was covertly supplied by the Sri Lankan government. During this time, the LTTE also (finishing what it had started) either absorbed or ruthlessly destroyed its separatist rivals, eventually emerging as the sole independent militant group left standing, with the remains of its shattered competitors subsequently allying themselves with the IPKF and, later, the Sri Lankan government. This also left the LTTE as the only group to which the (by this time) quite large Sri Lankan Tamil diaspora could funnel their support, and so the LTTE's coffers filled. In 1990, the IPKF, several thousand soldiers poorer, withdrew, and soon the LTTE, after a brief interlude of talks, was again fighting the Sri Lankan state.

At this point, the LTTE redoubled its efforts to police its supporters – or, in a sense, the Tamil nationalist public sphere – by using sophisticated propaganda campaigns and dramatic public rituals such as "Great Warrior Day" (Cheran 2001: 16) to mobilize diasporic Tamils; and by using finances and, sometimes, muscle to buy out or intimidate Sri Lankan Tamil media rivals both inside and outside the country. To talk to its public, the LTTE made sophisticated use of video, radio (it bought stations), newspapers, newsletters, and, by the early 1990s, via chat rooms and early websites, the internet – the first, faltering steps, if you will, at cyberinsurgency. All this was clearly aimed at influencing and mobilizing the Tamil diaspora, and through them Western sympathy, more than at Tamils in Sri Lanka – who were, for the most part, well enough motivated by the Sri Lankan army's violent counter-insurgency tactics. Of course, the LTTE used violence to enforce conformity too, as it did, (to pick only one example), with its assassination of Neelan Tiruchelvan, a moderate, in 1999. It was by violence, also, that the LTTE tried to strike at the will of the Sinhala populace (and, sometimes, of Muslim people in "Tamil" areas) through periodic expulsions, bombings and massacres. But all these actions would eventually prove counter-productive as they would allow the Sri Lankan government, in the context of America's growing concern with "terrorism", to win the external propaganda war by having its characterization of the LTTE as a "terrorist" organization accepted by the Western media and, eventually, by important Western states such as the US and Britain.

At roughly the same time, the Indo–Lankan Accords sparked a revived and more nationalist group, the JVP to vie for power in the south. The JVP, or the "People's Liberation Front" (*Janatha Vimukthi Peramuna*), was and remains a neo-Marxist, opportunistically nationalist, mostly Sinhalese, and periodically violent party. The JVP saw the Indo–Lankan Accords as a sterling opportunity to rally the Sinhala masses to its anti-Indian and revolutionary cause. In the resulting dirty war (1987–90) between the Sri Lankan government and the anti-government JVP (sometimes covertly aided by the LTTE) both sides to the conflict employed equally indiscriminant tactics, and both killed tens of thousands of people, (mostly noncombatants, including many prominent Sinhala leftists who had been sympathetic to Tamil structural complaints). This knocked yet another nail in the coffin of inter-communal discussion. As some of those killed were well known media figures, such as the famously handsome TV newsreader, actor, poet, and journalist Richard de Zoysa (Wijesinha 2000), the counter-JVP terror also sharpened the Sri Lankan government's hegemonic control over the press and the intelligentsia. Still, while many Sinhalese journalists, unsurprisingly, knuckled under, others continued criticizing the government – but warily. One former Sinhalese reporter, for example, a columnist at the time, told me he avoided (what he believed to be) an otherwise inevitable rendezvous with the anonymous white vans of the government death squads by never sleeping in the same bed on successive nights.

Yet, paradoxically, this intra-Sinhala terror provided a creative opening to some Tamil journalists, at least in the Sinhala-owned English-language press. For it was during this confusing time that Dharmeratnam Sivaram, at the suggestion of de Zoysa, and under the pseudonym Taraki, began writing a column on military affairs for *The Island*, one of Sri Lanka's few privately-owned dailies. Sivaram's columns were an immediate success because of his ability to explain clearly the tactics and politics behind often-complicated military events. He could do this because he was a former member of both the military and political wings of the People's Liberation Organization of Tamil Eelam, one of the groups decimated by the LTTE in the late 1980s, and he was therefore drawing from often bitter experience. Eventually, early diasporic Tamil internet chatrooms and mailing lists such as the *Tamil Circle* (also called the *Sri Lankan Tamil Interest Digest*), and early websites such as *Tamilcanadian.com*, began posting his articles on the web, and so his reputation began to spread among the mostly English-speaking refugee public as well. For Sivaram, then, the closing down of the Sinhala public sphere really was a kind of opening. Nevertheless, for the most part, direct and indirect control of the press in Sri Lanka continued to grow through the early nineties, reaching its peak, perhaps, when the government briefly imposed censorship in the mid-to-late 1990s in response to reverses on the battlefield. By that time Sivaram's Taraki column, like everyone else's, began to sport large sections that had been dramatically blacked out by the government censors.

Meanwhile, the Sri Lankan government, with a great deal of American and European aid, was also expanding the size of its armed forces from 14,000 to 120,000, and rearming itself with Russian T-55 tanks, BMP armored personnel carriers, various long-range mortars and howitzers, jets and helicopters. The army's command personnel, at the same time, were also being retrained by various foreign specialists – British, Israeli, and American – in standard Western counter-insurgency doctrine; training that was intensified in the mid-nineties when the US began sending small special forces teams to organize Sri Lankan counter-insurgency forces (Whitaker 1997: 203; Vijayasin 1999: 6). The result was that the Sri Lankan army, like the LTTE, also began to fight the war in a two-pronged manner: one fork aimed at reducing the LTTE militarily, the other at beating down the will of the Tamil people. What this meant, in effect, was confronting the LTTE with overwhelming fire-power in increasingly conventional military battles (which, by 1999, the government was losing) while imposing draconian civic intimidation tactics on Sri Lankan Tamils – tactics that came to include routine torture, massacre, "ethnic cleansing", village relocation, and disappearances.

Was this further hardening of counter-insurgency tactics a *consequence* of US training? It is difficult to say for sure. Raj Vijayasin, a Sri Lankan army officer who in 1999 accepted a trip to the US Army Command and General Staff College in Fort Leavenworth, Kansas, where US Counter-Insurgency Doctrine is produced, sees Sri Lankan army battlefield excesses as stemming, rather, from a failure to follow the softer, more political approaches to counter-insurgency laid out in US Army field manuals on "Low Intensity Conflict" (Vijayasin 1999). But although standard US military counter-insurgency doctrine in the late 1990s did hold – at least in theory – that persuasion (i.e.

"hearts and minds") should figure more largely than brute force (Vijayasin 1999: 29), Lesley Gill (2004). In her ethnography of the infamous School of the Americas, argues that since the Reagan administration military practice in the US has increasingly emphasized the coercion of noncombatants, and this is certainly the lesson that both the Sri Lankan military (and the LTTE) took to heart. The last two phases of the war (1990–95, 1995–2001) therefore were marked by a kind of odd, geopolitically-aided, military schizmogenesis: with, that is, both the Sri Lankan army and the LTTE adapting similar, opposing tactics (leading, eventually, to an increasingly bloody military stand-off). By 1996, then, two hegemonic forces were confronting each other, both militarily and ideologically, as masters of their respective public spheres – but not of each other: this was the Gramscian political context that confronted *TamilNet.com's* creators.

TamilNet.com and the internet's normative Habermasian context

TamilNet.com's creators, most of whom very much wish to remain anonymous, were all products of the civil war. Software engineers and computer entrepreneurs scattered about Europe and North America, they were all pushed out of Sri Lanka by the war, part of the great flight of Sri Lankan Tamil professionals in the mid-1980s. Fluent in the languages of the countries in which they have now resided for well over ten years (e.g., English and Norwegian), and linked to each other through kinship ties, phone cards, nationalism, and shared memories of home, they began to believe among themselves that the accounts of Sri Lanka appearing in the Western media were becoming either increasingly hostile toward Sri Lankan Tamils (particularly toward the LTTE) or, more often, simply indifferent to the whole conflict. As one young Tamil man in Toronto told me, "The press here is useless. They say nothing or they say rubbish about Sri Lanka". With this distrust in mind, they decided to establish *TamilNet.com* in 1995 as a kind of news–clipping and nationalist commentary site. One of them – who desires his name to be known, Mr. Jeyachandran of Norway – designed the site to be attractive, interactive, and easy to use. It was all those things; and yet it was a flop – no hits.

They debated whether they should close the site down. But one of them, a successful computer entrepreneur, suggested that they bring in a professional to rescue the site, and named "Taraki", the columnist well known to them all, as a possibility. Dharmeratnam Sivaram, consequently, was flown from his small house in Colombo to the spacious, North American suburban home of one of the *TamilNet.com* creators, to help them rethink the matter. Ironically, the cost of this flight was born by the US Department of State: Sivaram, and a number of other "Third World" journalists, were being given a tour of America to learn (as Sivaram told me afterwards, chuckling – for this was during the O. J. Simpson media frenzy) America's objective, democratic, journalistic practices.

Now I have discussed the events surrounding the restructuring of the site elsewhere at great length (Whitaker 2004b), so I will not give a blow-by-blow account of their deliberations here. Let me just outline what they discussed. Basically, Sivaram identified two problems with the old site and two possible solutions. First, the old site, as he put it, lacked "ground information" about the real situation in Sri Lanka. He suggested they could fix this by turning the site into a kind of Sri Lankan Tamil "wire service" by training and hiring a string of Tamil reporters in Sri Lanka, and then providing them with laptops and digital cameras. He knew that a pool of talent for this task was currently present in the Sri Lankan hinterland, in the form of Tamil reporters already acting as stringers for Western news agencies, and in the many local Tamil intellectuals – clerks, poets, local pundits and school teachers – who could be easily trained to write stories. To get around the censorship then constraining Sri Lankan newspapers (and "Taraki's" own columns), they agreed that the website should be managed from *outside* the country, and that editing should be done all over the world by various sub-editors, linked by email and cell phone. All this would make the site impossible to control or shut down by normal means, and would also allow them to post breaking news faster than Western news agencies and thus allow them to lead coverage of events.

Second, the old site, Sivaram felt, was "circumscribed by a world of opaque expatriate Tamil nationalists", and therefore written in a rhetoric that made it too off-putting to outsiders. He suggested that the new site should be free of obvious nationalism in both rhetoric and practice, and should adopt, instead, the "objective neutral" tone and professional practices of the Western press. He meant here, of course, more than merely a change in style. He argued, and they all realized it was true, that the site would have to remain formally and financially independent of any political organization, including the LTTE; otherwise its reports would not be taken seriously. Beyond this, in practice, the site would have to be as fastidious about factual accuracy as the Western press *claimed* to be. They all knew, he argued, that the Western press was not really objective or unbiased in its coverage of Sri Lanka since the direction of its attention (when Sri Lanka could capture it at all) was determined by political and market forces that lay, decisively, elsewhere – in the West. But by making what he called "ironic use" of Western "objective neutral" news practices, but directing them toward Sri Lankan Tamil concerns rather than Western ones, those very market forces could also contain the key to penetrating and altering Western coverage of Sri Lanka. For if *TamilNet.com* could provide cheap (actually, free) but recognizably "professional" news stories at moments of crisis, the Western press – constrained by its own market logic – would be unable to pass up using them.[7]

What remained unsaid, though it was equally important, was the role to be played in all this by the normative Habermasian, political context of the internet, with its relatively universal access, its disregard for the rank of participants, and, in a rather more complicated way, its emphasis on "rational" (or pluralistic) debate. On the one hand, newspaper reporters and columnists in Sri Lanka were spending much of the nineties dodging various attempts to shut down or control their activities. But there were, then, no police or regulations on the internet capable of limiting content providers. Similarly, international media coverage of Sri Lanka was dominated by Western concerns, first with the Cold War and, later, with terrorism. Given the vast economy-of-scale problems – all those satellites, TV stations, and printing plants owned by transnational, Western media corporations – shifting Western preoccupations through competition or persuasion would be impossible. But on the internet such economy-of-scale problems fall away; anyone with a laptop and some basic competence in HTML can post news that looks as well-packaged and accessible as the products of, say, the BBC or Reuters. Similarly, within the Tamil diaspora, all public talk about Sri Lanka was constrained by the interests of the LTTE and funneled through its many media outlets, which tended to mandate a discursive style more effusive than deliberative, more inward looking than outwardly engaging. But while *TamilNet.com's* creators shared many, even most, of the LTTE's goals, they also felt the need to speak not only for themselves but also to outsiders, something only possible on the internet; and this, again, turned their expressive practice, their journalism, in a more accessible direction. Moreover, the sheer fact of *TamilNet.com's* cross-cultural and inter-public ambitions, and the success they might achieve thereby, would swiftly make necessary the appearance of other sites, stemming from other constituencies, attempting the same trick. The result would be a "conversation" between contending sites, and eventually between such sites and the press in Sri Lanka and abroad, that, however raucous and uncivil, would still be (in Habermas' sense) at least the beginnings of a "rational" (i.e. a nonviolently pluralistic)[8] conversation.

And so it proved. After the site reopened in 1996, under Sivaram's editorial direction but without editorials, hits soared and, more importantly, Western news agencies – and eventually, even the Sinhala-controlled press in Sri Lanka – began to use and react to its material (albeit with appropriate cautions about the stories coming from a "pro-rebel" site). Why? They used *TamilNet.com's* stories because, as one reporter for *The Hindu* put it, they were "99 per cent accurate", because their writing style was completely professional, and because their stories and pictures were all free. You could see the site's new style on display, for example, in its bland coverage of the following story from 1998.

Garment factory to employ disabled soldiers [*TamilNet*, 10 December 1998 19:02 GMT]
Sri Lankan Deputy Minister of Defense Gen. Anurudha Ratwatte ceremonially opened today a large scale, modern garment factory called "Ranaviru Apparels", at Yakkala, for the benefit of the disabled soldiers.
Six hundred and sixty disabled soldiers will be employed in this factory which is expected to produce 27,000 army uniforms monthly and a net

income of Rs 1.3 million.

The soldiers are provided with accommodation, and health and sports facilities. The factory will be managed by a board comprising army officers.

Speaking at the ceremony, Ratwatte said that the disabled soldiers will again serve the country by producing the necessary uniforms required by the soldiers in the battle fronts.

Minister of Industries C. V. Gooneratne and the army commander Lt. Gen. Rohan Daluwatte were also present at the opening ceremony.

Here the oblique comment about just why so many disabled Sinhalese soldiers needed to be employed was simply left unsaid. Similarly, and in equally neutral language, Tamil.net gave up-to-the minute details about Sri Lankan army–LTTE battles ("Seven killed in Vanni clashes", 10 December 1997), chronicled the effects counter-insurgency tactics were having on Tamil civilians ("Elderly woman held over scenic prints", 10 December 1997, a story about a woman arrested at a checkpoint for having "suspicious" pictures, in fact prints bought in a Colombo art shop), and illustrated attempts to intimidate the Tamil press ("Another journalist arrested", 20 July 1998) – all stories, that is, which indirectly called into question the claims the Sri Lankan government was making at the time about progress toward ending the war and its associated human rights abuses. Yet because *TamilNet.com*'s stories were accurate, and uncluttered with nationalist rhetoric, professionals concerned with the insurgency both inside and outside of Sri Lanka soon felt compelled to check the site to see what was on it – and to do so every day. In this way, Dharmeratnam Sivaram and the other creators of *TamilNet.com* were able to make their internet site an independent addendum to the ongoing nationalist struggle. Their cyberinsurgency worked by sneaking their own perspective – through what stories they chose to report – into the considerations of geopolitical and Sri Lankan elites, and thus shifting how the war was reported in the Western press and debated by the various governments involved in the struggle between Sri Lanka's dueling nationalist hegemonies.

Conclusions: contexts in collision

One hot day in March 2004, Sivaram and I headed for an outdoor beer and *arrack* shop in Sri Lanka's Batticaloa District so he could sit down and handle a breaking news story. Several days earlier the LTTE's eastern military commander, Colonel Karuna, had split from the LTTE, intending, as he claimed in a leaflet, to set up his own "south-Eelam". This action was popular with some Batticaloa people, particularly small businessmen and professionals, and reflected a long-standing tension between Tamil Sri Lanka's semi-cosmopolitan north and its more rural east. In any case, the move had come at a critical time in Sri Lankan affairs because the country was facing elections. President

Kumaratunga's party (United People's Front Alliance) was on the offensive, and seemed headed toward (and would eventually win) a marginal victory at the hustings by claiming that its opposition, the United Front Government (which had been holding a tiny majority in Parliament), had been overly accommodating to the LTTE in the stalled peace talks. The Karuna rebellion, however, tossed all those cards into the air. Did either side want to grab the anti-LTTE opportunity Karuna's rebellion seemed to offer, and that their rhetoric seemed to invite, and risk a resumption of the war? Were the US and India somehow involved? Would the Norwegians, who had been overseeing the peace talks, pull out? What was going to happen?

What was fascinating to me at the moment, however, was watching Sivaram, over his slowly dwindling bottle of *arrack*, handle the resulting national and international journalistic firestorm with his cellphone. His phone could be linked, of course, to the internet, and, with its front flipped down, Sivaram could work a tiny keyboard with a toothpick stylus in between making and receiving hundreds of calls. Calls to and from, to cite just a few examples: *TamilNet.com* reporters in Jaffna, Colombo and Kandy; journalists from other agencies in London, Paris, Delhi, Madras, and New York; a Karuna spokesman hiding somewhere (with his cellphone and internet link!) in the jungles of Batticaloa's hinterland; Sri Lankan government and army spokesmen; and, finally, the *TamilNet.com* software people in Norway. At one point the BBC called and conducted an interview with Sivaram in which he (intemperately, I felt) blasted Karuna for being an idiot; at another point someone called to say that Karuna had just threatened his life. I began to look nervously around at the other tables where men sat drinking, some staring at us.

"Ah, Sivaram, don't you think we should move . . . somewhere else"?

"No, *machchang*,[9] this is just fine. Fine".

Eventually, so many calls came in from so many locations, and so many stories were being written and edited by him at the same time, that he started using my cellphone as a back-up, neatly maneuvering between the two phones, his stylus, and his glass of arrack without missing a beat. He was a spider in his own web, and he loved it. As he uploaded another *TamilNet.com* story, he looked at me and laughed.

"Ah, *machchang*, this is what it means to be alive. To be really alive".

"Well, for some people I suppose".

He laughed, hard.

Lately, some anthropologists have expressed a reasonable skepticism about the utopian claims early internet theorists made about the possible liberating and empowering effects of the internet, pointing out that states are now learning how "to regulate and control internet-based access to information" (Wilson and Peterson 2002: 4). I think this skepticism is well founded. At the same time, however, I believe it misses the ultimate significance of the internet for people locked in desperate Gramscian political contexts and struggles: that is, that its

normative Habermasian presence as an *alternative but proximate* political landscape provides a counter-context in which different possibilities can be
displayed by people who would otherwise be constrained from speech, and who
can now speak to audiences they would otherwise be unable to reach. In other
words, the key fact about the internet lies not in (controllable) *passive* access to
it but in (harder to control) *active* participation in it. Hence, for Dharmeratnam
Sivaram, *TamilNet.com* was always a form of "counter-counter-insurgency", to
use his term; that is, an institutionalized way of circumventing the restrictions
the Sri Lankan government had placed on access to its official public sphere,
and to the larger, net-linked and net-dependent, geo-political public arena (of
the Western media and global think-tank seminars) in which the fates of small
communities are often discussed and, too often, determined. But in Sri Lanka
now all sides have their websites – the LTTE, the government, local NGOs, and
even Karuna (see *thenee.com* and *tmup.org*) – and many now are even
attempting the "objective-neutral" news style and practice of *TamilNet.com*,
albeit with various degrees of effectiveness. Hence, all can play to that larger
geopolitical audience that hovers around the edges of their local conflict in
dangerous, unpredictable, or sometimes-supportive ways; and, because that is so,
all must also engage more than tangentially with each other's challenges and
ideas.

This last, perhaps, can be seen best in the wake of the tsunami that rolled so
pitilessly over Sri Lanka's coasts on 26 December 2004, drowning tens of thousands of people – Sinhalese, Tamil, Muslim and Christian alike – and wiping
away whole sections of coastline, including much of the low-lying Batticaloa
District. On the day of the disaster, *TamilNet.com* was one of the first news
agencies in Sri Lanka to report directly from the north and east, its first article
appearing within hours of the event ("At least 500 feared killed by Tsunami
waves in Sri Lanka", 26 December 2004). Afterwards, it was able to document
in graphic, personal terms how the wave destroyed the lives and livelihoods of
thousands (cf. "Navalady – A village turned graveyard", 8 January 2005). And
it quickly pointed to irregularities in the dispersal of aid funds to the north and
east (cf. "Authorities hinder help to Tsunami affected regions", 29 December
2004), thus getting in at the beginning of a debate on the politics of relief
funding that quickly spread to other Sri Lankan newspapers, websites, and to
the international media. This may not be Habermas' hoped-for, perfectly realized "rational debate", but it is a marked expansion of Sri Lanka's embattled
public sphere; and it is online.

A sad postscript

Journalist Sivaram murdered [*TamilNet*, 29 April 2005 02:37 GMT]
The body of abducted journalist Mr. Dharmaretnam [sic] Sivaram was
found with severe head injuries in Himbulala, a Sinhala suburb between
Jayawardhenapura hospital and the Parliament building in Colombo Friday

morning. The location is about 500 meters behind the parliamentary complex and lies inside a high security zone. Mr Sivaram, a senior editorial board member of *TamilNet*, was abducted Thursday evening around 10:30 PM by unidentified persons in front of the Bambalapitya Police Station in Colombo.

Family members visited the scene and have identified the body . . .

Notes

1   In memory of D.P. Sivaram.
2   In 1991, the last year a reliable census could be taken of the entire island, there were 19.6 million people living in Sri Lanka of whom 74 percent were Sinhalese, 18.2 percent were Tamil, and 7.4 percent were Muslim — "Muslim" here designating both a religion and an ethnic identity; see Whitaker (2004: 407).
3   Dharmeratnam Sivaram preferred, for various reasons, to appear under his own name. Among those reasons was that he was already a well-known public figure in Sri Lanka. Beyond this, however, Sri Lanka is a dangerous environment for journalists. So we talked about it and arrived at the hope that having his name out and about in other publications might actually make his job a bit safer. Obviously, we were wrong.
4   I am, of course, combining here the figures for the various Sri Lankan government-Tamil separatist wars and the Sri Lankan government-JVP war. Hence, for example, the National Peace Council of Sri Lanka (2003) and Médècins Sans Frontieres (2002) both estimate that between 60 and 65 thousand people – mostly non combatants – were killed during 20 years of ethnic civil war. At the same time, Bruce Van Voorhis (2003) of the Asian Human Rights Commission concludes that between 30 and 60 thousand people "disappeared" during the anti-JVP terror – and, of course, the JVP killed many people themselves. My combined total of 100,000, therefore, is probably conservative.
5   Allen (2002) and Wilson and Peterson (2002) have pointed out that lately states have been more successful in suppressing this openness by both controlling access to the internet and by putting pressure on internet providers to censor content. Nevertheless, as we shall see, while such controls may work within a state's boundaries, states tied to substantial diasporic communities – as Sri Lanka is to its far-flung migrant worker and refugee populations – cannot exert such control. Besides, *TamilNet.com* was not aimed at Sri Lankans but at the geopolitical players surrounding Sri Lanka. This was why it was so effective.
6   How many groups? Gunaratna estimates there were at least 37 groups by the end of 1983, and I know he missed several east coast groups (Wilson 2000: 126; Gunaratna 1993).
7   It is very important to emphasize that I am not claiming that *TamilNet's* reports are objective and neutral in some universal and absolute epistemological sense. Nor were *TamilNet.com's* creators striving to achieve such a thing. Sivaram's use of these terms, for example, was always completely and knowingly "ironic" (although he was never ironic when he used the word "professional"). In any case, *TamilNet's* creators were all nationalists, sympathetic (at the moment) to the LTTE, and all convinced that disunity among Tamils worked to the advantage of the Sri Lankan government. Therefore, they designed *TamilNet* to reflect these political beliefs, and tended to not report on stories detrimental to the LTTE, such as the LTTE's well-known use of child soldiers. Their argument is that this kind of strategic selectivity is characteristic of even the most vaunted of Western press organizations. Nevertheless, they

have remained independent of the LTTE, even fighting off an attempt at control by the LTTE's London office in 1998, a crisis that required releasing two subeditors.

8   The word "rational", of course, has a troubling history in anthropology, especially for postcolonial and feminist theorists; and for good reasons, since invocations of rationality's supposedly absolute character were often used to bludgeon nonWestern and non-male discourses down. But Habermas, I think, in his later discussions of communicative action seems to anticipate much of this and, in the context of his discussions of a *normative* model of the public sphere, seems to mean by "rational" something like "thorough-going, pluralistic conversation without violence". In any case, this is all I think "rational" can mean on the internet. As for terms like "objective" and "neutral" that Sivaram uses, remember that all of these terms are ironically invoked.

9   i.e. cross-cousin, male friend, or buddy.

References

Publications

Allen, Stuart (2002) "Reweaving the Internet: Online News of September 11", in B. Zelizer and S. Allen (eds), *Journalism After September 11*. London: Roli Books, pp. 119–40.

Cheran, R. (2001) *The Sixth Genre: Memory, History, and the Tamil Diaspora Imagination*. Marga Marga Monograph Series on Ethnic Reconciliation, No. 7 of 19. Colombo: Marga Institute.

Crehan, Kate (2002) *Gramsci, Culture and Anthropology*. Berkeley: University of California Press.

Fuglerud, Ovind (1999) *Life on the Outside: The Tamil Diaspora and Long Distance Nationalism*. London: Pluto Press.

Gill, Lesley (2004) *The School of the Americas: Military Training and Political Violence in the Americas*. Durham, NC: Duke University Press.

Gramsci, Antonio (1971) *Selections from the Prison Notebooks*. Q. Hoare and G. N. Smith (eds). New York: International Publishers.

Gunaratna, Rohan (1993) *Indian Intervention in Sri Lanka: The Role of India's Intelligence Agencies*. Colombo: South Asian Network on Conflict Research.

Habermas, Jürgen (1989) *The Structural Transformation of the Public Sphere: An Inquiry into a Category of Bourgeois Society*. Cambridge, MA: MIT Press.

——(1992) "Further Reflections on the Public Sphere", in C. Calhoun (ed.), *Habermas and the Public Sphere*. Cambridge, MA: MIT Press, p. 1–50.

Haraway, Donna (1996) *Modest Witness @ Second Millenium. Female Man Meets Onco-Mouse TM*. London: Routledge.

Médècins Sans Frontières (2002) "Conflict in Sri Lanka: Sri Lanka's Health Service is a Casualty of 20 Years of War", *British Medical Journal* 324(7333): 361. Available online: www.pubmedcentral.nih.gov/articlerender.fcgi?artid = 1122281

National Peace Council (2003) *Costs of War: Challenges and Priorities for the Future*. Ratmalana, Sri Lanka: Vishva Lekha.

O'Baoill, Andrew (2000) "Slapshot and the Public Sphere", *firstmonday* (an internet peer-review journal). Available online: www.firstmonday.org/issues/issue5_9/baoill/index.html

Taussig, Michael (1987) *Shamanism, Colonialism, and the Wild Man*. Chicago: Chicago University Press.

Van Voorhis, Bruce (2003) *Sri Lanka's Reign of Violence: The 1988–1992 Disappearances in Human Rights Solidarity*, vol. 13. Available online: hrsolidarity.net/mainfile.php/2003vol13no06-2004vol14no01/2305/

Vijayasin, Raj D. (1999) *A Critical Analysis of the Sri Lankan Government's Counterinsurgency Campaign*. MA thesis: U.S. Army Command and General Staff College, Fort Leavenworth, Kansas.

Whitaker, Mark (1997) "Tigers and Temples: The Politics of Nationalist and Non-Modern Violence in Sri Lanka", *South Asia*, 20, Special Issue: 201–14.

——(2004a) "Sri Lanka", in G. Palmer-Fernandez (ed.), *The Encyclopedia of Religion and War*. New York: Routledge.

——(2004b). "Tamilnet.com: Some Reflections on Popular Anthropology, Nationalism, and the Internet", *Anthropological Quarterly* 77(3): 469–98.

Wijesinha, Rajiva (ed.) (2000) *Richard de Zoysa: His Life, Some Work . . . a Death*. Sabaragamuwa: Sabaragamuwa University Press.

Wilson, A. Jeyaratnam (2000) *Sri Lankan Tamil Nationalism: Its Origins and Development in the 19th and 20th Centuries*. Vancouver: UBC Press.

Wilson, Samuel M. and Peterson, Leighton C. (2002) "The Anthropology of Online Communities", *Annual Review of Anthropology*, 31: 449–67.

Articles from TamilNet.com

"Seven killed in Vanni clashes", 10 December 1997
"Elderly woman held over scenic prints", 10 December 1997
"Another journalist arrested", 20 July 1998
"Garment factory to employ disabled soldiers", 10 December 1998
"Colombo hasn't spent a cent on Jaffna's development", 27 December 2003
"Jaffna GA denies TamilNet Report", 31 December 2003
"Colombo hasn't spent a cent on Jaffna", 4 January 2004
"At least 500 feared killed by Tsunami waves in Sri Lanka", 26 December 2004
"Authorities hinder help to Tsunami affected regions", 29 December 2004
"Navalady – a village turned graveyard", 8 January 2005

Chapter 15

Cyberethnography

Reading South Asian digital diasporas

Radhika Gajjala

Today, with globalization in full swing, telecommunicative informatics taps the Native Informant directly in the name of indigenous knowledge and advances biopiracy.

(Spivak 1999: ix)

Introduction

This chapter is a discussion of South Asian digital diasporic exchanges as cyberethnographies and self-writing online. In this chapter, I define what I mean by cyberethnography and discuss my experimental approach towards doing and writing a cyberethnography that examines the gendered postcolonial subject emerging online.[1] The perspectives that I bring into the chapter are situated within the context of ongoing debates concerning the issue of speaking for, speaking with and speaking about less empowered people in the world (Alcoff 1991–92; Mohanty 1994; Spivak 1994; Stacey 1988). Based upon my prior empirical and theoretical engagements with studying online communities (see Gajjala 1997, 1998, 2002a, 2002b), my attempted cyberethnography further draws upon my work with founding and moderating email discussion lists. My discussion highlights the question of whether women-only safe spaces can exist online, and seeks to problematize the issue of the online representation of the Other. I further ask under what conditions (if any) online encounters between peoples from contradictory worlds might lead to real dialogue. I argue that, while the internet allows for the possibility of the Other's engagement with and talking back to the hegemonic Western(ized) Self, the internet performances and exchanges visible currently do not show evidence of this happening often enough to change the tendency for structural and discursive appropriation of the Other's self-narratives.

Cyberethnography

Ethnography is a research method used by various disciplines that engage in the study of human interactions and the re-presentation of cultures. While ideally the goal of ethnography is to faithfully re-present a social situation or reality, in practice ethnography inevitably re-creates it, thus constructing a *new* version of reality. Simply put, cyberethnography is a study of online interactions; yet, the nature of the medium/technology raises unique issues about such interactions and the ways of researching them. For example, issues that have traditionally engaged anthropologists and sociologists (and other scholars studying human relations) have, as Jones points out, become "a part of [internet] discourse, for it becomes necessary to cover ground concerning participant observation, privacy, biography" (Jones 1995: 3). With cyberethnography, we are forced to question our assumptions and methods in order to respond to this new technologically-mediated ethnographic situation and the methodological and ethical dilemmas that arise (Ward 1999).

Some of the issues arise from the internet medium/technology itself, with its blurring of the boundaries between print and broadcast media and, further, between private and public. Technologies and their uses must be examined contextually if we are to understand how they aid or inhibit specific communities' democratization and material progress. As Slack (1989: 339) argues:

> [T]echnology is not simply an object connected in various ways to the institutional and organizational structures from within which it emerges to be reconnected in a new context, but it is always an articulated moment of interconnections among the range of social practices, discursive statements, ideological positions, social forces, and social groups within which the object moves.

Some of the issues confronting cyberethnography relate to the nature of the texts/subjects that are online. Discursive subjects are not anthropological subjects in the traditional sense: they are partial, online presentations of real-life agents who interact within various online contexts. At the same time, online texts are not traditional texts but are changing interactive subjects who are able to speak for themselves. Since cyberethnography studies these subjects/texts, the ethics of cyberethnography must engage issues raised by both copyright laws and human subjects review boards. Moreover, online interactions blur the boundary between the ethnographer and the ethnographic subject, allowing subjects "under study" to talk back as the process of study is going on. Talking back thus becomes an integral part of the cyberethnographic process. In this manner, cyberethnography confronts new challenges to the researcher's "authority", and to modes of re-presenting and writing the Other. The relative empowerment of participants makes the cyberethnographic research process especially reflexive (Ward 1999: 5). Cyberethnography might thus be defined as an internet technologically mediated and enabled hypertextual/intertextual performance.

In defining and doing cyberethnography it is important to avoid a dichotomy between "real life" and "virtual life" in order to examine how they are becoming inseparable in emerging hybrid, discursive-material spaces that are "neither physical or virtual but a combination of the two" (Ward 1999; see Gajjala 1997). This hybrid space occurs within a "glocal" (global–local) digital cyberspace mediated by the dominant power relations in place in today's unavoidably interconnected yet unequally-networked world. In other words, cyberspatial social life is situated within digital capitalism. In his discussion of the indivisibility of the cultural and economic spheres, Schiller writes: "Cultural, no less than automobile, production has its political economy" (1991: 13). Likewise, Grossberg (1997) places media-cultural imperialism as part of a broader system of imperialism. Such approaches are especially useful in the examination of the nature of the subject within the digital (post)modern culture/economy: a subject influenced by socio-cultural discourses, power relations and technologies that divide the privileged from the less privileged. These divisions occur along cultural and material formations of classed, raced and gendered subjectivities and not simply along a First-World/Third-World geographical divide. These divisions further "speak for" and mediate the subjectivities of "subaltern" Others: those largely disenfranchised peoples who, on the basis of class, race, gender, etc. have unequal access to power.[2] It has been proposed that information-communications technologies will help empower subaltern voices, and thus perhaps bridge the divisions between contradictory worlds. In considering this prospect with regard to the perspectives of subaltern South Asian women, my work questions whether feminist place(s) for connected thinking and acting in profoundly contradictory worlds (Haraway 1991) are possible online.

An attempted cyberethnography of SAWnet

In the spring of 1994 I began a study of an email discussion list called the South Asian Women's network (SAWnet).[3] This study was to be part of a larger project that would focus on the centrality of notions of gender and sexuality and the importance of representations of socio-culturally and economically less-empowered women in what I can only describe as an extremely productive and provocative manner by some of the participants of the email discussion list. However, in the summer of 1995, this study was interrupted by what I call the "SAWnet refusal" (see Gajjala 2002a). The issues leading to this interruption highlight several important questions in relation to ethnographic practices online and to the feminist movement and its practices of re-presentation.[4] The interrupted research itself further brought forth concerns related to the politics of enunciation within diasporic spaces and the possibility and/or illusion of safety online.

SAWnet is a forum for South Asian women, taken to include women originally from or still resident in Bangladesh, Bhutan, Burma, India, Nepal, Pakistan and Sri Lanka. The mailing list is restricted to women by the consensus vote of the members. The group is not, however, restricted to South Asian women – all women with an interest in South Asian issues are welcome to join. Since most SAWnet subscribers live outside South Asia, the discussions tend to focus on a mixture of general and personal issues centered around the experiences of "being away" or of "home", but all topics are welcome. Topics under discussion have included: literacy for women in South Asia; changing one's name upon marriage; wearing ethnic clothes to work; how to design a non-sexist wedding ceremony with traditional South Asian overtones; dealing with stress, abortion, female infanticide; writing poetry; gay/lesbian/bisexual issues and so on. The mailing list is moderated, and posts are rejected if they are abusive or purely provocative in nature; however, they are not edited in any way. Moreover, group accounts, shared accounts, or a woman using another person's account, cannot be subscribed.

In the case of my experience with the attempted cyberethnography of SAWnet, it bears note that before I became a researcher I had been an active participant, and for over a year had posted fiction and poetry to the list (thus I arguably already shared an ethos with other listmembers). It could be said that, as a South Asian woman living and working in "the West", I was an ethnographer on "my own territory". I launched my cyberethnography by posting a survey on SAWnet with the intention of finding out how the nature of the online community had changed since its formation in November 1991 with 40 original members. I wanted to examine what kinds of topics were being discussed, and what (if any) topics were being marginalized or unintentionally silenced. My concern with the issue of speaking and silencing was related to my larger interest in the use of the label "South Asian" (namely, here, the "South Asian Women's Network" as an online community). I wanted to better understand how these women identified themselves as "part" of a larger South Asian region, and how this influenced their online interactions and discourses.[5] While the intention behind naming SAWnet may have been to forge strategic coalitions between women of that region, it had appeared to me as a member/participant that there was a kind of hierarchy among the active participants, a hierarchy that privileged the voice of diasporic women from India. This could be seen as a replication of Indian hegemony in relation to other South Asian countries, since India is often seen by its neighbors as imperialist. In focusing on the question of diversity, one of my main goals was to discern any "overtones of domination and exclusion" (Bhattacharjee 1997: 309) that might have the effect of marginalizing other viewpoints. To begin my formal study, I posted online my intention of writing a research article about SAWnet. I was already aware of the posted SAWnet rule stating that discussions could only be shared with non-members of SAWnet if the person(s) posting the messages gave permission; and I had obtained permission to cite posts. I did not, however, foresee that writing an overall general description about SAWnet would become a matter of controversy for its members, since this did not involve the use of any one person's messages.[6]

In the spring of 1995 an anthropologist from New Zealand (a non-South Asian) also announced her decision to study SAWnet; and contacted some members of SAWnet personally to ask for permission to quote them. This sparked a series of discussions about the value of studying a group like SAWnet. Some women protested. They wanted to be "left alone" in what they perceived as a private space. Discussions began to get very interesting and even heated. I decided to remind members of SAWnet that I too had been writing about SAWnet since 1994. My entry contributed to and further complicated the discussion.[7] One or two members of SAWnet asked to see our work. Both the anthropologist from New Zealand and I sent our articles to at least fifteen members of the group (I had already planned to invite reactions to my research in the long run, so the discussions on SAWnet simply accelerated the timetable). At this same time, a message was posted by an anonymous poster who informed the participants of SAWnet that she had been studying the various writing styles of the members for a while. She claimed that she had done a "psychiatric" analysis of various contributors based on their writing styles and wished to publish her study. She later confessed that this was a prank. However, I think that this intervention made many participants even more aware of how little control they/we might have over our messages, over how they might be interpreted and used by researchers, and over the findings of studies conducted about SAWnet in general. The discussions led to a vote. The three options suggested and voted for were:

1   Studies of Sawnet are specifically forbidden.
2   Studies of Sawnet are permitted, as long as no post is quoted without explicit permission from its author.
3   Sawnet should be studied, but Sawnet members together will choose someone to study us. Only that person has the authority to do the study.

There were approximately 350 members at the time of the vote (at the time of this writing there are approximately 800 SAWnet members). Sixty-nine members voted; of this number, thirty-nine voted for option number one, twenty-nine voted for option two, and one person voted for option three.

Based on this vote, it was decided not to allow anyone to make "global state-ments" about SAWnet – that is, it was decided that "no one is allowed to generalize based on any of the posts on the discussion list". Researchers would need to obtain permission from individual members if we wished to use their messages. The current SAWnet policy statement linked to the SAWnet website records this policy decision.

What happened in this voting could be interpreted as an attempt to define and control community by certain participants of SAWnet. But it was also a panic. Some of the members clearly panicked upon realizing that, despite the illusion that SAWnet was a safe haven, it was/is not. It was/is as vulnerable to intrusion by researchers as any other type of public gathering. The vote reflected the larger issue that the SAWnet online community was suddenly faced with the fact that their women-only discussion was not necessarily a private space, despite SAWnet's stated privacy rule. The implicit protection promised by such a rule seemed to have lulled participants into thinking that the list discussions were like conversations in a friend's living room, where their privacy could not be invaded by unwanted researchers or nasty encounters that might have "real-life" consequences beyond the artificial boundaries of cyberspace. However, the internet cannot be confused with real spaces in this way. This is especially true of email lists. Messages that we post to email lists are sent to all subscribers of the list. "Speaking" on an email list is like speaking in a living room that has microphones to many other living rooms. Your message is being transmitted all over the world, to people you barely know.

The objections to my study of SAWnet revolved around questions regarding methodology, concerns over privacy and concerns about how I would represent the members of SAWnet. For some women, there was confusion over the issue of SAWnet being considered a "text". From the messages I received asking me how I considered the exchanges on SAWnet to be a text, I gather that the women who questioned me in this regard might have thought of "text" as a formally published document. If I had been studying documents written by these women and published in printed form, there would have been no doubt about the documents being texts. However, when studying texts produced online, the researcher necessarily takes on an "approach in which the object of study is a process (the changing text) rather than a project (the static text)" (Aarseth 1994: 82). However, as I discussed above, not only does the online researcher study a changing text, s/he also interacts with an anthropological subject (Gajjala 1998). SAWNet members, in questioning my methodology, further wanted to know how I would "validate" my findings and make sure that I was presenting the "correct" picture of SAWnet, since my audience might not be able to verify the truth of what I was saying by accessing the archives of SAWnet.[8] Some women did not think I should be representing them, and making generalizations about their lives. They felt that what I had written was not their experience. Some of the women who were objecting to the study appeared to have felt betrayed by a co-member (not just as a co-member of SAWnet, but a co-member of the South Asian community). Most importantly, they were concerned that my narrative regarding South Asian women would be received as representative, whether I intended it to be so or not. JV, a member of SAWnet who responded to several drafts of my work before and after the SAWnet refusal, wrote:

> Looking back, I feel that the debate that ended in the decision for "the vote" arose largely because some of the dominant personalities at the time were resistant to others' attempts to characterize the South Asian women's community (or at least the community comprised of sawnettors) . . . perhaps out of a somewhat naive fear of mis-representation, or out of a distrust of (and disdain for?) the field (and jargon) you represented.

When the SAWnet community came to a crisis, the members were forced to face the fact that their online communication might possibly have material consequences and repercussions. In this case, some members attempted to control the image of "community" (thus proving that they were indeed a community). The concept of a virtual community may have different characteristics, but none the less it still performs the "dual function of compromising and marginalizing" (Senft 1997: 265) like any face-to-face community. Several feminist studies have chronicled instances of women's marginalization online, and many have suggested that women-only spaces can be seen to be alternative safe-spaces (see, e.g., Spender 1995). I would argue that not enough attention has been paid to the power dynamics and micro-dynamics within women-only spaces; nor to the politics of inclusion and exclusion that operate therein. What does it mean to define a "safe" women-only social space; what are the inclusions and exclusions implicit in the notion of being "safe" online; who speaks for whom, and so on? Such issues were encountered in my attempted cyberethnography and in the SAWnet refusal. The SAWnet refusal raised the issue of not wanting to be represented or scrutinized by power (in the form of myself as a member of the university academy and thus afforded a certain degree of authority to speak). Interestingly, it was just this issue of representation, and who was being represented (or not) on SAWnet, that I had sought to research. In this matter, my own complicity, as a creative writer and an academic, in producing certain images of South Asian women also became an issue to be interrogated. The medium of the internet with its lack of face-to-face contact, as well as the transnational nature of access to the community I was studying, was relevant in this regard. I would like to interrogate my own complicity by examining the article that I circulated to SAWnet members and the reactions it sparked (Gajjala 1998).

The article I had circulated analyzed the discourses (which were often diverse and contradictory) on SAWnet regarding the educated, professional South Asian woman's position within Western societies and within South Asian ones.[9] I sought to situate their discourses with respect to two dominant narratives (one scholarly and one geopolitical) about South Asian/Indian "Third-World" women. I wrote that Indian women are forced to cope with the tension between Indian nationalism's discursive positioning of the *Bharatiya Nari* (Woman of Bharat/India) on the one hand, and with Western feminism's complicity with colonial discourses on the other. The Indian woman's expression of agency is complicated by the fact that both these discourses speak for and about her, but do not allow her to speak for herself. Indeed, my own initial (and unexpectedly aborted) SAWnet research was partly an attempt to see just what kind of subject positions (particularly through online forums) might be allowing the South Asian woman to speak for herself as an acting agent. Both the nationalist and the feminist discourses, each in its way, contributed to the production of the monolithic notion of the "Third-World woman". Several scholars have critiqued this notion, and its use by First-World feminists using "the West" as the point of reference for their theories and praxis. Mohanty (1994) criticizes the appropriation and codification of stories of "Third-World women" by Western feminists and argues that the analytic principles used by "Western feminists" (a category which well includes non-Western feminists) end up distorting feminist political practices. This limits the goal of furthering a global feminist initiative. What is needed, according to Mohanty, is to form strategic feminist coalitions across class, race and national boundaries. On a related note, Alcoff (1991–92) discusses the significant epistemic impact that the location of a speaker has on shaping the paradigms of interpretations. She argues that it is not possible to avoid "epistemic violence" simply by refusing to speak for the Other; instead she calls for spaces where "dialogic encounters" might be made possible. She hints that information-communications technologies may have the potential for making possible these dialogic encounters.

One particular SAWnet discussion – about feminism and feminist issues – seemed to me to provide an ideal example to explore these two dominant narratives, as well as to see whether communications technologies could indeed provide spaces for more dialogic encounters between South Asian women in diaspora. The article I distributed to SAWnet members focused on this SAWnet discussion of feminism. Given the great diversity of their opinions on this topic, it was my conclusion that one could not apply a single, blanket description to SAWnet members. However, it was also my conclusion that the views highlighted the fact that SAWnet women (like many South Asian women in diaspora) were relatively economically privileged and to some extent Westernized; and were not representative of South Asian women in general. SAWnet thus provided data to refute the simplistic "Third-World women" notion – even here, among women sharing relatively similar class positions and likely educational backgrounds, there was a plurality of voice. However, I also argued that while SAWnet (as a virtual community of a number of South Asian women) did indeed have a potential to provide a space for "dialogic encounters" between South Asian women of all classes and backgrounds, it could also risk becoming a social space for elite South Asian/Indian women. As such, it might unintentionally marginalize the voices of others deemed to pose a challenge or threat to the Indian emigrant society's (idealized) vision of itself in "the West". Indeed, my article suggested that SAWnet discussions tended to do just this (i.e. to marginalize certain types of discourses) and to be exclusionary. For instance, the heterosexual, North American-based Indian focus on this list would implicitly exclude perspectives from lesbian South Asian women or from women located in other diasporic or non-diasporic South Asian contexts.

Borrowing the concept from Narayan, I described SAWnet members as being positioned by the "dark side of epistemic privilege" (Narayan 1989). By this I meant that, given their privileged situations (relative to other South Asian women "back home" in respective "Third-World" countries) SAWnet members had, by default, greater opportunity and voice to speak. This resulting "epistemic privilege" to determine the content of discourse and frame paradigms carried with it the dark side that, in the process, SAWnet women might be interpreted as, and/or come to view themselves as, speaking on behalf of South

Asian women in general. The dark side thus encapsulated a moral dilemma about the prospects of eclipsing (whether intentionally or not) the voices of their South Asian sisters, whose lives were characterized by radically different experiences. While I suggested that SAWnet came close to running this risk, I also noted that, in all fairness, there was/is a broad range of opinions on SAWnet, and members often critique each other's views. Hence, from a larger perspective, SAWnet refuted the monolithic notion of the Third-World woman, while somewhat paradoxically being positioned in a privileged way to inadvertently contribute to and perpetuate just such a notion. Thus, SAWnet may or may not be in a position to further a global feminist initiative that is truly inclusive of subaltern voice.

The veiling of the subaltern and the problem of representation

While SAWnet is a successful space for the communicative exchanges of a relatively exclusive, if nevertheless diverse, number of South Asian women, it cannot be taken as a representative example of Third-World women's empowerment through the internet. That spaces such as SAWnet are often seen as signposts of diversity and multiculturalism online is precisely one issue that my attempted cyberethnography critiques (for more on this, see Rai 1995; Gajjala 1998; Lal 1999; Bahri 2001). Contrary to the celebratory rhetoric concerning the heteroglossic and dialogic possibilities of hypertext and virtual community, postcolonial collectivities online display a show of what Clifford would call a "romanticized multiculturalism" (1997: 273).

> The Net will be a more colourful, exotic place for us with Venkatavva flashing her gold nose pin, but what good will it do her? The Net, as it is, has a perception of Southern women as "brown", "backward" and "ignorant". A frequent, kinder, depiction of them is as victim of their cultural heritage. Is being exposed to such images going to help Southern women by encouraging them to fight, with self-respect, or will it further erode their confidence in a fast-changing environment?
>
> (Gajjala and Mamidipudi 1999: 14).

The existence of marginalized peoples' voices in public spaces does not in itself provide "evidence of decentering hegemonic histories and subjectivities. It is the way in which they are read, understood, and located institutionally which is of paramount importance" (Mohanty 1994). We live in a global hegemony that continually appropriates, re-appropriates and objectifies voices from the margins, tokenizing them and celebrating the enabling of their "voice" and "empowerment" through structures of modernity and Western liberal thought. It can be remembered that hegemony operates through the appropriation, "incorporation and neutralization of contradictions, not on a purely monological discourse"

(Beverley 1993: 25). If so, then how are we to interpret and situate the experiences of the Other – in this context, of South Asian subaltern women? Such concerns about the process and ethics of representation are central to both feminist theorizations and the goal for a global feminist project. This crisis of representation, in parallel fashion, is also central to the doing of ethnography/ cyberethnography. Stacey suggests that the feminist ethnographer's dilemma is that "feminist researchers are apt to suffer the delusion of alliance more than the delusion of separateness" (1988: 23). The ethnographer, in such cases, "betrays" (and perhaps even feels betrayed by) a feminist principle and by the subjects of her ethnographic study. Similarly with respect to the issues raised through the above-described experiences, the question for both ethnographers and feminists arises: are we ventriloquizing the voice of the "subaltern"? That is, do we speak as "representative" Others or are we appropriating the voice of the Other? If we are, what are the possible consequences of such an appropriation?

> is it in the saying
> or in you
> or in the understanding
> of
> perpetual half truths
> virtual and imagined truths
> who's to say whether
> western or indian
> i refuse to be either
> i dont dare laugh
> i might lose my balance
> . . . but once in a while
> behind hands that strive to hide
> the nervousness
> i giggle a little giggle..
> not at you
> or me
> but at the process of
> being scrutinised . . . observed . . . "understood"
> as we perform
> like monkeys
> producing hamlets. . . .
> or
> chicken littles
> muzzling wolves. . . .
>   (Annapurna Mamidipudi, *cyberdiva.org*)

Macherey points out that "[s]ilences shape all speech" (Macherey 1986: 85), and if so it is the silences of the subaltern that shape bourgeois speech. But can speech "reveal... silence" (Macherey 1986: 86)? And if silence is indeed revealed, does this mean that the speech itself is invalid? According to Macherey, the attempt to reveal the latent (the silent):

> ...simply means that the latent is not another meaning which ultimately and miraculously *dispels* the first (manifest) meaning. Thus we can see that meaning is in the *relation* between the implicit and explicit, not on one or the other side of the fence.... What is important in the work is what it does not say. This is not the same as the careless notation "what it refuses to say"... what the work *cannot say* is important, because there the elaboration of the utterance is acted out, in a sort of journey to silence.
>
> (Macherey 1986: 86-7)

Discourses thus run the risk of performing a "veiling" function in relation to the materially and culturally underprivileged subaltern populations. Even as, for instance, voices of Third-World women scholars are increasingly included and allowed into academic structures dominated by Westernized fields of knowledge and inquiry, these "gestures of inclusion ... instead often functioned to contain our voices within predefined space. Discursive, institutional, and ideological structures preempt" our discourse and determine what we are permitted to say and whether we will be heard when we speak (Amireh and Majaj 2000: 1). The writing-up of ethnographies into academic form is in itself a political act based on (conscious, strategic) choices made by the researcher. What is as important as what is actually said and written (both in the discourses on internet spaces and in academic or creative works by women of comparative cultural and material privilege) is what is *not* said, and, even when said, what is not heard.

> From: radhika@cyberdiva.org
> Subject: Re: (no subject)
> Date: Sat, 10 Jun 2000 21:23:02-0400

> websites with links that go no
> where
> don't go
> elsewhere
> celebrating our speech
> we silence the rest
> framing my speech,
> you silence me
> you program how i celebrate my
> so-called speech
> the silences speak volumes
> but how do i make you invested in hearing it?
> >was i supposed to understand

>or respond
>
>cyborgwati says "i don't understand that"
>cyborgwati says "come again?"
>
>cyborgwati sips virtual coffee and sits back on virtual furniture ignoring
>the rest of the world
>
>@more
>
>cyborgwati says "there is no more"
>
>cyborgwati says "can you repeat that please?"
>
>POOF cyborgwati blows a virtual fuse.
>reality is insane.

From: "Annapurna M"
To: sa-cyborgs@lists.village.virginia.edu
    Subject: Re: so..

my silence is response
to your speech
a weapon
against your ignorance
a taunt
to your insensitivity
a plea
for understanding
restraint
against your arrogance
discretion
in the face of your strength i find i like my silence more than your
speech . . .

Cyberethnography and self-writing

Cyberethnography as a method of study/performance unfolded for me during my
attempts at studying this South Asian women-only email discussion list. It
continues to "unfold" as a process of understanding cross-contextual internet
mediated/enabled communication – both in online public spaces and via
private exchanges over the internet (see, e.g., Gajjala and Mamidipudi 1999).
My project began as an attempt to study South Asian women's use of and
inhabitation of the internet, but the very doing of the research provoked a

controversy. My encounter with the SAWnet refusal raises several issues relevant to the doing of cyberethnography in general, as well as to the concerns of feminist initiatives and the politics of the internet. It further raises questions about my own role as a participant "native" ethnographer and a Third-World academic producing my work within the Western academy. Visweswaran (1994) discusses the struggles and difficulties she likewise faces as an intellectual who locates herself "in a field of power (the West) and in the production of a particular knowledge (about the East)". She advocates a deconstructive ethnography, where the ethnographer pays careful attention to silences, refusals and betrayals. She further suggests that ethnographers need to consider ways to "disrupt" their own authority; and that this would help work toward a critical feminist epistemology. Narayan argues for the *"enactment of hybridity* in our texts" (1997: 23, italics in the original). This hybridity is intended as a negotiation between "the world of engaged scholarship and the world of the everyday" (Narayan 1997: 23). She writes:

> [W]hat we must focus on is the quality of relations with the people we seek
> to represent in our texts: are they viewed as mere fodder for professionally
> self-serving statements about a generalized Other, or are they accepted as
> subjects with voices, views, and dilemmas – people to whom we are bonded
> through ties of reciprocity and who may even be critical of our professional
> enterprise?
>
> (Narayan 1997: 23)

These and other related strategies are useful for the ethnographer who is a participant-observer. But how to build this "quality of relations" with women I know mainly (if not solely) through my email communications with them? One of the steps I have taken is to continually share my work with South Asian women online (in electronic spaces), and face-to-face in the US and when I am in India. I seek to incorporate the critiques and feedback I receive as part of an interrogation of my academic work and my creative (poetry and fiction) writings about South Asian women. In the autumn of 1996, I presented parts of this work-in-progress at a major Conference on South Asia. The organizer of the panel, most of the members of the panel and some of the members in the audience were members of SAWnet. Many of these members apparently had not exercised their option to vote on the issue raised in the autumn of 1995. Some implied that, had they voted, they would have voted in favor of studies. This raises the interesting question regarding the validity of the vote over time.

What, then, does "betrayal" mean in the context of SAWnet as a virtual community? Is there a "betrayal" involved in my continuing to write about this community? For Stacey, "fieldwork represents an intrusion and intervention into a system of relationships, that the researcher is far freer than the researched to leave. The inequality and the potential treacherousness of this relationship are inescapable" (Stacey 1988: 21). In the case of a virtual community, however, both the researcher and the researched are free to leave. As Mitra points out, "there is no Internet audience[/participant] who is also not empowered to become an agent to mold the space as he or she wishes" (Mitra 1997: 60). In the case of the real-life community that this virtual community (SAWnet) is embedded in, neither I as "native" ethnographer, nor my resistant subjects, can "leave". Undoubtedly, my work is an intrusion and an intervention into a system of relationships, even an invasion of privacy of sorts. However, it is not an intrusion and intervention similar to the power dynamics in the case of an anthropologist who infiltrates a group of indigenous people who have little or no access to the power field (academia) within which the anthropologist will represent them. The women on SAWnet can and do speak as "representative" of their/our "native" cultures. Their narratives (as much as mine) are appropriated and re-appropriated in various ways within the hegemonic frameworks that favor "Western" structures of thought and cultures. Some of these women are scientists, engineers and doctors. Others are students, professors (humanities and the sciences), anthropologists, rhetoricians, writers (fiction and non-fiction), artists and film-makers. All of us re-present our Third-World heritage in some form or other. Even when we reproduce narratives in everyday conversation, our words are quite often given more weight and authenticity than those of a less culturally/materially privileged woman speaking from the geographical "Third World".

Hence, the women on SAWnet are as well-versed as I am in producing various versions of our lives to fit rhetorically within certain contexts. In this regard, they (as much as I) are native informants reporting not just about our own diasporic communities within and outside of our communities as participant-observers, but also "anthropologists in reverse" (John 1996) who carry "field notes" about our host society/culture back to our birth-countries. I would further argue that email lists, Usenet bulletin boards, websites, web-conferences and so on can be regarded as ethnographies of the self and of the other (see Gajjala 1998). One of the SAWnet participants, whom I call "C", suggests:

> SAWnet itself [i]s a space of representation. This is by virtue of its being a discursive space that depends on some shared conceptions of identity (imagined, as you note). And because the medium is not quite [face-to-face] so that for all of us, participating in Sawnet itself is an act of imaginative reading. And that implies mental maps/representations to oneself of the meaning of South Asian female identities based on how one interprets the mails. In effect, SAWnet itself exists because of our self-representations . . . which we assume will translate into a space where our narratives of opinion and experience will be comprehensible to unseen people – perhaps even "more" comprehensible than to those we encounter in real life! This implies that we are all partaking in acts of re-presentation. Why else share our narratives in texts with unseen collaborators in conversation – we must be imagining our readers when we write, and we must similarly imagine the writers when we read.

Conclusions

In the context of the larger South Asian diasporic community of which SAWnet is very much a part, I feel that the story of the SAWnet refusal needs to be told. On the one hand, it is a story of a virtual group of well-educated, mostly professional postcolonial women refusing to be subjects of studies. They are very articulate and have shown that they can speak for themselves and be heard within the public sphere. On the other hand, there is the issue of the attempt and perceived need of emigrant communities to control the image of community. Behind this need lies a history of complex postcolonial identity negotiations within a mainstream Western power field. Various scholars and writers (Sara Suleri, Trinh Minh-ha and others) have discussed the process by which non-Western (non-white, non-bourgeois) women are "Othered" and "interpellated by difference" (John 1996: 23). At the same moment as we are "Othered" we also learn to be the ideal Other, complicitous with the existing status quo and the process of "Othering". As the ideal native informants who have been indoctrinated into the cultural and linguistic system through our post-colonial education and our "sanctioned ignorances" (John 1996), we learn to produce narratives about our so-called Othered selves that will fit appropriately within hegemonic narratives concerning Third-World cultures. We thus contribute actively to the reproduction of colonial discourses by being fashionably multicultural. It is this habitual, even unwitting, complicity that needs to be interrogated.

The lure of cyberspace, not unlike the lure of immigrating to the West, promises a dream of individual freedom and upward mobility that becomes a possibility for the Other – namely the culturally or ideologically assimilated and materially-privileged Other. In performing this "global village", the Other "morphs" into a deracinated, degendered entity, allowed the freedom to "express" his or her cultural difference. These performances take place within the politically-correct and apparently multicultural (yet ahistorical) postmodern paradigm, which nevertheless serves to idealize emigration from the Third World to the West. Anyone browsing the web or reading a list or the archives of the Usenet groups available online can view these tokenized performances. It is little wonder that Westernized, post-colonially constructed communities feel free to express identity online.

Cyberspace provides a very apt site for the production of shifting yet frozen homes for South Asians (as for countless other peoples): shifting as more and more people get online and participate; frozen as their narratives remain on websites and list archives in a timeless floating fashion. At the time of the SAWnet research, the South Asian online presence was dominated by subject positions located in diaspora. Their discourses were colored by themes of nostalgia and re-constructions of postcolonial migrant identities invoked in contexts of diaspora and travel shaped by transnational capital and labor flows. South Asians visible in digital diasporic contexts, therefore, exist in an ethos of continual reconfiguration and shifting of narratives in relation to "home" society and "host" society. Sometimes implicitly, other times explicitly, the narratives are about "not having left home [yet]" or "having Arrived" (i.e. having made it in the Western world). These various reconfigurations occur "through the forming of [virtual] communities that create multiple identifications through collective acts of remembering in the absence of a shared knowledge or a familiar terrain" (Ahmed 1999: 329), and through collective acts of storytelling and sharing of knowledge and experience of the "unfamiliar" and "new" terrains. As we have seen, one such virtual community is SAWnet.

These self-narratives by model native informants who have moved "away" from home, yet who fetishize "home", celebrate this moving away and arrival as a measure of socially-upward mobility in a developed country. They perform the dual function of "modernizing" yet also making "exotic" the postcolonial (i.e. under-developed) subject. Such narratives and their sharing within diasporic communities are not "new": it is the speed of exchange and potential interactivity of internet-based communications, as well as the publicness of online interactions, that are "new". Yet these new media also introduce the possibility of disruption to these entrenched narratives. Increasingly, cyberspace is a "space" that contains the possibility for disruptive digital-diasporic encounters. Ever greater numbers of non-diasporic South Asian women are getting connected and going online while living in their respective homeland (that is, having "never left"). In the digital diaspora, those who have left home and have taken on the role of native informant (thus speaking for, while silencing, narratives from "back home"), thus potentially face the "real" in the form of counternarratives from this "back home". The real places and their counternarratives, however, are not the same (and are arguably more dynamic) than the memory of the diasporic storyteller.

This work, therefore, is not about "the subaltern". It is rather about the privilege of being able to speak, to write in hegemonic spaces, including cyberspace. Yet it is also about the silences – the unsaid and the cannot-be-said. It is not only about what "position[s] of authority we have been given", taken or enabled, and at whose expense we speak, but implicitly it is also a questioning into how we might be able to negotiate from within our speech and our silences in order to transform or disrupt hegemony. It is about negotiating from within to work towards a critical ethnography and feminist initiative. It is about resistance and complicity and responsibility. It is important for us to examine the speaking roles we are assigned as well as the location from which we speak. While the non-subaltern Third-World woman (as the "Other" of the Western woman) finds a point of entry into the hegemonic sphere, she must remember that her speech could be used as representative of a subaltern who is not located within the same sphere of material and cultural privilege. Silencing ourselves, however, is not the solution: silence would be a betrayal of another kind. As an e-colleague pointed out in response to one of my papers, "[i]f we remain silent, that is not going to make the subaltern heard". Further, as a SAWnet member wrote:

The question about "what is *our* right to speak?", while it *looks* like a question that places the Subaltern/Other on the map, doesn't after all produce the spaces *from* which the Subaltern could speak.

By turning away from the questions and issues raised by this project, I would be taking the easy way out by not forcing myself and perhaps even some of my readers to confront some of the issues related to our complicity, as researchers, with structures of oppressive social, cultural and discursive practices. The post-colonial feminist ethnographer should strive to acknowledge the unavoidable balancing act between complicity and resistance, to be vigilant and self-reflexive so as not to fill subaltern absences with her own self-interested speech, thus veiling the subaltern (see Gajjala 1998; Gajjala and Mamidipudi 1999). I have here argued for the importance of contextual, self-reflexive ethnographies that examine the political economy and cultural dynamics of cyberspace. Issues of voice and voicelessness, as well as of marginalization, ventriloquizing and Othering based on gender, race, class and geographical location, emerge as central concerns. While, as yet, cyberspace is still characterized by Western (masculine) hegemonies and notions of modernity, in digital diaspora there is arguably a potential balancing of power between the researcher and the researched. Here, non-diasporic subaltern cybersubjects may be in a stronger position to "talk back" and challenge the assumptions both of the ethnographer/researcher and of their compatriots in diaspora.

Notes

1   My use of the term postcolonial is situated in conversations and controversies within the field of "postcolonial studies". As Ashcroft, Griffith and Tiffin (1998) write, the concept is "now used in wide and diverse ways to include analyses of European territorial conquests, the various institutions of European colonialisms, the discursive operations of empire, the subtleties of subject construction in colonial discourse and the resistance of those subjects, and, most importantly perhaps, the differing responses to such incursions and their contemporary colonial legacies in both pre- and post-independence nations and communities" (Ashcroft, Griffith and Tiffin 1998: 187).
2   The term "subaltern" is used by the "Subaltern Studies Group", an interdisciplinary organization of South Asian scholars, and is "a name for the general attribute of subordination in South Asian society whether this is expressed in terms of class, caste, age, gender and office or in any other way" (Guha 1988). See Spivak (1994) for relevant discussions of "the subaltern" and her answer to the question "Can the subaltern speak"?
3   There is an increasing, even overwhelming, amount of research being done regarding the internet at present; yet when my work on SAWnet began in 1994, internet researchers had very little to draw upon to inform our methodologies. Researchers using a postcolonial feminist perspective have since examined the internet as the empirical site for topics related to South Asian diaspora, to Sikh diaspora, to Hindu diaspora, to Tamil diapora, to Muslim diaspora, to Indian diaspora, and so on (see for instance, Rai 1995; Mitra 1997; Lal 1999).
4   See http://www.cyberdiva.org/erniestuff/sanov.html for more on this.
5   In exploring the phrase "South Asian" (and problematizing my own use of it with respect to the "diaspora") I find Bhattacharjee's explanation insightful. She writes:

the "label's attraction for South Asians such as myself lies, to a large extent, in its ability to subsume more than one nation. It is thus seen by those skeptical of oppressive conditions of nationhood as something less rigid; it has little institutional authority (such as a flag or an embassy) and less solidified cultural homogeneity. In the competing ethnic realities of the United States, it is also a way to amass numbers" (1997: 309).

6   It has been argued that the SAWnet website is the public face of SAWnet and that it is okay to describe or write about the website, but that the email list is private and so no one should write about the list. However, the website itself carries a description of the SAWnet list, and if this description is an authorized one (and therefore more legitimate than any other SAWnet member's description of the list) then the question is who authorized it, and what was the process by which it was approved?

7   JV, a member of SAWnet, wrote, "I wonder if the vehemence of the reaction to your wanting to study sawnet was not in part exacerbated by the fact that just around that time (or was it before your query) the white (?) researcher had wanted to do so as well".

8   Incidentally, any woman can become a member of SAWnet and (at the time of this writing) ask to receive a copy of all past SAWnet digests. Therefore any woman can "verify" that the discussion I am writing about really did occur.

9   In fact email lists like SAWnet have been adopted by researchers wishing to point to the "diversity" of women's voices in cyberspace. See, for instance, the work of Leslie Shade (http://www.vcn.bc.ca/sig/comm-nets/shade.html).

References

Aarseth, Espen J. (1994) "Nonlinearity and Literary Theory", in G. P. Landow (ed.), *Hyper/Text/Theory*. Baltimore: The Johns Hopkins University Press, pp. 51–86.

Ahmed, Sara (1999) "Home and Away: Narratives of Migration and Estrangement", *International Journal of Cultural Studies* 2,(3): 329–47.

Alcoff, Linda (1991–92) "The Problem of Speaking for Others", *Cultural Critique*, Winter 1991–92: 5–32.

Amireh, Amal and Majaj, Lisa Suhair (eds) (2000) *Going Global: The Transnational Reception of Third World Women Writers*. New York and London: Garland.

Ashcroft, Bill, Griffith, Gareth and Tiffin, Helen (1998) *Key Concepts in Postcolonial Studies*. London: Routledge.

Bahri, Deepika (2001) "The Digital Diaspora: South Asians in the New Pax Electronica", in M. Paranjpe (ed.), *Diaspora: Theories, Histories, Texts*. New Delhi: Indialog, pp. 222–34.

Beverley, John (1993) *Against Literature*. Minneapolis: University of Minnesota Press.

Bhattacharjee, Anannya (1997) "The Public/Private Mirage: Mapping Homes and Undomesticating Violence Work in the South Asian Immigrant Community", in M. J. Alexander and C. T. Mohanty (eds), *Feminist Genealogies, Colonial Legacies, Democratic Futures*. New York and London: Routledge, pp. 308–29.

Clifford, James (1997) *Routes: Travel and Translation in the Late Twentieth Century*. Cambridge, MA: Harvard University Press.

Gajjala, Radhika (1997) www.cyberdiva.org/erniestuff/define.html

——(1998) *The Sawnet Refusal: An Interrupted Cyberethnography*, PhD dissertation, University of Pittsburgh. Dissertation Abstracts International, 99-00131.

——(2002a) "An Interrupted Postcolonial/Feminist Cyberethnography: Complicity and Resistance in the 'Cyberfield'", *Feminist Media Studies* 2(2): 177–93.

——(2002b) "Interrogating Identities: Composing Other Cyber-spaces", *International and Intercultural Communication Annual* 25: 167–88.

Gajjala, Radhika and Mamidipudi, Annapurna (1999) "Cyberfeminism, Technology and International 'Development'", *Gender and Development* (7)2: 8–16.

Grossberg, Lawrence (1997) "Cultural Studies, Modern Logics, and Theories of Globalization", in A. McRobbie (ed.), *Back to Reality?* Manchester: Manchester University Press, pp. 7–35.

Guha, Ranajit (1988) "The Prose of Counter-Insurgency", in R. Guha and G. Spivak (eds), *Selected Subaltern Studies.* New York: Oxford University Press, pp. 45–88.

Haraway, Donna (1990) "Manifesto for Cyborgs: Science, Technology, and Socialist Feminism in the 1980s", in L. J. Nicholson (ed.), *Feminism/Postmodernism.* London and New York: Routledge, pp. 190-233.

——(1991) *Simians, Cyborgs, and Women: The Reinvention of Nature.* New York: Routledge.

John, Mary (1996) *Discrepant Dislocations: Feminism, Theory and Postcolonial Histories.* Berkeley: University of California Press.

Jones, Steven G. (ed.) (1995) *CyberSociety: Computer-Mediated Communication and Community.* Thousand Oaks, CA: Sage.

Lal, Vinay (1999) "The Politics of History on the Internet: Cyber-Diasporic Hinduism and the North American Hindu Diaspora", *Diaspora* 8(2): 137–72.

Macherey, Pierre (1986) *A Theory of Literary Production,* trans. G. Wall. London: Routledge.

Mitra, Ananda (1997) "Virtual Commonality: Looking for India on the Internet", in S. G. Jones (ed.), *Virtual Culture: Identity and Communication in Cybersociety.* London: Sage, pp. 55–79.

Mohanty, Chandra Talpade (1993) "Defining Genealogies: Feminist Reflections on Being South Asian in North America", in The Women of South Asian Descent Collective (eds), *Our Feet Walk the Sky: Women of the South Asian Diaspora.* San Francisco: Aunt Lute, pp. 196–220.

——(1994) "Under Western Eyes: Feminist Scholarship and Colonial Discourses", in P. Williams and L. Chrisman (eds), *Colonial Discourse and Post-Colonial Theory: A Reader.* New York: Columbia University Press.

Narayan, Kirin (1997) "How Native is a 'Native Anthropologist?'", in L. Lamphere, H. Ragone and P. Zavella (eds), *Situated Lives: Gender and Culture in Everyday Life.* London: Routledge, pp. 23–41.

Narayan, Uma (1989) "The Project of Feminist Epistemology: Perspectives from a Nonwestern Feminist", in A. M. Jaggar and S. R. Bordo (eds), *Gender/Body/Knowledge: Feminist Reconstructions of Being and Knowing.* Trenton: Rutgers University Press, pp. 256–72.

Rai, Amit S. (1995) "In On-line: Electronic Bulletin Boards and the Construction of a Diasporic Hindu Identity", *Diaspora* 4(1): 31–57.

Schiller, Herbert I. (1991) "Not Yet the Post-Imperialist Era", *Critical Studies in Mass Communication* 8: 13–28.

Senft, Theresa M. (1997) "Introduction: Performing the Digital Body – A Ghost Story", *Women and Performance: A Journal of Feminist Theory* (1)17: 263–8.

Slack, Jennifer Daryl (1989) "Contextualizing Technology", in B. Dervin, L. Grossberg, B. O'Keefe and E. Wartella (eds), *Rethinking Communication. Volume 2: Paradigm/Exemplars.* Newbury Park, CA: Sage, pp. 329–45.

Spender, Dale (1995) *Nattering on the Net: Women, Power and Cyberspace.* North Melbourne: Spinifex.

Spivak, Gayatri Chakravorty (1994) "Can the Subaltern Speak?", in P. Williams and L. Chrisman (eds), *Colonial Discourse and Post-Colonial Theory: A Reader*. New York: Columbia University Press, pp. 66–111.

——(1999) *A Critique of Postcolonial Reason: Toward a History of the Vanishing Present*. Cambridge, MA: Harvard University Press.

Stacey, Judith (1988) "Can There be a Feminist Ethnography?", *Women's Studies International Forum* 11(1): 21–7.

Visweswaran, Kamala (1994) *Fictions of Feminist Ethnography*. Minneapolis: University of Minnesota Press.

Ward, Katie J. (1999) "The Cyber-Ethnographic (Re)Construction of Two Feminist Online Communities", *Sociological Research Online* 4(1). Available online: www.socresonline.org.uk/4/1/ward.html.

Chapter 16

Postscript: *Vox Populi* from the margins?

Kyra Landzelius

Navigating center and periphery

The contributors to this volume have, each in our way, grappled with the trials and tribulations of venturing into virtual *terra incognita* without methodological charts. Like anthropology's early pioneers who conceived "participant-observation" methods over a century ago largely due to circumstance, so too did many of us accidentally find ourselves virtual pioneers on a twenty-first-century threshold – not necessarily setting out to do fieldwork in/of/about cyberspace, yet somehow finding ourselves there (in several cases because the "natives" were there first)! Such a lesson should serve to debunk simplistic notions about center–periphery relations, notions that may indeed prove to be toppling at the speed of clicks and bytes: as one of the founders of the Oneida Indian Nation's website, Dan Umstead, jokes: "we were the first sovereign Indian nation to put up a web page [in May 1994] . . . Even the White House homepage wasn't up yet!" (quoted in Polly 1998). To the extent that "ethnography is strengthened by the lack of recipes for doing it", our forays add to the growing list of ethnographic first encounters to study the worldly aspects of information-communications technologies – studies that arguably are revealing them to be "more interesting, more nuanced, more differentiated and more dull than futurologists would have us believe" (Hine 2000: 13).

These chapters, each in its way, provide us with an ethnographic snapshot (however fleeting) to situate hyper-modern media technologies in the lives and localities of indigenous and diasporic peoples – subjects long marginalized from modernity's promises, yet nevertheless mediating and mediated by its powerful global flows and histories. In these chapters, we have witnessed ICTs catering to remote indigenous neighborhoods and to transnational coalitions; servicing traditional medicine alongside radical environmentalism; circulating facts as well as fictions. We have encountered examples of ICTs variously recruited: to fantasize about forbidden homelands or to romance former ones, to author alternative histories or to re-write today's news, to practice domestic politics "at a distance" or to participate in global political movements. We have traveled along ethnoscapes that stretch identity into new zones of contact and dialogue, and traveled along others that risk "ghettoizing" identity within hermeneutic online forums. We have watched cyberactivism rehearse tradition or reinvent it, protect heritage or perform it, stage periphery or ignore it, unmask power or mimic it, heal the wounds of war or fan the flames of conflict. In "worlding" a few select bits of cyberspace (Fischer 1999; see also Whitaker 2004: 475) these vignettes give a glimpse, if you will, of the virtual faces of indigeneity, and trace the silhouettes of diasporas linked digitally.

So what can we glean from these studies concerning the broader picture of indigenous cosmopolitanism and virtual diaspora? The "big questions" (harking back to our introductory chapter) still linger: Can indigenous peoples make a home in cyberspace; and will they feel themselves at home there? And what about diasporic peoples: Can virtual media assimilate disparate homes for peoples widely scattered from (actual or fantastical) homelands? While at first glance "indigenous" (subjectivities "rooted" in home) and "diasporic" (subjects "routed" from home, cf. Clifford 2001) seem counterposed, we have emphasized how both are keenly enmeshed in the politics of place and attuned to fragile "dynamics of positioning" (Miller and Slater 2001: 10, 18–20 and *passim*). We might in both respects pose the question of whether the internet can be "indigenized": implying by this term not just whether it can be reworked to articulate local traditions or agendas, but also whether it can be meaningfully enrolled in the production of locality – a never-static enterprise that necessarily coordinates manifold trans-localities and discordant temporalities. Locality, as we recall from the opening chapter's discussion, is here conceived less as some dwelling place or referential point on the map, and more in terms of the feelings, properties and cosmologies of a group, whose "tasks of producing locality" are exposed to contradictions and challenging "new elements" spurred and spawned by globality (Appadurai 1995: 213, 221). Conceived thus, locality is both a "spatial fact" and a sensibility, yet equally a transit point (Appadurai 2000: 6 and *passim*). Increasingly, it seems, global technologies and intercourse of all kinds further challenge, stretch, condense, disperse, warp and what-have-you not only locality's production, but its very definition and phenomenology, leading to re-positionings in the experiencing and significance of centers and peripheries, and the meanings accorded them.

Indigenizing the net?

Questions about the potential of ICTs to be indigenized inevitably interface with questions about power: implicating its direct and indirect manifestations, its material and ethereal forms. Power comes in many shapes and sizes, of course: state, corporate, military, popular, bureaucratic, ideological, etc.; each sporting its own intensely context-dependent orientation *vis-à-vis* the infrastructures of new media. In launching here our empirical studies with an overview of plans to cultivate ICT hardware, software and wetware in the outback lands of Australia's Aborigines, Latukefu (Chapter 2) puts the issue of power squarely on the table. Latukefu's candid musing about the specter of an

ICT panopticon is doubly keen for calling attention to the prospect of surveillance over subjects, but equally to the possibility that subjectivities might be at risk for ideological (self-)disciplining. As the comparatively more tangible apparatus of domination, surveillance in/of/through computer networks is a routine (if not necessarily uniform) occurrence: spanning from institutional spying upon employee email to government patrolling of "subversive" sites or even the entire "wired" citizenry in some countries. The argument that ICTs could pose a "colonizing" (Hall 1999) apparatus – a decidedly less measurable (thus arguably more insidious) manifestation of power – implicates the hegemonic reach of dominant logics and their proposed importation into local sensibilities and spaces. This raises questions as to the cultural neutrality (or lack thereof) of any given technology: specifically, the extent to which ICTs (and their attendant praxes and idioms) are assimilable into local values and lifeways; or conversely the extent to which dominant modes of thinking and doing are embedded in their very matrix, luring users into an inescapable ICT hegemony.

These are not rhetorical questions for academic speculation; on the contrary, indigenous activists, authors, politicians and lay people themselves are preoccupied about just this matter of adaptability versus authority. To wit: "the technologies can leave the West but can the West leave the technologies?" (Rogers 2000). In many an indigenous community crossing the digital divide, lively debate has ensued about the plasticity of the internet to translation and re-signification, on the one hand, or its systemic fidelity to mainstream code, on the other. Those skeptical about the prospects of indigenization are apt to argue that ICTs are necessarily inscribed by and radiate dominant culture paradigms. Some caution that conventional hierarchies are reproduced, perhaps even essentialized, online (Becker and Delgado-P. 1998). Some predict that indigenous societies will be conscripted into ICT mass-mediation and commercialism (Fair 2000). Some object on the grounds of cultural dissonance: emphasizing how new media reflect Western values of individualism, the privileging of texts and the commodification of knowledge – trends that run counter to and likely threaten many indigenous traditions (cf. Bowers et al. 2000).[1] Some opponents see dangers in the very act of self-exposure; the Saami teacher, Nora Bransfjell, goes so far as to claim that reclusiveness has been the guardian of Saami culture, and further questions whether state governments will be prone to "tap into" indigenous communications as a form of electronic espionage (quoted in Forsgren 1998). Some critics problematize the issue of exposure by declaring the internet a "two-edged sword" (Maybury-Lewis 1998), or by pinpointing the dangers of "half-truths" that have the potential to "take on a life of their own" in cyberspace (Downey 2001). Gibb's study (Chapter 9) of Harari immigrants in its way touches upon the problem of half-truths by demonstrating how a particular kind of "half-truth" – that which homogenizes identity for youth in (second generation?) diaspora – may put these youths at risk of cross-cultural misunderstandings, whilst also delimiting opportunities or incentives to indigenize ICT resources and cater them to the production of these youths' respective localities of residence. Landzelius (Chapter 6) strikes a similarly cautious note concerning the possibility of an unambiguous victory in cybercampaigns like that of the U'wa. By exposing the specter of a postmodern "noble savage", she queries the extent of participatory freedoms and/or tyrannies mediated online. Even *TamilNet's* ironic mimicry of Western journalism's alleged neutrality, which Whitaker discusses in Chapter 14, can arguably be read with "two minds" regarding the nature and criteria of the indigenizing potential of ICTs. On the one hand, to diversify coverage of Sri Lanka's ethnic conflict by broadcasting the little-heard local perspective certainly betokens a savvy indigenizing; on the other hand, the "packaging" of this resistance strategy attests to the entrenched constraints of having to fight hegemony on its (and not necessarily indigenous) terms. Even if ICTs prove intractably biased in their architecture, however, this does not necessarily prevent their deployment against power – in a manner akin to "using the master's tools to take apart the master's house".[2]

On the other side of the indigenization argument we find advocates for the autonomy of ICTs from their originary sources/forces. These proponents make a strong case for the adaptability of new media technologies to fit indigenous agendas (Trahant 1996), and point to a growing inventory of indigenous uses, such as story-telling and language pedagogy, political empowerment and environmental protection, heritage mapping and property reclamation, person-to-person socializing and pan-indigenous networking. We considered a range of similar examples in our introductory chapter; and several authors herein elaborate upon such creative enlistments of ICTs for indigenous aspirations: witness the re-engineering of Carib indigeneity by means of performative homepages and hyperlink endorsements (as demonstrated by Forte in Chapter 7). The successful positioning of the Zapatistas' "keyboard is mightier than the sword" cyber-victory (discussed in Chapter 5 by Belausteguigotia) underscores that the "subject" under panopticon surveillance may on occasion turn out to be, not an indigenous peasant on the periphery, but a central apparatus of power – to wit, the Mexican military. Gideon's presentation (Chapter 3) of how First Nation Canadians are seeking ways to "morph" traditional healing with high-tech medicine in the delivery of e-healthcare gives us an additional example, and one that highlights the bi-directionality of morphing. For assimilation is typically a two-way street: by frequently mandating the design of new symbols, sound files, software and the like, indigenous exercises are also pushing the technological frontier and influencing the direction of ICT innovation (cf. Young-Ing 2003; Donaghy 1998). In addition, the pioneering exploration of the interface between traditional and computer-generated art is posing unique challenges to the already tricky, and as yet largely unresolved issues of copyright rules and protections in cyberspace (McMahon 2001). Digital reproduction raises similar conundrums with respect to the communal ownership and/or production of much indigenous art (see Radoll 2001). In short, indigenization means not just enlisting ICTs to do things with tradition, but enlisting tradition to do things with ICTs. In keeping with the general tenet of human–machine relations, indigenous ICT users may tend to cognize and manipulate these tools differently based upon and in accordance with indigenous idioms.

At home in new media worlds

As should be apparent, the gist of debate surrounding the indigenizing potential of ICTs parallels in kind the debates regarding its emancipatory versus hegemonic aspects. The ethnographies in this volume weigh in, by and large, on the side of indigenization – with early examples of the engagement of ICTs in a wide range of locality-producing agendas. In some cases, we get hints of how these engagements interweave with the structures of feeling, ideologies and properties of social life that configure locality, as we (following Appadurai's lead) have approached it here. Inuit family homepages, for example, are firmly anchored within the everyday course and discourse of community-building, acting in certain respects as just another prosthesis upon established communicative channels and personal relationships, as Christensen (Chapter 4) shows (in a manner not unlike the two-way radio of yesteryear, which historically afforded a crucial tool of Arctic communications; see Searles 2001). Inuit homepages nonetheless forge dialogic bridges – however superficial – across vast geographical and cultural divides, in what I have likened to a fashion of "home-paging the Other" (Landzelius 2001). The chat relays taking place between Tongan youth in diaspora (See Lee in Chapter 8) evince impassioned commitments to a collective exploration of "Tongan identity", especially in relation to querying the role of native language. At the same time, they articulate ideological resistance to normative structures (e.g., royalty, sexuality, gender) that have been intrinsic properties of traditional Tongan culture. To cite another locality-producing initiative, we can recall how participant-members of/on iGhana "descend" (virtually-speaking) upon "real-life" Ghana to intervene in domestic politics (the chimpanzee repatriation scheme that Schaefer presents in Chapter 11). Given their oft-superior financial, symbolic and political capital, their connections to Western institutions and organizations, plus their greater command of geopolitics and cross-planetary media, Ghanaians in diaspora likely wield more clout than locals. Indeed, ex-patriates have long played a major role in developments "back home"; and external interventions are certain to intensify in the age of ICTs and diasporic digerati. In turning to Assyrian and Turkoman virtual nation-building, we find that "home" is precisely the niche cyberspace vicariously fills. For some cybernauts, locality (if not quite tangibly produced) is certainly symbolically performed and imagined – not intended as simulacra, but as dress-rehearsals or scripts for the real thing, as Fattah examines in Chapter 10. The participants in/on the SAWnet discussion group for South Asian women in diaspora were so dedicated to protecting their (sense of) intimate locality online – a locality textualized and filtered in relation to ideas and feelings about "imagined community" homelands – that they barred its scrutiny by trespassing researchers: namely Gajjala, our aspiring cyberethnographer of Chapter 15. To take a somewhat inverse example: it was to virtually escape a conflict-ridden locality, in order to safely reflect "back" upon and diplomatically restore it, that *Burundinet* and the *Burundi Youth Council Forum* were founded and designed to be dialogic meeting places for Hutus and Tutsis at home and in diaspora (see Kadende-Kaiser in Chapter 12). Turning our attention to a completely antithetical case, we discover that it is violent disputes over and for locality – for geographical places and their real and symbolic control – that motivates tit-for-tat hacking on the part of pro-Palestinian and pro-Israeli website defacers, where actions are fueled by a deep moral indignation that inscribes identity (and conceptions of alterity) on both sides of the conflict (see Taggart in Chapter 13).

Taken collectively, our empirical snapshots lend support, by and large, to the "yes" vote regarding the indigenizing potential of ICTs. That is to say, the chapters herein convincingly illustrate the adeptness of subaltern counterpublics to weave electronic networks, digital images, HTML languages, homepages, hyperlinks and the like into local agendas, for diverse puposes and with varying degrees of "success", assuredly. A growing number of indigenous peoples are clearly making themselves a(t) home in new-media environments, whilst also altering these environments in the process. Likewise, it seems that a virtual homesteading, of sorts, has come, to complement the diasporic condition, whereby we might suggest that many a person/community in diaspora is finding/ forging "a home away from home(s)" in cyberspace.

All of this is not to imply that these settings and trajectories are in any way straightforward or inevitable, nor are they presumed to be enchanted or disenchanted, prescriptive or permissive, nor necessarily empowering. While much of our discussion has orbited around issues of empowerment, our examples also underscore the fragile, ephemeral, subjective, and context-dependent nature of power and empowerment. Still, it seems incontrovertible that some gain in experiential or representational freedom(s), is prerequisite to making claims about the indigenization of any technology with respect to its usage by indigenous and/or diasporic peoples. The ethnographies presented here envince empowering moments and effects, in the form of relatively successful resistance to government oppression, corporate exploitation, (perceived) neo-colonialism, environmental degradation, disenfranchisements of various kinds, and even to the constraints of tradition. Nevertheless, they also make clear that there is no simple algorithm to power equations (nor to their "fix"); and apparently this adage rings equally true on- and offline. Apropos of this, as we espy First Nation Canadians at the (rhetorical, at least) vanguard of federal ICT-development (jobs and other) programs, we justifiably find cause to welcome an anticipated liberation from unequal welfare dependency (among other gains). Yet we might also find ourselves troubled by a nagging worry that, via such schemes, ICT-competent indigenous publics might (in the eyes of some bureaucrats or policy-makers) be presumed ideally positioned to "take advantage of global trends in outsourcing infotech work via the Net".[3] Given a corresponding shift towards corporate and away from state regimes, the prospect of indigenous peoples as telemarketing laborers pivots the question of emancipation *from* (what?) to one of emancipation *to* (what?). To take another example of the relativity of emancipation and its multiple positionings, we can consider again the empowerment demands of indigenous women in the Zapatista movement. A victory for "women's rights" in this case is one that accomplishes an interesting dual objective: to problematize (even reject) tradition; and to displace Western feminism's emphasis on the "right to work" with a local emphasis on the "right to rest". The complicated calculus of power/empowerment is similarly attested to in the case of Carib revitalization movements. On the one hand, in the light of growing indigenous calls for autonomy, resource-rights, repatriation and the like, such campaigns to "(re)engineer" indigeneity might be apprehended as a threat to nation-state sovereignty. On the other hand, indigenous groups with a theatrical presence might well prove welcome tourist attractions with potential to boost local and regional economies. And so it goes; as virtually-mediated "real-world" considerations expose the polymorphous architecture of center–periphery relations, we are led again to query the nature of ICT indigenization. In speculating on what changes ICTs might bring to the Native American Hopi tribe, one Hopi man with whom I spoke[4] put forth the interesting proposition: that, as Hopi availed themselves of online shopping in lieu of traveling considerable "off-rez" distances (i.e. to stores located outside the Hopi reservation), regional merchants might conceive a greater respect for Native Americans as a valuable consumer public whose business they should be loathe to lose. The upshot, in this Hopi's opinion, could improve face-to-face relations between ethnic groups in the regional marketplace and other arenas. Following this line, it seems fair to conclude that indigenous engagements with ICTs are more apt to reconfigure existing power relations in unpredictable ways, rather than to simply rehearse or alternatively erase them. They are also likely to introduce new asymmetries and hegemonies even whilst redressing or toppling extant ones.

As the above discussion seeks to illustrate, minority ICT uses and users (like all uses and users) are situated in webs of power, a situatedness that thwarts any simplistic formulas to calculate just what constitutes empowerment. Utopian or dystopic postulates about new media worlds are tempered by the exigencies of lived realities and perspectival truths; correspondingly, victories (and defeats) are best assessed on a case-by-case basis.[5] Rather than interpreting these technologies in sweeping terms, it may be keener to conceive of fleeting, localized "islands of utopia" – digitized variants along the lines of what Bey (2001) calls "pirate utopias" (see also Ludlow 2001). In such enclaves, emancipatory moments – experiments in collective enlistment of ICTs for meritorious or righteous local agendas – can be and assuredly are being achieved; and, whilst memorable and sometimes revolutionary, in the scale of things many such instances likely remain islands in a larger sea of "technopoly" (i.e. the monopoly of technology and bureaucracy in the service of global capitalism, see Postman 1993). The indigenizing potential of ICTs may well mirror their emancipatory potential in analogous manner. Accordingly, we might conceptualize "islands of indigenized engagement" where traditions are being reinvented, re-invigorated and/or re-articulated. Or we might talk about "pirate indigenization", whereby ICTs are meaningfully enrolled in the production of locality. It remains to be seen, however, to what extent indigenized islands in the net will chart new geographies, or simply re-map old dominant codes. Given that ICTs are undergoing rapid evolution and diffusion, and given that it is as yet unclear how they will transform the fabric of everyday life and personhood for peoples historically on the margins of power, perhaps it is prudent (if admittedly dull) to sound a note of caution. There is space and place for hope, but in this case hope's best ally may prove to be a healthy suspicion and creative circumvention of "the machinery of power and the power of the machine" (Landzelius 2003).

Indigenous cosmopolitanism and virtual diaspora?

Continuing along this path from the empirical to the conjectural, in closing we might hazard some reflections upon the future directions of indigeneity and diaspora in the age of digerati. Turning first to the future of diaspora, one feels on firm ground (and indeed in ample company[6] to declare ICTs phenomenally situated to *effectively virtualize the diasporist experience*: to attenuate diaspora in such ways and in such cases that displacement – as fact and concept – assumes elasticity, as it were, becoming ever more open to navigation, ever more pliable to technological morphing. On the one hand, given the communicative immediacy, ready accessibility, "real-time" dialogue and so forth that characterize ICT connections, distances that orchestrate diaspora may be diffused or even transcended in multiple and collective acts of virtual returnings and the phantasmagoria of "home" they likely conjure. On the other hand, given a solidarity based in shared diasporist identities and the likelihood that events "back home", estrangement from home and/or returnings to home shape discussions, "distance" may be intensified and dwelled upon, emotionally (re)lived or symbolically rehearsed in and through connectivity itself (and the discourses, sentiments and habits it spawns). Nowadays, more than ever, people in diaspora command a battalion of communications and transport tools – ranging from sophisticated to mundane, from ubiquitous to exquisite – in order to figuratively "come and go": to be, if not literally present, then at least participant; if not sufficiently visible, than persistently vocal. Such perennial, polymorphic comings and goings (both online and off) present locality and its productions(s) with a radical ontological challenge. This is a challenge uniquely met by the crisscrossing itineraries linking here, there and everywhere/anywhere/nowhere (in cyberspace). To follow the meaning-makings of diasporist selves and communities is to appreciate that locality increasingly trafficks in itself, to form and inform a kind of cartographic *modus vivendi* – the embodied map-making that indexes diaspora today.

Turning lastly to ponder the future of indigeneity in a digital age, we equally find ICTs well suited to *tangibly cosmopolitanize indigenous identity*. As we have seen, digital media technologies are proving useful conduits and catalysts for the activities and agendas of indigenous persons and groups. Viewed from the perspective of temporary localized "pirate utopias" in cyberspace, indigenous cyberactivism holds potential to introduce a veritable archipelago of indigenized islands on the net. Hyperlinked and heavily trafficked along mediascapes and ideoscapes, these islands may well form chains, fashioning an indigenous "cosmopolitics" (Cheah and Robbins 1998) for the twenty-first century – one ICT-equipped and mediated to definitively map indigeneity into/onto geopolitical scenes. This view is premised on an understanding of indigeneity as an idea (and influence) whose "time has come". That indigeneity represents a (revamped) ideological and situational emergent, a debut global *presence*, is convincingly demonstrated by the exponential rise, over the past two decades, in indigenous-rights movements (and/or movements that claim and/or frame themselves in such terms). These have taken place throughout the Americas (Churchill 1996; Ramos 1998; Brysk 2000; Warren 1998; Martin 2002; Warren and Jackson 2003), across the African continent (Hodgson 2002), in pockets of Asia and the South Pacific (Kalland and Persoon 1999; Kolig and Mückler 2002; Weiss and Hassan 2002; Ganguly and Macduf 2003), in Europe and globally (see Niezen 2003). These trends have spawned a proliferation of special-interest associations around indigenous matters (e.g., arts, crafts, politics, literature, languages, lands, artifacts, etc.) and have mobilized a host of civil society and non-governmental organizations working to promote indigenous empowerment (of such caliber as the United Nations Task Force and its Declaration on the Rights of Indigenous Peoples) (Roulet 1999). Given their growing prominence as technologies increasingly recruited to these trends, ICTs play an ever-expanding role not just to mediate, but to substantiate "indigeneity"; not just to broadcast its messages, but to fundamentally recast its meanings and values. It is such semantic shifts in indigeneity (indigeneities?) that establish the moment as no less than a revolution in the fate of an identity marker – one with a notable measure of success, thus far, in making itself a(t) home in new media worlds.

As I argued in the introductory chapter, we are all – from one perspective – equally "native on the net" (echoing, in certain respects, the Zapatista movement-inspired slogan "We are all Indians"). Nonetheless, the question might be raised as to whether "some are more equal (more native?) than others?" For it has been argued that indigenous peoples may represent "the first global group to legitimately utilize the electronic media to strive for equivalence in living standards and self-determination" (Westblade 1998). This is to suggest that historically marginalized peoples are not only taking roles, but in certain respects taking the lead, as savvy, technoscientific actors themselves "colonizing" global media channels and converting them into fertile habitats for the exercise of identity and voice across distances.

Digital technologies and computer-mediated communications are accordingly firmly situated in the *quest* for "indigeneity within globality", as they progressively take center stage in framing the *question* of indigeneity within globality. Indigeneity's "moment" may have come, but it remains to be seen whether this moment will prove intractable or ephemeral, weighty or inflationary, validated or violated. For, to digitally chaperone *vox populi* from the margins and onto the geopolitical scene depends not only on who is speaking, but equally on who is listening and on the nature of dialogue being worlded.

Notes

1   To complicate matters further, at least one author has raised the counter point that importation of Western ICTs without attendant cultural values may itself prove problematic; the example being given is that of the vitriolic "infowars" waged between Armenian and Azerbaijani hackers, which (Rogers [2000] asserts) have spurred disproportionate over-reactions due to a failure of both sides to put into perspective the actor/activist "serious fun" involved in the rogue theatrics of disinformation.

2   Paul Gilroy makes this point in a related context (see Gilroy 1998).

3   The quote is borrowed from George Sadowsky, who deploys it in the context of advocating ICT advantages and expansions in countries "like Tunisia" (see Rao 2001).

4   The informant in question had regular dealings with regional merchants, and preferred to remain anonymous in granting me permission to here re-present his perspective. My travels on Hopiland were graciously assisted by the Hopi Tribal Council. I am also grateful to Miguel Vasquez and Sean Downey, both of Northern Arizona University, for sharing with me their writings about Native Americans and ICTs.

5   The situation is comparable to ICT usages elsewhere/everywhere: where examples of emancipatory moments abound, alongside ample evidence of surveillance and crackdown attempts. For example: the Chinese government's digital regulatory system is robust and has certainly taken its share of prisoners, but state enforcement mechanisms, in toto, are inadequate to block the free flow of information, given the availability of "anti-blocking software, mirror sites, remailers, secret Usenet groups, anonymous e-mail services" and the like (Lacharite 2002). Similarly, the Burmese regime has successfully censored a great deal of ICT activity within the nation's borders, but finds it much more difficult to police "hard copy" printouts from the internet that are strategically leaked across its Thai border (a timely reminder, as well, that a great deal of the new media's impact works via older media genres) (see Fink 1998). In a related vein, wealthy Saudis have been known to circumvent government online eavesdropping by using their buying power to purchase connectivity from foreign servers (Fandy 1999).

6   Examples of the myriad uses to which ICTs have been put in re-orchestrating the diasporist experience span across disciplines; studies have addressed: development and reconstruction (Brinkerhoff 2004; Hanafi 2005), war and conflict (Stubbs 1999; Axel 2004), sovereignty (Spoonley *et al.* 2003), spatiality (Adams and Ghose 2003; Parham 2004), identity and social networking (Ignacio 2000; Hiller and Franz 2004), and social activism (Shi 2005).

References

Adams, P. C. and Ghose, R. (2003) "India.com: The Construction of a Space Between", *Progress in Physical Geography* 27(4): 414–37.

Appadurai, Arjun (1995) "The Production of Locality", in R. Fardon (ed.), *Counterworks: Managing the Diversity of Knowledge*. London: Routledge, pp. 204–205.

——(2000) "Grassroots Globalization and the Research Imagination", *Public Culture* 12(1): 1–19.

Appiah, Kwame (1998) "Cosmopolitan Patriots", in P. Cheah and B. Robbins (eds), *Cosmopolitics: Thinking and Feeling Beyond the Nation*. Minneapolis: University of Minnesota Press, pp. 91-116.

Axel, Brian Keith (2004) "The Context of Diaspora", *Cultural Anthropology* 19(1): 26–60.

Becker, Marc and Delgado-P., Guillermo (1998) "Latin America: The Internet and Indigenous Texts", *Cultural Survival Quarterly* 21(4). Available online: www.cultural-survival.org/publications

Bey, Hakim (2001) "Temporary Autonomous Zone", in P. Ludlow (ed.), *Crypto Anarchy, Cyberstates and Pirate Utopias*. Cambridge, MA: MIT Press, pp. 401–34.

Bowers, C. A., Vasquez, Miguel and Roaf, Mary (2000) "Native People and the Challenge of Computers: Reservation Schools, Individualism, and Consumerism", *American Indian Quarterly* 24(2): 182–200.

Brinkerhoff, Jennifer M. (2004) "Digital Diasporas and International Development: Afghan-Americans and the Reconstruction of Afghanistan", *Public Administration and Development* 24(5): 397–413.

Brysk, Alison (2000) *From Tribal Village to Global Village: Indian Rights and International Relations in Latin America*. Stanford: Stanford University Press.

Cheah, Pheung and Robbins, Bruce (eds) (1998) *Cosmopolitics: Thinking and Feeling Beyond the Nation*. Minneapolis: University of Minnesota Press.

Churchill, Ward (1996) *From a Native Son: Selected Essays in Indigenism 1985–1995*. Cambridge, MA: South End Press.

Clifford, James (1997) *Routes: Travel and Translation in the Late Twentieth Century*. Cambridge, MA: Harvard University Press.

——(2001) "Indigenous Articulations", *The Contemporary Pacific* (13)2: 468–90.

Donaghy, Keola (1998) "Olelo Hawai'i: A Rich Oral History, A Bright Digital Future", *Cultural Survival Quarterly* 21(4). Available online: www.culturalsurvival.org/publications

Downey, Sean (2001) *Ethnography of Hopi Culture and Computer Technology*. Unpublished manuscript.

Fair, R. S. (2000) "Becoming the White Man's Indian: An Examination of Native American Tribal Web Sites", *Plains Anthropologist* (45)172: 203–13.

Fandy, Mamoun (1999) "CyberResistance: Saudi Opposition Between Globalization and Localization", *Society for Comparative Study of Society and History* 41(1): 124–47.

Fink, Christina (1998) "Burma: Constructive Engagement in Cyberspace?", *Cultural Survival Quarterly* 21(4). Available online: www.culturalsurvival.org/publications

Fischer, Michael M. J. (1999) "Worlding Cyberspace: Toward a Critical Ethnography in Time, Space, and Theory", in G. Marcus (ed.), *Critical Anthropology Now: Unexpected Contexts, Shifting Constituencies, Changing Agendas*. Santa Fe: School of American Research Press, pp. 245–304.

Forsgren, Aanta (1998) "Use of Internet Communication among the Sami People", *Cultural Survival Quarterly* 21(4). Available online: www.culturalsurvival.org/publications

Ganguly, Rajat and Macduf, Ian (eds) (2003) *Ethnic Conflict and Secessionism in South and Southeast Asia: Causes, Dynamics, Solutions.* London: Sage.

Gilroy, Paul (1998) *Between Camps: Raciology and National Cultures on a Planetary Scale.* Paper presented at the Second International Crossroads in Cultural Studies Conference, Tampere, 28 June–1 July.

Hall, Martin (1999) "Virtual Colonization", *Journal of Material Culture* 4(1): 39–55.

Hanafi, Sari (2005) "Reshaping Geography: Palestinian Community Networks in Europe and the New Media", *Journal of Ethnic and Migration Studies* 31(3): 581–98.

Hiller, Harry H. and Franz, Tara M. (2004) "New Ties, Old Ties and Lost Ties: The Use of the Internet in Diaspora", *New Media and Society* 6(6): 731–52.

Hine, Christine (2000) *Virtual Ethnography.* London: Sage.

Hodgson, Dorothy L. (2002) "Introduction: Comparative Perspectives on the Indigenous Rights Movement in Africa and the Americas", *American Anthropologist* 104(4): 1037–49.

Ignacio, Emily Noelle (2000) "Ain't I a Filipino (Woman)?: An Analysis of Authorship/Authority through the Construction of 'Filipina' on the Net", *Sociological Quarterly* 41(4): 551–75.

Kalland, Arne and Persoon, Gerard (eds) (1999) *Environmental Movements in Asia.* London: Routledge/Curzon.

Kolig, Erich and Mückler, Hermann (eds) (2002) *Politics of Indigeneity in the South Pacific: Recent Problems of Identity in Oceania.* Hamburg: LIT.

Lacharite, J. (2002) "Electronic Decentralisation in China: A Critical Analysis of Internet Filtering Policies in the People's Republic of China", *Australian Journal of Political Science* 37(2): 333–46.

Landzelius, Kyra (2001) *Going Native on the 'Net: Wired Outbacks and the Digitalization of Indigeneity.* Paper presented at New Technologies and Social Welfare Symposium, 17 December, University of Nottingham.

——(2003) "Paths of Indigenous Cyber-Activism", in "Indigenous Peoples and Information Technology", Special Theme Issue: *Indigenous Affairs.* Copenhagen: International Work Group for Indigenous Affairs, 2(03): 6–13.

Ludlow, Peter (2001) "New Foundations: On the Emergence of Sovereign Cyberstates and their Governance Structures", in P. Ludlow (ed.), *Crypto Anarchy, Cyberstates and Pirate Utopias.* Cambridge, MA: MIT Press, pp. 1–23.

Martin, Pamela (2002) *The Globalization of Contentious Politics: The Amazonian Indigenous Rights Movement.* London: Routledge.

Maybury-Lewis, David (1998) "The Internet and Indigenous Groups", *Cultural Survival Quarterly* 21(4). Available online: www.culturalsurvival.org/publications

McMahon, Michael (2001) "Indigenous Cultures, Copyright and the Digital Age", *Indigenous Law Bulletin.* Available online: www.austlii.edu.au

Miller, Daniel and Slater, Don (2001) *The Internet: An Ethnographic Approach.* Oxford: Berg.

Niezen, Ronald (2003) *The Origins of Indigenism: Human Rights and the Politics of Identity.* Berkeley: University of California Press.

Parham, Angel Adams (2004) "Diaspora, Community and Communication: Internet Use in Transnational Haiti", *Global Networks: A Journal of Transnational Affairs* 4(2): 199–217.

Polly, Jean Armour (1998) "Standing Stones in Cyberspace: The Oneida Indian Nation's Territory on the Web", *Cultural Survival Quarterly* 21(4). Available online: www.culturalsurvival.org/publications

Postman, Neil (1993) *Technopoly: The Surrender of Culture to Technology*. New York: Vintage Books.

Radoll, Peter (2001) *Copyright of the Internet: Australian Indigenous Art*. Unpublished manuscript.

Ramos, Alcida Rita (1998) *Indigenism: Ethnic Politics in Brazil*. Madison: University of Wisconsin Press.

Rao, Madanmohan (2001) "E-Dinars, E-Tijara: Tunisia Embarks on Ambitious Internet Plan", *On the Internet* Jan/Feb. Available online: www.isoc.org/oti/articles

Rogers, Richard (2000) "'Internet & Society' in Armenia and Azerbaijan? Web Games and a Chronicle of an Infowar", *First Monday* 5(9). Available online: firstmonday.org/issues/issues5_9/rogers/index.html

Roulet, Florencia (1999) *Human Rights and Indigenous Peoples: A Handbook on the UN System*. Copenhagen: International Work Group for Indigenous Affairs.

Searles, Edmund (2001) *Igloos and the Internet: Reconfiguring Inuit Identity and Tradition in the Information Age*. Paper prepared for the American Ethnological Society Annual Meetings, 3–6 May, Montreal.

Shi, Yu (2005) "Identity Constructions of the Chinese Diaspora, Ethnic Media Use, Community Formation, and the Possibility of Social Activism", *Journal of Media and Cultural Studies* 19(1): 55–72.

Spoonley, Paul, Bedford, Richard and Macpherson, Cluny (2003) "Divided Loyalties and Fractured Sovereignty: Transnationalism and the Nation-State in Aotearoa/New Zealand", *Journal of Ethnic and Migration Studies* 29(1): 27–46.

Stubbs, Paul (1999) "Virtual Diaspora?: Imagining Croatia On-line", *Sociological Research Online* 4(2).

Trahant, M. N. (1996) "The Power of Stories: Native Words and Images on the Internet", *Native Americas* 13(1): 15–21.

Uimonen, Paula (2001) *Network Culture & Pioneer NGOs: Internet Frontiers of Laos, Malaysia & Geneva*. Paper presented at the International Workshop on Indigenous and Diasporic Internet Use, 8–11 June, University of Gothenburg.

Warren, Kay B. (1998) *Indigenous Movements and Their Critics: Pan-Maya Activism in Guatemala*. Princeton: Princeton University Press.

Warren, Kay B. and Jackson, Jean E. (eds) (2003) *Indigenous Movements, Self-Representation, and the State in Latin America*. Austin: University of Texas.

Weiss, Meredith L. and Hassan, Saliha (eds) (2002) *Social Movements in Malaysia: From Moral Communities to NGOs*. London: Routledge/Curzon.

Westblade, Brett (1998) *Cyber Camp: A Reflective Phenomenological Ethnographical Case Study of Visual and Auditory Enhanced On-line Communication for Remote Indigenous Community Leaders*. Unpublished manuscript.

Whitaker, Mark (2004) "Tamilnet.com: Some Reflections on Popular Anthropology, Nationalism, and the Internet", *Anthropological Quarterly* 77(3): 469–98.

Young-Ing, Greg (2003) "Perspectives on the Indigenous Tradition/New Technology Interface", in "Indigenous Peoples and Information Technology", Special Theme Issue: *Indigenous Affairs*. Copenhagen: International Work Group for Indigenous Affairs, 2(03): 14–17.

Index

A. G. Kiosk 83
Aalborg 84
Abbasid Caliph 191
Abbott, Jason 153
aboriginality 19; digital representations of 145–49; *see also* indigeneity
Aboriginal mechanism 43–44
Aboriginal Peoples of Australia 6–7, 19, 43–58, 58n3, 241, 293; and ICTs [access 48–50; development 44, 50–53; politics 53]; communities [Desert Mob 58n4; Freshwater Mob 58n4; Gurindji 47, 59n5; Kimberley Mob 58n3, 58–59n4; Pilbara Mob 59n4; Saltwater Mob 58n4]; cultures 46–47, 51; diversity 46, 51; governance 43–46, 51–55, 62 [Office of Aboriginal Economic Development, Aboriginal Health, and Aboriginal Education 53]; history under colonialism 45–47; households 7; language groups 46, 51 [Bardi-Jawi 58n4; Gidja 58n4; Nyul-Nyul 58n4]; leadership 44, 46, 50, 58n8; lifeways 7, 46; literacy 8; media 50; politics of place [Aboriginal and Torres Strait Islanders Commission 53; Native Title 59n8; *Statement of Commitment to a Just Relationship* 53]; rights 47; self-determination movements 47, 55–58; workers 58n5; *see also* Australia, Outback Digital Network, Stolen Generations
Aboriginal Peoples of Canada 7–8, 61–78; and ICTs [access 67–68, 72; links 68; usage 66–68]; and e-health 68–76 [as thing vs. environment 72–75; ownership of 68, 70–74]; demographics 62; governance 63–64; health [and infant mortality rates 64; inequities 61–66, 69; statistics 64–65; status 7, 61, 64, 69; surveys 64–65, 69]; healthcare [Indian Health Policy 65; National Aboriginal Health Organization 69; Nunee Health Authority 71; providers 64–66, 68–71; traditional 61, 65–66, 69–76]; history under colonialism 62–64; politics of place [Constitution Act 64; Indian Acts 62, 64; Royal Proclamation 63; White Paper 63–64]; self-determination struggles 63–64; *see also* Canada, First Nations, Inuit, Métis, Smart Communities Aboriginal Project(s)
abortion 231–32; as online discussion topic 26, 164, 228–29, 231, 275
academic(s) 105, 133, 146, 203, 278; authority 278, 285; circles 202; institutions 99, 106–7, 133, 135, 155–56, 188, 245, 256, 284; literature 242; productions 282–84; Third-World 284
activism 104, 126, 193, 227–28; costs 126–28; cyber-2, 5–16, 19, 23, 99, 104, 107, 122–24, 239, 243, 256, 293, 300; environmental 16, 89, 109n7, 112–29, 246, 292; online 36n15, 108, 244, 253; *push-button* 123; social 301n6
activist(s) 5, 15, 35n8, 100, 107, 109n6, 113, 118, 120, 125, 133, 145, 202, 238, 294; animal-rights' 204, 210, 216; assassination of 117; Burundian woman 230; cyber-15, 107, 200, 239, 257; embodied 107, 118; electronic chain of 107; feminist 107, 110n10; feral 202; First World 122; grassroots 15, 17, 105, 112, 116–20; militant 99, 112–29; potential 123; serious fun of 301n1; social 109n7; street 117, 239–40; Third World 196; web 123, 144, 189, 227, 242–43; youth 228

Africa 2, 137, 202, 207–9, 212, 222; coast
  of 207–8 [gold 216n6]; continent 300;
  as dumping ground 205, 207; generic
  209; returning to 208–9; views of 205–
  8
African(s) 147n4, 176–77, 180, 208–10,
  232; atrocities upon 207; diaspora 208;
  websites 176; wildlife 204
African-American(s): and employment
  209; as heritage tourists 209; in Back to
  Africa movement 208–9, 216n6
Age of Discovery 20, 44
agriculture 171; farming 120, 178, 229
  [and farmers 221]
aid: communications 147n1; foreign 152,
  210, 262; funds 268; mutual 74; of
  supporters [for U'wa 114; for Zapatistas
  98]
Akoto, Francis 202–3
Al-Aqsa Intifada 239, 242–43, 249; see
  also Palestine
Alaska 88–89, 94n5n6, 144
Alcoff, Linda 279
Ali, Muhammad 216n7
alienation(s) 1, 20, 22; cultural 233; over-
  coming 27; resistance to 91
Allah 179
Allen, Stuart 269n5
Almarales, Beryl 138
Al-Rasheed, Madawi 195
alterity 2, 19, 126, 297
Álvarez, President Luis Echevarría 108n3
Alvarez, Sonia 129n1
Amazon 16, 112–29; peoples of 18, 112,
  117; see also rainforest
America(s) 2, 138, 147, 172, 179, 197,
  238, 245, 261, 300; Central 142; North
  36n12, 63, 88, 138, 147, 172, 175–79,
  181, 183n8, 193, 203, 256, 263; South
  138, 142, 147
America-Israel Public Affairs Committee
  (AIPAC) 243
American(s) 177, 202, 207, 212, 214, 225,
  232, 250–51; aid 262; military 260,
  262; see also United States of America
American Colonization Society 216n6
American Red Cross 245
Amerindian(s) 132–47; ancestry 136–37,
  140, 143; Carib(s) 18–19, 132–34;
  cultural heritage 137–38; extinction
  18, 132–36, 142–47 [vs. survival claims
  18, 132–36, 142–47]; (re)engineering
  132, 138, 146–47, 298; tribes in

Guyana 133; website(s) 135; see also
  Santa Rosa Carib Community,
  Taino(s)
Amerindian Peoples Association 133–34
Amerindian Trail 134
Amharic 171, 182n2
Ammassalik 89
Amnesty International 190
ancestor(s) 98, 112–16, 140–41, 180, 224
Anderson, Benedict 182, 187, 211
animal(s) 117, 204–7; feral 205 [case of
  pigs 205; case of rabbits 205]; figures
  144; husbandry 205; rights [activists
  204, 210; organization 25]
annihilation 195; collective 121, 124; self-
  118, 122
anthropology/anthropologies 4, 11, 270n8,
  292; and its subjects 36n16, 277; and
  taboos [against going native 4, 31–33,
  36–37n17]; as object of critique 36n16,
  37n17; at home 36n16; auto-36n16; in
  cyberspace 30; metareflexive turn 29–
  30, 36n16; pioneers of 292; textbooks
  11; see also ethnography
anthropologist(s) 2, 30, 37n17, 92, 195,
  216n9, 256, 267, 273, 275–76, 285;
  cyber-29, 31–33; in reverse 285; native
  3, 36n16; Scandinavian 37n17; semi-
  nomadic 81
Aotearoa 47
Apostolic Church 187
Appadurai, Arjun 3, 175, 211, 296
Arab(s) 176, 186, 193, 198, 252; and Iraqi
  Assyrians 193–99; and Iraqi Turcomans
  192; civilization 193; conquests 193,
  196, 198; countries 27; dress 242; environment 192; websites 27, 176, 191,
  240, 244; youth 27
Arab American Institute 193, 198
Arabic language 175, 191, 197
Arafat, Yasser 26, 243, 251–52
Arawak peoples 143
architectonic constructions 84
Arctic 2, 7, 12, 63, 67, 80–81, 88–93,
  93n3, 94n5, 94n6, 94n7, 296
Arima 136; Borough Council of 136–37
Armenia 191
army/armies 191, 225; Abbasid historical
  191; Amhara 170; chimp 209; Harari
  170, 182; Hutu militia 222; Israeli 252;
  Liberation Tigers of Tamil Eelam 255,
  260; national 224; of India 260; of
  Mexico 108n6 [revolutionary 99,

108n2; Zapatista 108n4, 109n6]; Sri Lankan 261–67 [officer(s) 262, 266; uniforms 266]; Turcoman 192; Tutsi 222–25; US 266; *see also* military, war

ARPAnet (Advanced Research Projects Agency Network) 241

art(s) 140, 167n10; and resistance movements 245–46; and street murals 245; computer-generated 295; graffiti 245–46; indigenous 9, 11, 35n7, 295, 300; life imitating 36n12; public 245–46; shop 266; traditional 295

artifact(s) 8, 300; cultural 30; technological 76

artificial intelligence (AI): lab 241; pioneer 241

Arusha 236n2

Ashcroft, Bill 288n1

Asia 300; Central 187; *see also* South Asia

Asian Human Rights Commission 269n4

assassination(s) 193; in post-colonial Burundi 221–22; of American activists in Colombia 117; of Assyrian political leaders 190; of Dharmeratnam P. Sivaram 268–69; of leading witness in massacre trial 253n3; of Neelan Tiruchelvan 261; of Prince Louis Rwagasore 225; of Richard de Zoysa 261; of Zapata 108n2; targeted 238

assimilation 62–63, 177, 183n9, 191–92; cultural 233, 286; forced 35n11, 171, 192; of diverse histories 186; policy 59n6; refusal of 194; voluntary 192

Assyrian(s) 24, 187–201; activism 193; as indigenous Christians 193–94, 198; civilization 24, 189, 193–96; émigrés 197; ethnic groups [Chaldeans 193–94; Maronites 193, 198; Syriacs 193–94]; history 187, 193–96; homeland 187, 194; ideological renaissance 24, 197; internal conflict 194; language 194; nation 199 [-building 296]; political parties [Assyrian Democratic Movement (Zowaa) 193–95, 199; Assyrian Democratic Organization (Mtakasta) 194–95, 198]; national agenda 189, 193–95; refugees 197; websites 187–88, 193–200 [*Assyria Online* 200n11; *Assyrian Forum* 196–97; *Zinda* 197, 200n6]; *see also* Iraq

Assyrian Empire 198

Assyrian International News Agency 190, 193–94

Assyrian National Church 195

Assyrian Orthodox Church 187

Assyrian Triangle 187

Atlanta 172

audience(s) 16, 71, 159, 200n7, 284; and truth questions 277; cyber-21; disembodied 106; global 268 [potentially 12]; intended 157, 161; internet 161, 285; literate vs. consuming 211; meta-consciousness about 37n18; national 134; reaching 47, 268 [electronically 2; new 196]; target 244, 255; virtual 11

audiotape(s) 256

Australia 2, 6–7, 43–60, 152, 172, 193, 203, 205, 217n12; founding [Act of Federation 46]; government(s) of [conservatives 59n8; Liberal Party 59n8]; National Census 46; politics vis-à-vis Aboriginal residents [Arbitration Commission 47, 59n5; Department of Aboriginal Affairs 53; Northern Territory Land Rights Act 59n5; White Australia Policy 46, 59n6]; regions of [Adelaide 52; Barkley 49; Brisbane 52; Broome 53; Bungle-Bungle Ranges 52–53; Cape York 52, 55; Fitzroy Plateau 52; Great Sandy Desert 52; Kakadu National Park 52; Kimberley 43, 48, 52–53, 58, 58n3, 58n4; New South Wales 52; Perth 52; Pilbara 48, 53, 58, 58n3; Queensland 49; Sydney 52; Tanami 49, 52; Top End of Northern Territory 52, 59n5, 59n8; Uluru 52]; Research Council 166n2; Union movement 59n5; *see also* Aboriginal Peoples of Australia

Austria 197

authenticity 13, 19, 32, 113, 124, 129n3, 143, 145, 166, 285; and language 155, 161, 164; contests over 115–16, 133; defense of 23, 35n7, 145–47; performances of 18, 91; *see also* V.E.R.A.city loop

Azerbaijan 189, 191

Azeri: groups on the net 191; hackers 301n1:-influenced Turkish dialect 187

Babylonia 197

Back to Africa movement 208–10, 216n6; as online discussion topic 208–10

Baghdad 191–92

Bahaman: claims to be 212

Bangladesh 274

Baranyanka: sons of 225
Barazani, Massoud 200n3
Bastian, Hilda 75
Bayn al-nahrayn 197
Bedouin 22, 241
Beirut 253n3
Belausteguigoitia, Marisa 15, 97, 295
Belgian(s) 225; colonialism 221; courts 253n3; monarchy 221
Belgium 253n3
Bell, David 34n3
Benhabib, Seyla 127
Bentham, Jeremy 56
Bet-Nahrain 190, 194, 197
Bey, Hakim 298
Bharath, Ricardo 136–38, 141
Bhattacharjee, Anannya 289n5
Bhutan 274
bin Laden, Osama 178
body/bodies 101, 104–5, 113, 116, 216, 243; and events in the flesh 99, 102; and voice 103–4; and speed inter-change 104; as weapon 112, 116, 123–24, 249; colonial 208; eco-112, 118; geographical 112; inscribed with home-land 181–82; internet interception of 103; legislative 65; native 103, 113, 116–18, 124, 285; of abducted jour-nalist 268–69; of activists 112, 118, 238; of earth 112, 119; of indigenous women 101; of soldiers 251; of suicide bomber 249; of the nation 104; of text 194;-politic 23–25, 112, 116 [of medicine 74]; on the line 128; repre-sentative organizational 54, 137, 141; virtual 128, 145
Bogotá 118
bombing(s): by Tamil separatists 261; Dolphinarium suicide 248–49; of Iraq 197; over Lockerbie 178
border(s) 35, 169; absence of 197 [for virtual communities 212–13]; across 170 [relationships 210]; and electronic frontier 170, 242; checkpoint(s) 238, 251; disputes 171; ideological 245;-lands 210; national 153–54, 170, 177, 211; of modernity 97; patrolling 174; state 9, 97, 99, 186, 205, 248, 301n5 [crossing 20; demarcated 212]; tech-nology 99; thinking strategies 97, 110n12; zone(s) 119, 247
Borrero, Chief Roberto Mucaro 141
Boscoe, Madeline 75

boundary/boundaries: and space 80–81; cyberspace 277; international 214; maintaining 120, 180;-markers online 37n18, 91–92; of code 242; of tradition 21; territorial 119–20, 269
Bransfjell, Nora 294
Bray, Hiawatha 217n10
Brazil 105
Britain 261; *see also* England, United Kingdom
British: annexation of Australia 45, 47; colonialism 45, 63; corporations 122, 129n4;-Dutch conglomerate 129n4; military 260, 262; monarchy 63; news-papers 117; North American Act 62; Parliament 64; protectorate 152; widow 205
British Petroleum Corporation 122
Browning, Barbara 208
Bruner, Edward M. 209
Buddhist 255
Burma 274
Burmese: in exile 36n15; regime 301n5
Burton, Sir Richard 183n5
Burundi 26, 220–37; and human rights struggles 232; and national reconstruc-tion 227, 235; Bururi region of 223–25; civil war 220–27, 235; ethnic groups of 221, 224; government(s) of 229 [and legitimacy 224; colonial 221; future 228; Ganwa monarchy 221]; history 221–22, 224; independence 221, 225–26; invasions of 224; National Assembly 229; opposition party 235n1; third world within 223; women's status in 228–31, 236; *see also Burundi Youth Council*, Burundian(s), *Burundinet*
Burundi Youth Council (BYC) 26, 220–36; as alternative forum 235; as internet community 222; discussion threads [conservative vs. liberal 232–33; on gender 229–31; on sexual orientation 229, 231–33; on women's rights 229–31]; goals 228; netiquette 221, 227; member-participant(s) 227–35 [demo-graphics 227; executives 227–29, 232–33; founding 227; resident in Burundi 220; resident in the West 220]; Peace Summit 222
Burundian(s) 37n18, 220–27, 235; cultural heritage 232–33, 235; politicians 228, 235; traditional sayings 226, 228; *see also* Hutu/Tutsi, Twa

Burundinet (*B-net*) 26, 28, 220–27, 233–
35; participant *B-netters* 223–26 [in
Burundi 220; in diaspora 220];
membership 220

Cabrales, Orlando 129n4
calendar(s): Christian 179; Gregorian 179;
Muslim 179
cameras 264
Canada 7–8, 10, 35n12, 61–78, 94n6,
134, 138, 153, 176, 178, 182n1, 193;
and ICTs [Community Access
Program 67; SchoolNet 67];
Department of the Interior 62;
Ministry of Health 65; National
Forum on Health 74; Special Forces
179; *see also* Aboriginal Peoples of
Canada, e-health
Canadian Women's Network 75
capital 208, 215, 286; financial 296; global
240; political 296
capitalism 45, 114, 205, 211, 298; digital
274; electronic-211–12; predilections
of 35n8; print-211
Caribbean 138, 208, 212; diasporic 133;
region 132–47
Caribbean Amerindian Centrelink
(CAC) 135
Caribbean Organization of Indigenous
Peoples 132
Carranza, Venustiano 108n2
Castells, Manuel 59n7, 152, 166
Catholic Church 49, 108n3, 187
censorship 23, 227–28, 235, 262, 264,
269n5, 301n5; absence of 235; by colonial history 116; free from 27; in online
forums 163, 166; *see also* freedom
center(s), *see* periphery
ceremony/ceremonies 138, 266; and
festival(s) 11, 140, 167n5, 174, 209,
238; marriage 275; *potlatch* 62; *pow-
wows* 18, 140, 142; sundance 62
Chaldean Church 187
chat(s) 22, 27, 29, 32, 85, 244–45, 253n1,
296; and privacy question 29; applications 217n16, 246;-rooms 4, 144, 156,
167n6, 167n7, 195–98, 239, 261–62;
sites 1, 21–22, 24; *see also* discussion
forum(s)
Chavakacheri 255–56
Cherokee: ICT projects 10
Chiapas 15, 97, 109n6, 110n10, 110n12
Chicanos 105

child/children 7, 46, 59n6, 62, 71, 82–83,
93, 102, 117, 152, 158, 161, 173–76,
180–82, 205, 209, 229, 238–40, 244,
251; abuse 164; of Harar 180; poster
122, 125, 129;-rearing practices 164;
soldiers 269n7; *see also* family, parents
chimpanzee(s) (chimps) 25, 202–10, 215–
16; and African homeland 209; and
discourses of ferality 205–6; army 209;
burger 206; Ghanaian wild 206; repatriation 203–10, 215–16, 296 [from
zoos and circuses 204, 206]; saga 204,
215–16; squad 206
Christensen, Neil Blair 8, 12, 80, 296
Christian(s) 171, 196–97, 268; Abyssinian
170; Assyrian 187, 195; in the Middle
East 197; Ethiopian 181; calendar 179;
ministry 179; nationalists in Ethiopia
171; non-147n7; superstition 179
Christianity 108n3, 187, 195, 198; *see also*
Christian(s)
church(es): in Tongan society 158, 164;
Palestinian 240; services for Hutu/Tutsi
222
Church of the East 187, 195
Cisler, Steve 133
citizen(s) 181, 234–35; Australian 43–47
[indigenous vs. non 55]; Burundi 228;
Caribbean 137; European 46; in
cyberspace 211; Lomarian virtual
36n12, 214; mainstream 1; modern 57,
141; of Colombia 119–21; of iGhana
202, 211–13; of Iraq 186, 192; of
Mexico 99, 105; of the metropolis 121;
of the US 178; of Western countries
213; participation of 68, 76, 93n5, 99;
rights 98; second-class 240
citizenship 36n12, 46, 97, 172, 200, 213;
as online discussion topic 217n12; non-
territorial 214; subaltern 126
city/cities: center 215, 238, 242, 248–49,
255; ancient 183n5; children of 180–
82; disputes over 192; of the
Eurocenter 204;-state 170; streets 249;
walls 172; *see also* urban
civil: disobedience 124; liberties 194;
society 103–4, 215, 300
civilization(s) 113–15, 124, 196, 200;
Arab 193; Assyrian 189, 193, 195, 198;
Mesopotamian 196; online 196;
Turcoman 189
civilizing mission 35n11, 46, 115, 206;
failures of 205

class 97, 105, 188, 203, 288, 288n2; and
educational equity 229; and socioeconomic background 162; and
subjectivity 274; bourgeoisie 216n5,
234; differentials among diasporists
203; feminist coalitions across 279;
Hararis as affluent 170–72; lines 99;
lower 203; middle 98, 106, 139, 203,
212, 217n16; online [masking 259;
reproducing 37n18]; under 216n4;
upper 139, 183n9, 203, 279; working-
204
Cleaver, Harry 101, 109n6
Clemmer, Richard O. 113–14
Clifford, James 92, 173–74, 280
clothes: ethnic 275 [khafiyyas 238; sarong
256]; traditional 101, 138, 145, 181; t-
shirts 109n9; used 207
code(s) 104, 239, 253; boundaries of 242;
building 53; mainstream 294, 299; of
conduct 227; open source 241; propri-
etary 241;-switching 37n18
Coalition of American Assyrians and
Maronites (CAM) 197
Colombia 16, 112–31; government(s) of
112, 116–23, 128; National Indigenous
Organization of 112–13; rebel groups of
117, 119; regions of [El Cocuy National
Park 118; Samore 118–19, 122, 125,
129n4]; see also U'wa
Colombian: Minister of Environmental
Affairs 123; Minister of Mines 129n4;
peoples 112, 119 [Open Letter to 117,
120]; resource nationalization 119;
venture 129n4
Colombo 255, 263, 266–67, 269
colonial: administrators 45, 53, 208; atrocities 25; discourses 278, 286;
domination 205; era 46 [experiments
205; legacies 59n7]; expansion 45, 205;
expeditions 207; institutions 51, 87;
invasion 224; language 25; locales 17;
master 225; rule 45, 63, 93n2, 113,
142, 221; typologizing 207–8; see also
postcolonial
colonialism 10, 25, 45, 57, 98, 115, 133,
143, 205, 221, 225; and enforced de-
traditionalization 35n11; and
modernity 211; agents of 225–26; as
online discussion topic 208; recast 10,
25; neo-10, 25, 27, 29, 113, 210, 297
colonization 45, 52, 62, 152, 170; de-225;
of the lifeworld 259; virtual 36n14

Columbus, Christopher 144
Comandante Esther 101, 110n11, 110n12
Comandante Ramona 110n11
Comandante Susana 110n11
Comandante Yolanda 110n11
Come, Chief M. Coon 8, 35n9
communication(s) 6, 44, 53, 67, 87–88,
94, 102, 105, 145, 159, 175, 235, 284,
287, 294; and agency 216; barriers 161
233, 283 [across 221, 223, 233]; fields
211; global 90, 153; inter-diasporic
176; mode 20–21, 43, 103–4, 156, 163,
174; see also information-communications technologies
communicative: action 234, 258, 270n8
communism 35n8
community/communities: autonomy 192;-
building 173, 296; defense of 154;
development 70; dispersed 154–55,
169–73, 182; emigrant 286; hacker-
defacer underground 239, 242, 244,
247; in global terms 69–70; notion of
52, 92; online 275–89; remote 43, 48–
50, 56, 60n10, 64, 76n1, 292; simu-
lacrum of 135; see also virtual
compatriots 25, 197; in diaspora 288
computer(s) 7–8, 11, 49, 57, 69, 81, 86,
93n5, 99, 118, 139, 152–54, 165,
183n8, 211, 217n16, 239, 258–59,
263–65; crisis 178; culture 241; enemy
[sabotage of 27, 36n14]; languages [C
246; Hypertext Markup Language
(HTML) 245, 259, 265; Java 214;
JavaScript 246]; literacy 36n14, 69,
100, 156, 211; networking 2, 213–14,
217n16, 294; operating systems 242–
44 [Linux 214, 241; UNIX 241, 246];
passwords 241; programming 214;
resources 7, 49, 99, 108n6, 139; scientists 256; scripts 239, 244; security
241; skills 27, 49, 69, 108, 244; software 167n8, 267, 293, 295 [engineers
263; free 85]; translations 244;
training 7–8, 70; users 72, 211,
217n10, 250 [in Mexico 99;
Trinidadian 139, 217n17; women 97,
105–10]; see also information-commu-
nication technology
computer-mediated communication(s)
18–19, 29–31, 97, 100, 152–53, 156,
163, 166n3, 167n8, 233–34, 300–301;
acronyms in 156; emoticons in 156;
equalization phenomenon 233

conflict 13–14, 27, 32, 54, 89, 133, 189, 235, 262, 293; Burundian 220–29; diagnosing 220–21; in Ghanaian chimp saga 203; online [and flaming 36n13; and offline dynamics 36n13, 293]; Palestinian-Israeli 36n13, 238–54 [cyberspatial periphery of 249]; resolution 26, 223, 226–27, 230, 297 [and ethnicity 26, 220; hindrances to 230; internet as resource in 220–21, 255]; Sri-Lankan 28, 255–71, 295; Taino 148n10; U'wa-Oxy 112–30; zones 36n16

Congreso Nacional Indígena 110n10

consumer(s): advertising 259; empowering 75 [via health informatics 74–75]; First World 112; goods 178; of media [vs. *participants* 252]; public 298

Consumer Network (of the Cochrane collaboration) 74–75

Coombs, Nugget 43–44

Copenhagen 81

corporation(s) 89, 113–17, 122, 125, 265, 297–98; media 49, 58n2, 85, 202, 252, 265; national [in Greenland 85, 93n2]; petroleum 122, 125–26, 129n4; *see also* Occidental Petroleum Corporation

cosmology 11, 16, 114, 118, 146, 293; Taino 144; U'wa 120

crime(s) 26, 129n2, 225, 250, 253n3

Croats 225

Crosby, Alfred W. 205

Crown Lands 59n5, 59n8

Cruzado, Juan Carlos Martínez 142

Crystal, David 153

Cuba 142, 204

cultural: displays 117–18, 132–47; dissonance 294; divides 296; expression 194, 280; heritage 232 [victims of 280]; homogeneity 289n5; hybridity 210; logic 2, 121, 130; privileges 195; relativism 233; revitalization 9, 19, 132, 136–38, 152, 200, 298; rights 188, 192–94

Cultural Survival Quarterly (journal) 34n5, 129n1

culture(s): and language 152–68; and space 214; computer 214; concepts of 36–37n16; cyber 214, 217n16; dead 241; diasporist 175–76; dominant 21, 162, 294; hacker 241–42; material 143; popular 100; predicament of 36n16;

traditional 13, 21, 43–53, 61, 70, 101, 231; writing against 36n16

cyberspace: and freedom vs. tyranny 295; and imagining 212, 253; and safety 26, 294; and status 37n18; as abstract organism 90; as field site 31–32, 165, 292; as home 296; centrifugal character of 107; cultural dynamics of 273–74, 288; demythologizing 34n2; gaining presence via 33, 155, 190, 193; giving voice to the silenced 103–5, 152, 163–66, 287; hackers as original occupants of 240; letting off steam in 198; lure of 286; impersonal arena of 176; political economy of 273–74, 288; visions of 81, 85, 90, 93n4, 159–61 [utopian vs. dystopic 34n2, 90]; worlding 3, 17, 27, 30, 293

DNA 142; and genetic continuity 142

Dallas 172

Daluwatte, General Rohan 266

Dances with Wolves (film) 118

Danish: colonial powers 93n2; language 82–83, 91; Kingdom 85, 93n2; Royal Arctic Line 82 [*Irena Arctica* 82]

data 136; collection 35n7, 73–74, 82, 222, 244–45, 279; ethnographic 20, 35n7, 136, 222–23, 232, 253n1; health 68; OCAP (ownership, control, access and possession) 70–71, 74, 76; management 56–57, 69; online 136, 222; production 136, 232; transmission 61

David and Goliath 114

Dávila, Arlene 141

death(s) 49, 114; due to injury 64; in Nigeria 129n4; plunge 115; squads 261; to native lifeways 112; toll in Sri Lanka 258; with dignity 116; *see also* victim(s)

Debord, Guy 116

defacer(s), *see* hacker(s)

Delhi 260, 267

Delphis, Ltd. 134

democracy 104, 127, 173, 183n7, 191, 215, 224, 233–34; banner of 194; digital 26, 233–34; lifeworld of 128; putative 205; real-world 234

democratization 89, 273

Denmark 84, 88, 93n2; and Danes 94n6; government(s) of [Home Rule government 85, 93–94n5; Social Democratic Party of 83]; *see also* Greenland

development(s): agencies 53, 210; and
reconstruction 235, 301n6; community
49, 70; cultural 132, 241; economic 49,
89, 98; ICT 7, 47, 49–56, 94n5, 297
[implications of 56]; infrastructural 48–
50; political 109, 116, 119, 122, 193,
215; politics of 229; rhetoric of 130n9,
208; schemes 50–52, 55, 117, 130n9,
210, 235; technological 76, 147n
De Waal, Alex 182n2
diaspora(s) 20–24, 209–10, 299; and
embodied map-making 299; and idealized return 169, 173; and identity 19–
20, 141, 299; and nostalgia 29, 181
[discourses of 286]; African 177, 208;
Assyrians in 24, 186–87, 193–200;
Caribbean 133; contexts of 286; digital
29, 272–89 [and power 288]; discourses
of 19–20, 29; from Ethiopia 169,
182n3; Ghanaians in 25, 202–16, 296;
global 169, 173, 246; Goans in 154;
Hararis in 169–85; Hindu 288n3; Hutu
and Tutsi in 26, 220–37, 297; idea of
169; Indians in 91, 288n3; Iranians in
21; Iraqis in 188–201; Jewish 182n3;
Kurds in 23; Muslim 288n3; paradox of
173; Sikh 288n3; South Asian 288n3
[digital 272; women in 272–89, 296];
Tongans in 21, 152–68, 296; Tamils in
256, 260–64, 288n3; Turcomans in 24,
186–87, 190–200; virtual 20–22, 293;
Western 175; see also return
digital divide 211 [crossing 6–8, 211–12,
215, 294]
Digital Equipment Corporation 202
Dire Dawa 171
discourse(s): about indigenous presence
137; analysis 147, 278; and identity
275, 278–79, 299; anti-racist 106,
110n11; anti-sexist 110n11; colonial
278, 286, 288n1; dominant 282 [chal-
lenging 234, 282]; epidemiological 205,
207–8; everyday 259; feminist 107,
278; global 110n11; hegemonic 246;
internationally-mediated 247; Muslim
181; nationalist 87, 182, 278; non-male
270n8; non-Western 270n8; nostalgic
286; of community-building 296; of
cultural exchange 208; of diaspora 19–
20, 29; of disease 207–8; of ethnicity
227; of exploitation 208; of indigeneity
146–47; of invasion 205; of Marcos
100; of modernity 104; of racism 205;

of sexuality 208; of Western individual
rights 231; online transformation of
220–21, 233–35, 282–83; political 203,
235; public 258–59; trumped by fear
259
discrimination 22, 105–7; and cultural
traditions 101, 235; against homosexuals 231–32; against women 106–8,
229–31; economic 47; racial 48
discussion forum(s) 139, 144, 154–66, 169,
174, 195–99, 202–19, 220–35; archives
286, 289n8; bulletin board(s) 144,
167n5, 220, 227, 285; democratic
nature of 215; expulsion from 212;
hermeneutic risk of 292–93; Usenet 91,
243, 285–86, 301n5; women-only
217n17, 274–80; see also chat
disease(s) 25, 64–65, 98, 129n3, 206–8;
cancer 207; diabetes 64; rates 64;
tuberculosis 64; see also health
displacement 20, 46, 98, 100, 108n6, 169,
174, 222, 240, 299; antidote to 20;
legacy of 18
dispossession 35n11, 109n7
distance learning 8, 9, 19, 56, 89
Divide et Impera 225
Dodge, Martin 34n3
Doheny-Farina, Steven 145
Dome of the Rock 239, 249
Dominica: Community of Caribs 133–34,
138, 147n1; internet portal [A Virtual
Dominica 134]
Dominican: émigré 134
dot.com: planet 21; industry 56; resistance
123
Downey, Sean 301n4
D'Souza, Dinesh 216n7
Dybbroe, Susanne 92

e-centres 67; First Nation [in Deer Lake
67; Fort Severn 67; Keewaywin 67;
McDowell Lake 67; North Spirit Lake
67; Popular Hill 67]
e-colleague 287
e-commerce 8–9
e-groups 166n3
e-health 61–78, 295; and training 76n1; as
extension 72–75; as innovation 72–75;
economic benefits of 76n1; governance
[Advisory Council on Health
Infostructure 68; Canada Health
Infostructure 68; First Nations and
Inuit Health Information System

(FNIHIS) 69, 71, 74]; in Fort Chipewyan 70–71, 74 [televisitation with Fort McMurray 71; videoconferencing therapy 70]; patients 7, 66, 68, 70–73; projects 69 [Baffin Health Network 69; Federal/Provincial/ First Nations Telehealth Project 69; *Ikajuruti Inungnik Ungasiktumi* Network 69; *Keewaytinok Okimakanak* Telehealth Project 69; Mental Health Evaluation and Community Consultation Unit 69; National Native Addictions Information Management System 69, 75; National Native American HIV/ AIDS Integrated Services Network 76; Nova Scotia Telehealth Network 69; SLICK – Screen for Limbs, I-Sight, Cardiovascular and Kidney Complications Using Mobile Diabetes Clinics 69]; telemedicine aspects 7–9, 56, 61 [electronic patient records 61, 68, 71, 73–75; videoconferencing 70, 74]; *see also* medicine
e-justice 8, 19
e-learning, *see* distance learning
e-nation 25, 36n12, 202, 210–14; *see also* nation
e-voting 7, 9
earth: body of 119; landmass 34n6 [and indigenous peoples 34n6]; March of the Color of 101; mother 112, 119–20; protection of 124; riches of 119; stewardship of 120–21
East: the 284
Ebonics 162–63; *see also* English
economy: and culture 274; and neo-liberalism 210; and social space 90; and values 58; Ghanaian 204–5; global 58; information 52, 54, 58; local 10, 298; market 35n11; Mexican 97–102; of Harar [as online discussion topic 182]; Tongan 152; peasant 98–99; rationalization of Australian 49; political [of culture 274; of cyberspace 288]; regional 298; wage 89
ecumene 36n16
education 1, 7, 9, 14, 35n11, 46, 89, 158, 220; and indigenous peoples [in Australia 48–50, 56; in Canada 63; in Mexico 98]; health 71; levels [among Tongans 155, 158, 172; in Greenland 93n5]; mandatory 63; postcolonial 286; and women [Burundian 229; Mexican

indigenous 106; South Asian diasporic 279]; *see also* literacy
Eickelman, Dale 181
elders 7, 10, 71, 155, 160, 165, 169–70, 176, 181, 227, 240, 266
election(s) 53–54, 108n6, 183n7, 204, 215–16, 223, 250, 260, 266; and cybertechnology 215
electricity 6, 59n8, 156, 178
electronic: communications 155, 212, 235, 246, 283 [and access to anthropologist 32; and interaction 75, 89, 211]; cowboys 242; espionage 294; generation of reality 144; network(s) 77n2; newsletters 144, 220; promotion 145; spaces 284
Electronic Library (journal) 34n5
elite(s) 29, 45, 57, 93n2, 94n7, 112, 139, 152, 165, 177, 191, 202, 234, 257, 266, 279; domestic vs. diasporic 203, 210, 215; hackers 244; indigenous 59n6; *see also* leaders
Elkins, A.P. 51
Elkins, David 153, 155, 166n1
email(s) 1, 5, 139, 144, 147n1, 156, 166n1, 174, 188, 227, 245–248, 250, 264, 284–85, 294; addresses 82, 222, 233, 245, 250; discussion lists 166n3, 169–70, 175, 243, 272, 274–89, 289n6, 289n9 [moderating 272; speaking on 277]; jamming 36n13; interviews 244–45; petitions 123; resistance 113; sharing offline 170
emancipation 298; from domestic drudgery 16; question of 297–98 [in cyberspace 37n18]; noble savage as 122–23
émigré(s)/emigrant(s) 134, 197, 181, 204, 210, 279; identity 170, 279, 286; communities 286; cross-border relationships 210; men as first-wave 174; would-be 36n12; *see also* migrants
employment 47–50, 59n5, 98, 209; un-48; *see also* jobs
empowerment 1, 15–17, 50, 61, 66, 72–74, 280, 295, 297–301; calculating 298; dis-274; of ethnographic participants 273; of subaltern voices 274, 280–81; online 285; *see also* self-determination
England 84; *see also* Britain, United Kingdom
English language 82–83, 109n6, 169, 191, 203, 244, 262–63; and code-switching 21, 23, 37n18, 82, 91, 153–54, 159–63,

222; big 204, 216n4; black 162; dictionary 206; dominance question 153–54; fluency 244, 263; Ghanian 216n5; newspapers 257; press 261;-speaking publics 153, 262

enslavement 46, 114, 209; *see also* slave(s)

environment(s) 52, 58n4, 63, 92, 124, 157, 174, 178, 181, 183, 241, 269, 280; and indigenous peoples [conflation of 129–30n6, 241]; as obstacle to development 7, 48; bioreserve 108n3; destruction of 10, 117, 128, 297; issues regarding 44, 48, 53, 119; protection of 295; science of 113

epidemiology 205, 207–8

equality 64, 76; in living standards 300; of wages 59n5; struggles for 97; *see also* inequality

Eritrea 171

Escobar, Arturo 129n1

Eskimo(s) 89, 93n3

ethics: environmental 129n6; fieldwork 30, 136, 273; local 11; of hacking 241; of informed consent 70, 273; of oil exploitation 117; of representation 29, 30, 36n16, 272–73, 281

Ethiopia 22, 170–83; and diaspora 182n3; Battle of Chelenko 182; ethnic groups of [Amharas 170, 183n6; Argobbas 183n6; Eritreans 183n6; Gurage 183n6; Oromos 183n6; Tigrayans 183n6]; government(s) of 169–73 [Dergue 169–70, 173, 182n2; Provisional Military Council 182n2]

Ethiopian(s) 169, 177, 182n2; political parties [Oromo Liberation Front 183n7]; revolutionary forces 169

Ethiopian Orthodox Church 171

ethnicity 98, 101, 126, 153, 166n1, 172, 183n6, 188, 199, 205, 226, 228, 234; and clan differentiation 221; and marriage 186; as fluid process 221; as political tool 228; claims 14, 16; debates about 233; explosive potential 26, 221, 223, 227; online [masking 233; pan-94n7]; mixed 228; naming 4, 19, 22; negotiating 187–88, 195; notions of 136; question of 221, 228, 232; victimization based on 227; *see also* indigenous, race

ethnographer(s) 32, 147, 281; auto-17; authority of 287 [disrupting 284]; cyber-297; feminist 281 [postcolonial 288]; native 29, 284; online 33, 136, 275 [challenges facing 146–47, 252–53, 253n2, 274]; *see also* anthropologist(s)

ethnographic: first encounters 292; governing telos 30; indeterminacy 30; methodology 3, 135–36, 147, 240, 244, 272–73 [and virtual ethnography challenges 27, 30–33, 175, 217n12, 222–23, 253n2, 273, 277, 288n3, 292; participant observation 135–36, 175, 273, 283–85, 292]; particularity 2; productions 284 [as invasion of privacy 285; as political act 282; sharing of 275–76, 278, 284; transparency regarding 36n16]; snapshot(s) 292; study 132, 171, 259, 272–73; subjects 29, 273

ethnography 245, 263, 272, 296–97; auto-11; critical 287; cyber 81, 133–36, 147, 155–65, 175–82, 222, 272–91, 273, 284–85, 288; deconstructive 284; goals of 272–73; interpretive 36n16; multi-sited 33, 175; of the self 285; *see also* anthropology

ethnoscapes 17, 118, 292–93

Europe 45, 88, 138, 172, 193, 197, 203, 211, 250, 256, 263, 300; imperialist 57; modernity of 211

European(s) 62–63, 147n4, 202, 207–8; aid 262; bourgeoisie 234; colonialism 206–7, 288n1; citizens 46; contact in New Worlds 63; ethnicity 147n4; fauna and flora 205–6; governments 197; ideology 45; professionals 202; public sphere 234, 259; rabbits 205; territorial conquests 288n1; tourists 208; travelers 170

European Economic Community (EEC) 94n6

European Union (EU) 9

Exetron Corporation 129n4

exile(s) 20, 36n15, 135, 137, 154, 169, 173–75, 180, 188, 193, 199, 209, 213

expatriate(s) 20, 135, 137, 154, 256–57, 264, 296

experiment(s): colonial-era 205; federal 190; in communication 26, 101, 114, 298; laboratory 206–7; medical 207; repatriation 209; technological 211–12, 242; with cyberethnography 36n16, 272; with identity 30, 34n4

extinction: of Caribbean Amerindians 18, 132–36, 142–47 [refutation of 18, 132–

36, 142–47]; of chimpanzees in Ghana 204

face(s): Indian 105; of indigeneity [4, 35n7, 293]; of resistance 249–50; of the dead 249; poor 204; public [of *SAWnet* 289n6];-to-face 26, 99, 105, 209, 222–23, 228, 232, 234, 246, 253n2, 284–85, 298 [community 278]
factory 265–66
family/families 80–85, 91, 93, 108n3, 110n11, 140–41, 152, 156, 158, 160–62, 172, 177, 181, 232, 241, 252, 269; displaced 240; neglect of 164; lands 229; legacy 142; loss of 226; reunions 172; Tongan royal 156; websites 80–84, 140; *see also* generation(s)
Faroe Islands 85, 93n2
Fattah, Hala 24, 186, 296
fatwa 178
fax 147n1, 188
Federation of Saskatchewan Indian Nations 71, 138
feminism 29, 107, 281; as online discussion topic 279; Western 278, 298 [complicity with colonial discourses 278]
feminist(s) 106, 281; agendas 107;-based NGOs 15; coalitions 107, 279; discourses 278; epistemology 284; ethnographers 281, 288; First-World 278; initiative 16, 279–81, 284, 287; political practices 279; places 274; praxis 278–79; studies 278, 288n3; theorists 270n8, 278, 281; Western 278–79; *see also* women's movement
Feral, Priscilla 205–6, 209
Ferguson, Tom 75
fieldwork 4, 27, 30–33, 37n17, 135, 166n2, 166n4, 175–77, 182n1, 238; ethics 30; multi-sited 36n16; notes 285; of non-places 36n16; online 2, 29, 133–36, 244, 253n2, 292 [creative observation 136, 146–47; with offline 3, 32–33, 81, 135, 248]; relations 135–36, 147, 284–85 [inequality of 284; issues involving 37n17]; *see also* methodology
Fienup-Riordan, Anne 89
Fink, Christina 36n15
Finland 202
First Footsteps in East Africa: or, An Exploration of Harar (Burton) 183n5

first nations 143; Santa Rosa Carib Community as 139
First Nations (of Canada) 7, 9, 14, 19, 61–78, 142, 295, 297; and ICT links [National First Nations Network 68]; communities 61, 65–75 [Saskatchewan 71; Southend 71]; cultural groups [Algonquin 62; Blackfoot 62; Blood 62; Carcross Tagish 70; Cree 62; Dene 62; Micmac 62; Mohawk 63; Saskatchewan 71]; e-centres [Deer Lake 67; Fort Severn 67; Keewaywin 67; McDowell Lake 67; North Spirit Lake 67; Poplar Hill 67]; governance [Assembly of First Nations 65–76, 138; Assembly of Manitoba Chiefs 138; Council of Elders 70]; *see also* Aboriginal Peoples of Canada
Fischer, Michael 30
fisheries 94n5
fishing 80, 87, 91, 120
flag(s) 289n5; digital 23; Hamas 238; Israeli 26, 252; Kurdish 23; Palestinian 238
Fong, Kevin 51–52
Foreman, George 216n7
Fort Leavenworth 262
Forte, Maximilian C. 18, 132, 295
France 105
French: *bourgeois* 216n5; factions 63; fur traders 62; language 222; peoples 225; philosopher 81; railway 171
Franklin, Marianne 167n10
Fraser, Nancy 126
freedom(s) 191, 197–98, 234, 297; from captivity 204; in research 285; individual 286; of choice 231; of expression 24, 166, 171, 195, 198, 228, 232–34, 286; of information 241; of the net 198; of the press 183n7, 205, 215, 234; participatory 295; political 188; religious 194; virtual 188
Freitas, Terrance 129n2
Friedman, Thomas 215
Friends of Animals (FOA) 204–10

Gaboro, Ninos 198
Gad, Alexander 22
Gajjala, Radhika 29, 272, 296
Gaia hypothesis 120
Galveston 216n6
gangs 105, 162, 245
Gaonkar, Dilip 216n8

Garvey, Marcus 216n6
Gates Foundation (Bill and Melinda) 7
gatherer(s) 221
Gay, Lahee'Enae 129n2
gays 105, 231–32
Gedicks, Al 129n1
gemeinshaft 84, 93n4
gender 97, 105, 126, 188, 230, 288, 288n2,
    296; and power 274; and subjectivity
    274; differences 233; interactions 230,
    234; issues 16, 228 [as online discussion
    topic 228–31]; male [and hacking 244];
    online [masking 233, 259; reproducing
    37n18]; notions of 274; relations 173
    [in Tongan society 164; in indigenous
    Mexico 106]; ratio 174
generation(s) 2, 115, 119, 132, 183n9; and
    language 157, 162; diasporic 22, 173;
    first-22, 158, 162, 173–74, 181; future
    34n6, 230; *H-net* 175; older 165; parent
    173, 178; relations between 156–64,
    173–74, 180; second 34n2, 35n7
    [immigrants 21–22, 164, 175]; Stolen
    46, 54, 59n6; trans-23; younger 10,
    157, 172, 181; virtual 195; *see also*
    elders, family, youth
Geneva 225
genocide 46, 251–52
geography: and identity 80–93; new 299;
    of medical clinic 74; physical 203
geopolitics 28, 88, 178, 208, 296
Gerlach, Allen 129n1
Germany 72
German: colonialism 221
gesellschaft 84, 93n4
Ghana/iGhana 25, 35n12, 202–19, 296; as
    space and text 210–13; ethnic groups
    of [Ewe 205]; government(s) of [Armed
    Forces Revolutionary Council 204;
    civilian 204–5; National Democratic
    Congress (NDC) 205; New Patriotic
    Party (NPP) 210; Provisional National
    Defense Council (PNDC) 204]; polit-
    ical lineages [Danquah-Busia 210;
    Nkrumahist 210]; regions of [Lake
    Volta Region 204–5; Western Region
    204]
Ghanaian(s)/iGhanaian(s) 25, 27–28,
    37n18; communities [diasporic opposi-
    tion vs. domestic political 203, 215];
    culture 203; domestic politics 202;
    economy 204; history 203;
    homepage(s) 202; in diaspora 202–16,

296; in Ghana 202–16, 296;-oriented
    websites 202–19 [*Ghana Forum* 202–
    19; *Ghanaforum* 217n10;
    Ghanaweb.com 217n10; *Say It Loud*
    202–19]; politics 203; public policy
    202; tourist industry 204
Gibb, Camilla 22, 169, 183n9, 294
Gibson, William 214
Gideon, Valerie 7, 61, 295
Gill, Lesley 263
Gilroy, Paul 301n2
Glick-Schiller, Nina 183n4
Gli-Gli Carib Canoe Project 134, 147n2
Global Islands Network 50
globalization 2, 18, 20, 33, 35n11, 44, 107,
    152, 272, 293; and space/time restruc-
    turing 183n4; anti-141; vs.
    homogenization 89, 152, 166, 244
Goa 154
Goan: identity 154; language 154; websites
    154
God 179, 209, 240
Gomes, Alberto 154
Gooneratne, C. V. 266
governance 1, 26, 46–53, 55–56, 70, 76,
    92, 100, 127–28, 143–44, 155–56, 221,
    228
Grabea, A'dnan 22
graffiti 245–46, 249
Graham, Mark 21
Gramsci, Antonio 257; and Gramscian
    259 [political and geopolitical context
    258, 263, 267]
graphic(s) 12, 26, 113, 117–18, 122, 124,
    140, 145, 243;-delivery system 145; *see
    also* photographs
grassroots 61, 75, 105–6, 122–23; environ-
    mental organizations 16, 89, 112–13,
    116–18, 124, 129; movements 74, 97,
    122; *see also* activist(s)
Great Warrior Day 260
Greenland 8, 12, 80–93; and ICTs [devel-
    opment 86–87; domains 88; usage rates
    88; websites 88]; Home Rule 85, 93n2,
    94n6; Information Technology Council
    93n5; nation [and identity 87; birth of
    87–88, 93n2, 94n6]; *see also* Inuit of
    Greenland
Greenlandic: content [on web 8]; family
    81–93; languages 82–83, 87, 91;-ness
    80, 87–88, 94n6, 94n7; web sources
    [*Atagu* 85; *Igloo* 82; *Santa Claus* 82]
Green Line 247–48, 252

Greenpeace 89, 94n6
Griffith, Gareth 288n1
Grim, Adam 80–93, 93n1, 93n4
Grossberg, Lawrence 274
Guatemala 10, 98
Guillen, Sebastian 109n8
Gunaratna, Rohan 269n6
Guyana 133–34

Habermas, Jürgen 130n8, 234, 258–59, 265, 268, 270n8; and Habermasian normative context 259, 263, 264, 268
habitats: endangered 124; native 117–18
haciendas 108n2
hacker(s) 26–27, 36n13, 239–54, 253n2; and counter-establishment ethos 241–42; and rock throwers 239–40; Armenian 301n1; as indigenous occupants of cyberspace 240–41; Azeri 301n1; culture 241–42; genealogy 246; military as 36n14; portrayal of 242;- terrorists 36n14; vs. crackers 242; *see also* script-kiddies, website defacers
Hacker Ethic 241; betrayal of 241
Hacker Quarterly (magazine) 242
Haile Selassie 170–71
Harar 169–74; as legendary city 170; as nation 176, 181–82; neighboring populations [Abyssinian Christians 170; Afar 170; Amharas 170–71; Argobba 170; Oromo 170–72, 183n9; Somali 170, 179, 183n9]; occupation of 170; *see also* Ethiopia
Harari(s) 22, 24, 169–85; army 170, 182; culture 169, 174, 183n9; homeland 170–72; immigrants 294; in diaspora 169–82; in Harar 170–74, 177; language 169, 174, 183n9; marriage practices 174, 183n9; National League 172;-ness 176–77, 183n9; religious practices 183n9; websites 169 [*Harari-Net* 174–82]
Harroy, John-Paul 225
Harvard University 114
Harvey, David 183n4
Hawai'i 141, 144, 205
Hawai'ian: ICT projects [Leok??? 10; Kualona 10]; identities 154; language revival 10, 154; websites 10, 154; woman 129n2
health: deficiencies 48, 61, 69, 98, 196; of Aboriginal peoples 46, 61–77, 98; of colonial administrators 208; destiny 65;

informatics 68, 74–75; narratives 70; practices 7, 75; public 46, 65, 72, 208; reproductive 196; research 64, 69; sector 61; self-determination over 66, 70; statistics 7, 64; and women [rights to 106; traditional roles in 65]; *see also* e-health
healthcare 1, 7, 61–76, 203, 208; Aboriginal programs 70–76 [First Nations and Inuit Longitudinal and Regional Health Survey 74]; authorities 66; for disabled Sri Lankan soldiers 266; governance 66, 68, 73 [Aboriginal Health (of Australia) 53; Alma-Ata Declaration on Primary Healthcare (WTO) 65; First Nations and Inuit Health Renewal Initiative (of Canada) 61; Indian Health Policy (of Canada) 65; Ministry of Health (of Canada) 65]; models 61, 66, 75, 77n2; resources 66–67, 120; rural 69, 71; sector 61, 66, 68; *see also* e-health, medicine
hegemony 123, 240, 246, 259–66, 280–81, 287, 295, 298; colonial 210; English-language 154; Gramsci's model of 257–59; ICT 294; Indian 275; masculine 288; media 252; of global capital 240; superpower 25; Western 44, 265, 285, 288
Heilmann, I. 84–85, 93n1
helicopter(s) 262; Apache 238; traffic 82
heritage(s) 11, 14, 23, 62, 295; Amerindian 137–38, 142; Assyrian 200; Burundian 222; mapping 295; mixed 228; performance of 293; protection of 293; Third-World 285; Tongan 158; tourism 209; Turcoman 200; U'wa 129; victims of 280
hero 294; culture 10; of independence 225
Hezbollah 250
Hijra 179–80
Himbulala 268
Hindu scriptures 91
Hine, Christine 30
Hispaniola 142
historiography 133
history/histories: anthropological 37n17; alternative 2, 10, 23, 292; books 143, 224; colonial 43, 116, 221 [post 286]; contests over 113–16, 187–88, 240–41; Ethiopian 169–72, 183n5; ever-morphing spectacle of 195–96; forgetting 195; Ghanaian 203;

Greenlandic 87–88, 93n2, 94n6; Harari 169–74; hegemonic 280; Hutu-Tutsi 222–24; in Trinidad 137; indigenous authorship of 10, 146; Iraq's multiple 186–201; lessons from 47; modernity's 292; of antiquity 195; of indigenous peoples [in Caribbean 143; in Mexico 98–99; of Mesopotamia 193, 199]; of Rwanda and Burundi 225; of Sri Lankan conflict 259–63; projections of 140, 144, 194, 199; reinterpretations of 198; recovery of 133; textual vs. oral 115; transmission of 176; uses and abuses of 187, 198–200
Hitlerites 246
HIV/AIDS 76n2, 207–8
Hobsbawm, Eric J. 145
Hoerder, Dirk 201
Holocaust 240
home(s) 3, 80, 107–8, 152, 164, 173, 228, 239–40, 263, 296; and field 31; away from home 297; back 198, 279, 296, 299 [counternarratives from 287]; countries 154, 189, 286–87; discussions of 275, 286–87; destruction of 247–48, 260; estrangement from 299; fetishizing 287; in cyberspace 3, 8, 22, 24–25, 293, 297, 300 [morphing into real 36n12]; in host country 20, 286–87; internet access 217n16;-lessness 169; of Palestinians 243; phantasmagoria of 299; returning 173, 178, 299; second-22, 174; shared memories of 263; see also homeland
Home of All Ethnically Cleansed Palestinians 243
homeland(s) 20, 22, 24–25, 27–29, 118, 128, 170–72, 187, 194, 197, 200, 287, 296; and memory 173; as mythological place 175; chimpanzee 208; connections with 173–82; debates about 182; distant 174; embodiment of 181; emotional ties to 213; forbidden 292; images of 175; Jewish 240; marks of 181; of Greenlandic homepages 80; relations with 174–76; romancing 177–78, 181–82, 292; virtual 193
homepage(s) 19, 93n4, 140, 154, 295; and guestbooks 90 [correspondences online 83–85]; and homepaging the Other 296; Ghanaian 202; Greenlandic Inuit 14–15, 80–93, 296; Kurdish 23–24; Tongan 156; visitors 84

Hopi 13, 298; Tribal Council 301n4
Hopiland 301n4
Hornborg, Alf 129n6
hospital(s) 65, 69–74: Jayawardhenapura 269
Houston 172
hunter(s) 92
hunting 80, 87, 93n2, 120
Hussein, Saddam 178, 188, 192, 197
Hutri, Hassan 249
Hutu(s) 26–27; militia 222; pro-226; see also Huti/Tutsi
Hutu/Tutsi: civilian casualties 222; common ground [establishing 235, 297]; conflict 220–37 [interpretations of 223–25]; ethnic relations 221–22, 226 [online 220–36, 297; success of 27]; shared cultural practices 222; socioeconomic roles 221–22; see also Burundi Youth Council (BYC), Burundinet (B-net)
hyperlinks 1, 6–7, 12–13, 15, 23, 44, 67, 81–91, 97, 109n6, 113, 116–17, 140–47, 156–57, 282, 300; endorsements via 18, 135, 144, 148n5, 148n8, 295

identity/identities: and home 3, 164; and language 152–68; and space 80–96; alternative 34n4, 235; beyond borders 170; claims 14; constructions 35n11, 102, 113, 132–47, 154–66, 169–83, 196, 199–200, 217, 223, 235, 294; debates about 186–87; encrypted 249, 252, 253n2; ghettoizing 292–93; hybridized 162; multiple 181–82, 233; national 61, 87–88, 170, 176, 211; online [indeterminacy of 210, 212, 222; hiding 212, 233; mutability of 233; protection of 75, 104; reclaiming 146, 152–54]; performances 10–14, 34n4; politics 198; transnational 170, 183n4, 189; virtual 234
ideology/ideologies 2–3, 23, 26, 55, 130, 198, 293, 296; European 45; colonialist 63; of Back to Africa movement 208; of cyberspace myth 81; of diaspora 21; of global Islam 245, 249; of indigeneity 146; state-centered 186
ideoscapes 118, 300
Illich, Ivan 76
imagined community 187, 202, 211–12, 296
Imagined Communities (Anderson) 187

imperialism 274–75; media-cultural 274
immigrant(s) 105, 244, 248; see also migration
incarceration 252
India 137, 154, 257, 260, 267, 274, 275; Woman of [Bharatiya Nari 278]
Indian(s) 109n9, 281, 300; East 147n4; hegemony 275; language 101; nationalism 278; of Mexico 97–108; of North America 138; Peace Keeping Force (IPKF) 260; Southeast Asian in diaspora 91, 272–89; tribe 241; women 278–79
indigene(s) 133, 146–47
indigeneity: and globality 33, 146 [quests for 18–19, 300–301; questions of 18, 300–301]; and indigenes 142, 145–48; as macro-phenomenon 139–41, 146, 300–301; claims upon 240–41; common to the internet 213; configuring 4, 14, 19, 33, 35n11, 89, 132–47, 213, 240, 295, 298 [dialectical with dominant society 17–18, 89, 113, 133]; diversity of 98, 126; future of 299–301; semantics of 4, 17–18, 143, 300; sustainability of 126; virtual 146–47 [face(s) of 4–5, 35n7, 293]; see also indigenous
indigenous: activists 125, 294; authors 4, 11, 294; cosmopolitanism 2, 18–19, 293, 299–301; cyberactivism 2, 4–5,10–23, 132–47, 256, 300 [inreach initiatives 5–6, 8–10; outreach initiatives 5–6, 8, 10–14]; cyber-presence 4–6, 35n7, 139, 144; definitions of 34–35n6, 241; movements 15–16, 97–111, 119–30, 130n6, 136–47, 300; networking 18, 132, 295; organizations 5, 18, 44, 112, 117, 138; public(s) 8, 11, 14, 120, 126–29, 257, 297 [sphere 28]; stereotypes about 102, 126
Indigenous Affairs (journal) 34n5
Industrial Revolution 8
inequality: gender 106–7, 228–31; in research 285; social 220–32
informant(s) 31–32, 139, 242–43, 245, 301n4; co-authorship 36n16; native 272, 285–87; relations with 37n17; 135–36, 147, 275–78, 283–86, 289; self as 136; virtual 29, 253n2
information-communications technologies (ICTs): access to 1–2, 6, 27, 29, 67–69, 72–73, 86, 94n7, 99, 133–34, 139,

147n1, 152–56, 165–66, 166–67n4, 169–70, 188, 211, 217n10, 217n16, 220, 250, 258, 299 [censoring 227, 267, 269n5; costs of 86, 259; passive vs. active 268; questions of 43–44, 47–57, 69]; among marginalized peoples 1–33, 147n1, 179, 234, 279, 292, 301n1; and connectivity 1, 6, 8, 43, 73, 215 [costs 86–87, 156, 301n5; speed 86, 217, 287]; and manipulation of distance 7, 11, 17, 25, 28, 32, 46, 57, 61, 174, 182, 292, 299–300; development [in remote regions 6–7, 44, 47–54, 61–78, 297]; hardware 293; hegemony 294 [vs. emancipation 296]; indigenizing potential of 2, 34n3, 34n5, 44, 57–58, 293–301; regulation 67, 156, 212, 264–65; server(s) 6, 86, 156, 202–3, 217n10, 243, 252, 301n5 [shut-downs 156, 246–47, 250, 264–65]; social nomadology of 253; wetware 293; see also internet
Information Superhighway 1, 30
Information-Technology Revolution 8
infrastructure(s) 6, 8, 45–49, 59n8, 68–69; breakdown of 179; civic 9; communications 7, 33–34n1, 43, 49, 54, 86, 293 [in Arctic 90, 296; in Australia 43, 48, 54; in Canada 61, 66–69; in Greenland 86]; semiotic 8; technologies of 20, 68; war-torn 188
injustice(s) 122, 191, 240
Innaarsuit 8, 86–87
insurgency 15, 258; counter-258, 261; [counter 28, 255, 268; doctrine 260; effects on civilians 266]; cyber 261, 266; deadly politics of 258; technologies of 258
intelligentsia 261, 264; see also urban professionals
International Monetary Fund (IMF) 204, 251
International Telecommunications Union 58n1
International Work Group for Indigenous Affairs (IWGIA) 34n5, 34–35n6
internet: as a border strategy 110n12; as a tool [for equality struggles 97–99; for social agendas 99; for solidarity 97; for virtual resistance 123; to embody indigeneity 145]; as arena for domestic politics 13; as colonizing apparatus 294; as culture and artifact 30; as cultural club 199; as democratic

medium 233–35; as ethnicity index
199; as homogenizing force 89; as ideal
public sphere 259; as instrument to
deliver pledges 24; as meeting space
30, 169; as mode of imaging future 24;
as outreach venue 14; as place where
imagination can speak 175; as political
barometer 199; as safe haven 24; as site
of mediation 103–5; as thing vs. as
new environment 72–75; as traditional
storyteller 10; as two-edged sword 294;
as virtual meeting place 199, 287; cafés
8, 86, 99, 107, 242; pioneers 202, 216–
17n10
Internet Corporation for Assigned Names
and Numbers (ICANN) 202, 216n1
Internet in Iraq: Limited, Appreciated (news
report) 200n2
Internet Protocol Suite (TCP/IP) 241
Internet Relay Chat (IRC) 239, 244;
modified Internet Relay Chatting
(mIRC) 245; I Seek You (ICQ)
217n16, 244–45
Internet Service Providers (ISP) 86, 88,
156, 202, 217n16, 239; attacks upon
250; accessing foreign 301n5
interview(s): ethnographic 129n5, 228,
232–33 [online 139, 141, 222, 240,
242, 244–45, 247, 253n1]; media [of
Tamil journalists 267; of Zapatista
leaders 108n5, 110n11]
Intifada, *see* Al-Aqsa Intifada
Inuit Circumpolar Conference 94n6
Inuit of Canada 61–77; communities
[Labrador 63; Northern Quebec
(Nunavik) 63: Nunavut 67, 69, 89; St.
Lawrence Islands 63]; demographics 63;
ethnic groups [Inupiat 63, 88; Yupik
63]; history 63–64; land agreements 63;
language 70; *see also* Aboriginal
Peoples of Canada
Inuit of Greenland 8, 12–13, 19, 37n18,
80–93, 93n2, 93n3, 241; and pan-Inuit
coalitions 94n6; communities
[Aappilattoq 80–83, 87–88, 92, 93n1;
Municipality of Upernavik 80–87,
93n1, 93n2]; governance 82–83, 85,
93n2, 94n6; homepages 12–13, 80–93
[guestbook 82–84; links 83–85]; landscapes 80–85; *see also* Greenland
Inuk 70
investment(s): foreign 119; in healthcare
61; in ICT development 53, 56, 68,

93–94n5, 264; in infrastructure 52, 55;
in homeland 174, 183n8
Iran 189, 191, 194, 197–98; Contra Affair
178
Iranian(s): Assyrian 197; in diaspora 21;
regime 195
Iraq 24, 186–201; and illegitimacy thesis
186, 199; during monarchy 186;
government(s) of 186–93, 195 [Baath
regime 186, 188–89; multi-parliamentary system 191]; multiple histories of
186–201; national communities within
186, 199; pre-modern 196; region(s) of
[Kurdish 188, 194; Turkomaneli 192];
territorial integrity of 192
Iraqi(s): nationhood 186–87, 195, 200;-
ness 199; state 187–89; textbooks 197;
website [*uruklink.net* 188]; *see also*
Assyrian(s), Kurds, Turcoman(s)
*Iraqi Assyrian Christians in London: The
Construction of Ethnicity* (Al-Rasheed)
195
Irbil 187
Ishi, the Last Yahi (Heizer and Kroeber) 241
Islam 170, 179, 186; brotherhood of 180;
concepts in 180; defense of 180; significance in diaspora 176–82; history of
176; image of 250; roots of 22; scholarship of 170; transnational symbols of
181; world of 250; *see also* Muslim
Islamabad 239, 245
Israel 22, 36n14, 197, 238; and Gaza 240,
245, 247–48; and indigeneity claims
240; and West Bank 240, 245, 247–49;
as nation 251–52; Defense Forces
(IDF) 252n3; modern 240; Mossad
244; Russian immigrants in 244; state
of 240, 250–51 [ethnically-plural 244;
founding of 242]; streets of 252
Israeli(s) 36, 238–54; army 252; check-
points 238; Commission of Inquiry
253n3; cyberactivism 243; discourse
248; diversity 252; election 250; flag 26,
252; intelligence forces 244, 250; military specialists 262; Minister of Defense
253n3; peoples 251; political parties
[Gush Shalom 248; Kach 248; Labor
248; Likud 248; Shas 248]; politician
239; public 241; right-wingers 252;
settlers 243, 252; soldiers 238; tank(s)
40; victims 251; war machine 243;
website(s) 240 [*womeningreen.org* 243]
Istanbul 187

Italy 110n10, 175
Italian language 175

Jackson, Anthony 18
Jaffna 256, 267
Jamaican: populist 216n6
Jammo, Sarhad 200n7
Jerusalem 239, 251; Old City of 239
Jews 172, 175, 240, 248, 250–52; and
    homeland 240 [as prevention of future
    Holocaust 240, as promised by God
    240]; in historic Palestine 240; religious
    vs. secular 251; right wing vs. left wing
    251–52; Russian 244, 248–50; ultra-
    nationalistic 240; see also Israel
Jeyachandran, Mr. 263
jihad 180–81
jobs 21, 48, 50, 119, 161–62, 209, 220,
    232, 247, 269n3, 297; see also employ-
    ment
Jones, Steven 30, 273
Jordan 248; Palestinian refugee camps in
    249
Journal of Assyrian Academic Studies
    (JAAS) 195
journalism 28; and alleged neutrality 295;
    elementary 256; counter-36n15;
    Western 295
journalist(s) 101, 105, 135, 256–57, 261,
    263–70; Third-World 263
justice 47, 75, 125, 128, 188; wrestlers for
    109n7 [Fray Tormenta 109n7; Super-
    Barrio 102, 109n7; Super-Ecologista
    109n7]

Kadende-Kaiser, Rose M. 26, 220, 297
Kageorgis 225
Ka'ili, Tevita 167n6
Kalaaleq 92
Kalaaliussuseq 87
Kalinago e.V. 134
Kami, Taholo 155
Kandy 267
Kangersuatsiaq 92
Kansas 262
Karuna, Colonel 266–67
Kashmir 239
Kashmiri: separatists 244
Keane, John 234
Kearney, Michael 182n3, 183n4
Khan, Sharukh 91
Khatami, President Seyyed Mohammed
    197

Khosravi, Sharam 21
King Menelik 170, 182
King Mwambutsa IV 221, 225–26
King of Tonga 152, 164
Kingdom of David 251
Kingdom of Elgaland 214
Kingdom of Vargaland 214
kinship 11, 49, 51, 91, 174, 183n9, 263;
    and clan(s) 221; and nationhood 177;
    terms [ahli 177, machchang 267, 270n9];
    see also family
Kirby, Jon P. 216n5
Kirkuk 190, 192
Kirundi 222, 232
Kitchen, Rob 34n3
Kluckhohn, Clyde 30
Kroeber, Alfred L. 30
KubarU'wa, Chief 117, 119–20
Kufor, John 216
Kuhmunen, Henrik Micael 9
Ku Klux Klan 216n6
Kumaratunga, President 267
kumete, see kava
Kurd(s) 23–24, 186–92, 199; and question
    of state 191
Kurdish: flag 23; homepage(s) 23–24;
    leadership 190, 200n3; nation-building
    efforts 190; organizations 23; paramili-
    tary190; political parties 36n13, 189–
    90, 194–95 [Kurdistan Democratic
    Party (KDP) 189, 200n3; Patriotic
    Union of Kurdistan (PUK) 189];
    websites 23–24 [www.aka.kurdistan]
Kurdistan: Iraqi 188–90; Regional
    Government of 189–90

laboratory/laboratories: artificial intelli-
    gence 241; of modernity 211; research
    25, 206–7
Lacandon Indians 108n3
lafo 167n6
Lake Tanganyika 224–25
Lakota: homepages 13, 16; declaration of
    war to wannabes 13; shamans 13, 16
La Neta 109n10
La Trobe University 166n2
land(s) 118–20, 122, 178, 300; accumula-
    tion 243; ancestral 112, 121, 192, 199,
    229; as social relationship 81; base 134;
    claims over 59n5, 63, 92, 128; conflicts
    over 98–99, 108n6, 242; expropriation
    190; expulsion from 98, 240, 243; farm-
    171; foreign 172; grants 136; no

person's 214; of diaspora 181; outback
293; ownership 170–72, 190 [women's
229]; promised 240; reservation 62–63;
return of 194; seasonal 63; subdivision
of 172; traditional 54, 59n5 [ITONGO
229]; see also property
Landzelius, Kyra 1, 16, 112, 217n11, 292,
295
language(s) 62, 85, 91, 104, 138, 140, 144,
152–67, 172, 195, 203, 206, 300; and
heteroglossia 37n18, 252, 280; and
macrons 167n8; and belonging 162; as
boundary marker 91; as cultural resistance 152, 154, 161; as unifying source
241; bureaucratic double-speak 207;
cyberpunk 214; debates 152–68;
fluency [and bilingualism 159, 165,
222]; heterodox 203; idioms 37n18,
246; mixing 37n18; pedagogy 295;
patois 154, 216n5; play 162–63; print-
211; revival 9–10, 154, 158, 165;
schools 190; scripts 153; slang 37n18;
street 162–63; translation 142, 160;
vulgar 163; world's 153
Lanier, Jaron 90
Las Abejas 108n6
Latukefu, Alopi 6–8, 293
Tefua 'a Vaka Lautala 158
law(s) 27, 51, 54, 59n8, 63, 99–100, 133,
253n3; calls for 98–99, 106, 229, 231;
copyright 273, 295
Lawson, Sean 36n13
Lea, Martin 233
leader(s): Assyrian 190; Australian
Aborigine 6, 44–47, 50; Burundi Youth
Council 222; Carib 136–38; corporate
122, 203; Ghanaian former 203; Harari
[from diaspora 174]; Hutu/Tutsi 221;
Kurdish 190; in Ethiopia 170–71; in
Mexican Revolution 108n2; indigenous 5, 7–8, 43, 46–47, 61, 63, 72, 117,
120; Iraqi 197; of Fatah 238; of Ku
Klux Klan 216n6; of Santa Rosa Carib
Community 136–39; Palestinian
former 243; spiritual 74, 250; Taino
141; Tongan 164; U'wa 117, 120;
Zapatista 100, 103, 108n6 [female 101,
110n11, 110n12]
leadership 4, 6, 15–16, 44, 50–51, 61, 65–
68, 101, 108n6, 136, 174, 190, 197–98,
221, 226, 235, 251
Lebanese: Phalangists 253n3
Lebanon 189, 198, 248, 250, 252, 253n3

Lee, Helen 21, 152, 167n10, 296
Lefebvre, Henri 81, 84, 89–91, 213
Lemarchand, Rene 221
lesbian(s) 231–32
Liberation Theology 108n3
Liberia 216n6
lifeways 17, 46; endangered 118; indigenous 7, 11, 13–14, 102, 112–14, 116,
126, 129n3; local 294
lifeworld(s) 128–29, 130n8, 259
Liqa' al-yawm (television show) 200n2
literacy 8, 45, 48, 59n6, 98, 100, 108, 211,
275; computer 6, 36n14, 49, 69, 100,
108, 211
locality/localities 12, 27, 31, 33, 223, 292–
93, 296; as spatial fact 293; as transit
point 293; escape from 297; in identity-
formations 87, 137, 293; production of
3, 5, 12, 19, 22, 30, 86, 91–92, 293–99;
questions of 17, 29; trans-293
London 117, 195, 267, 270n7
Lopez, José "TureyCu" 142
Los Angeles 117, 172, 245
Louvre Museum 195
Lower Zab River 187

Macherey, Pierre 281–82
Madras 267
Madrid 105
Malik, Lincoln 193–94
Malinas, Anna 234
Mamidipudi, Annapurna 281, 283
Mandali 187
Maori 14
map(s) 11, 22, 80–83, 92, 240, 288, 293;
electronic 23; mental 285; of
Aappilattoq area 82; of Greenland 82;
of Israeli expansion 243; of Kurdistan
23
marches 238–40; Zapatista [March of the
Color of the Earth 101; Xi'Nich 99]
Marcos, see subcomandante Marcos
market(s) 112, 130n8, 172, 203, 222, 229;
and commerce 1, 45, 170–71, 252; and
merchants 301n4; economies 35n11;
forces [and Western media 28, 264];
logic 258, 264;-place 127, 170, 298;
telecommunications 60n9; value 196
Markham, Annette N. 217n17
marriage: and Métis peoples 62; and name
changes 275; Harari preferential 174,
183n9; in historic Iraq 186; in indigenous Mexico 102

martyrdom 116, 128, 249
mask(s): dialectics of 109n8; internet as 104; of Mexican state 98, 103; Pre-Colombian 102; Zapatista use of 102–5, 107, 109n8, 110n11
massacre(s) 194, 252, 253n3, 261–262
Maundi, Mohammed Omar 236n2
Maya Project 10
McLaughlin, William 132
Mecca 179, 181
Médecins Sans Frontières 269n4
media: attention 125; broadcast(s) 49, 215 [vs. print 273]; control over 211, 258, 274 [corporate 252]; governmental 228, 261–62]; electronic 28, 72, 211, 300; figures 261; international 268; mainstream 132–33, 242, 250; manipulation 259; mass 137, 251; new 4, 19, 33n1, 34n3, 170, 212, 287, 293–300 [combined with old 211–12, 301n5]; participants 252; popular 210; rivals 261; visibility 100; Western 208, 240, 250, 257, 261, 263–66, 268 [and alleged neutrality 264]; see also news, print
mediascapes 2–3, 118, 249, 300
medicine: evidence-based 74; traditional 65–69, 74, 77n2, 102, 292 [morphing with high-tech 295]; Western 61, 65, 72–74; see also e-health
Medina 179–80
Melbourne 158, 166n2
memory: in 269n1; of homeland 20, 173, 287; women as bearers of 102
memoryscapes 92
men: and cooperation with women 230; and kava 164; and martyrdom 249; and Muslim diaspora 176; as first-wave emigrants 174; bourgeoisie 234; business-208; diasporist Tamil 256; repatriation among Harari 174; war tally of Hutu 222
Mengistu Haile Mariam 182n2
Menominee 129n2
Meriage, Larry 122
Mesopotamia 193, 196–97
mestizos 98
metaphysics of presence 130n9
Métis: and Canadian Confederation 63; communities [Northern Territories 63, Ontario 63, Prairies 63, West Coast 63]; ethnicity 62–64, 69 [Cree 62; English 62; French 62; Irish 62; Ojibwa

62; Salteaux 62: Scandinavian 62; Scottish 62]; history 62–63; leadership 63; Michif language 62; self-determination movement [and Red River Valley defeat 63]; see also Aboriginal Peoples of Canada
Mexico 97–111, 245; and Mexican Revolution 108n2; army of 108n2, 295; Congress 101; government(s) of 15, 98–105, 110n11, 110n12; Indian ethnic groups in 98–101; states of [Michoacan 110n10; Tampico 109n8, Tehuacan 110n10; Veracruz 110n10]; see also Zapatista(s)
Mexico City 99
Meyrowitz, Joshua 72
Microsoft Corporation 85
Middle East 36n14, 137, 193, 196–99, 240, 245
migrant(s) 20, 152–53, 158, 173; identities 286; incoming 20–21, 63, 105, 244, 248, 294; workers 269n5; trans-170, 182; see also émigré(s)/emigrant(s)
migration(s) 45, 152, 158, 169, 172, 216n6, 244; idealizing 286; out-208; permission for 197; policies 152–53
Mi'kmaq: cultural revival 10
military 45, 63, 106, 108–9n6, 171, 182n2, 260, 266, 293, 295; advisor 100; and counter-insurgency doctrine 262–63; as potential hackers 36n14; coercion of noncombatants 260–63, 266; contractors 207; coups d'état 204, 209, 223–24; equipment 209; intelligence 36n14; para-119, 190, 209; schizmogenesis 263; theorists 258, 262; training manuals 260; tribunal 204; uniforms 102, 266; see also army, war
Miller, Daniel 2, 24, 34n3, 154, 217n17
Minh-ha, Trinh 286
minority/minorities 1, 17, 24, 36n15, 45, 126, 145, 162, 170, 180–81, 186–89, 191–96, 221, 225, 255, 298
missionaries 208
MIT (Massachusetts Institute of Technology) 241
Mitchell, Timothy 216n8
Mitra, Ananda 91, 285
Mobutu, Sese Seko 216n7
modernity/modernities 45–47, 81, 89, 113, 121, 280, 288; and indigeneity 17, 121; alternative 216n8; bypassing 6; discourse of 104; failure of 35n8;

history of 57, 211–12, 216n8;
languages of 127; late-208 [anthropolo-
gies of 31; transnational flows of 208];
limits of 97; phantasy of 124–25; post-
6, 89, 92; promises of 292; two faces of
113–21, 124–29; victims of 89
Mohanty, Chandra Talpade 278–79
Mohawk 138
Mongols 191
Montes Azules 108n3
Morse, Margaret 213
Mosques 240
movements: aboriginal protest 47; anti-
globalization 141; Back to Africa 208–
10, 216n6; democratic 45; environmental 112–22, 126, 129–30n6;
Freedom 239; grassroots 74, 97, 122;
health 74–75; independence 257;
indigenous 16, 97–111, 119–30, 136,
300; Native American 141–42; Open
Source 241; political 215 [global 292];
resistance 245, 249; revitalization 298;
separatist 260; social 16, 36n16; Union
59n5; women's 15–16, 105–10; youth
228; see also Zapatista
Murdoch (Western explorer) 88
music 21, 145, 250; channels 27; hip-hop
245–46; karNAtaka 91; Harari
wedding 179–80; rap 162, 239, 246;
Tongan 158; traditional 52, 145, 158
Muslim(s) 171, 176, 179–81, 243, 261,
268; Africans 169, 177; brotherhood
27, 250; calendar 179; city-state 170,
183n5; community 176; discourse 181;
image of 250; online networks 22;
principles 181; racism against 178;
Shi'a 187, 199; space 180; state 177;
Sunni 186, 199; websites 176; see also
Islam
myth(s) 46, 52, 117, 243; and reality 88–
90, 93n4; countering 243; cyberspace
81, 90; figures from 10; of extinction
142; of past 24; of progress 35n8; of
return 193; origin 114

Narayan, Kirin 284
Narayan, Uma 279
narrative(s) 208, 224, 277, 285–86;-
counter 287; device 180; dominant 14,
137, 278–79; grand 45; hegemonic
286; historical 191, 193; of lamentation 24; of state power 186; personal
23, 272, 287

nation(s) 56–57, 137, 152–53, 177, 181,
195–96, 210–12, 224–25, 251;-building
24, 88, 186–88, 190, 211; e-25, 36,
202, 211;-hood 63, 170, 176–77, 182,
186–201, 289n5 [and identity 61, 170,
176, 186–88, 199, 211; and unity 224];
idea of 177, 195; micro-214, 217n13;
postcolonial 202, 288n1; reconstruction of 227, 235; sovereign 9, 171, 143;
within diaspora 173–77; see also
nation-state
nation-state(s) 14, 19, 23–24, 45–46, 51,
119, 181, 186, 193; administration 211;
and anti-documents 36n12; as
autochthonous 210; as imagined
community 187, 202, 211–12; facsimile
of 35n12; federation of Australia 45;
origins of Mexican 98; project 61;
sovereignty 298; super-structure 57;
Western 44, 152–53, 155, 204–5, 211
National Indigenous Organization of
Colombia 112
native(s) 6–33, 37n17, 117–18, 120, 292,
300; anthropologists 3, 36n16; arts 11,
35n7; cultures 9–12, 124 [speaking for
285]; ethnographer 29, 284–85;
habitat(s) 117, 122; identity 116, 244;
language(s) 10–11, 18, 101, 157–58,
190, 296; meta-112, 117–18, 124;-ness
4, 14, 19; Other 17, 125; pagan 147n7;
peoples 8, 50, 112, 115, 121, 198;
population(s) 7, 193; voice 103; see also
indigenous
Native American(s) 37n18, 76n2, 129n2,
144, 241, 301n4; as consumer public
298; colleges 7; movement 141–42;
organizations 76n2 [National Native
American HIV/AIDS Integrated
Services Network 76n2]; publications
142; Summit 13; Title 59n8; websites
144, 148n8 [Hopi Links' Native
American Resources 148n8; Indian
Nations 148n8; Native American
Timeline 148n8; USA Tribal
Governments 148n8]
nature 81, 92, 124, 145; and natives 118;
reserve 25
Navajo Nation: ICT projects 7
Navalady 268
N-dignes 133, 146–47
Nelson, Diane M. 241
Nepal 274
netizen(s) 25, 118, 202, 206, 212–13

net-savvyges 88–89
networking 1–3, 5, 9, 14–15, 18, 23, 30, 49, 54–56, 73, 75, 100, 107, 134–35, 138, 141, 144, 295, 301n6
New Age 35n7, 120
New Agers 13
New Jersey 141
New York (City) 117, 134, 141, 178, 216n6, 267
New Yorker (magazine) 212
New Zealand 14, 18, 47, 152, 158, 275–76
news 9, 24, 67, 116–17, 133, 137, 156–57, 166n3, 167n5, 202–3, 220, 230, 255–70, 292; agencies 100, 257–58, 264, 268 [Al-Jazeera 200n3, 247; Associated Press (AP) 257; BBC 200n3, 247, 250, 257, 265, 267; CNN 200n3, 247, 251; C-SPAN 179; Reuters 257, 265; *TamilNet.com* 255–71]; editor 124, 257, 264;-groups 144, 235n1; headlines ¡Basta! 99; print 100, 114, 117, 122; wires 116, 264; *see also* media, newspaper(s)
newspaper(s) 70, 87, 99, 102, 104, 114, 117, 256, 261; Danish tabloid 82; Israeli 252; Sri Lankan 255, 264–65, 268; *Atuagagliutit* 87; *Avangnâmiok* 87; *Boston Globe* 217n10; *Cambio 16* 108n5; *Chicago Tribune* 193; *Le Figaro* 108n5; *New York Times* 108n5, 251; *San Francisco Chronicle* 108n5; *San Jose Mercury News* 193; *The Ghanaian Chronicle* 205, 215; *The Hindu* 257, 265; *The Island* 262; *The Mirror* 216n4; *Washington Post* 251
Ngati Awa: and ICTs 18
Nigeria 129n4
Noah 179
non-governmental organizations (NGOs) 5, 15, 17, 34–35n6, 101, 106, 109–10n10, 110n12, 134, 147n1, 188, 204, 214, 268, 300
North American Free Trade Agreement (NAFTA) 98–99, 103
Northern Arizona University 301n4
Northern Ireland 245
Norway 263, 267
Norwegian(s) 267; language 263
Nukit 93n5
Nuttall, Mark 92
Nuuk 86

O'Baoill, Andrew 258–59
Occidental Petroleum Corporation (Oxy) 112–23, 125–30; Chief Executive Officer 123; company spokesperson 122; shareholder(s) 23 [meeting 117]; *see also* U'wa
Occupied Territories 27, 243, 247, 252; *see also* Israel, Palestine
Ocupas 105
Odense 82
offline, *see* online-offline
oil 16, 112–22, 125, 178
Oklahomans 216n6
Oneida Indian Nation: ICT projects 10; website 292
online: activism 18, 36n15, 244; attacks [fears of 232]; autoethnographic encounters 11; brokering [of diaspora 20–30, 37n18, 286]; campaigns 34n4, 90, 97, 99–108, 108–9n6, 112–13, 116–18, 123, 133–47; communications 47, 100, 104, 216n9, 234 277–78, 287 [and anonymity 75, 175, 210–13, 233–34, 163, 198; and intimacy 296; material consequences of 278]; communities 241, 275–89; court proceedings 14–15; debates 152–66, 205–10; discourse transformation 220–35; distanciation 234; homes 8, 12, 36n12; isolation 234; living 214; marginalization of women 278; nicknames 212; persona 16; phonebook 167n5; pseudonyms 232–33; self-actualization 188; self-writing 272; shopping 89, 298; survey 94n5; testimonies 133; texts 167n8, 277 [-subjects 273–74]; visibility 134, 139, 143–44; worlds 13
online/offline: binaries 81 [deconstructing 3, 81]; cooperation 141; conflicts [spill-over effects 36n13, 148n10, 190, 301n5]; indigenous engagements 4 [facets of 4–20, 34n5]; nexus 133; recursive relations 32–33, 84, 87–90, 138–39, 144, 158, 163, 294, 299
Ontario 63, 67
oppression 98, 107, 172, 193–95, 209, 297; faces of 105, 108; forms of 108n6; lyrics of 246
origin(s): city of 173, 181; community 191; culture of 21; ethnic 182, 221; land of 169, 173, 182, 223; mixed 142; national 182; of European nationalism 211–12

Organization for Economic Co-operation
and Development (OECD) 98
Organization of American States 138
Orinoco River 147n2
Ottoman Empire 191
Our Right to Take Responsibility (Pearson)
54
Outback Digital Network (ODN) 6, 43,
49–58, 58n2; agendas 50–55; and
indigenous [empowerment 50–53;
ownership 50; public services 54; right
to responsibility 55]; constituents
[Balkanu Cape York Development
Corporation 49, 58n2; Broome
Aboriginal Media Association 49,
58n2; Tanami Project 49, 58n1; Tenant
Creek Regional Infrastructure Project
49, 58n1; Top End Aboriginal Bush
Broadcasting Association 49, 58n2];
funders 43 [Networking the Nation
54]; management 54–55 [community
51; Goolarri Media Enterprises 52;
strategies 51–52]
Oxy, *see* Occidental Petroleum
Corporation

Pacific Islanders 160, 165; languages of
160; region 155; websites 155, 165
Pacific Ocean 152
paenga 167n6
Pahl, Raymond E. 93n4
Pakistan 27, 239, 244, 260, 274; Hacking
Club 243; urban 244
Pakistani: hackers 243; nationalists 246;
youth 250
Palestine 27, 36, 239; and Gaza 240, 245,
247–48; and West Bank 240, 245, 247–
49; historic 240; Ministry of Education
242 [defacement of website of 242];
Mukhabarat 242; streets of 243
Palestinian(s) 238–54, 253n3; Christian
240; computer users 250; dispossession
240; families 240; indigeneity claims
240–41; Muslim 240; nation 251;
National Authority 249; opinion(s)
243, 247; peoples 240, 250–51; political
parties 248 [Fatah 238, 247; Hamas 238,
247, 250; Islamic Jihad 238, 247;
Popular Front for the Liberation of
Palestine (PFLP) 238, 247]; public 241;
refugee(s) 240, 247–49; resistance
movements 238, 245, 249; self-determination 250; victims 251; websites 243–

44 [*electronicintifada.net* 243, 250;
hamas.org 250; *Palestineremembered.com*
243; *al-aqsa.org* 242]; youth 238–40, 250
panopticon: and optical surveillance 56;
ICTs as 56–57, 294–95
Papal Bull *Inter Caetera* (of 1493) 141,
147n7
parent(s): and child-rearing practices 164;
and ICTs [exclusion from 160; training
7]; and homeland 175–77 [as bearers of
culture 173, 181]; emigrants as 22 [and
native language pedagogy 158, 161–62,
165]; generation 173, 178, 228; grand-
120; *see also* children, family
Parents Learning Technology 7
Paris 195, 267
participation: and inclusion/exclusion 187;
barriers to 258; community [in healthcare 76]; electoral 7; freedom of 295; in
resistance 126; of subaltern citizens
126; political 72, 268; public sphere
114, 126, 128; tyranny of 126–29, 295
[and of non-participation 128]
pastoral: industry 59n5
pastoralism 52
Pathmanathan, S. 255–56
peace 63, 120, 173, 230, 252, 255; accord
251; and ceasefire agreement 255, 258;
and cohabitation 223; approaches to
220;-building efforts 227, 229–30, 255,
260 [and absence of women 229–30];
BYC Summit for 222; fragile [in Sri
Lanka 258–67]; partners for 252; return
of 235; talks 267
Pearson, Noel 54–55
peasant(s) 15, 98, 105, 108n2, 142, 295;
economies 15, 98–99
Peña, Gómez 100, 109n7
performance(s): cyberethnography as 283;
of identity 34n3, 286; of indigeneity 3,
23; of modernity 118; of resistance 28,
109n7, 118 [and performative competence 16, 125; Zapatista strategies of
100, 103]; of tradition by women 101–2
periphery/peripheries: and
Greenlandicness 86–89, 94n7; and
center(s) 31, 94n7, 171, 285, 292–93,
295, 298; cyberspatial 249; ignoring
293; staging 12, 293 [and resisting 12,
293]
personhood: and ICTs 1, 213, 299
Peterson, Leighton C. 269n5
Phillips, Susan A. 245

Phoenicians 198

photographs: posted online 23 [of locality 80–84, 90–92; of Zapatista women 110n11; of U'wa 117–18, 129n3; of Taino 140]; *see also* graphic(s)

pirate: indigenization 299; utopias 298, 300

Piscatori, James 181

poet(s) 261, 264

poetry 140, 155, 158, 275, 284

police: forces 249; online 265; secret 242; station 269

politician(s) 67, 82–83, 94n5, 94n6, 100, 123, 137, 192, 216n4, 228, 235, 294; *see also* leaders

politics: alternative modes of 235; bread and butter 247; domestic 202, 209, 292, 296; Ethiopian 171; Ghanaian 203; indigenous 300; local 247; offline 144; of development 229; of Jewish groups 248; of identity 198; of inclusion and exclusion 278, 281–82; of national reconstruction 235, 255–56; of place 293 [and dynamics of positioning 293]; of relief funding 268; of the internet 284; practice of 235

Polynesian(s): peoples 14, 159–65; pan-[identity 21, 165]; roots 162–63; *see also* Tonga

Pope 147n7

population(s): animal 206; civilian 225–26; challenges of virtual 213; displaced Burundi 222, 235; estimated diasporic Tongan 153; flows 20; Ghanaian wildlife 204; global dispersal of Harari 169, 172; human 206; Inuit 93n3; Iraqi [Assyrian 200; Turcoman 190, 200]; of Canada 62–65, 69, 75; worldwide [of indigenous peoples 34–35n6; of internet users 153; with telephone service 58n1]; of Sri Lanka 269n2; of Trinidad and Tobago 147n4; prison 56; Tamil [killed in conflict 260–61; in diaspora 256]

pornography 250

Portugal 147n7

postcolonial 11, 25, 59n7, 98, 113, 202, 205–6, 288, 288n1; critique 159, 165; education 286; guilt 210; studies 288; subject(s) 272, 280; theorists 270n8; women 286; *see also* colonial

Poster, Mark 30, 72

postscript(s) 179, 268–69; as resistance strategy 104; Zapatista use of 102–8

poverty 48, 98, 179, 209

power(s) 1–3, 5, 8, 32, 35n12, 37n17, 46, 56–58, 72, 118–19, 123–29, 180, 225, 233–34, 293–99; abuses 209; and domestic politics 209; and geopolitical competition 257; apparatus of 295; at-a-distance 25; bid 210, 215; center/periphery 94n7, 171, 285; colonial 93n2; communicative 106; corporate 241, 293; electoral 53; games 13, 209; government 241; ICT *mana*-like 31; imperializing 235; in cyberspace 253 [balancing of 288]; locus of 223; machinery of 299; manifestations of 293–94; mimicking 293; of networking 56; operation of 105; policing 122; questions about 293; regulatory 62; relations 105, 221, 274 [among women 278; in classic anthropology 285; reconfiguring 298]; sources of 233–34; state 186, 211, 293; struggles 221–22, 226, [Machiavellian 257]; super-25; tools of 44, 57; unequal access to 274, 285; unmasking 293; usurping 204–5; webs of 298; Western 17 [fields of 284, 286]; women's access to 229

Powers, Marla 13

prayer(s) 122, 140, 238

pregnancy: teenage 232; as online discussion topic 26, 228, 231

press, *see* news

Primarily Primates 204

primitive, *see* savage

print:-capitalism 211;-languages 211; media 43–47, 87, 114, 117, 122, 139, 211–12, 215, 273, 277 [combined with electronic media 139, 212, 273, 301n5; garnering attention of 100]

printing press 43, 45, 259; and printing plants 265

Progressivists 13

Project Underground 113

propaganda 126, 171, 207, 242–43, 260; war 261

property: boundaries 120; communal 98, 102, 118; issues of 37n17; ownership 113 [logic of 119]; private [abolishment of 171]; privatization of Mexican 98; reclamation of 295; rights 70; sub-surface mineral 113, 121; *see also* land(s)

Prophet Muhammed 179–80, 243
Protestant Church 187
public: authority 234; debate 257; development agencies 53; discourse 258–59; enemy number one 178; health 208; institution 234; life 230, 235; opinion 28; perceptions 247; policy 47, 202; relations 6, 11, 16, 116, 129n2 [disaster 129n4]; rituals 260; sector 55, 258; services 49, 54, 56, 93n5; space(s) 123 [online 283]; spending 48; sympathies 124; visibility of indigenous women 101
publics: dominant 126–29; global 28; indigenous 11, 28, 124–29, 257, 297; interloper 127; subaltern 126
public sphere(s) 26, 124, 126–29, 233–35, 286; activism 128; alternative 28; as arena of democracy 234; competing 258; cyber 128; genealogy of 234; European 259; Habermasian normative model of 258 [rational debate in 258, 264–65; regardless of rank 258–59, 264; universal access to 258, 264]; hegemonic 257; indigenous 28; language 234; micro-234–35; potential 234; radical-democratic 259; Sinhala 261–62; Sri Lanka's 255–71 [embattled 268; Tamil vs. Sinhala 260]; studies of 234
Puerto Rico 134, 140–42, 144
Puerto Ricans 132, 134; see also Taino

Qaanaaq 84
Quaynor, Nii 202, 216–17n10
Queen Elizabeth 64
Qur'an 243, 249

race(s) 97, 126, 188, 212, 239, 288; and homosexuality 232; and power 274; and skin color 225; and subjectivity 274; and the negro problem 208; collaboration across 99, 105; feminist coalitions across 279; human 239; issues of 209; transference over in cyberspace 37n18; see also ethnicity, indigenous, white
racism 46, 102–7, 179, 181; allegations of 209; deliverance from 208; language of 178, 196, 205; perceived 180; postcolonial 205
radiation 206

radio 50, 70, 87, 114, 211, 215, 228, 250, 261; station 259, 261; two-way 296
rainforest 16, 127; Amazon 16, 112–13, 117–22; Lacandona 98, 100
Rainforest Action Network (RAN): and U'wa Tribal Links campaign 116–18, 122–26, 295 [dramaturgy 117, 122, 124; high stakes of resistance 124–26; noble savage themes 116–19, 124, 129n3; poster child 122, 129; push-button activism 123]; see also U'wa
Raitt, David 34n5
Ramallah 238, 242, 249–51; central [Manarah 238]
Rankin Inlet 89
rape 229, 231; as online discussion topic 231
Ratwatte, General Anurudha 265
Rawlings, Jerry 204–5, 210, 215–16
reconciliation 227, 230; talking 27; virtual 26
reconstruction 188, 227, 235, 301n6
reflexive: dialogues 29; projects [in indigeneity 18]; self 22, 154, 288 [ethnographies 288]; turn in anthropology 30, 36n16
refugee(s) 36n12, 153, 173, 180, 188, 197, 214, 220, 248–49, 260; camps 240, 247, 249; cause 36n12; collection points 197; economic 203; populations 269n5; public 262; temporary 220
Refugee Camps 253n3
reindeer herding 9
Reinsborough, Patrick 129n5
religion 13, 18–19, 138, 171, 176–77, 181, 187–89, 195, 269n2; conflict over 242
repatriation 174; chimpanzee 203–10, 296; cross-generational attitudes towards 174; experiments 209; idea of 173; issue of 177–78; of indigenous peoples in Mexico 108n3; question of [for Palestinian refugees 248]; rates 174
reporter(s), see journalist(s)
representation(s): acts of 29, 285; crisis of 36n16, 202, 278, 281, 283–84; diplomatic 214; ethics of 20, 30, 281; of the Other 11, 17–18, 28, 133, 208, 260, 272, 285–88 [mis-16]; of the future 187, 199–200; of the past 187–95, 198–200; politics of 3; questions of 97; self-5, 11–13, 19, 132, 135–44, 217n12, 285; spaces of 285; strategies of 104

Republic of Lomar 35–36n12, 213–14; as
    nonterritorial entity 213–14; citizen-
    ship 36n12; passport 35n12
research 73–74, 136, 195, 207, 214–15,
    242, 256, 272, 275–76; and controversy
    283–84; challenges posed by online
    135–36, 146–47, 222, 253n2, 292;
    institutions 207; interrupted 274; inter-
    views 222; resources 135
researcher(s) 68, 275–77, 282, 289n7,
    289n9; and complicity 288; and
    freedom 285; and researched 288;
    unwanted 277, 297
Reserve Lands 59n5
resistance 20, 25, 27, 101, 108–9n6, 112,
    124, 152, 172, 250, 287, 296–97; and
    art 245; and complicity in research 90,
    288; and question of ICTs 32; costs of
    122–29; cyber-239; dot.com 123; email
    113; expression of 252; legacy of 115;
    marketing of 124; movements 28, 105–
    8, 238, 245, 249; of postcolonial
    subjects 288n1; symbolic 240; theatrics
    of 113, 116–18, 124–27; to alienation
    91; virtual 123
resource(s) 6, 49, 97, 126; anonymity as
    26; disjunctures 3; financial 43; health
    61–62, 66, 74–75; human 43, 48; guide
    243; ICT 3–8, 83, 85, 220; manage-
    ment 89; material 48; nationalization
    policy 119–20; native body as 124;
    park 209; rights 120, 298; social 48;
    stewarding of 121; symbolic 138, 143
Ress, David 221
Reston 207
return: to homeland 175–82, 206, 225
    [and Back to Africa movement 208;
    desire 182n3; idealized 20–21, 169;
    ideology 208; imperative 172–74, 181;
    law protecting 27; literal vs. symbolic
    175; long-awaited 24, 200; myth 193;
    notion 169, 173; option 169, 174;
    virtual 33, 299]
Revolutionary Armed Forces of Colombia
    (FARC) 129n2
Revolutionary Women's Law (of
    Zapatistas) 99, 106
Rezaei, Siamak 36n13
rhetoric(s) 206, 209–10, 242, 264, 267;
    about hypertext 280; about welfare
    210; deliberative 145; indigenous 17;
    infinities of cyberspace 27; militaristic
    209; nationalist 29, 264, 266; of

ecotourism 208; of empowerment
    130n9; of online diversity 280; rights
    13
Richberg, Keith B. 216n7
Richter Scale: of spectacles 124
Riel, Louis 63
right(s) 35n12, 46, 51, 55, 119, 189, 195–
    99; abortion 231; animal 25, 210; citi-
    zens 97; civic 193; constitutional 194;
    cultural 188–94; discourses 13, 231;
    economic 46, 193; environmental 126;
    human 17, 119, 128, 171, 191, 195,
    199, 229, 231–32 [abuses 169, 190,
    240, 266; organizations 128, 190, 214];
    indigenous 14, 34n6, 43, 47, 51, 55,
    63–66, 97–108n3, 126–28, 194, 300
    [groups 124, 147n7]; individual vs.
    collective 113, 121, 187–88; land 14,
    47, 59n5, 59n8, 70, 99–101, 108n2,
    108n3, 147n7, 229, 298; language 190,
    192; law of 99; national 192; of
    conquest 147n7; of man 45; political
    194; resource 119–20; to data owner-
    ship 73; to privacy 29; to rest 16, 106,
    110n11; to self-govern 47, 92, 100,
    171–72, 177; to speak 288; to work
    298; women's 100–101, 105–8, 229–
    31, 298
Robins, Kevin 90
Rousseau, Jean-Jacques: tableaux of 118
Roy, Loriene 34n5
ruler(s) 56; Aboriginal in Canada 63, 65–
    68; Canadian 61–68; Colombian 112,
    116–22; democratically established in
    Ethiopia 171–73; European 197;
    federal in Australia 55; of Ghana 204–
    5, 215–16; of Guyana 134; Iraqi 186–
    201 [questions of 188]; Mexican 15,
    98–105, 110n11, 110n12; monarchical
    of Burundi 221; of the United States
    178; of Tonga 152, 164; of Trinidad
    136; official of Greenland 83; socialist
    dictatorship in Ethiopia 169–72
Rumaliza 224
Rumble in the Jungle (boxing match) 216n7
rural: and urban 6 [life 93n4]; communities
    43–44, 48–56, 64, 67; healthcare 69–
    72, 76n1; peasant populations 108n2,
    142; region 256, 266; women 229
Rushdie, Salman 178
Russia 248
Russian: Jews 244, 248–50; language 244;
    T-55 tanks 262

Rwagasore, Prince Louis 225–26
Rwanda 225

Sabra 252, 253n3
Sackey, Valerie 205
Sadowsky, George 301n3
safe: havens 188–90, 201n2, 228 [internet as 23–25, 226, 233, 272, 276–78]
safety: online 9, 26–27, 232–34, 272 [possibility of 274–75, 278]; physical 232; virtual 233–34, 258 [vs. exposure 294]
Safran, William 182n3
Salgado, Liliana 198n1
Salinas, Carlos 98
Sam, Chief Alfred C. 216n6
Sámi: ICT projects [*Project@stoahppa* 9; *Sámásta-project* 9]; peoples 9; teacher 294; website [*SameNet* 9]
Samper, President Ernesto 129n4
San Cristóbal de Las Casas 101, 110n12
Santa Rosa Carib Community (SRCC) 132–48; indigeneity 132 [online 146–47]; traditions [promotion of 134]; and cultural revival 138; agendas 136–38; as representatives of national diversity 137; formal charter 136; leadership 137–38; pan-indigenous networking 138 [online 18, 138–39]; *see also* Amerindian(s)
satellite(s) 6, 8, 25, 32, 69, 82, 85, 188, 200n3, 265
Saudi Arabia 175; Ministry of Health 248
Saudi(s) 301n5; and ICT censorship 301n5
savage(s) 113; noble 45, 116, 118, 121, 124–29 [postmodern 295]; of the electronic frontier 242
SAWnet 29, 274–80, 284–89, 296; and privacy 277, 284–85; and representation 278–88; archives 277, 289n8; as safe haven 276; as text 277; attempted cyberethnography of 275–87; crisis 277; discussion topics 275–80; formation 275; policy statement 276, 289n6; refusal 29, 33, 274, 277–80, 284–86; research 278; public face of 289n6; subscriber/members 274–76, 289n7; vote 276–77, 284
Schaefer, John P. 25, 35–36n12, 202, 296
Schiller, Herbert I. 274
scholar(s) 11, 17, 35n8, 109n6, 114, 142, 170, 195, 273, 278, 282, 286, 288n2

school(s) 8, 21, 49, 62, 67, 86, 88, 105, 137, 156–58, 162, 164, 196, 202; language 190; remote 156; teachers 264
science(s) 285; and technology studies 36n16; environmental 113; of man 37n17; secret 109n8; social 132–33; Western 208
script-kiddies 239–40, 244; *see also* hacker(s)
search engine(s) 4, 85, 88; Google 214; Greenlandic 82
security 68, 229, 241, 252, 269
Sejersen, Frank 88
self-determination 14, 23, 34n6, 35n11, 43–58, 66, 70, 93n2, 94n6, 94n7, 100–101, 113, 124–29, 171, 250, 300
Seminole peoples 138
Serbs 225
sexuality 208, 296; alternative modes of 235; discourses of 208; notions 274, 275, 279; teenage [as online discussion topic 164]
sexual orientation 233; as online discussion topic 126, 164, 228–29, 231–33; hetero-279; homo-231–32
Shade, Leslie 289n9
Shah (Persian) 191
shaman(s) 13, 16, 148n9
Shan, Jamal 190, 192, 200n3
Sharon, Ariel 239, 250–52, 253n3
Shatilla 252, 253n3
shekel 239
Shell Oil Corporation 29n4
ship(s) 209, 216n6
Siberia 88, 94n6
silence(s) 99, 110n12, 242–43, 281–84, 287; as mediation 109n8; as weapon 283; subaltern 281–84; *see also* speech
Silva, Armando 245–46
Simpson, Mary 71
Simpson, O. J. 263
Sinhala 255, 257
Sisimiut 86
Siumut 83
Sivaram, Dharmeratnam P. 256, 261–69, 269n1, 269n3, 270n8; as Taraki 261
Slack, Jennifer Daryl 273
Slater, Don 2, 24, 34n3, 154, 217n17
slave(s) 20, 209, 224; capturing 224; forts 209; trader(s) 224
slavery 83n5
Smart Communities Aboriginal Project(s) 67–69; and Nunavut 67 [*Igalaaq,*

Community Access Centre 67; *Ikajuruti*; Leo Ussak Elementary School 67]; *Kuh-ke-nah Network* 67 [e-government 67; e-health 67–76; e-learning 67]; *see also* Aboriginal Peoples of Canada

social: divisions 235; forces 253, 273; ills 234; inequality 220–21, 227–84; life 3, 23, 274, 296; science 132–33; services 14, 65; structure 11, 161, 230–32; welfare 15, 210

socialism 169–71, 204, 210

society: Australian 50; civil 103–4, 215, 300; Burundi 221, 228–35; closed 198; dominant 19, 53, 104, 107, 180; Ghanaian 204; Greenlandic 87, 91, 93n2, 94n7; host 159, 164–65, 285, 287; Mexican 15, 100–106; networked 56; South Asian 278; Tongan 164; Trinidad 137; Western 278

society of the spectacle 116, 123, 128

Soja, Edward W. 213

soldier(s) 20, 110n11, 191, 208–9, 238, 259–60; bodies of 251; child 269n7; disabled 265–66

solidarity 6, 15–16, 18–19, 23, 27, 105, 107, 118, 160, 173; and ICT tools 18, 97, 109n6, 299; threats to 258

Somalia 175, 179

Sorenson, John 182n3

South American: tribes 120

South Asia 245

South Asian(s) 286, 289n5; digital diasporas 272; issues 274; region [identification with 275]; women 28, 274–89 [in diaspora 272–89, 296; non-diasporic 287;-only discussion lists 274–89]; scholars 288n2; *see also SAWnet*

South Pacific 300

sovereignty: campaigns 6, 16; ICT-mediated 14, 23, 214, 301n6; of Fourth World peoples 34n6, 35n8, 143; state 211, 298, 301n6

space(s): and culture 214; architectonic constructions of 84; communicative 202, 227–28, 234, 285; contests over 115–16; diasporic 274, 287; for dialogic encounters 279–80, 282; hegemonic 287; hybrid 274 [discursive-material 273]; everyday 80; geo(physical) 12, 24–25, 80–86, 128; homogeneous 214; hyper-182; limitations of 182; lived 80;

local 81, 86, 88–89; mapping online 80–86; Muslim 180; (non) 33; of a speech act 215–16, 287–88; of interaction 232; of representation 285; private 276; public 123; real 244; social 12, 83–85 [online 36, 283];-time 1–2, 10, 169 [transformations in cyberspace 169]; trialectic model of 213; virtual nation as 210–13; virtual 234–35, 241 [creation of 241; vs. physical 234]; women-only 278, 283

Spain 147n7

Spanish: conquest in the Americas 98, 114; Crown 142; language 100–101, 109n6

spatiality 23, 30

Spears, Russell 233

speech: act(s) 282 [extended online 215–16]; and location 287; and representation 268, 287–88; and silence 281–83 [disrupting hegemony 287–88]; as cultural signifier 181; bourgeois 281; of Comandante Esther 110n11; privilege of 287; public 110n12, 158; rights to 288; therapy 70; *see also* silence

spirituality: and healing 76n2; and resurrection 173; Lakota 13; tele-74

Spivak, Gayatri Chakravorty 272, 288n2

Sri Lanka 28, 255–71, 274; and intra-Sinhala terror 261–62; census 269n2; ethnic groups within [Sinhala-speaking majority 255, 261; Tamil minority 255]; government(s) of 255, 257–62 [and LTTE 258; Jayawardenan 260; international news coverage of 257, 263–66; National Peace Council of 269n4; political contexts [Habermasian vs. Gramscian 259, 264–65, 267–68]; public [discourse 259; sphere 268]; regions of [Batticaloa District 256, 258, 266–68; Northern Province 255]

Sri Lankan: conflict 295; Constitution 260; Deputy Minister of Defense 265; government [agent 255; censorship 258, 261–62; spokesmen 267]; Minister of Industries 266; Parliament 260, 267, 269; political parties [People's Liberation Front (JVP) 261; United Front Government (UNF) 267; United People's Front Alliance (UPFA) 267]; separatist movements 260 [Liberation Tigers of Tamil Eelam (LTTE) 255–71];

state 260 [Bambalapitya Police Station 269]; *see also* Tamil(s)
Stacey, Judith 281, 284
Stallman, Richard 241
state 34n6, 234, 247; and Kurdish peoples 191; anti-247; as distinct from nation 187–88; centralization 186; decentralized 192; democratic 187–88; disciplinary regimes 35n11, 297–98; less 214; power 186 [over internet 269n5]; quasi 214; reformulated Iraqi 187–89, 193; resistance to 252; sovereignty 211; systems 259; use of print media 211; welfare 210
Stephen, Lynn 108n2
Stolen Generation 46, 54, 59n6: and informationalism 59n6; and National Inquiry into the Separation of Aboriginal and Torres Strait Islander Children from their Families 59n6
Stoler, Ann Laura 211
street(s): demonstrations 16, 99, 113, 117–18, 122–24, 239–40; graffiti 246; language 162–63; of Israel 252; of Palestine 238–39, 240; of the metropolis 117; talk 162
structures of feeling 8, 23, 213, 296
student(s) 100, 105, 135, 155–56, 164, 256, 285
study/studies: DNA 142; geological 117; of societal phenomena 11, 30, 34n2, 75, 123, 217n16, 234, 278, 288n1, 292–93, 301n6; of *SAWnet* 276, 284, 286
subaltern 1–2, 11, 29, 126, 281, 287; absences 288; counterpublics 126, 297; cybersubjects [and talking back 288]; non-287; subjectivities 274; veiling of 280, 282, 288; voices 281, 287–88 [inclusion of 280–83]
Subaltern Studies Group 288n2
subcomandante Marcos 15, 100–107
subjectivity/subjectivities: and ICTs 2–3, 7; alternative modes of 235; challenges to 128; classed 274; decentering 280; diasporist 20–22; gendered 274; of subaltern others 274; raced 274; rooted in home 293
subject(s): anthropological 29, 31–32, 245, 253, 273, 277, 284; discursive 273 [as partial online presentations 273]; in diaspora 22, 286; postcolonial 288n1 [gendered 272; modernizing vs. exoticizing 287]; postmodern 274; research

34n4; resistant 285–86; review boards for human 273; routed from home 293; texts 273; textualized 30; under surveillance 294–95
suffering 226, 252
Suleri, Sara 286
suicide: mass political 112, 114, 121–22; rates in Canada 64; ritual 116
surveillance 56, 294–95; ICT-based 27, 212, 301n5
survey(s): health 64, 69; online 89–90
survival: assertion of 133, 143; biological 142 [chances 178, 235]; cultural 19, 142, 174; issues of 228; of customs 142; of hacker culture 241–42; of indigenous groups 133; political 198; recognition of Taino 141–44; representation of 145
Switzerland 226
Sydney 172
symbolic capital 18, 36n12, 125, 296
Syria 189, 191, 194, 198–99, 248
Syrian(s): on the net 191; nation 195

taboo(s) 243; against going native 31, 36–37n16; broaching online 21, 26, 163, 235
Taggart, William C. 26, 238, 297
Taino(s) 132–49; aboriginal groups 140–44 [Native American Taina Tribe of Aymaco, Borinken 142; Jatibonicu Taino Tribal Nation (JTTN) 140–44; Turabo Aymaco tribe 142; United Confederation of Taino People (UCTP) 134, 141, 148n8]; and ancestry [Cacike Orocobix 141]; homepages 140; identity 132 [constructions 140–44; diasporic 141]; leadership 141; pan-indigenous networking 141–44; political petition 142; transnational activism 141; website(s) 134, 139–44 [*Baramaya* 140; *Biaraku* 140, 142; *Bohio Bajacu* 140; hyperlinks 148n5; *Maisiti* 140; of the Taino Ancestry Legacy Keepers, Inc. 140; *Presencia Taina* 140, 148n10]; *see also* Amerindian(s), Puerto Rico
Tamil(s): Batticaloa District 256; diaspora 260–61, 263; internet [chat rooms 262; news agency 257]; journalists 261–62; language 255, 257; minority 255; nationalist public sphere 260; negotiations with government [Indo-Lankan

Accords 261]; separatist groups 260
[Liberation Tigers of Tamil Eelam
(LTTE); People's Liberation
Organization of Tamil Eelam (PLOTE)
262]; problem [final solution 260];
refugees 262; websites [*Tamil Circle*
261; Tamilcanadian.com 262]; *see also*
TamilNet.com
Tamil Nadu 260
TamilNet.com 28, 255–71; and mimicry of
Western journalism 295; as addendum
to nationalist struggle 266; as indigenous public 257; as international news
wire service 274; creation of 263–66;
cross-cultural ambitions 265; political
context 257, 264–65
Tanzania 236n2
Taraki, *see* Sivaram
Taussig, Michael 109n8, 259
technology 30, 36n16, 66, 76, 155, 167n4,
245, 273; access 29 [questions of 43];
and competence 49, 69, 100, 108, 169,
175; and contexts 273–74, 293–99; and
culture 8 [questions of neutrality 55–
58, 294–99]; and innovations 45; and
morphing 299; and power 293–99; and
unequal privilege 274; border 99;
digital media 300; global 293; infrastructural 20; interactive 235, 273;
interpreting 298; new 102, 147, 295
[and identification with the nation
211; experimentation with 211–12]; of
insurgency and counter-insurgency
258; problems 155; transfer 7; *see also*
information-communications technologies
technopoly 298
Tel'A'far 187
Tel Aviv 248
telecommunications 47, 60n9; broadband
44, 49, 68; manufacturers [Swedish-
based Ericsson 48]; markets 60n9;
preferential nature 211; providers
[TELE Greenland 86; Telecom
Australia 48; Telecommunications
Commission of Canada 67; Telkom
South Africa 217n10; Telstra 48, 54];
sector [in Australia 60; in Greenland
93–94n5; in Iraq 188]
telemarketing 297–98; outsourcing 297
telephone(s) 6–7, 43, 48–49, 58n1, 188;
cards 263; companies 67; connections
7, 139; mobile 86, 264, 267

television(s) 50, 102, 104, 114, 166n1,
183n8, 200n3, 211, 228, 261; stations
265
Terra Nullius 47
terrorism 178–79, 261; cyber 252; 9/11 (11
September, 2002) 28, 178
terrorist(s) 28, 36n14, 178–79, 250–51;
attacks 28, 178, 245 [Dolphinarium
248–49; 9/11 178, 245]; cyber-242;
organization [LTTE cast as 261]; virtual
26–27, 36n14
territory/territories 23, 34n2, 57, 67, 69,
122, 125, 144, 146, 211, 275; and citizenship 214; and deterritorialized
[experiences in diaspora 213; groups
175; peoples 169, space 170, 182]; and
indigenous [definition of 34–35n6;
revitalization 132]; claims over 14, 27
[ancient 10, 120, 183n10]; conquests of
147n7, 288n1; cyberspace as 23, 32 [for
deterritorialized peoples 169–82, 213];
defense of 25, 108n6, 113; expansion of
170; governance of 49, 57; integrity of
191–92, 211; of body 116
Texas 204
text(s) 31, 91, 104, 114, 137, 194, 196,
242, 277; analysis 147;-based communications 246, 285; changing vs. static
277; ethnographic 138, 284 [*enactment
of hybridity* in 284]; hacking replacement 239, 250, 252; hyper 280;
interactive 30; mainstream cultural
235; narrative 178; online 167n8 [vs.
traditional 273]; privileging 294;
virtual nation as 210–13
theatrics: of disinformation 301n1; of
resistance 113, 116–18, 124–27
Tiffin, Helen 288n1
Tigris River 187
time: contests over 106, 113–15; frozen in
118; in healing process 227; transformations in cyberspace 170
Tiruchelvan, Neelan 261
Tobago 137–39, 147n4; *see also* Trinidad
Togo 205
tolerance 13, 26, 230, 232
Tololyan, Khachig 175, 181, 182n3
Tonga 21, 152–68; government(s) of 152,
164 [British Protectorate of 152; King
of 152, 164; monarchy 164]; power
structures within 164
Tonga Language Journal (*Tefua 'a Vaka
Lautala*) 158

Tongan(s) 37n18, 152–68: being 21;
culture 21, 152–68, 296; etiquette 165;
heritage 158; in Melbourne 158;
language 21, 157–66 [ability 161, 164–
65; and Tonglish 161–63; expressions
161–62, 167n6, 167n9; fluency among
migrants 157–58; greetings 158, 167n9;
identity 296; macrons 167n8; slang
162–63, 167n9; speech-making forms
158; swear words 159]; Parliament 152;
royalty 152, 158, 164, 296; US-based
155–56, 159–61; values 156, 161;
websites 156, 166n3 [iTonga 163; Kava
Bowl 21,155–66, 166n3, 166n4, 167n5,
167n6; Planet Tonga 155–58, 162–63,
165, 167n5; Polynesian Café 155; Tonga
Online 155–56, 166n3; Tongan History
Association Forum 155, 166n3; Tongan
Youth Forum 157, 165; Tongatapu on the
Net 166n3]; youth 21, 152, 155–68,
296; see also Pacific, Polynesian(s)
Tönnies, Ferdinand 93n4
tool(s): analytical 30; Arctic communication 296; ethnographic 32; governance
50; ICT 8, 11, 34n3, 43, 49, 67, 72,
296; internet as 7, 74–75, 99, 104, 123;
language as 155; master's 295; of
communication 97; of conviviality 75–
76; of informationalization 56n6; of
management 56, 57; of participant
observation 135; of power 28, 44, 57; of
solidarity-building 18, 97; optical 56;
political 123; transport 299; written
word as 115
Torres, Cacique (Chief) Pedro Guanikeyu
141–42, 144
Toronto 172, 175–76, 263
torture 262
tourism 10–12, 50, 52–53, 101, 134; and
disease 208; and jobs 209; as space of
encounter 209; eco-25, 204 [rhetorics
of 208]; heritage 209
tourist(s) 208; attractions 298; sites 209
toxic waste 207
trade 62–63, 88, 98; coffee 98, 183n5;
corn 98; free 15; fur 62–63; in political
ideas 88; liberalization 215; monopolies
170–71; schemes [neoliberal 15];
tobacco 88
tradition(s) 15, 46, 109n8, 115–16, 138–
40, 177, 193, 210, 294; challenging 21–
22, 26, 70, 163–66, 228–35, 298
[gender-biases in 229–30]; digitaliza-

tion of 8–10, 295–96; disavowed 116;
footsteps of 115; globalizing 132, 193;
invention of 145, 293; keepers of 137,
163; knowledge of 52; literary 158;
local 293; lost 138; morphing with
high-tech 7, 295–96; oral 10; resur-
recting 132–38; rehearsal of 293; rights
to 190; safeguard of 13, 23, 102; vs.
civilization 115–16; women as bearers
of 101; see also culture, traditional
traditional: clothing 101, 117, 138, 145,
181; beliefs 50, 61, 68, 231; ceremonies
62; communities 52, 59n6; culture(s)
13, 21, 44, 53, 70, 101, 231, 296;
exchange systems 102; governance 51,
221; knowledge 9, 50–51, 134 [harmo-
nizing with Western 50–51, 295]; lands
54, 59n5; media forms 50, 295;
medicine 65–69, 74, 77n2, 102, 292,
295; morality 232; occupation 9; practices 9, 22, 46; sayings 226, 228;
sociocultural relationships 52, 59n4,
174; storytelling 10; systems 51, 54,
102, 174; values 61, 76; women's roles
65, 101–2, 106
Traditionalists 13
transactionalism 135
transnational 19, 170, 173, 181–82, 191;
activists 127; coalitions 15, 292;
companies 85; connections 154, 156,
189, 278; defacer groups 244; dimensions 92, 189; environmental groups
113; flows 208, 286; forces 225;-ism
and identity 189, 191; media 265; news
116; symbols 181; virtual neighborhood 23
Trinidad 3, 132, 136–39, 147n4, 154,
217n17; demographics 147n4; govern-
ment(s) of [People's National
Movement (PNM) 137, 147n6]; see
also Santa Rosa Carib Community
tsunami 268
Tunisia 301n3
Tupac 239
Turcoman(s) 24, 187–201; community
origin 191; connections with Turkey
190–91; homeland 187 [calls for 190];
in cyberspace 190; nation 189 [-
building 296]; political parties 190
[Iraqi Turkoman National Party 190,
192; Iraqi Turkmen Front 190;
Turkmen Peoples' Party 191]; politics
[First Turcoman Congress 187];

websites 187; 190–93, 198–200 [*Iraqi Turkman Front* 200n5; *Turkmen People Party* 201]; *see also* Iraq

Turkey 189–91, 194, 198

Turkish: agents 190; expansion 191; government 190; groups on the net 191; language 187, 191; peoples 187; political presence in Iraq 198; regimes 195; soldiers 191

Turkle, Sherry 34n4

Turkmenistan 187

Tutsi(s) 26–27; army 222, 224; clan exclusivity 224; communities [Northern vs. Southern communities 223–24]; pro- 226; regionalism 224; *see also* Huti/ Tutsi

Twa 221, 224

tyranny: of non-participation 128; of participation 126–29

Uimonen, Paula 217n10

umma 176, 180–81

Umstead, Dan 292

United Kingdom (UK) 80, 188, 195; *see also* Britain, England

United Nations (UN) 35n6, 64, 142, 188; Declaration of Rights of Indigenous Peoples 194; Development Fund for Women (UNIFEM) 236n2; Development Program 134; Educational, Scientific and Cultural Organization (UNESCO) 138; International Day for the World's Indigenous Peoples 141; representative in Palestine 252; Safe Haven in Iraqi Kurdistan 188–90; Task Force on Indigenous Peoples 5, 300 [Declaration on the Rights of Indigenous Peoples 300]; website 252; World Health Organization 65; World Intellectual Property Organization 138

United Native America 144

United States of America (US) 35n12, 105, 132, 138–39, 141, 143–44, 152–53, 171, 178–79, 188, 193, 197, 199, 202, 205–10, 212, 216n6, 248, 257, 261–62, 267, 284, 289n5; Army Command and General Staff College 262; Census Bureau 141; Central Intelligence Agency (CIA) 179, 238; Counter-Insurgency Doctrine 262 [field manuals 262–63]; Department of Defense 241; Department of State 263;

government(s) 199 [Reagan administration 263]; media 199; National Air and Space Agency (NASA) 204; National Guards 179; National Institutes of Health (NIH) 207; School of the Americas 263; Pentagon 245; Senate 179; Thule Airbase 94n6; White House [website 10, 14, 292]; *see also* America

Universal Negro Improvement Association (UNIA) 216n6

University of Melbourne 166n2

University of Oxford 182n1

University of Puerto Rico 142

University of Tampere 202

University of Texas 109n6

University of Villanova 200n7

Unknown Image Archive 23

urban 22, 64, 99, 118, 121–22, 172, 244–46; and rural [continuum 6; divide 43; perspective 93n4]; dwellers 152, 180, 183n9; guerilla movement 100; life 93n4; professionals 203, 256, 266 [woman 278, 285–88]; sub-214, 263

Urciuoli, Bonnie 162

Urdu 244

utopia(s): claims of 267; islands of 298 [in sea of technopoly 298–99]; vs. dystopia 34n2, 90, 298

U'wa(s) 16, 19, 112–30; activist campaigns 112–30; ancestors 114–15; as interloper public 127–29; as meta-native 121–22; cosmology 120; demographics 112; governance 117, 120–21; lands 112, 122–25 [Cliff of Glory 116; Samore 118–19, 122, 125, 129n4];-Oxy contests 112–31 [over history 114–16; over individual vs. collective rights 114, 118–20]; political participation 122–24 [tyranny of 126–28]; stewardship of earth 120–22; threat of mass suicide 112, 114–16; website 128; *see also* Occidental Petroleum Corporation, Rainforest Action Network

Valtierra, Pedro 110n11

value(s) 2, 21, 31, 35n11, 53, 58, 72, 75, 128, 276; broadened 76; cultural 49, 91, 128, 130n8, 138, 156, 161 [and importation of ICTs 301n1]; indigenous 128; individual and collective 120–21; local 294; market 196; of history 294; of ICTs

49–50, 104, 139, 144; placed on indigeneity 138, 294, 300; politics of 35n8,
138; publicity 124; therapeutic 71; traditional 61, 76, 102, 163–64; Western 294
Vanity Fair (magazine) 108n5
Vanni 266
Vargas-Stehney, Valery (Nanturey) 140,
142
Vasquez, Miguel 301n4
Vatican 147n7
Vázquez, Richard 143
ventriloquism: and the subaltern's voice
281, 288; in Zapatista movement 97,
104
V.E.R.A.city loop 145–47, Figure 7.1
victim(s): Israeli 251; of Al-Aqsa Intifada
240; of Burundi civil war 222, 226; of
cultural heritage 280; of Dolphinarium
terrorist attacks 248–49; of modernity
89; of 9/11 terrorist attacks 245;
Palestinian 251–52; status [claims to
240]; of warfare in Sri Lanka 260–61,
269n4; tsunami 268
victory 192, 215; electoral 250, 267; cyber-
295; for women's rights 298; grassroots
122, 129n4, 295
video 261;-conferencing 49, 58n2, 70, 74
Vienna 197
Vietnam 225
Vijayasin, Raj 262
village(s): forced relocation 262; global
93n4, 286; in Iraq 190, 194; Palestinian
[eradication of 240]; Southeast Asian
37n17
violence 117, 186, 221, 223, 226–31, 251–
52, 258, 261; aftermath of 220; against
children 164; against Indians 108–9n6;
cycle of 242; domestic 15, 164, 228–31;
epistemic 279; eyewitness accounts of
223–24; in Aboriginal communities 48;
interethnic 26, 220–34, 269n4; real or
potential 257; to enforce conformity
261; traumas of 226
Virginia 207
virtual: colonization 36n14;
community(ies) 22–24, 135, 155–56,
165, 166n1, 175, 212, 214–15, 246,
278–79, 284–87 [dialogic possibilities
of 280; ethnic 153, 163, 166n1]; diaspora 2, 20–22, 293, 299–301;
environment 73, Table 3.1, 226; ethnographer 27, 30; ethnography 30, 222;
face of indigeneity 4, 35n7, 293; field

site(s) 30–33, 136; fieldworker 33;
homesteading 297; identities 234;
informants 29–30; life 31, 273; media
32, 293; nation(s) 35–36n12, 202,
210–14 [building 297; policing 212];
occupation 26, 249–52; pioneers 292;
reality 90, 170, 182, 214 [MOOs
(Object-Oriented Multi-User
Dungeons) 214, 217n16; MUDs
(Multi-User Dungeons) 214, 217n16];
safety 233–34; space(s) 234–35, 241;
taboos 30; *terra incognita* 29; terrorist
26–27; tricksters 30; war of words 113;
worlds 12, 23, 93, 188, 213, 222
Visweswaran, Kamala 284
voice(s): alternative 104; counter 36n16;
eclipsing others' 279 [moral dilemma of
280, 284]; extension via mediators 105;
from the margins 280–81, 300; Indian
104; issues of 288;-lessness 288; new
235; of the Other 281; of the silenced
103–5, 152, 163–66; subaltern 280–81;
via website defacements 252; women's
106, 230, 279–80, 282, 289n9
Voorhis, Bruce Van 269n4
Votenow.com 7
vox populi 292, 301

Wade, Peter 130n6
Waldron, Sidney 171
war(s) 45, 98–99, 102, 170, 190, 238–40,
250, 262–66, 301n6; and formation of
Israel 240; Balkan-style 179; cessation
of 173; cyber 26, 221; declarations
[*Declaration of War Against Exploiters of
Lakota Spirituality* 13; *Zapatista
Declaration of War* 99, 106]; holy 180–
81; effects of 235; info-301n1; low
intensity 258; machine 243; of words
25, 113; on taxes in Mexico 99; on
terror 178; propaganda 261; shadow
258–61;-time 173;-torn 188, 255;
widows 229; wounds 28, 293
War: Burundi civil 26, 220–27, 235; Cold
43, 178, 260, 265; Gulf 188–91, 199;
Mexican Revolution 108n2 [and Plan
de Ayala 108n2]; on Terror 257, 260,
265; Operation Babylon 197;
Operation Iraqi Freedom 197; Sri
Lanka's civil 255–69, 269n4; World
War II 93n2 [post-243]
Warhol, Andy 116
Warschauer, Mark 154

Washinawatok, Ingrid 129n2
Washington, D.C. 117, 172, 207, 209, 217n12, 222
Wave Hill 59n5
weapon(s) 100, 260; and targets 239; B-52 94n6; BMP armored personnel carriers 262; body as 112, 116, 123–24, 128; burning tires as 238; cyberspace as 25; educated black man as 239; hacking as 36n14, 239; helicopters as 238, 262; howitzers 262; jeeps 238; Kalashnikov 249; keyboard as 295; long-range mortars 262; Molotov cocktails 251; nuclear 94n6; of mass destruction 197; public as 234; rhetorical 28; rubber bullets 238–39; rocks as 238–40, 250; silence as 283; tanks 240, 262
web: administrators 155, 163, 212, 227–29, 272; applications 239; bugs 239;-cruiser 4, 13; gatekeeping 216–17n10, 227;-masters 85, 134, 140, 202–3, 212, 217n10, 247 [Dutch 203]; rules of engagement 221; surfing 197, 202, 214; targets 239; traffic 85–88, 135, 140, 202–3, 300; vandals 242; see also website(s)
website(s): About.com 143; Arab 27, 176, 191, 240, 244; Assyrian 187–88, 193–200; by and for Hutu and Tutsi groups 26, 28, 220–36; by and for indigenous Caribbean 132, 137, 139–47; by and for South Asian women 274–89; design 76, 134–35, 156–57, 167n5, 263; geocities.com 88; Ghanaian 202–19; Goan 154; Greenlandic 82; Harari 169, 174–82; Hawai'ian 154; Hopi 148n8; in non-English languages 154; Iraqi 187–88; Islamic 176, 249; Israeli 240, 243; Kualono 10; Kurdish 23–24 [www.kurdistan.org 23]; Native American 144, 148n8; of the Oneida Indian Nation 292; Pacific 155, 165; Palestinian 243–44, 250; PeaceNet 109n6; Sámi 9; Sri Lankan-oriented 268; Taino 139–44; Tamil 255–71; Turcoman 187, 190–93, 198–200; Tongan-oriented 155–67; Zapatista-oriented 109 [for women 110]
website defacement mirrors: alldas.org 244, 246–48; attrition.org 244, 246–47
website defacers 239–53; Dr. Nuker 243; Macwiz 239, 245, 253n1; n00gie 247; Pakistani 243; pro-Israeli 26–27, 36,
297 [mOsad team 243–44, 247–49, 251–52; InfernoZ 243–44]; pro-Palestinian 26–27, 36, 297 [GForce Pakistan 243; LinuxLover 243; Silver Lords 243, 245; The World's Fantabulous Defacers (WFD) 239, 243, 247, 250–52]
Webster's Dictionary 241
welfare 15, 47, 54, 98, 119; state 210 [dependency on 35n11, 48, 55, 297]
West 22, 24, 29, 118, 154, 159, 175, 179, 196–97, 215, 220, 264, 275, 279, 284, 286, 294; vs. the Rest 153–54
Whitaker, Mark 28, 255, 269n2, 295
white: Australia 59n6; countries 208; culture 46; forum participant 212; leader of Zapatistas 103; non-286; opinion 216n6; people 120; researcher 289n7; separatists 208; South African man 217n12; see also race
Wickens, Kathryn 216n9
Wilson, Samuel M. 269n5
Wired World of Iraqi Kurds (news report) 200n1
women 65, 251, 286; abused 230–31; and land ownership 229–30; and marginalization 278; and public life 230; and power 229, 274, 278; and reproductive freedom 231; as bearers of tradition 101; as embodiment of homeland 174, 181 [and genital circumcision 181]; as partners in development 235; Canadian 62; for Israel 243; in Burundi 229–33; in governance 26, 228, 230; Western 286 [interpellation of 286];-only spaces [diversity of 289n9; politics within 278; safety of 278]; rights of 229, 231 [victory for 298]; roles of indigenous Mexican 101–2, 105–7; rural 229; South Asian 28, 274–89; Tongan 164; violence against 164, 229–31; voices of 106, 230, 279–82, 289n9; Zapatista 15–16, 97, 101–11, 298
Women for Israel's Tomorrow 243
women's movement 274; global 16; Western 15–16, 298; Zapatista 15–16, 105–10, 298
world wide web 18, 21, 32, 33n1, 84, 114, 123, 129, 153–54, 156, 243, 253, 256; as field of dreams 24, 199; as graphics delivery system 145; re-negotiating history via 187–200

World: First 35n8, 43, 98, 112, 122, 274;
     Fourth 35n8, 112, 122; New World 98,
     147n7, 208–9; Second 35n8; Third-
     35n8, 211, 274, 279, 285–86 [academic
     284; activist 196; city 178; cultures
     286; debt relief 119; heritage 285; jour-
     nalists 263; woman 29, 278–82, 287]
World Bank 210, 251
World Trade Center Towers 178, 245
World Trade Organization (WTO) 60n9

xenophobia 208

Y2K millennium shift 85, 178–80; and
     computer crashes 178
Yakkala 265
Yankah, Kwesi 204, 216n4
Yassin, Sheikh Ahmad 250
youth(s): and hacking 240, 244; American
     214; Arab 27; Bedouin 22; Burundi 26,
     227–38; culture 21; development 228;
     diasporic 22; Ghanaian 215; Harari 22,
     173–82, 294; Mexican 99; Pakistani
     250; Palestinian 27, 238–40, 250; pro-
     Israeli 244–47; pro-Palestinian 239,
     244–47, 250; Russian-Jewish 27, 240,
     244, 247, 249–50; Tamil 260; Tongan
     21, 152, 155–68, 296
Yugoslavia 199

Yupiit 89

Zaire 216n7
Zapatista(s): *Declaration of War* 99, 106;
     ethnic groups associated with [Choles
     98; Tojolabales 98; Tzeltales 98;
     Tzoltziles 98]; movement 15, 97–111;
     National Liberation Army (EZLN) 97–
     105, 108n4, 109n6; negotiations with
     government [San Andrés Accords 100–
     101];-oriented websites [*Chiapas95*
     109n6; *Enlace Civil* 109n6; *Ya Basta*
     109n6; *Zapatistas in Cyberspace* 109n6];
     peoples 19, 97–111; solidarity groups
     [Accion Zapatista 109n6]; women 15–
     16, 97, 101, 105–10; women-oriented
     websites [*Creatividad Feminista* 110n10;
     *Plataforma de solidaridad con Chiapas de
     Madrid* 110n10; *Red de Apoyo Zapatista
     en Madrid* 110n10; *Ya Basta, Italy*
     110n10; *Zap Women* 110n10]; *see also*
     Mexico
zemis 144, 148n9
Zionism 243
Zionist: goals 251; pro-242
Zoysa, Richard de 261

2Pacalypse Now 239
700 Club 179